Apollo's Swan and Lyre

Five Hundred Years of the Musicians' Company

I. Granted 15th October 1604.

Apollo's Swan and Lyre

Five Hundred Years of the Musicians' Company

RICHARD CREWDSON

THE BOYDELL PRESS

First published 2000
The Boydell Press, Woodbridge

ISBN 0 85115 766 1

The Boydell Press is an imprint of Boydell & Brewer Ltd
PO Box 9, Woodbridge, Suffolk IP12 3DF, UK
and of Boydell & Brewer Inc.
PO Box 41026, Rochester, NY 14604–4126, USA
website: http://www.boydell.co.uk

A catalogue record for this book is available
from the British Library

Library of Congress Cataloging-in-Publication Data
Crewdson, Richard, 1932–
    Apollo's swan & lyre : five hundred years of the Musicians'
Company / Richard Crewdson.
       p.   cm.
    Includes bibliographical references and index.
    ISBN 0–85115–766–1 (hardback : alk. paper)
    1. Worshipful Company of Musicians – History.   I. Title.
ML28.L8 W6743 2000
780'.6'0421 – dc21   99–054373

This publication is printed on acid-free paper

Printed in Great Britain by
St Edmundsbury Press Ltd, Bury St Edmunds, Suffolk

CONTENTS

ILLUSTRATIONS

TO GERALDINE

ACKNOWLEDGEMENTS

Without the help and goodwill of a great many kind people this book could never have been written, and it is a pleasure to recall them with gratitude and to record their names, although I know that I shall be mortified to find that I have forgotten others whom I should have mentioned.

In the early days of my research I became fascinated by the complexity of musical life in 18th century London, and was promised help by Professor 'Corky' McGuinness, Professor Simon McVeigh and Professor Colin Timms, which sadly I was unable to take advantage of, because it proved to be the period when the Company's own records began to fill the stage. I did however benefit greatly from another of Royal Holloway's luminaries, Dr Fiona Kisby, who shared with me her great knowledge of 16th century London musicians. Dr Andrew Ashbee and Dr David Lasocki were kind enough to read the first half of the book in its original draft, and to make many extremely constructive comments, which enabled me to rework the text with a great deal more confidence than I had felt first time round. The views expressed are, however, still my own.

Several offers of help turned what I had feared would be a rather stodgy account of the 19th century and the years leading up to it into what I hope is now a good deal more lively and interesting. John Denison kindly introduced me to Charles Burney's detailed report of the 1784 Handel Commemoration, with all the musicians named. John Cruft generously sent me copies of the Royal Society of Musicians History and list of members, which brought to life the little band of professionals who still belonged to the Company around the turn of the century. And Professor Brian Trowell alerted me to Sir Frederick Bridge's autobiography, which dovetailed beautifully into the Minutes and other official papers of the Company covering the 1890s and the early years of the 20th century.

In the same way, Arthur Hill's Diaries for the same period transformed the events of the day and the people involved into three dimensions, and I am immensely grateful to Charles Beare, who is now the owner of the diaries, for allowing me to quote some extracts from these unpublished papers.

This is perhaps the moment to express my appreciation for all the research into the Company which Arthur Hill commissioned and initiated nearly a century ago. The records which he had made, and carefully preserved, cover virtually all the primary sources of the Company's history up to 1700. My father also undertook extensive research in 1948–49, and his notes have been immensely helpful to me. It has been a privilege to be able to make much fuller use of all this material than either Arthur Hill or my father were able to do themselves, and it has of course made my task infinitely simpler, especially when faced with a whole mass of 'secretarial' script!

My thanks go to Hubert Chesshyre, Clarenceux King of Arms, for his help with the Company's heraldry, to Andrew Gillett for information about the Founders Company, to Hugh Cobbe of the British Library, for his great interest in the book, to my old and dear friend Walter Ficker for his comments on the draft and for lending me his archive of Company papers, to Paddy Dunn, for lending me his father's files relating to his Mastership and the Duke of Edinburgh, to Mrs Rena Cuddigan for information of great interest concerning the Skilbeck family, and to David Hill for kindly supplying the photograph of Arthur Hill in his Master's robes.

Libraries are the feeding troughs of writers, and I cannot commend highly enough the assistance which I have received from all those that I have used: the Barbican Library, the Library at Cecil Sharp House, the Music Library of the Somerset County Council at Yeovil, and the London Library from whence it is hard to come away without at least one needed book. But very special thanks must go to Stephen Freeth, Keeper of the Manuscripts at the Guildhall Library, and Andrew Riley, his lieutenant, for both of whom nothing has been too much trouble, although I bothered them a lot, and to John Fisher of the Prints Department who did so much to seek out the sort of illustrations which I was looking for. My thanks go also to Dr Amanda Bevan at the Public Record Office for guiding me through a difficult filing system.

Simon Waley and Margaret Alford have made me constantly welcome in the Clerk's Office, despite the chaos which I regularly caused there in searching through the Company's own boxes of papers and relics.

The difficulty of finding a publisher was something I never had to worry about, thanks to the kindness of Sir David Willcocks in introducing me to Bruce Phillips at Oxford, and then to Bruce's own kindness in putting me in touch with Richard Barber at Boydell & Brewer. I (and the Company) are fortunate to be in their hands.

I acknowledge with gratitude the permission of the Bodleian Library for permitting me to use and quote from MS Rawlinson D.24, a document of great interest to all City Livery Companies, and the Britten-Pears Foundation's permission to publish Benjamin Britten's letter to Lord Astor.

Finally, and perhaps more important than all, I have had so much moral support to be thankful for from the members of the Court, from the Quincentennial Committee, and especially from my wife, to whom, because she has had to put up with the demands and distractions of the Company for forty years, I have with utmost gratitude and affection dedicated this book.

ABBREVIATIONS

CLB	Corporation of London Letter Books
CL Jor	Corporation of London Journals
CL Reps	Corporation of London Repertories
GSMD	Guildhall School of Music & Drama
RCO	Royal College of Organists
RMA	Royal Musical Association
RSM	Royal Society of Musicians
TCL	Trinity College of Music, London

INTRODUCTION

According to the historian Plutarch, Numa, the second king of Rome, at the end of the 8th century BC, organised eight groups of artisans in the city into Guilds, and the first in seniority were the Musicians. This may be a totally irrelevant piece of information for a book about the London Guild of Musicians. On the other hand even if Plutarch (1st century AD) made it up, it does show that guilds and musicians have both been active in Europe for a very long time and that the Worshipful Company, in London, as it celebrates it Quincentenary, is carrying on a very ancient tradition, which deserves to be put on permanent record from time to time.

Fifty years ago, my father, Alastair Crewdson, who was then Clerk to the Company, wrote his 'Short History' of the Company, which has been an invaluable work of reference for freemen, liverymen, guest speakers and, indeed, his successors in office as Clerk, including myself. It was, however, strictly the story of the Company in isolation, and for historians and others who find the context in which an institution evolves as interesting as the subject itself, there was something lacking, as my father readily acknowledged in the Preface to his book. He wrote:

> I have had to resist the temptation to branch off into the history of the Minstrels on the one hand and of the City Guilds on the other . . . I hope that if a second edition is ever required, I, or some successor of mine, may be able to include some notes on these fascinating subjects.

I confess that before rediscovering what my father had written, I had already made this my intention. There has been such an enormous outpouring of books and articles on music history and musicology since the 'Short History' was published, that it might have seemed to be a blinkered exercise not to widen the horizons of the new book. The reader will therefore find that woven into the Company's history there are two subsidiary themes, music in London and the City of London itself.

I had hoped to include also some reference to English composers and the development of English music, but this was too ambitious; I was finding that where I proposed to write a paragraph, half a chapter was needed, which had already been written by a much more expert hand than mine. So this idea was abandoned, but I still found that in trying to paint a wider picture, I was running into problems. Five hundred years is quite a long time to hold the reader's interest, together with a sketch of the preceding two hundred years (which must be included because of the minstrels' activities in London during that time) and great care had to be taken not to 'branch out too far'. While I have tried therefore to work only from primary sources so far as the Company itself is concerned, I regretfully came to the conclusion that I did not have the time to do the same for the subsidiary themes, for which I have freely acknowledged my debt throughout the book to the very many excellent scholars whose work I have relied upon.

In this respect (and no doubt in many others also) I shall be found wanting by musicologists and music historians, whose standard of scholarship is of the highest order, and whose appetite needs original material to be satisfied. But I cannot pretend to have had any training in musicology, and this book has been written primarily for the members of the Musicians' Company, whose interest in joining the Company is derived from so many rich and diverse sources, of which Academia is only one. If I have been able to hold their attention up to the last page of the book (whether they bother to refer to the numerous Appendices or not) my principal objective will have been achieved. At the same time I hope that here and there a nugget or two of new information may be found which will divert or provoke the musicologist or the historian.

In the year 2000 the Company celebrates its five hundredth anniversary, and the publication of this book will be timed to coincide with this celebration. It is for this reason that I have chosen to focus the spotlight first of all on the moment, half a millennium ago, when the Company was incorporated according to the procedure of the City of London, before I turn back in Chapter 2 to the earlier origins of organised minstrelsy in London and elsewhere. I hope that this will not cause any confusion or disorientation.

I know that I shall be criticised for my decision to modernise the spelling in the old documents that I quote from. To those who find this offensive I apologise, but stand unrepentant, because for me quotations reproduced in their original ancient spelling are a distraction. The word 'quaint' always crosses my mind; I find that I am amused by the spelling while losing the gist of what is being said, and tempted into a feeling of superiority over those lesser mortals who did not know how to spell. To risk experiencing such feelings is harmful, and I believe that the original writer is respected more, and his words make more impact, if the distraction of unconventional (for us) spelling is removed. I have not made any word substitution, except in one or two very special cases where the original wording was unintelligible to a modern reader.

I have also used the modern calendar throughout, so that every year begins on the 1 January, although in reality the English year began on 25 March until 1751: this was 169 years after the introduction of the Gregorian Calendar (which changed the New Year to 1 January) in Rome and most of Catholic Europe.

Some readers may be unfamiliar with the arcane terminology associated with the City of London livery companies, particularly in their earlier days, and a word or two may help to clear away some obscurities. The words 'guild', fraternity', 'brotherhood', 'fellowship', 'mistery' will be found in close association and in many cases are interchangeable. 'Guild' or 'gild' is probably the earliest name for an association of persons with a common interest (not necessarily in connection with a craft or trade), dating back to Saxon times. 'Fraternity' was originally used more commonly in relation to groups with a religious object, and 'brother-hood' was the Anglo-Saxon synonym for the same word. Fraternities or brother-hoods tended to exist before the formation of craft guilds, and the guild or livery company in the 14th and 15th centuries might be formed 'on the back of ' the fraternity, soon evolving into a separate body with the specific purpose of exer-cising control over a trade or craft. A 'mistery' was the trade or craft itself, although the use of the word was often extended to those permitted to exercise it. 'Fellowship' was a term which could be used in almost any context relating to members of guilds and fraternities with a common interest. In the 17th century the word 'Society' began to be used in a similar sense.

Then there is the ancient usage of 'art' and 'science', which is of special impor-tance to the Musicians' Company because its mistery was always described as 'the Art *or* Science of Music'. 'Art' did not correspond to the modern sense of the word at all. It had nothing to do with aesthetics, and was often used synony-mously with 'craft'. It is not easy to distinguish between the two parts of the defi-nition, because by the time they were being applied to music in the context of the Company the meanings of the two words were becoming confused and were sometimes transposed. The clearest distinction, which may be a little archaic, is to allow the word 'art' to be applied to the set of rules and theory which underlie the practice of Music, and 'science' then means the acquired skill and 'know-how' necessary to practise it.

Readers of this book will find that the problem of the Company's credentials runs like a submerged reef all the way through, causing shipwreck when it rises above the surface and anxiety and embarrassment at other times. It was a problem which was only finally resolved in 1950, with the obtaining of the new Royal Charter. The lack of Company records makes it unusually difficult to interpret the circumstances associated with the various grants – the 1469 Royal Charter, a Charter for *City-based* King's Minstrels, the 1500 City Act and Ordi-nances, for City minstrels, and the King James Charter of 1604, again for the City Minstrels or Musicians.

The case against the Company put by Nicholas Lanier in 1634 was that the 1604 Charter was obtained by fraud, in disregard of the 1469 Charter; this was duly recorded, along with the forfeiture of the Charter, in Hawkins's History in the late 18th century. I am convinced that the allegation was false and was made in bad faith. It is my belief that the purpose of the 1604 Charter, obtained in a unique climate of good fellowship and cooperation between the City Musicians and the King's Music, was to embrace within the Company the native-born members of the King's Music and all other London musicians, and that this was then frustrated by the development of the exclusive masque-culture within the Stuart Court, and the gentrification and caste-consciousness of the royal house-hold musicians of Lanier's circle. It is a hypothesis which I have not gone to great lengths to prove, because the evidence is slim, to say the least. I hope however that in due course further research will help either to disprove or to uphold this interpretation.

The last chapter of the book, covering the whole of the 20th century, is a long one, but I am afraid that some of my colleagues on the Court of the Company will be disappointed that I have written so little about recent events. It was a deliberate decision, as it is usually very difficult to draw a line between instant history and journalism, which everyone knows is altogether lacking in perspective. The Company's last twenty years have been full of incident, but this will be for the author of the next edition to interpret and describe.

1

The Year 1500

ON Christmas Eve 1499, Pope Alexander VI Borgia went in solemn procession to the *porta aurea* of the basilica of St Peter's and knocked three times on the door with his papal staff, crying: 'Aperite mihi portas justitiae', 'Open unto me the Gates of Righteousness'.[1] The door opened, and the Pope who planned to bring all Italy under his political rule through his children, Cesare and Lucrezia, had inaugurated the Jubilee Year 1500, when pilgrims to Rome could purchase from the Pope full absolution for their sins.

In Ferrara, about 250 miles away, Isabella d'Este, Duchess of Mantua and sister to Alfonso, Duke of Ferrara (shortly to become Lucrezia Borgia's third husband), was promoting the making of 'families' of viols for consort playing. Apart from reputedly being the most beautiful woman in Italy, she was in her time the outstanding patroness of artists and musicians. She and her brother were also accomplished performers, and may have been the first high-born amateurs to play in consort. For Isabella and Alfonso the 'noble' music had to be played not on wind but on stringed instruments (i.e. the viols), and the dance music on the new violins.[2]

Also in Ferrara, Josquin des Prez, the greatest composer of his age, had been enjoying the benefit of the Este patronage, until in 1500 Louis XII, king of France, invaded the north of Italy with a great army, wreaking havoc on the Duchy of Milan, and Josquin is next heard of in the king's service in France. Born in Hainaut about 1445, and trained in St Quentin, he had emigrated to Italy as a young man, working first in Milan and then in Rome from 1486 to 1494. During his time in Italy he developed his exceptional innovative skill in polyphonic composition.

In 1500 Martin Luther was in his last year at school at St George's, Eisenach,

---

[1] Psalm 118 v. 19. The ceremonial for 1499/1500 was newly devised.

[2] Peter Holman, *Four and Twenty Fiddlers, The Violin at the English Court 1540–1690* (Oxford: Clarendon Press 1993), pp. 13–18. The dating of the advent of the 'modern' violin is a controversial subject outside the scope of this book. Holman takes the extreme early view. For a contrary view in an English context see Brian Harvey, *The Violin Family and its Makers in the British Isles* (Oxford: Clarendon Press 1995), p. 13.

(where he sang in the church choir) before taking up a place as a law student at the University of Erfurt in the following year. Here he excelled himself as a lute player. Erasmus, aged 34, had just arrived in Paris where he compiled a book of quotations for his first patron, William Blount, Lord Mountjoy. He too had had a musical training in his boyhood as a chorister in Utrecht, under the guidance of Jacob Obrecht, then a young choirmaster and organist, who, like his compatriot Josquin, settled in Ferrara and died there of the plague in 1505.

Western Europe was an 'open' Continent, and artists and scholars travelled extensively, bound by no ties of nationality.

In London a group of minstrels whose identity and number is unknown were planning to apply to the Corporation to be incorporated as a Fellowship or livery company. After nearly half a century of civil war, England in 1500 was peaceful, in a way that could not have been predicted two or three years previously. Perhaps this is why Erasmus had accepted Lord Mountjoy's invitation and paid the first of his many visits to England and Oxford in the spring of 1499.

Peace had come at last after the first fifteen years of Henry VII's reign which were as turbulent as, and in some respects a continuation of, the Wars of the Roses.

Generations of English schoolchildren have been taught that the Middle Ages died with Richard III in 1485 on Bosworth Field, and that that was when 'Modern History' began. This is in fact a gross over-simplification, and no contemporary observer of English politics would have been conscious of any decisive change when Henry VII acceded to the throne. There was no good reason then for assuming that the Wars of the Roses had come to an end; the new king had taken the throne by right of conquest, and he was just as much a usurper as Henry Bolingbroke (Henry IV, the first of the Lancastrian kings) nearly one hundred years before, and Henry Tudor had a good deal less royal blood in him. There was an entirely valid prior claimant to the throne, Edward, Earl of Warwick, the Duke of Clarence's son, if he could distance himself from the attainder attaching to his late father. But the young earl was unlucky, because his uncle, Richard III, had imprisoned him in the Tower of London in the year before Bosworth, and Henry made sure that he stayed there.

The threat to his throne came therefore not from the Earl of Warwick but from the two 'Pretenders', Lambert Simnel (pretending to be Warwick), and the more troublesome Perkin Warbeck (pretending to be Richard of York, the younger of the 'Princes in the Tower') who for seven years enjoyed the support successively of the Emperor Maximilian, the king of France and the king of Scotland.

Civil strife finally came to an end in 1497 when the king defeated the rebels and Warbeck was captured. Two years later, in November 1499, both the Earl of Warwick, who had been trapped into treasonable communication with Warbeck, and Warbeck himself were executed. Thus the real House of Plantagenet became extinct, and the now self-confessed fraudulent Yorkist 'Duke of York' removed from the political stage. Henry VII was at last secure on the throne. He was not a popular king, because he lacked 'charisma' and his methods of taxation were extortionate, but by 1500 he had finally brought to an end the dynastic wars which had bedevilled the second half of the 15th century, thus bringing security also to his subjects, none of whom appreciated this more thoroughly than the citizens of London. Round numbers and tidy dates are abhorrent to historians, but the fact remains that the Middle Ages can more realistically be said to have ended not in 1485 but with the turn of the Century, and the Musicians' Company therefore came into existence in the first year of the new era.

In that year Londoners with long memories could look back to the comparable 1470s, the last decade of Edward IV's reign, when there had been a time of peace, trade suddenly boomed and there was a palpable growth in prosperity.[3] Unpredictable though it may have been at the time, the City would see a resumption of growth and prosperity which continued through the 16th century, coupled with a huge increase in population, transforming it from its mediaeval ambience, which still made it, in 1500, an attractive place to live. It then had quite a small population, probably about 50,000, which would have been rather smaller than Florence and about half the size of Venice and Naples. There was a surprising amount of space. Although certain parts of the City were over-crowded and full of mean hovels and narrow passages, building regulations had been in existence for over 300 years, and street sweepers ('scavengers' and 'rakers') were regularly employed.[4] Fine buildings, particularly the Livery Company halls and the City churches, were built with room to circulate around them. One could stand back and admire their proportions. The Tower of London and the principal ecclesiastical foundations occupied huge areas of the town, both within and outside the walls, and although these mostly stood within their private precincts, they would have imposed a sort of 'cathedral close' atmosphere on their immediate surroundings.

Looking, for example, at the sector of the City lying to the south-west of St Paul's Cathedral (itself a vast building much longer than the present cathedral and with a spire fifty feet taller than Salisbury), it was virtually a royal and ecclesiastical enclave as far as the City Wall. Closest to the Cathedral was the Wardrobe, a cluster of buildings then consisting of offices and warehouses for the royal household. To the south was Baynards Castle, a royal residence. Just to the west, stretching from Ludgate down to the river and extending to the Fleet river was the Blackfriars friary. Across the Fleet there was marshy land on which Henry VIII would build the Bridewell Palace, and beyond that the Whitefriars friary, reaching to the boundary of the Inner Temple.

Moving clockwise around the Walls, to the north-west of St Paul's were the Greyfriars inside the Walls, and outside them the Priories of St Bartholomew

3   Customs revenues increased by one third during the years 1471–80. See J.H. Ramsay, *Lancaster and York* (Oxford 1892), vol. II, p. 470.
4   John Schofield, *The Building of London from the Conquest to the Great Fire* (London: British Museum Press 1993), p. 79.

1. An early 19th century engraving of the northern half of London Bridge and the City in about 1500. The engraver has reconstructed the view of the background from the well-known manuscript illustration of the Duke of Orleans in the White Tower (British Library, Royal 19 F II folio 73), which dates from that time.

and St John, the Charterhouse (a Carthusian monastery) and the Clerkenwell Nunnery. Further to the east were the Austin Friars, the Hospital of St Anthony, which we shall revisit later in the chapter, and St Helen's Priory close to Bishops-gate. In the north-east sector, with a boundary wall running most of the way from Bishopsgate to Aldgate, and with the parish church of St Katherine Cree (which still abuts onto Leadenhall Street) built into its walls, there was the immensely wealthy Priory of the Holy Trinity, which owned the whole of Port-soken Ward, and whose Prior, because of his importance as a landowner, was *ex officio* an Alderman.[5]

All this monastic glory, which would have been taken for granted as part of London life in 1500, was to disappear in the next reign and this would affect dra-matically the way in which the Fellowship of Minstrels would evolve during the 16th century. At the time of incorporation the livelihood of City minstrels was dependent to a very significant extent on the regular observance of feast-days and other religious festivals, which were an inseparable part of the life of every community in the late Middle Ages. Journeymen and apprentices did not enjoy

---

5 Schofield, p. 46.

vacations, in the sense of leaving home for a holiday, but they certainly stopped work to celebrate many holy days during the year.[6]

The first impressions of a visitor to the city at this time would have been made by the huge crowd of extremely busy pedestrians who would be constantly hustling and jostling him as he made his way though the wide and narrow streets. There would of course be carts and heavy traffic in the main streets as well, not to mention livestock 'on the hoof' on the way to market or slaughter, but it would be the pedestrians, all rushing about their business, who would be predominant.

Those who were not so active might be of sufficiently 'worshipful' standing to have time to engage in conversation with their colleagues and rivals; others, including minstrels, would be plying their trade on the street. So would street-sellers using the traditional street-cries. It would be another hundred years before English composers thought of fitting the traditional street-cries into their compositions (Percy Scholes found 150 different cries represented in this way), but they were featured in a mid-15th century poem by John Lydgate, and must have been in continuous use, even if they evolved a little in the meantime.

Every trade and craft was represented within the City Walls, many with their own street or precinct from which the peculiar noises or smells of their mistery would give pain or pleasure to the senses of passers-by. The most notorious areas of production were the lower end of Walbrook for the skinners, the junction of Gracechurch Street and Eastcheap for butchers, and the west end of Cheapside for goldsmiths. Some trades were kept as far away from the centre as possible. The tanners were secluded on the west side of Old Bailey, between the street and the Fleet river, and in 1478 the Whitetawyers, who were the specialist makers of white leather, were ordered to carry on their trade outside the City altogether, 'inasmuch as they cannot exercise their art within the same without annoying their neighbours'.[7]

Besides being a centre for trade and crafts, London was the biggest port in England, so the same streets which provided homes, shops and workshops also had to accommodate export and import and coastal traffic on its way to and from the wharves along the river, dominated by cartloads of woolsacks on their way to the Staple ports of Calais and Pisa. There was also an increase in traffic at this time because many liverymen of the Great Twelve and other major companies had developed entrepreneurially, which meant that wholesale and retail operations in the same trade coexisted within the City but in different locations, greatly increasing the numbers employed and the movement of goods.

The City of London had been self-governing since the 12th century, and jealously guarded its privileges which had been won from the king and carefully noted down over many years. There was, nevertheless, a constant neurosis

---

6   See pp. 26–7.
7   CLB Letter Book L, p. 155.

regarding the possibility of the king in Parliament taking these privileges away, and this anxiety contributed to the maintenance of high standards of local government, achieved mainly by a careful regard for custom and precedent, coupled with an appropriate use of spectacle and symbolism.[8] The high standards had been matched over the centuries by the most scrupulous record-keeping. Because of the structure of the City Corporation, three parallel records were maintained, the Repertories, recording the proceedings of the Court of Aldermen, the Journals, recording the proceedings of the Court of Common Council, and the Letter Books, which served as an *aide-mémoire* and a record-book for anything to which the officers of the Corporation might wish to refer at a later date. The Letter Books came to be used most regularly to record elections of successive Mayors and Sheriffs and other officers, and also to record private bond deposits by citizens, mostly in relation to gifts to children contingent on coming of age or marriage. But there is a great variety of other information, especially regarding the livery companies. Unusual crimes and punishments also feature in the Letter Books, as for example the fate of William Campion,[9] who in 1478 'unlawfully tapped a conduit pipe' and brought water into his house in Fleet Street. Sentence was passed that Campion should be brought out of Bread Street Compter (gaol), and:

> set upon a horse with a vessel like unto a conduit full of water upon his head, the same water running by small pipes out of the same vessel and that when the water is wasted new water to be put in the said vessel again; and further that he should be conveyed to divers parts of the City and proclamation made in each place of his misdoing.

The Corporation records are claimed to be the best local government records in Europe, and in the absence of any records of its own dating from this time anyone researching the history of the Musicians Company during its first two hundred years must rely heavily upon them.

It is therefore to these records, specifically Volume 10 of the Journals, folios 183–5, that we now turn, in the hope of coming to a tentative conclusion as to why the Petition which resulted in the incorporation of the Fellowship of Minstrels was presented in June 1500, and not at some other time. It may be helpful to identify first the main objects which the Act of Incorporation was designed to achieve, and then to turn back to the preamble which set out the Petitioners' grievances and explained (ostensibly) why they were seeking relief.

The regulations containing the main objects are as follows (I have numbered the paragraphs for convenience):

---

[8] See Sheila Lindenbaum, 'The London Midsummer Watch' at pp. 174 and 179–182 in *City and Spectacle in Medieval Europe*, ed. Barbara A. Hanawalt and Kathryn L. Reyerson (Minneapolis: University of Minnesota Press 1994).

[9] CLB Letter Book L, p. 160. Later entries in Letter Book L show that Campion was by then a respectable Grocer of some standing. He *may* have been an ancestor of Thomas, born in London in 1567!

1.   That no manner of foreigner of whatsoever condition he be occupy any minstrelsy, singing, or playing upon any instrument within any parish of this City or franchise upon any church holidays, or dedication days hallowed or kept within the parish; nor at any churchings, weddings or brotherhoods made or kept within the City or franchise upon pain every such foreign minstrel after warning to him given by the Wardens to pay 3s 4d for every time that he should be found doing contrary to this Act, the one half to be paid to the common use of the City and the other half to the common box of the said Craft.

The word 'foreigner' does not mean alien. It means anyone who did not have the freedom of the City, unless employed by or apprenticed to a Freeman.

Franchises or Liberties were areas outside the City (such as Smithfield) which came under City governance, and enjoyed the same privileges.

It is interesting to note that the restriction on making music was limited to special occasions. 'Busking' on an ordinary working day seems to have been excluded.

2.   That for good order and honest Rule . . . the Fellowship of Minstrels, being Freemen of the City, have power and liberty to assemble in a convenient place on a predetermined day every year for evermore to choose two able persons of the Fellowship to be Wardens of the Fellowship for the year following. If any person so chosen Warden refuse and forsake the said office to pay 20s, half to the City and half to the common box.

Note that at the outset the Company had no Master, just the two Wardens. At some time between 1500 and 1518, probably in the first year,[10] the most senior office of Master was established.

3.   That the Common Box of the Fellowship be from year to year in the custody of the Wardens. And of all such money as they shall receive in the term of their Wardenship, the Wardens shall deliver an account in writing to the whole Fellowship, or the greater part of them, within one month after being discharged from office, upon pain to pay 20s [divided as before]. The keys of the box to be in the keeping of two honest freemen of the craft such as by the common voice of the Fellowship . . . shall be named or assigned.

This would have been a safe (if inconvenient) way of preventing fraud.

4.   Every Freeman or brother of the said craft pay yearly towards the supportation of the charges of the said craft 12d by year that is to say 3d at every quarter day. Every person not paying this manner of quarterage [sic] at every quarter day or within 20 days next and immediately following to pay as often 3s 4d [to be divided as before].

This is the first use of the expression 'freeman or brother of the said craft' which is discussed under Article 6.

It is always difficult to relate to fees paid or charged in times remote to one's own; it may be helpful to note that in 1500 the annual basic salary of a City Wait was £1. 6s. 8d,[11] to which of course would be added performance fees for any

---

10 See p. 41.
11 See Walter Woodfill, *Musicians in English Society from Elizabeth to Charles I* (Princeton: Princeton University Press 1953), p. 37.

occasion which was not part of the Waits' regular function. Waits were well paid in comparison with the ordinary City Minstrel. The annual quarterage might therefore be the equivalent of two weeks' earnings, and the default fine about 3 months' earnings, which would be crippling, if the Wardens were able to collect it.

5.   Every Freeman of the said craft shall present every of his apprentice to the Warden of the said craft within a month after any such apprentice shall be bound, paying at his presentation to the common use of the craft 20d, and if any person be found negligent and do not present his apprentice within a month paying the fine of 20d as aforesaid such person to forfeit 10s [divided as before].

Presumably the apprentice's master would have the right to present to whichever Warden happened to be available or whom he knew best.

6.   If any person enfranchised in the said craft or brother of the same warned by the Beadle to come to the quarter days or to any assembly of the Wardens without reasonable excuse absents himself or is not willing to come, to pay on each occasion 2s. [divided as before].

This is the first mention of a Beadle. Unfortunately there is no record of his name. The words 'enfranchised in the said craft or brother of the same' suggest that there may have been two different 'classes' of Freemen, but there is no clear answer to what the distinction may have been. It seems from Article 8 that both definitions related to practising minstrels. Could it perhaps represent the difference between those who had served their apprenticeship within the Fellowship and those who had purchased their freedom 'by redemption'?

7.   That no enfranchised person or brother rebuke, revile or grieve with slanderous words or words of villainies the Wardens or any other person brother or freeman of the Fellowship upon pain to pay at every time that any of them shall be found culpable of such unfitting language 6s 8d [divided as before].

At this stage it is not stated that the adjudication in such a case could be made by the Company's officers, and therefore it would be necessary to have the case heard before the Mayor's court. Later the officers of the Company would have the right to levy the fines in such cases.[12]

8.   That none of the Fellowship whether enfranchised minstrel or brother of the said craft teach or inform any other person than his own apprentice in any point of the feat of minstrelsy [offenders to be fined 20s to be divided as before], nevertheless if any Gentleman or Merchant be disposed to learn anything for pleasure it shall be lawful to inform and teach every such Gentleman and Merchant.

The notion that any musician should be at liberty to teach as many amateurs as he wishes (such pupils representing no threat to the profession) while being restricted to one apprenticed professional, was a restricting practice and a long

___

[12] See pp. 42–3.

way from any recognition of the need for group teaching of future professionals. Members of the Musicians' Company consistently failed to look beyond the traditional confines of the apprentice system, as we shall see, and made matters worse by limiting apprenticeship to a one-to-one relationship.

9.　That no Freeman take any servant by year or in covenant for any term more or less or otherwise than by apprenticeship for 7 years according to the laudable custom of this City upon pain &c [fine of 40s, divided as before].

The limit of one apprentice was not spelt out in the original regulations, but was specifically introduced in 1518.

PROVIDED THAT these Acts and Ordinances extend not to or be prejudicial to the King's Minstrels, the Queen's the Princes' the Queen Mother's or to any Minstrels of Lords in the Parliament, but they and every of them use and occupy the feat of minstrelsy within the same City as they did or ought to do before the making of this Ordinance so they be not resident, inhabit or continually conversant within the City.

Although Henry VII had effectively moved his court to Westminster (and Greenwich and Richmond), and had much less to do with the City than Edward IV, the minstrels of the royal household had an absolute right to play when in attendance on the king, wherever that might be, as for example when he took up residence in his City palace, Baynards Castle, at the time of his elder son Arthur's marriage to Catherine of Aragon in 1501.

The 'Princes' were Arthur and Henry, each with their own minstrels. The reference to the 'Queen Mother' must be to the king's mother Lady Margaret Beaufort (who was never queen), not to Edward IV's widowed queen, Elizabeth (Woodville), the king's mother-in-law, who had died in 1492. Lady Margaret survived until 1509.

These were the ordinances which comprised the original regulations of the Company. In some respects they resembled the ordinances of other Livery Companies, which are recorded in great quantity in Letter Book L, sometimes in the form of a completely new set of ordinances and at other times recording certain new provisions requiring the approval of the City Corporation. This was the result of a decree by the Corporation late in 1487 forbidding 'Misteries' to make or introduce new regulations without the approval of the Corporation. The Letter Book then notes that:

Wardens of Misteries brought in their books of ordinances that had not been approved by the Court of Aldermen, and those ordinances were cancelled, and the leaves of the books on which they were recorded were cut out.[13]

Whether the increased activity influenced the Minstrels in deciding to incorporate with ordinances of their own is debatable, but they could not have been

---

[13] CLB Letter Book L, p. 246.

unaware of what was going on. On the other hand fourteen of the Companies which asked the Court for approval for their new ordinances did so in 1488, and although a few others followed in more leisurely fashion, the pressure had eased off by 1500.

What then were the alleged reasons for the Minstrels' Fellowship wishing to incorporate? Here is the preamble to the Petition:

To the Right Honourable Lord and Worshipful My Lord Mayor and Aldermen:-

In humble wise showing and complaining unto your good lordship and masterships, your daily bedesmen the wardens and fellowship of minstrels and freemen of the City, that whereas the continual recourse of foreign minstrels daily resorting to this City out of all the countries of England occupying here at more liberty than freemen, causing your said suppliant freemen to be brought into such poverty and decay that they have not the ability to bear charges to pay lot and scot and do their duty as other freemen do because their living is taken from them by such manner of foreigns

And where also as these foreign minstrels be accustomed to do great displeasure and grievously annoy the Citizens of this City as in pressing to their tables upon the churchholidays dedications Churchings Weddings and other feasts malgre the owners of houses where they resort without desire of any person sometime five or six without cunning standing unware at abodes and to the great grief displeasure of the Citizens and of their honest friends and neighbours as happen to be present, and to the great hurt and hindrance of your said suppliants

Please it your Lordship and Masterships in consideration of the premises and to the intent that your said suppliant freemen might have some furtherance and relief before foreigns to grant enact and establish these Articles following as far as they be reasonable in reverence of God and of Saint Anthony their patron to whom they shall continually pray for the prosperous state of you and of this noble City.

The minstrels were in good company, so far as the grounds of their complaint was concerned. In May 1493 the Skinners had complained that:

journeymen, freemen of the Craft, were unable to obtain work owing to the great influx of strangers and foreign journeymen.[14]

Next year it was the turn of the Tailors, whose grievance was that:

freemen journeymen of the Craft were unable to obtain work owing to the influx of persons as well as alien strangers as Foreign journeymen; and further that a great number of strangers 'botchers' infested the City, each keeping daily in his house 3 or 4 strangers occupying the same handicraft, to the great prejudice of the King's liege subjects, who would gladly undertake the work if the strangers were not there.[15]

The question is whether these complaints were genuine, or whether this was a standard ploy designed to prove hardship, causing the petitioners to fall into a

---

[14] CLB Letter Book L, p. 295.
[15] CLB Letter Book L, p. 302.

state of 'poverty'. Poverty, or the threat of it, was an essential ingredient in the formation of a trade fraternity or guild. There had to be an element of protection for the poor oppressed members of the craft which if the petition were not granted would not be forthcoming. If the need for this could not be shown, the Licence in Mortmain, which was customarily available to City guilds because it had always been regarded as a charitable act to allow them to form an association for their own protection, would not apply, preventing the guild from holding property 'in perpetuity'. Looked at from the point of view of modern jurisprudence the whole process had become little more than a legal fiction, but it was part of the custom of the City of London, and vigorously defended as part of its privileges as well as being necessary for the promotion of trade and industry.

One can be reasonably sure therefore that the drafting of petitions such as the minstrels' was in the hands of experienced professionals, who knew the formula that would succeed with the Mayor and Aldermen, and enable them to collect their fee. Not all such petitions however had the touch of local colour which some skilful hand had introduced into the minstrels' preamble. The thought of half a dozen cacophonous rustics pushing their way in, uninvited, at a church holiday or wedding celebration – it was a nice touch, and should have produced a smile or two and won the sympathy of the Court from the outset. Whether occurrences of this kind were common, and if they were, whether they would actually have had a significant effect on the City minstrels' earnings, is very questionable. A greater threat, as is shown by subsequent ordinances, came from freemen of other companies who purported to be minstrels, but did not perform to the required standard.[16]

A careful examination of these ordinances provides some interesting information about the Company at its inception. We have already noted that the Fellowship had no Master, but from the preamble it is clear that the first Wardens had already been appointed. They would either have been chosen just in time to present the petition, or else the fact that they were in office indicates that there was already an unrecognised Fellowship in existence,[17] and that some set of circumstances now made it necessary to incorporate according to the custom of the City. There were many such Fellowships, Fraternities and Guilds in London, for example the Guild of St Nicholas, to which most church musicians belonged.[18]

It is clear from the petition that the most important, and probably the most vulnerable, earnings source for the City minstrels were the religious feasts referred to; the church holidays, dedication or patronal festivals, churchings and weddings; also 'brotherhood' occasions, such as livery feasts. There were of course no concerts in the modern sense of the word. The official city music was the prerogative of the City Waits, and church music was sung and played by church musicians, the 'conduct' and the clerkes. The 'three Ds', dining, drinking

16 See pp. 48–9.
17 See p. 31.
18 See p. 45.

and dancing, whether on church feast-days or other occasions, were therefore the principal source of the London minstrels' livelihood.

The reference to St Anthony as patron of the Fellowship is of particular interest, because he features also in the 1469 Charter to the King's Minstrels.[19] It is the only self-evident link between the two bodies, but it is a significant one because it lends credence to the supposition that the Fellowship was an offshoot of the King's Minstrels, deliberately established because the latter no longer had any part to play in City life.

The Hospital of St Anthony (of Vienne, not the Egyptian hermit or of Padua), which stood at the junction of Threadneedle Street and Broad Street, was built on the site of a synagogue in the 13th century, when Henry III granted it to the brotherhood of St Anthony. It was used as a hospital and became a Royal Free Chapel in the reign of Henry V. Shortly afterwards a school and almshouses were added, and the whole institution was annexed to the Collegiate Church of St George's Windsor by Edward IV in 1475. By 1500 it was a school of some renown at which both John Colet and Thomas More had been pupils,[20] and it had a flourishing song school, the records of the Guild of St Nicholas showing a succession of Masters of Choristers. It could therefore have been through the musical excellence of the services at St Anthony's that the saint had acquired the patronage of music and minstrels in London.

The church itself had been rebuilt in 1499. The minstrels would surely have been associated in some way with the funding for this work. Is it stretching speculation too far to suggest that because the minstrels hoped that they might be granted part of the Hospital as a site for a Hall, they felt, when the church was rebuilt, that it was time to become incorporated for reasons of mortmain?

Sadly, we have no facts to work on which would put this hypothesis to the test, and all one can say is that it was as good a reason as any for seeking incorporation at this time. We can probably rule out the sudden inrush of 'foreigns' for reasons which have already been discussed. There may have been some concern at the arrival from Flanders and other parts of the Continent of new music forms and instruments, leading to defensive action by the City minstrels, but the trickle had not yet developed into a flood, as it did in the next reign.

The peace, which was referred to at the beginning of this chapter, might have been enough to induce the minstrels to seek the benefit of incorporation. If this was the reason, then the ostensible complaints in the preamble may carry a little more weight. It would have meant that the ending of all hostilities and of the threat of their resumption would have restored the freedom of minstrels from all parts of the country to resume travelling, with London as their prime destination. Again there is no evidence, apart from the petition itself, that this did occur.

We are left therefore with an undisputed, but unexplained fact that on 4 June

---

[19] See p. 30.
[20] Peter Ackroyd, *The Life of Thomas More* (London: Chatto & Windus 1998), pp. 17–25, 72.

1500 the Fellowship of Minstrels, which after a hundred years shed its first coat and became the Worshipful Company of Musicians, was incorporated and has continued ever since in uninterrupted existence. What it had been immediately prior to incorporation, how many members of the Fellowship there were, and what were their names, we may never know, although some tentative assumptions are put forward at the end of the next chapter.

The purpose of this book is to track the progress of the Fellowship through five centuries. Sometimes the tracks disappear, sometimes the Company itself appears to have been at risk of expiring. Certainly until the 20th century the word 'progress' carried with it little sense of improvement in the Company's fortunes. In fact there is a case to be made that the minstrel/musician was better off in the Middle Ages than he has been in more modern times. To test this hypothesis before moving forward into the 16th century, it will be necessary to take a look at minstrels and music-makers in London and elsewhere in earlier years.

2

Making their Minstrelsy

'MINSTREL' is a beautiful word, and would probably still be in common par-
lance if it had not been smeared with disreputable connotations in the 16th
century, as we shall see in the next chapter. The word was derived from the mediaeval Latin word 'ministrellus' and meant 'a little servant' (by implication) of the
king or of a feudal magnate. It therefore embraced confidential messengers and
personal servants and attendants as well as entertainers in the royal and noble
households, and it was not until the 14th century that its use was generally
limited to players of musical instruments.

If the Musicians' Company were now still known as 'The Worshipful
Company of Minstrels', one wonders if the term would be used in the exclusive
sense, so that it comprised only musicians, or would it be inclusive, thereby
opening the door to poets, media artists and comedians, members of Equity,
impresarios and play producers, theatre proprietors, circus performers, and the
Magic Circle, all of whom are the true descendants of the story-tellers, fools and
clowns, jugglers, acrobats and dancers, actors, conjurors and exhibitors of performing animals, who were classified as minstrels in the High Middle Ages? In
addition, in line of descent from the confidential messengers, sergeants-at-arms
and the heralds, who were also within the definition, there would be the Diplo-
matic Corps, MI5 and MI6 and the College of Heralds.

Members of the Company will perhaps be thankful that at its inception it was
an exclusive guild for musicians, but there may be some who have joined the
Company as amateur musicians or out of their love for music who could now
claim that if the wider definition applied they too, through the nature of their
work, would be in the right 'trade guild'.

By the time of Henry V, in the early 15th century, the list of minstrels who
travelled to France in his entourage appears to have been composed almost
entirely of performing musicians.[1] Nevertheless the Marshal of the King's Minstrels at the end of Edward IV's reign, Alexander Mason, who continued in office

---

[1] See Rymer's *Foedera*, 29 May 1415.

under Richard III and Henry VII, was a 'geyster', which means either a story-teller or a jester.

Minstrels skilled in music had to be adaptable; they had to be able to sing and dance as well as play a variety of instruments, and at least until the 14th century the 'harper' was synonymous with the storyteller. Most of them would have drawn the line at tumbling or circus-keeping. If they were household servants they also had to follow their lord around, in peace and in war, and would be trained for a role on the battlefield, as well as at court. The waits on the other hand, who were the civic equivalent of the household minstrels and were also categorised as minstrels, had a fairly static responsibility, as it was their job to keep the watch in their respective cities at night, and to sound the alarm on loud instruments which far exceeded the maximum amount of noise of which the human voice was capable. From these unmusical origins sprung their secondary function of providing musical entertainment on official occasions, and it was in this role that they spent much time augmenting their wages by travelling to engagements at some distance.[2]

Whatever their actual individual status, prior to the 14th century the vast majority of minstrels were servants, as the word 'ministrellus' indicates, and this meant that unless and until they achieved some degree of autonomy there would have been little opportunity or initiative to form associations among themselves.

There was however at least one example at a very early date, not in England but in the Flemish wool and cloth market city of Arras, and such was the mobil-ity of minstrels and others around Europe throughout this period that it is possi-ble that the Arras Fraternity may have set the precedent for the minstrels' guilds subsequently formed in other Northern European towns and cities, although it has been suggested that it was nothing more than a religious brotherhood.[3] At this early date it is difficult to distinguish between a religious fraternity and a trade or craft guild, and it is perhaps idle to try to do so, as church observances were so tightly linked to everyday life. What is important is that an association of minstrels and others was formed under a 'communal' city government. Like the cities of North Italy at this time, Arras was virtually an independent city-state and had established a commune at the beginning of the 12th century. During the struggle to maintain its independence it is said that two minstrels saved the town from capture in 1105 by the miraculous intervention of the Virgin Mary, who gave them a candle, which was known as 'le joyel d'Arras'. This moment of glory set the Arras minstrels up with sufficient status to form a minstrels' guild, and apparently local and foreign minstrels 'flocked to join', as well as the Arras bour-geoisie.[4] A song contest was instituted in about 1120, and this continued for at

---

2 J. Southworth, *The English Medieval Minstrel* (Woodbridge: Boydell Press 1989), pp. 128–9.
3 See Nigel Wilkins, *Music in the Age of Chaucer* (Cambridge: D.S. Brewer 1979).
4 See Anne Sutton, 'Merchants, Music and Social Harmony', *London Journal*, vol. 17, no. 1, 1992.

least two hundred years. The guild built an elaborate stone tower for itself in 1200, and there is a copy of its statutes dating from 1224.

Around the end of the 13th century, when a similar celebration was instituted in London,[5] the principal function of the Arras guild was to hold the Festival of the Puy, which took place just after Trinity Sunday and lasted for three days, with a programme of plays, satires, *chants royaux* and what might be called 'party games', of varying degrees of coarseness and refinement. The *chant royale* or 'chansoun reale', as it was called in London, was a special five-verse song, and in its original form in Arras was a song in honour of the Virgin Mary composed by each entrant in the competition.[6] In London, where the conditions of entry were broadened, it was a chivalrous love song. The song competition was the central feature of the 'Puy', the winner of which would be chosen by an expert jury and would be crowned amid feasting and dancing. What was interesting was that the competitors, certainly in London, were usually not minstrels at all, but merchants, who in 1304 also formed the majority of the jury. In Arras it seems that those participating were a mixed band of minstrels, merchants and others.

The link between merchants and music and conviviality is not perhaps immediately obvious, but it had existed from earliest times.[7] Perhaps if one visualises the plodding train of mediaeval pack-horses and then superimposes on this ancient scene recent memories of commercial travellers and their way of life, the picture begins to come into focus. The mediaeval merchant had to be at the point of sale of his product, and have it with him. Whether he took it himself, or rode on ahead and waited for his drovers to bring it along behind, he would have time to kill. What better way to fill the hours than to make up a song for the next gathering of merchants (there must have been some merchants who were unmusical, but if music was an integral part of their life, it might have actually been a factor in the selection and training of apprentices). After the fair or market, when business was done, celebration would follow. In Arras, Amiens and London, the celebration was formalised into the Puy competition, known in London as the 'Feste du Pui'.

A fraternity was established in London around the event, complete with its own ordinances providing for a yearly mass in St Helen's Priory, a common box, and a chaplain who was paid to say masses for the souls of deceased members.[8] Whoever won the competition became the 'prince' for the year, and had twelve 'assistants' who would be his drinking companions and his supporters in the processions and formal ceremonies during the year. This may have been a conscious imitation of the structural pyramid of the earliest craft and trade guilds,

5   See George Unwin, *The Gilds and Companies of London*, 4th edn (London: Frank Cass 1963), p. 98.
6   Sutton, p. 4.
7   Sutton, p. 11.
8   Unwin, p. 100.

such as the Weavers and the Fishmongers. It would have been too early for the Mercers (1394) or the Merchant Taylors (1327). By the time the Merchant Taylors came into existence as a guild, the London Puy was extinct, and was never again revived in England. In France however the custom continued in a somewhat spasmodic way, and one revival there is of particular interest as it appears to have been the first recognition of St Cecilia in Northern Europe. The date was 1571, and the celebration on St Cecilia's Day took place at Evreux in Normandy. The Foundation that organised the event, which continued for at least 20 years, was known as 'Le Puy de Musique'. Prizes for composition were awarded annually from 1575.[9]

Beginning at about the same time as the London Puy, citizens of Florence, who were members of one of several 'companies', which were associated not with a craft or trade but with a particular church, would spend much time learning to sing *laude*, devotional songs written in Italian specifically for the laity.[10] It would be interesting to know whether the original idea travelled to Florence from Arras with a consignment of cloth, in which case the Florentine practice, which lasted until the time of Napoleon, may have had the same origins as the London Puy.

London at the turn of the 13th century, near the end of a great king's reign, seems to have been awash with music. It is almost as if the merchants decided to do their own entertaining because the minstrels were too busy elsewhere. There was a splendid double royal wedding in 1290, when Edward I's elder daughter Joan was married to the Earl of Gloucester, followed by the wedding of a younger daughter, Margaret, to the Duke of Brabant. After the celebrations were over, 426 minstrels were paid off by Walter de Stertone, the king's harper, at a cost of £100.[11] The last great celebration of the reign took place at Whitsun in 1306, on the occasion of the knighting of the Prince of Wales and many of his contemporaries, before the king's departure from London on a penal expedition to subdue the Scots. Here is the scene as described by Nigel Wilkins:

> There were players on harps, lutes, psalteries, tabors, fiddles, organs, trumpets, nakers, gitterns, bells, citoles, crowds and flutes; there were minstrels from the service of the Count of Warwick, the Bishop of Durham, the Patriarch, the Prince, the Count and Countess of Hereford, Lord Percy, the Count and Countess of Lancaster, the Count of Arundel and of several lesser households; minstrels came from all directions, including from across the channel – Champagne, Boulogne, Brabant, Quitacre, Leylonde, Blida, Duffelde, Swylingstone, Normanville, Colecestria, Salopia, Trenham, Brayles, Chorleye, Scardeburghe etc; some had delightful

[9] See William Henry Husk, *Musical Celebrations on St Cecilia's Day in the 16th, 17th and 18th Centuries* (Bell & Daldy 1857), chapter 6.

[10] See Blake Wilson, *Music and Merchants: the Laudesi Companies of Republican Florence* (Oxford: Clarendon Press 1992).

[11] Southworth, p. 62.

'professional' names such as Matilda Makejoye, 'Perle in the Eghe',[12] or Reginald 'le Menteur'.[13]

The event has been the subject of a detailed study of minstrelsy by Constance Bullock-Davies in her book *Menestrellorum Multitudo*.[14] Two separate payrolls, one in Latin and the other in French listing all the minstrels present at the ceremony have survived, and the book analyses the list and provides whatever biographical information is available in relation to each of the persons who 'made their minstrelsy' at the feast, as well as a description of the historical events leading up to the ceremony and its aftermath. The book's special interest is that it relates to a moment in English history which was the high water mark for minstrelsy as a solo act. In examining the list of the minstrels who were instrumentalists, and excluding the trumpeters and drummers, as their function was ceremonial, there were almost as many harpists present (twenty-six) as all the other instrumentalists put together (thirty, excluding two organists and a bell-ringer). The harpists, therefore, were predominant in the musical entertainment, using their small harps to accompany themselves in solo song. It was the old minstrelsy, derived from the harper and troubadour tradition, characterised by the solo performance (like a music hall 'turn'), on terms of assumed (or sometimes real) familiarity with the presiding host. Its music would be partly memorised, partly improvised. After the death of Edward I the following year, this form of entertainment went out of fashion and it was the vielle-players and crowders who could play together for dancing and did not sing, who were most in demand.[15] It was the beginning of ensemble playing, in groups of two or three related instruments, only the bass or percussion instruments, if used, being outside the 'family'. David Munrow, in the companion volume to his famous album *Instruments of the Middle Ages and Renaissance*, talked about 'the dazzling variety of musical instruments shown in the hands of angels by religious painters of the 14th and 15th centuries', and wryly commented 'Such angel concerts belong not to this world but to paradise, and they bear little relation to contemporary . . . practice.'[16]

In another respect also the individual minstrels were at a peak in terms of social standing at this time, and their favoured status survived through the reign of Edward II. For record purposes the members of the royal household were

---

[12] According to Bullock-Davies (see note 14, below) Matilda Makejoy and Perle in the Eghe were not 'professional' names at all. Makejoy was a known surname; Matilda was a famous acrobatic dancer. Perle in the Eghe was a blind minstrel, suffering from cataracts. Bullock-Davies suggests (p. 146) that both may have been London-based minstrels.

[13] Wilkins, pp. 139–40; the detail is from *Annales Londoniensis*.

[14] Constance Bullock-Davies, *Menestrellorum Multitudo: Minstrels at a Royal Feast* (Cardiff: University of Wales Press 1978).

[15] Bullock-Davies, p. 28.

[16] David Munrow, *Instruments of the Middle Ages and Renaissance* (Oxford: Oxford University Press 1976), p. 5.

divided into three classes, and some of the minstrels were recognised to be in the first class, and of the same standing as the knights bachelor, clerks, sergeants and squires.[17] The daily wage of these 'squire-minstrels' was 7½d per day. Lesser minstrels ranked with the king's falconers and huntsmen, and received 4½d per day. When Edward III came to the throne he reduced all minstrels to the lower rate.

Despite the chaos and the political disasters of Edward II's reign, the early part of the 14th century was an important time of change for minstrels outside the royal and noble households. Because of the vast amount of information preserved in the records of the royal household, music historians tend to concentrate on the court musicians from earliest times until the end of the 17th century. In the 14th century information about minstrels in the city of London is practically non-existent, but one cannot therefore assume they did not exist, or that they were not hard at work keeping up with the latest developments in the practice and performance of music. We have noted the 426 minstrels at the royal wedding in London in 1290. Most of these would have been outside the royal household. We know that some of the minstrels at the 1306 Knighting were wealthy, worked part-time and had property in London.[18] From the City's own records a Letter Book entry for 1334 shows a payment of 68s 8d to 'minstrels'.[19] Of a different order, but of equal interest is the account of a fight in Cornhill in 1324 when:

> a dealer in skins named Thomas de Lenne was so angered at the music of a minstrel named Thomas Somer that he struck him with a door-bar and pursued him to kill him, only to be stabbed himself by the same Somer. It was playing and not singing that moved him to such violent criticism.[20]

Minstrels travelled extensively (most of them were not 'wandering', but going purposefully from one place to another), and this tradition, which increased their sense of corporate fellowship, continued in the 14th century until interrupted by war. Minstrels gathered regularly from all over Europe in Flemish cities and elsewhere. Their meetings were known in French as 'escoles', and indeed their principal purpose was to enable the minstrels to renew their repertoire. The gatherings usually took place during Lent, when music at court was banned. There was one such gathering in Ypres in 1313, another in Bruges in 1318, and a 'School for Fiddlers' in Malines in 1328.[21]

Writing about minstrels in the 14th century Nigel Wilkins says:

> This was above all a time of consolidation for the profession, of the formation of guilds, of tighter organisation, and most performers were attached to royal or

---

17 Bullock-Davies, p. 15.
18 Bullock-Davies, pp. 93, 114.
19 CLB Letter Book F, p. 4.
20 Wilkins, p. 131, quoting from E. Rickert, *Chaucer's World* (New York 1948), pp. 17–18.
21 Wilkins, pp. 134–5.

influential households or to a town as their employer, received regular income and wore a distinctive livery.[22]

This is a fair summary of the overall position, but it contains one or two contradictions. The initiative for the formation of guilds would not have come from employed household musicians. As we have already noted they were servants, and concepts of trades unions were unheard of at that time. Nor did members of guilds wear a livery because they received a regular income or salary, but as a sign of solidarity among a group of self-employed persons in the same profession. This is borne out by the signatories to the Statutes of the Paris Guild of Minstrels, the earliest of the regulatory guilds, which was formed in 1321. There are thirty-seven names, including four married women and three waits. Apart from the three waits there is nothing to suggest that the others were in full-time employment. The statutes themselves are reproduced in summary form in Appendix 1, as they provide an interesting comparison with the 16th century Ordinances of the Musicians' Company, and also may be taken as an indication of what sort of regulations the London fraternity may have added to their original 'Agreement' of 1350. It will be observed that the Paris minstrels were of sufficient standing to have a street named after them.

When considering why the minstrels of London chose to set up their fraternity in 1350, it may be of significance to note that it was during the first half of the 14th century that many of the more influential crafts and trades set up their own guilds or fraternities. These included the Barbers (1308), the Blacksmiths (1325), the Carpenters (1333), the Cutlers (1344), the Grocers (1345) and the Glovers (1349). In 1327, at the very beginning of Edward III's reign, the Girdlers, Goldsmiths, Skinners and Tailors (later the Merchant Taylors) were all established in the same year.[23]

Unlike the religious fraternities, which changed little until the Reformation when they were dissolved, the craft and trade guilds very quickly obtained regulatory ordinances and disciplinary powers from the Corporation and so evolved into prototype livery companies with the right to control their 'mistery' (i.e. the craft or trade in which they were engaged). Half of The Great Twelve companies also obtained royal charters from Edward III.[24] The benefit of the Royal Charter, in contrast to City Ordinances, was that the powers could be exercised as widely throughout the kingdom as the charter provided. Ordinances were limited in scope to London and its 'liberties'.

---

[22] Wilkins, p. 126.

[23] These dates are taken from the official Corporation of London booklet 'The Livery Companies of the City of London', published in 1997, except for the Grocers, for whom the booklet gives the date of the first charter (1428), although the Company's own history (see note 26) records the 1345 Ordinances, when the Pepperers turned themselves into the fraternity of Grocers.

[24] Goldsmiths, Skinners, Tailors (and Girdlers) in 1327; Drapers, Vintners and Fishmongers in 1363–64. See Unwin, p. 79.

2. The 1350 Ordinances of the Minstrels Fellowship as presented to the Parliamentary Inquisition in 1389; preserved in the Public Record Office, together with many other similar documents relating to London guilds existing at the time. The document, on parchment, is written in Norman French.

Reverting to the Minstrels and their fraternity, and the Ordinances of 1350, it is instructive to consider in what way these differed, if at all, from those of other craft guilds established at about the same time. Is there any reason to suppose that the fraternity was simply a guild set up for religious purposes?

The wording of the Ordinances[25] (in modern translation) is as follows:

---

[25] The Ordinances written on parchment are held in the Public Record Office under reference C47/46/470. There is, unfortunately, a gap in the modern archives of the Company, so that there is no explanation apart from one paragraph in Alastair Crewdson's book (p. 23) as to how the document was found. Arthur Hill appears to have been unaware of its existence.

To the honour and in the name of our most gentle Lord Jesus Christ and of his Blessed Mother Saint Mary, our advocate.   Amen.

Know all people who this writing shall see or hear that there is an agreement between the Minstrels of London and other good people dwelling in the same city in the year of the Incarnation of our gentle Lord Jesus One thousand three hundred and fifty, in the year of the reign of our Lord King Edward the Third after his conquest the twenty-fourth;

This preamble is somewhat unusual, in referring to an 'agreement' between the minstrels 'and other good people'. At first sight it suggests an element of inse-curity, as if the minstrels were hesitant about standing on their own feet. Who could these 'other good people' be?

That is to say that they have ordained and established between them a Fraternity to endure for the term of their lives;

Taken at its face value, the fraternity would cease to exist on the death of the last of the original group.

And by their common consent they have ordained a common box to which each one of them aforesaid during their lives and the life of each one of them shall place every year thirteen pence sterling, commencing the first time on the feast of the Nativity of St John the Baptist next ensuing after the date of this;

The feast day falls on 24 June. As we do not have the exact date of the deed, we do not know whether the annual contributions were to start in 1350 or 1351.

And the said box shall remain in the keeping of one of the company. And two others shall each of them have a key of the said box in their keeping. And they shall be dwellers in the city. And from year to year each one after the other elected shall have the said box and also a paper in which the names of the said company who pay to the said box are con-tained. And two others [shall have] the two keys without refusal or demur when their turn shall come. Or otherwise let it be permitted to him who desires to refuse the custody of the said box or two keys to be discharged for the year when his turn shall come, paying to the said box for the year in which it shall come into his hands eleven pence for the support of their alms within fifteen days of being discharged, unless there be excuse of poverty or for other good cause

And moreover the before-mentioned keepers of the box and of the keys, or three others of the said company in the absence of the others, shall have power in the name of the whole of the said company to ordain and do that which they shall deem most profitable and most safe for the whole company for the increase of the box

The arrangements for safeguarding the Company's wealth correspond closely to those in the 1500 Ordinances, except that there is one treasurer instead of two. But the discretionary power to do what is 'most profitable . . . for the increase of the box' is rather more adventurous, especially in time of war, as this was. Perhaps there was good money to be made out of provisioning the army in France.

Also it is ordained that if any one of the said fraternity [suffer] by chance of poverty, illness, robbery, maiming, old age, or loss of property or false imprisonment or by any sudden event by the hand of God, and he himself be not the cause of his loss, he shall have each week fourteen pence sterling from the box by the consent of all the companions aforesaid. And then after he is able to work the said company shall lend him from the money in the box, if there be any therein, a sum by their common consent to aid him to recover.

This weekly benefit would be close to the average weekly wage of a skilled labourer. The recovery loan represents generous thinking, even if the box is empty when the time comes!

Also it is agreed among them that if anyone of the said fraternity or of those who are companions of the said fraternity is unwilling to perform the covenant in accordance with the form aforesaid and fails of his payment for a whole year and eleven days and is dwelling in the said city or suburbs of London and is able to pay;

Or if any one of the said company shall offend or cause strife with another and refuse to make amends after having been three times requested so to do and fairly admonished by the said companions and will yet persist in his conduct and malice; That they then expel him from the said fraternity without re-admission. In which case no question shall be raised as to the money he shall have put into the said box but he shall be named and enrolled among the benefactors inscribed in the obituary roll of the Carmelite Friars of the said city so that the benefits conferred upon the said fraternity shall not be lost sight of nor forgotten, but shall always be remembered.

There is a healthy 'rough justice' balance in the equation:

Expulsion = Forfeiture of contributions = Commemoration as benefactor!

The 'roll of the Carmelite Friars' would have been maintained at White Friars, on the south side of Fleet Street.

And in case any one or many desire to enter the said fraternity and they are deemed worthy and loyal to the said company, they shall be received, doing and paying to the box aforesaid in all things as the wardens and the said companions may deem good for the maintenance of their well-being and for the honour of God and of his Mother.

Although in the second paragraph the duration of the fraternity was defined as 'the term of their lives', the ability to 'receive' new members without restriction except as to worthiness and loyalty would in effect make the fraternity self-perpetuating, and this must have been what was intended.

This paragraph contains the first mention of wardens, who, as the next paragraph explains, are the wardens of the 'box'.

In like manner the aforesaid companions will and guarantee to each one of the said fraternity that [if he suffer loss and be in need of] money the wardens of the said box shall lend him a sum, on a sufficient security of its value or more, until a certain fixed day. And in case he fails to repay the said money on that day the security shall be taken to recoup the box for the sum thus lent.

Likewise it is agreed that if any one of the said companions should be impleaded in any false suit made against him by way of malice or wrong, the wardens shall help to effect a reconciliation between the parties, but if they are unwilling to give cheerful assent or to be guided by them, let the common law settle it between them in the name of God.

An article of this nature would normally state that it applied only to disputes between members of the fraternity,[26] and one should perhaps read this into the text, as the wardens would have no standing in regard to a disputant who was not of the guild.

And at what time any one of the said company who now are or shall be is summoned by God let all the company assist in burying him. And within the third day of his decease let there be said from the common box aforesaid thirty masses for his soul and the souls of all Christians.

Although there seem to be remarkably few references to it in the official city records,[27] it is worth noting that these Ordinances were drawn up just as the worst effects of the Black Death had passed. Estimates of the death toll in the previous two years vary between 30% and 50% of the city's population.

And this covenant and ordinance well and loyally to maintain and keep in the form aforesaid the companions of the fraternity have sworn.

And touching the goods and chattels to the same fraternity belonging:-
>There is in the box – xliiiis. vd.
>Also a security on which they have lent money viiis.
>And they have for the company a special garment

Taking a multiple of 500, which sometimes gives the right answer, the equivalent amount of start-up capital in current terms would be £1200, and the loan £200.

None of the names of the oathtakers has survived. If it had not been for the fraternity producing this document for the parliamentary inquisition into the guilds in 1389, the fact that the document is neither signed nor dated would make it difficult to assert with confidence that it was more than a draft or an uncompleted document. The submission of the document in 1389 does however overcome that problem. What cannot be answered with certainty is whether this was truly a craft guild, or just a benefit society.[28] The indications are that it was a craft guild, and a couple of comparisons may be apposite.

If one looks at the Ordinances of the Grocers Company of 1345, it is interesting to see that these too give the appearance of being more appropriate to a mutual benefit society, but in 1346 and in subsequent years the true nature of the guild becomes more apparent. In 1346, the wardens were given power by resolution of the first annual assembly to impose fines. In 1348 it was decided to

---

[26] See, for example, the Grocers' Company ordinances.
[27] In Letter Book F there is one entry for November and there are three for December 1349. CLB Letter Book F, pp. 199 and 210.
[28] I should perhaps put on record that my father in the *Short History* (p. 24) took the view that the fraternity was not a trade guild because the ordinances contained no regulations. I am reluctant to come to the same conclusion.

appoint a beadle, and to fine any member who ignored the beadle's summons. The wardens were not to travel overseas while in office, and not to lend the company's money, except at their own personal risk.[29] By 1351 the Grocers were among the chief misteries who were summoned to elect six representatives to sit on the Common Council.

In the original Ordinances of 1345, the only provisions which do not also appear in those of the Minstrels relate to an annual assembly at the Hospital of St Anthony (under whose patronage the Grocers' fraternity rested) on the saint's day in May, assistance with burial expenses if necessary, arrangements for taking apprentices and an annual supply of livery.[30] Of these it is only the reference to apprentices which puts the nature of the guild beyond doubt, and there is no reason to suppose that the Minstrels did not follow up their original Ordinances with supplementary rules and regulations along the same lines in subsequent years.

Another example worth noting is the Drapers, who formed a fraternity in 1361 called 'the Brotherhood of our Lady of Bethlehem' only three years before obtaining a Royal Charter. They had been late in setting up a guild, despite the presence of many wealthy drapers in the city, but they lost no time in moving from the fraternity to the livery company in 1364 (although the brotherhood continued to exist).[31]

Unwin summed up what was taking place at this time as follows:

> The Grocers' fraternity of St Anthony, and the Drapers' fraternity of St Mary of Bethlehem, were in existence before those companies received their charters, and there is a strong presumption that the same is true of the Skinners' fraternity of Corpus Christi. As far as the greater crafts go, then, there is little reason to doubt that the privileges they procured from the king, and the influence they acquired in the city, were due to the strength of fraternity organisations acting in their names.[32]

Although there was never any question of the Minstrels seeking a charter at this time, it seems logical to assume that the 1350 fraternity was an 'organisation acting in their name'. Unfortunately except for the 1389 inquisition the guild and its ordinances disappear totally from sight, and we have no way of knowing how it fared during the intensely political and violent times of Richard II's early years as king, nor how long it survived after proving its lawful existence in 1389. That it was remembered in 1469 there is no doubt (and perhaps this can be taken to mean that it ceased to exist within what would then have been living memory). The Charter to the King's Minstrels contains the following grant:

29 Baron Heath, *Some account of the Worshipful Company of Grocers* (London: private publication 1869), pp. 50 and 53–4.

30 Heath, pp. 44–8.

31 A.H. Johnson, *The History of the Worshipful Company of the Drapers of London* (Oxford: Clarendon Press 1914), vol. 1, p. 94.

32 Unwin, pp. 95–6.

We . . . by these presents do grant and give licence . . . to the said Walter Haliday &c
. . . to found, to continue and to increase a certain perpetual Brotherhood or guild
(such as we learn that brothers and sisters of the Fraternity of Minstrels of our
Kingdom in times past formed, established and ordained) . . .

This is of course further evidence of the status of the fraternity as a craft guild.
Two possible reasons may be adduced for its failure; either economic difficulties,
competition and a decline in the number of minstrels in London made it unvi-
able, or it may have failed for the very opposite reason – that business was so
good, especially with the opportunities that arose after the French defeat for
working in France during the duarchy (the period from 1420 to 1436 when the
two kingdoms were united), that there was no longer a need for a mutual protection society.

Some recent research indicates that the second alternative may have been the
more likely cause. In his book *The Rise and Fall of Merry England*[33] Ronald
Hutton begins the final summary of his conclusions with the following interpre-
tative statement:

> During the late Middle Ages a religion which embodied the concept of salvation by
> works encouraged a tremendous elaboration of sacred buildings, ornaments and
> rites. In turn, and perhaps assisted by propitious economic factors in some areas,
> the fashion grew of utilizing communal merry-making and semi-secular calendar
> customs to raise money for the parish. It was a society in which ritual and festival
> was utilized for many different purposes at many different levels.[34]

The evidence which Hutton examines in the first chapter of his book suggests
that there was a huge increase in the popular celebration of religious feasts and
festivals at about this time, and although they were not always welcome at some
of the more solemn and sacred festivals, minstrels were able to exploit to their
own advantage not only the cult of processions but also the newly developed
form of moral instruction (and crowd-puller) the biblical play.

The 15th century calendar of Feasts[35] began with the Twelve Days of Christmas, leading on to Plough Sunday, and then to Candlemas and Shrovetide, all of
which would have been celebrated with processions or merry-making or both (a
day which began with a solemn procession to church for Mass would often end
with a feast). After the wild excitement of Shrove Tuesday it was Lent, and there
would be no music for six weeks. This would be the time for professional musicians to meet together, as already mentioned. In the North of England the Bever-
ley guild of minstrels, which was open to membership for any 'honest minstrel'
living between the Rivers Tweed and Trent, held its annual assembly 'on the

---

[33] Ronald Hutton, *The Rise and Fall of Merry England: The Ritual Year 1400–1700* (Oxford:
Clarendon Press 1994).
[34] Hutton, p. 261.
[35] All the information in the following paragraph is extracted from the excellent and much
fuller description in chapter 1 of Hutton's book.

rogation days of Lent'. When the Lenten fast finally ended there would be the Palm Sunday processions, and a variety of observances at Eastertide. The next festival was St George's Day on 23 April, celebrated in the 15th century as never before. This was followed soon after by the once-pagan festival of May Day, which opened a season of merry-making lasting for the next two months. The festivities, which of course varied from parish to parish, were known as May ales or May games, church ales or summer plays. They were celebrations of 'summer and of communal life',[36] and were (like the village fete today – can one imagine a village fete without music?) a source of revenue for parish funds. These summer festivities were largely ignored in the London parishes, but this may have been because of the Midsummer Watch, described in the next chapter.[37] Whitsun seems to have been the favourite time for the ales and games. In the church calendar in late spring Rogation would have been observed as a fast, followed closely by the Feast of the Ascension. At midsummer, the comparatively new Festival of Corpus Christi was celebrated with processions (the Host being paraded through the streets), and also very commonly with biblical or 'mystery' plays. These were often the responsibility of the craft guilds in the cities and towns. In Coventry, for example, it is known that 'the city's crafts spent lavishly on costumes and musicians', and there were forty craft guilds.[38] By contrast there is no record of Corpus Christi plays in London. The Corpus Christi festival was followed almost immediately by the festivities of St Peter's Eve on 28 June.

Late summer brought the time of harvest and harvest fairs (including London's St Bartholomew's Fair which lasted for a fortnight from 24 August), continuing into October. At the end of that month there would be a sombre, but sometimes splendid, observance of the Feast of All Souls, with which solemn music would be associated. Advent was another time of fasting, but some communities broke the fast on St Nicholas' Day and celebrated with elaborate 'Boy Bishop' ceremonies. And so back to Christmas. The pattern that emerges is of an almost continuous flow of communal festivities (except during fast-time), demanding participation by minstrels all over the country. The music provided would be fairly basic and high standards of musicianship would not be needed.

There was some resentment and resistance on the part of employers in London to the proliferation of feast days (the Church expected labourers to stop ordinary work on those days; this meant that employers in the 15th century lost about 45 working days per employee per annum, one reason perhaps why London was in the forefront of the Reformation movement).

The more the nation's labourers feasted and danced the more the minstrels lined their pockets and purses, and in these fortunate circumstances we can leave the original fraternity to rest in its redundancy. The profession was doing well without it. But as the editors of the City Corporation booklet, 'The Livery Com-

---

[36] Hutton, pp. 27–8.
[37] See p. 35.
[38] Hutton, p. 42.

panies of the City of London', have graciously extended the life of the Musicians' Company by one hundred and fifty years[39] it would perhaps be appropriate at this point to attempt to put beyond doubt the lack of continuity between the 1350 Fraternity and the 1500 Fellowship.

When basing an argument on documents that are silent, it is hard to be conclusive, so the evidence of the Calendar of Letter Books may not carry sufficient weight on its own. However the extract from the 1469 Charter already quoted, which leaves no doubt that the former Fraternity was then extinct, confirms what the Letter Books appear to be saying. Book K, covering the reign of Henry VI, contains numerous lists of 'Masters of Misteries sworn', with the names of masters and their companies. There is no mention of Minstrels. Virtually every page of Books K and L contains entries relating to one company or another. Minstrels are conspicuous by their absence. The only entries for minstrels relate to three individuals who at different dates are excused jury duty through age and infirmity,[40] and entries like the following from 1423 which vividly demonstrates the lowly function which some minstrels in the city were expected to perform (and which they probably enjoyed):

> Alison Boston condemned to stand in the pillory three market days for an hour each day, being brought thither from prison with pipes or other open minstrelsy, for having let to hire for immoral purposes her innocent young apprentice.[41]

In the absence of any new evidence to the contrary, it does appear that minstrels of London at this time practised an 'art', but had no need of livery. For whole-time or part-time minstrels who were permanent members of a community, whether rural or urban, the same conditions may have applied, but if a minstrel decided not to pursue a professional career in London, but had ambitions beyond his own town or village, then he would be obliged to enter into the service of some lord whose livery he could wear, or else find employment as a wait in one of the many towns and cities up and down the country that required such services. Without livery or a wait's chain of office, the itinerant minstrel would have no standing, and would find it difficult to obtain admittance to grand houses or to towns with their own liberties and government.[42] On the other hand for those who could show that they were liveried or had their badges of office, the annual round was part of their way of life and a principal source of remuneration. Whether, as the 15th century continued, the need for this sort of patronage was reduced, as communities became more sophisticated, individual instrumentalists' reputations spread, and the interest and fascination for new instruments grew, is something which requires further investigation. It certainly did not disappear, even in the 16th or 17th centuries, because the companies of

---

[39] See note 23. The comparable date for the Musicians is given as 1350.
[40] See, for example, CLB Letter Book K, p. 24.
[41] CLB Letter Book K, p. 17.
[42] See Southworth, chapter 9.

dramatic Players were able to stay together as a troupe only if they were under noble patronage, and the Vagrancy Acts of Henry VIII and Elizabeth, which we shall come across in the next chapter, made it practically impossible from then on for a minstrel to 'go solo'. Nevertheless when one sees the record of the Smiths guild in Coventry paying at the St Loy's Day dinner in 1453 the sum of 8d 'to a luter',[43] it does look as though at this time a solitary performer on an unfamiliar instrument could make a living by himself.

By concentrating in this chapter on the minstrels who were not on the royal payroll during the 14th and 15th centuries we have effectively marginalised the King's Minstrels, who appear to have acquired this official title early in the 15th century (but having the same function and disposition as the royal household musicians who were referred to at the beginning of the chapter). Before moving on to the Tudor period in the next chapter we must bring the King's Minstrels centre-stage, at the moment when they were granted a Charter by Edward IV in 1469. This was the first royal charter to be granted to a body of musicians in England. When we were looking at the 14th century the suggestion that minstrels employed in the royal household might take the initiative in establishing a guild was dismissed, on the basis that the security afforded by employment within the household made the protection of guild membership superfluous. What held good in the 14th century did not necessarily apply in the uncertain times of the Wars of the Roses. Even before the war began, the King's Minstrels had petitioned the king, complaining of the abusive and unauthorised use of the king's livery, to which the official response (of an uncertain date between 1446 and 1452) was as follows:

> Whereas many rude husbandmen and artificers of England feigning to be min-strels and some of them wearing the King's livery and so pretending to be the King's Minstrels collect in certain parts of the realm great exactions of money of the king's lieges by virtue of their livery and art and though they be unskilled therein and use divers arts on working days and receive sufficient money thence, they fare from place to place on festivals and take the profits from the King's Min-strels and others skilled in the art of music whereby they using no other labours or mysteries should live,
> The King has appointed William Langton (Marshal) Walter Haliday William Haysham Thomas Radcliff Robert Marshall William Wykes and John Clyff King's minstrels to enquire throughout the realm except the County of Chester[44] touch-ing all such and so punish them holding the said inquisition themselves or by deputies.[45]

The King's Minstrels were therefore commissioned by the king to search out those who were unlawfully passing themselves off as trained minstrels, or worse, as the king's servants wearing his livery, at festivals. If this abuse was widespread

---

[43] Southworth, p. 129.
[44] The County of Chester was excepted for special historical reasons (see Appendix 5).
[45] Calendar of Patent Rolls Henry VI, 1446–52, p. 262.

and causing concern, it would fit with the pattern of music-making and merry-making described earlier in this chapter. Is it entirely credible? It presupposes a certain gullibility on the part of those who allowed themselves to be deceived, especially by those dressed up as King's Minstrels. On the other hand one has to bear in mind that the 15th century was a time when lordship over land was the essence of power, even for the king when threatened by mighty dynasties as well-endowed as himself. Patches and pockets of royal domain, large and small, were dotted all over the country, each with its own castle and skeleton household. It would not therefore be so difficult for imposters to claim that they were the minstrels from this or that royal castle.

There is no evidence that William Langton and his colleagues were able to take any action. Perhaps the king's first attack of insanity and the disruption of civil government which led to the Wars of the Roses interrupted any plans they may have had to enforce the powers given to them. If so, the Edward IV Charter granted in 1469 must have been the next step taken by the King's Minstrels with a view to exercising some control over the profession throughout the realm. The text of the Charter is set out in Appendix 2. The first two paragraphs are a virtual paraphrase of the previous complaint, only the reference to the wearing of the king's livery being omitted.

From the point of view of the Musicians' Company the 1469 Charter was the great 'might-have-been'. If it had been viable and effective the minstrels would have had powers and liberties which would have gone far beyond what most other livery companies enjoyed, and these would have been jealously retained, at least until the time of the Commonwealth. In the first place, although the Charter makes it clear that the centre of operations would be London, the guild would derive title not from the Mayor and Corporation but from the king. Those members who worked in London would not even have had to obtain the freedom of the city. The guild would be under the patronage of St Anthony, whose Chapel in the middle of London was a 'royal peculiar', outside the control of the Bishop, and again free from City interference. Except for Chester, the guild's supervisory powers covered the whole country. It could regulate its own membership, and penalties and fines levied on members went entirely to guild funds. All members of the guild would have the prestigious title of 'King's Minstrel', whether members of the royal household or not.

We cannot of course be sure that the minstrels named in the Charter were representing or allied to the majority of the other minstrels who worked and lived in London, but it seems likely to have been the case, as no counter-measures are recorded in the corporation archives. The Charter would be the bigger prize, and one can perhaps assume that the expression 'our other minstrels' in the second paragraph of the Charter is equivalent to the phrase 'others skilled in the art of music and using no other labours' in the earlier document setting up the commission.

It was a grand design, but hopelessly unworkable. In the first place the officers of the royal household were not likely to welcome an indefinite number of musicians who were entitled to call themselves 'King's Minstrels' but were not within the royal establishment. There would be friction and confusion between those who were employed in the household and those who were not, and even within the household there was by 1478 a delineation between those few who were permanently employed and those who were retained on a part-time basis.[46] Secondly the City would make things as difficult as possible for a rogue body which controlled a not insignificant number of city workers but had no obligation to conform to city custom and practice.

What actually happened is uncertain. The Charter was certainly confirmed in 1520. According to Nicholas Lanier and his colleagues in 1634, it remained in full force and effect, but was carried off to Westminster by the King's Music in Tudor times, so that it governed no one but those in royal employment. Whether this was a legal fiction will be discussed in Chapter 5. There is no evidence that the minstrels used the nation-wide powers contained in the Charter at any time. What is plausible is that the guild established by the Charter continued as one of the many guilds not officially recognised by the city, with St Anthony's Hospital as its meeting-place. The repairs and refurbishment to the Chapel in 1499 have already been mentioned. One year later the Fellowship was incorporated, still with St Anthony as patron. It is logical to suppose therefore that the original Wardens and members of the Fellowship were the cast-off members of the Chartered guild, left behind after those who were fortunate enough to be on the establishment of the royal household went off to Westminster, taking the Charter with them. Deprived of the protection of the royal charter, the marooned remainder would be conscious of the necessity of putting themselves beneath the umbrella of the City Corporation.

---

[46] *The Household of Edward IV: the Black Book and the Ordinances of 1478*, ed. A.R. Myers (Manchester 1959), pp. 131–2.

3

Tudor Revolution

THE newly established Company (which is how the Fraternity or Fellowship will be described from now on) lost no time in asserting its authority in the City, and it was not long before the City Waits felt compelled to appeal to the Court of Aldermen for protection against the Minstrels. In April 1502 they presented a petition in which they claimed that by custom 'time out of mind' the Waits had been treated as freemen of the City by reason of their service, and complained that the Company was refusing to allow them to 'occupy and buy and sell' unless they became freemen of the Company. This was of course quite beyond their means, and therefore if the Lord Mayor and Aldermen were not prepared to allow them to be admitted to the freedom of the Company free of charge, they would have to go and find ways of providing for their living elsewhere. And, by the way, could they please have their summer livery which had been promised to them 'at their coming to London'.[1]

The tone of the petition is not a little cynical, but the Waits, named as John Maschall, John Broun, William Palling, Nicholas Kyppes and John Nayler, must have relied on the Corporation not putting up much resistance when faced with the threat of mass resignation by the City's official musicians. The petition was granted and a link was established between the Waits and the Company which continued until the last appointment of a City Wait was made three hundred years later in 1802. The City decision was in any event correct; it would have been unreasonable to subordinate the City Waits to the supervision and control of the Company. Although few in number, and officially limited to six in the early 16th century, the Waits were in the City Corporation's permanent employment. Their original role had been as night watchmen for the City and they continued to perform this duty for three months in the year, but their more important task was to provide the music for official civic occasions. This gave them a status above the ordinary minstrel/musician, and it is generally accepted that in Tudor and Stuart times the City Waits ranked in terms of performance second only to the Royal Musicians. From time to time a City Wait was promoted to the King's

---

[1] CL Rep 1, fol. 98b.

Music, one of the first being Robert Baker the elder, who was appointed Wait in 1588 and then became a Royal musician in 1594.[2] Thomas Morley, the composer and organist of St Paul's, dedicated his book *The First Booke of Consort Lessons* to the Lord Mayor and Aldermen, and in his dedication wrote:

> the ancient custom of this most honorable and renowned City hath been ever, to return and maintain excellent and expert Musicians, to adorn your Honour's favours, feasts and solemn meetings.[3]

That this fulsome compliment refers to the City Waits, and not to the Company at large, is proved by the fact that elsewhere in the Dedication the Musicians whom Morley is referring to are described as 'your servants'. Some Waits did become actively involved in Company affairs, for example Robert Strachey, who was Master of the Company in 1596. As we shall see, he had a difficult year.[4]

The Waits' petition in April 1502 was a minor event, with a happy end to the story. But there is a curious coincidence which may possibly indicate that they felt more threatened at that time than is readily apparent. The Accounts of the Treasurer of the Chamber, who was responsible for routine payments to musicians employed by the king, show that for six years from 1496 one or two regular payments were made every year to the 'waits of London'.[5] The amounts were small, but the regularity of the payments suggests that the Waits had some recurring function in the royal calendar. The Waits received their last payment in April 1502, shortly after the presentation of the petition. If this has any significance at all it must mean that from that date the royal household had no further need of City music, the Westminster establishment now being quite self-sufficient, in stark contrast to the position in 1469 when the King's Minstrels were clearly city-based. In terms of royal favour, therefore, the Waits were in no better position in 1502 than the founders of the Company had been two years previously.

Not all Waits became freemen of the Company. It was a jealously guarded custom of the City that so long as a citizen enjoyed the freedom of one company, he or she was permitted to practise the trade or craft of any other, and there are numerous examples in the 17th and 18th centuries of Waits who were free of other companies, despite being professional musicians. Towards the end of the 16th century, for example, a Joiner, Arnold Pinckney, was admitted 'drumster' in 1597, and Edward Tydder, Clothworker, was admitted 'fife'. In 1598 another drummer, John Molde, Draper, was admitted. Despite strenuous efforts on the part of the Company to prevent it, which will be referred to as we follow the Company's progress through the next two centuries, professional musicians in

2   Walter Woodfill, p. 44.
3   See Holman, p. 135.
4   See p. 56. For a full account of the City Waits see Woodfill, chapter 2.
5   Andrew Ashbee, *Records of English Court Music*, vol. VII (Aldershot: Scolar Press 1993), pp. 156–71.

the City are commonly found, quite apart from the Waits, who were members of other companies, especially at times when the fortunes of the Company were set about with trouble.

Nine years after the Company's incorporation King Henry VII died, not greatly mourned except by his mother, Lady Margaret Beaufort (who outlived him only by two months), but immensely rich. His elder son Arthur had died in 1502, and his younger son, who had lived in fear and awe of his father, succeeded to the throne, at the age of seventeen, as Henry VIII. So in 1509, in an atmosphere of relief and relaxation, wealth and abundance, under the guiding light of such men as Erasmus, John Colet and Thomas More, there began a new reign under a young and handsome Prince. It began promisingly, but it became the most tyrannical reign in English history, one from which no social class or subject escaped unscathed. This was a harsh enough fate in itself, but what made this and successive reigns during the 'Tudor century' peculiar and distinct was the continuity with which the whole dynasty, without exception, were able to exercise absolute power. In stark contrast to the patchwork of monarchs good and bad, weak and strong, in previous centuries, and the Stuart dynasty whose absolute sovereignty was a grand illusion, the Tudor kings and queens were adept at grinding down their people, often mercilessly and with great cruelty. Jasper Ridley in his biography of Henry VIII quotes Holinshed, the Elizabethan historian, as saying that in Henry's reign 72,000 thieves and vagabonds were hanged, and he goes on to show that this figure was probably no great exaggeration.[6] If correct, it represents about 2% of the population, and would undoubtedly have included a number of minstrels of the poorer sort, who in a later, Elizabethan, Act were to be specifically linked with the crime of vagrancy.[7]

Many of those who suffered this fate would have been guilty of nothing more than membership of a community which was dependent on one of the rural monasteries, and of being left with no work when these were shut down by order of the king.

At the other end of the social ladder, nobles, gentry, priests and other persons of influence were being condemned to public execution at a hitherto unprecedented rate. This bestialising experience was perhaps the most extreme symptom of the revolution which the king himself had initiated, a revolution (concealed under the banner of the 'Reformation') against spiritual, not temporal, authority.

The revolution was not just a simple matter of the king and his people

---

[6] Jasper Ridley, *Henry VIII* (London: Constable 1984), p. 281.

[7] 1572: 'An Act for the Punishment of Vagabonds and for the Relief of the Impotent and Poor'. The definition of 'rogues and vagabonds' included 'all Fencers, Bearwards, Common Players in Interludes and Minstrels not belonging to any Baron of this realm or towards any other honorable persons of greater degree'. It also included 'all scholars of the Universities of Oxford and Cambridge that go about begging, not being authorised under the seal of the said Universities'. That begs a few questions!

espousing the Reformist doctrines of Martin Luther. Henry had one over-riding obsession; that no one, not even the Pope, should stand in the way of his divorce from Catherine of Aragon and his marriage to Anne Boleyn. The people rejoiced at the overthrow of the princely Cardinal, Thomas Wolsey, the butcher's son from Ipswich, who had so shamelessly amassed and displayed such a gross amount of power and wealth. Cranmer and the new theologians translated and ritualised the revolution into a rejection of the errors and venality of the ancient church and its traditional year of feasts, fasts and saint's days. The customs of the 15th century, with its rites, celebrations and processions, were condemned wholesale.[8] Although there were many places in rural areas where these survived for a time, the demand for minstrelsy within the calendar of annual religious feasts and festivals faced an inevitable decline. Musicians would have to find alternative sources of work.

In London, as we have seen, there was already some resistance on the part of masters and other employers to the constant stoppage of work caused by religious festivals, and this meant in particular that spectacles such as the Corpus Christi plays were not part of the ritual year in the City. There was however another reason for not celebrating the Corpus Christi Festival in London. The date coincided with the old London custom of the Midsummer Watch, which was more splendid, but completely secular. It was in fact the forerunner of the Lord Mayor's Show, but held at a different time of year, and by torchlight, between 11pm and 2am on Midsummer Eve. It originated from a precautionary watch to prevent the customary Midsummer bonfires from getting beyond control and setting light to city premises. It then developed into a procession which became the responsibility of the Livery Company to which the Lord Mayor for the year belonged. The Lord Mayor and the Sheriffs rode in state in the procession. Vast sums of money were spent on the pageant which included floats and tableaux vivants, morris dancers, halberdiers, a dragon or a giant (or several), together with all the Livery of the sponsoring company properly dressed in the company's colours. In 1521 the pageant, organised by the Drapers, included a symbolic castle manned by soldiers fending off a Moor called 'Soldan' who was pursuing them with a 'very long tin sword tinged with blood'. The soldiers used twenty-eight pounds of gunpowder to repel the Moor.[9]

For the Midsummer Watch in 1541, the Drapers, the organising company once again, employed eighteen minstrels and seven morris dancers, the minstrels playing flutes, shawms, harps and drums.[10] It was customary also for some of the floats or pageants to be provided by other companies, who would provide their own music.

---

[8] For a full account of the destruction, in a very un-decadent society, see Eamon Duffy, *The Stripping of the Altars: Traditional Religion in England c.1400–c.1580* (New Haven, Conn.: Yale University Press 1992).

[9] Lindenbaum, p. 175.

[10] Johnson, vol. II, p. 277.

Not even this unique City celebration was immune from the king's jealous interference. On two occasions he used the festival for his own purposes, once as entertainment for foreign royalty and once as an opportunity for propaganda, and in 1539 he actually cancelled the Watch and called a muster in St James's Park instead.[11] As an occasion for restating and reinforcing the City's rights and liberties the Midsummer Watch therefore began to lose its 'punch', and it went into serious decline towards the end of Henry's reign.

By then many of the traditional occasions for minstrelsy in the City had been whittled away. In 1524 Church Dedication days were amalgamated and reduced to one common day in the year, and the City Waits, who lost a lot of work in consequence of this change, petitioned the Corporation for a substantial rise in their annual salary in compensation.[12]

As one window of opportunity was closing for the minstrels, new ones were opening for musicians, or 'musitioners', as they were at first called. Henry was neither the first nor the last tyrant to value human life so cheaply and be passionately dedicated to music. He had inherited this love from his Beaufort grandmother (who had maintained a musical establishment as large as the late king's), and was respected by his courtiers for his prowess as a singer, instrumentalist and composer. When he became king, he inherited the musicians who had served his father. These included seventeen minstrels,[13] about half of whom were aliens, including a Flemish *alta* group[14] (or loud wind band), playing on shawms and sackbuts. Three years later in 1512 there is a comment on the Christmas Revels at Greenwich, where the music included 'tambryns and rebecs', and 'six minstrels with strange sounds'.[15] Here were the beginnings of a transition, and perhaps through his contacts with the French court, where one recalls that Josquin was still in the king's service, Henry was becoming dissatisfied with the resources at his disposal. Within four years the complement had changed and now included three members of the van Wilder family from Flanders, Matthew, and Peter and Philip who are thought to have been Matthew's sons. They were certainly lutenists, but may also have been responsible for introducing the first consort of viols to the court.[16] There was also a sackbut player from Flanders, Nicholas Forcyvall, and an organist from Venice, Dionisius Memo, as well as the famous blind harper, William More, who was one of the last survivors of the old tradition. In 1518 John Savernake, a French rebec player was taken into the king' service. The King's Music therefore now included the *alta* (which by 1525 had become a

---

[11] Lindenbaum, p. 182.

[12] CL Jor xii, fol. 281.

[13] Ashbee, pp. 25–7.

[14] 'A polyphonic improvising dance ensemble of 15th Century Northern Europe' (see Holman, p. 59).

[15] Holman, p. 63.

[16] Holman, p. 71. There are frequent entries relating to payments to 'stringminstrels' in the accounts for Henry VII's reign, but the players were probably fiddlers rather than violists.

proper consort of sackbuts, with the addition of six Italians[17]), a consort of viols, a rebec consort, several lutenists, a harper and an organist. It seems likely that the viol consort was strengthened in about 1522 with the arrival of two Germans, Hans Hossenet and Hans Highorne. The existence of three separate consorts is significant because it was becoming commonplace at this time for composed music to be 'written in a neutral style'[18] and in a limited range, so that it could be played on as many different types of instrument as possible.

Coinciding with the inflow of so many foreign musicians, new dances were arriving at court from the Continent. In the previous century each 'basse dance', the dignified or stately type of dance then enjoyed by the European courts, had had its own music, steps, pattern and duration. Within the overall pattern, the sections into which each dance was divided had their own idiosyncratic lengths and special features. Everything had to be thoroughly learnt and memorised.

In the 16th century, with the introduction of dances such as the pavane, branle and galliard, the choreography became more standardised, and the dance was made up of short sections, each of the same length. The setting was also regularised so that each dance could be performed in the same space. This made the new dances easier to teach and learn and more accessible to those outside the court circle.[19] Of even more significance would be the introduction of the violin, with the arrival of the Italians in 1540, as the ideal instrument for playing dance music.[20]

At this time the king had his viol consort, his loud wind band, his lutenists and privy chamber music and his blind harper (he also had a jester, the famous Will Somers). His musical appetite was still not fully satisfied, and when members of the Venetian Bassano family visited England in 1531, and performed as a sackbut consort, he coveted them too. One of them, Anthony Bassano, may have stayed in England for four years, but they were all back in Venice in 1536. Anthony returned to London permanently in 1538. The following year, despite the refusal of the Venetian authorities to allow them to leave, four Bassano brothers secretly travelled to England, with a recommendation from the king's agent in Venice, Edmond Harvel, that 'they were the best musicians in Venice'.[21] Forsaking their former prowess as a sackbut ensemble, 'Alvise, John, Anthony, Jasper and Baptista de Bassani, brothers in the science or art of music' were established in April 1540 as the court recorder consort.[22]

Later in the same year a group of most excellent violists arrived from Northern Italy. Their names were recorded at the time as Alberto and Vincenzio de

---

[17] David Lasocki, *The Bassanos* (Aldershot: Scolar Press 1995), p. 6.

[18] Holman, p. 29.

[19] Holman, p. 30.

[20] Holman, p. 24.

[21] Lasocki, p. 9.

[22] Lasocki, p. 10.

Venetio, Alexandro de Mylano, Zua Maria de Cremona and Ambrose de Milano. The family name (actual or attributed to them in England) of the Venetians was Kellim, of the Milanese, Lupo, and the name of the family from Cremona was anglicised as Comy or Comey. In 1545 they were joined by a violinist, Mark Antony Galliardello from Brescia. These families together with the Bassanos all came to settle in London.[23] It is now believed that they were not native Italians, but that they came from families of Sephardic Jews who had been expelled from Spain in 1492, and had then taken refuge in the independent cities in North Italy where they would be somewhat protected from anti-Semitic persecution.[24] Since that date Northern Italy had become a transit camp for the invading armies of Catholic kings and emperors, and post-Reformation England would therefore offer the younger generation the security which they feared they might now have lost in Italy, especially in view of the growth in the activities of the Inquisition. In London, although officially England was closed to Jews, the musicians and their families could lead 'a life of relative security provided they were prepared to conform to the established religion'.[25]

What makes the arrival of these Italian musicians (and others from France and Flanders) of special significance is the fact that, although they had to be available for duty at all times at Westminster or Greenwich or wherever the king happened to be, none of them appears to have lived in Westminster. Almost without exception they lived in the City of London, and later in the 16th century representatives of the families were playing an important part in parish life there, just as if it was their principal place of business. Mark Anthony Galliardello, for example, who was noted as arriving in London in 1545, was elected Church-warden of Holy Trinity Minories in 1568, and another Italian, Anthonia Maria, succeeded him in that office in 1570. Both of them are recorded in the Church-wardens' accounts as giving generously to the church for repairs.[26] Most of the alien musicians naturally tended to find a place to live in those wards which had the largest number of expatriates from the same country. One such area in the City, in the extreme south-east and nearest to the quays and relatively undeveloped, comprised the wards of Tower and Portsoken. This included the parishes of St Olave Hart Street, where some of the Bassano family settled, All Hallows Barking (the home of John Savernake, Philip van Wilder and Nicholas Lanier the elder, among others) and Holy Trinity Minories where, apart from two Galliardellos and Anthonia Maria, there was another Lanier, John, and Henry Troches. Altogether the records for the years from 1520 to 1600 show thirty-one foreign

[23] Holman, p. 79.

[24] R. Prior, 'Jewish Musicians at the Tudor Court', *Musical Quarterly*, vol. 69, No. 2 (1983), pp. 253–65.

[25] Holman, p. 87.

[26] I have been greatly assisted in this survey of royal musicians in the City by Dr Fiona Kisby, whose unpublished dissertation, 'The Royal Household Chapel in Early Tudor London 1485–1547', is one of the most comprehensive studies on this topic.

and fourteen English musicians in the royal household who lived in the City. This raises the tantalising question, what contact did the royal musicians have with the City minstrels?

It seems to be a question which cannot yet be answered with any degree of assurance. There is plenty of evidence of pre-Reformation contact between the singing men, the gentlemen of the Chapel Royal, and their counterparts in the City churches. This would have occurred mainly through the Guild of St Nicholas and its *alter ego* the Parish Clerks Company. Indeed it appears that within that Company certain customary duties were reserved for performance by the royal singers, as for example the festal mass which was celebrated in Ascensiontide after the annual election of the Master.[27] Some gentlemen were freemen of leading City Companies; others were men of property. None of the Chapel Royal gentlemen, so far as one can tell, were freemen of the Musicians Company, and few if any had their permanent residence in the City. If, however, professional singers in the royal household who were not resident in the City maintained close contact with City choirmen and other non-musical men of business, to what extent were the instrumentalists in the royal household, who did live in the City, fraternising with their opposite numbers?

Negative evidence comes from the Wills registers, which often give an indication of a close relationship between a testator and his 'overseers' (sometimes but not always synonymous with 'executors'), from which some general conclusions can be drawn as to the trust placed by one person in another. There are a number of cases where the royal musician has appointed another royal musician as overseer, as one would expect. Many non-musicians are appointed. There does not appear to be a single case where a City minstrel is appointed as overseer for the estate of a royal musician living in the City. The explanation cannot simply be one of nationality or location. It is true that one would not expect an Italian-born Bassano, living in the parish of St Olave in the south-east, to appoint as overseer a native Londoner working as a City minstrel and living in St Giles Cripplegate in the north-west. But apart from the aliens there were the native royal musicians, mostly trumpeters, who did live in parishes much closer to St Giles. It is not apparent that they chose to appoint City minstrels as overseers either. The only contrary evidence occurs in 1570 when Anthony Tyndall, a City Wait, collected the wages of a royal musician, Ralfe Greene.[28] The conclusion would seem to be that whatever relationship may have existed, it was not a close personal one, and one may assume that the difference in status between the royal 'gentlemen' and the City yeomen would have had something to do with it. But professional connections are not thereby ruled out, and could Tyndall perhaps have contracted a debt on behalf of his friend or colleague Greene?

The only piece of evidence that has so far been found for a professional con-

---

[27] Westminster City Archives MS E1, pp. 450–1.
[28] Ashbee, vol. VI, p. 102. I am grateful to Dr David Lasocki for drawing this to my attention.

nection is the entry in the Corporation Repertories for 3 October 1510, which reads as follows:

> At this Court it is granted that John Chambre, Marshal of the King's Minstrels, shall be admitted into the liberties of this City in the craft of Minstrels and that the Chamberlain shall charge himself with 40s on his account, and he to take no more of him but 3s 4d for his said liberty.[29]

It is very clear that this was an exceptional event, and that whether spontaneously or in response to a royal 'command', the Corporation was honouring the Marshal of the King's Minstrels with something approaching the Honorary Freedom of the Company. If an ordinary royal minstrel were being admitted to the freedom of the company, it would not warrant an entry in the Repertories. It is possible to interpret this sign of goodwill in a number of ways. It may have been a mark of respect for someone well known in the City, as John Chambre may have had connections with St Anthony's Hospital.[30] It may have resulted from the initiative of the Company, who wanted to 'keep well in' with the royal musicians at the beginning of a reign in which music was clearly going to play a more important part. It is unlikely that it was simply an honour offered to the head of another group of musicians with which the Company had no close links, because although named officers of the Company at this time are rarely to be found, we know that when the Company applied to amend its Ordinances in 1518, John Chambre was one of the Wardens, although he was no longer Marshal, having been displaced in 1514 by John Gilmyn.[31] He must therefore have been interested in playing an active part in the Company's affairs during the intervening period.

The only other piece of evidence existing from this early period which reflects the exercise by King's Minstrels of some control over the profession in the City is an obscure reference in the City Repertories for 1522,[32] where it is recorded that two King's Minstrels, Thomas Grennyng and Thomas Spence, entered a petition to prevent three persons named John Feld, Charles Maynard and John Laurence, but otherwise unknown, from setting up a rival fraternity. Spence was by this time of a great age, but still in service. He had served Henry VII as a 'still minstrel' for virtually the whole of his reign. Grennyng is first mentioned as a 'still minstrel' in 1503, but was still signing for exchequer payments in 1526.[33] The names of both Spence and Grennyng follow immediately after that of the new Marshal John Gilmyn in the record of the confirmation of the 1469 Charter on

---

[29] CL Rep 2, fol. 98b.

[30] A few years later a 'physician' of the same name, who was also a Canon of St Stephen's Westminster was Master of St Anthony's. (See Hugh Baillie, *Some Biographical Notes on English Church Musicians*, RMA Research Chronicle, vol. 2 [1962], p 42.) But there were probably two men with the same name.

[31] Ashbee, vol. VII, p. 44.

[32] CL Rep 5, fol. 78.

[33] Ashbee, vol. VII, pp. 2 and 332.

23 January 1520 which is referred to in the next paragraph. On whose behalf, therefore, did they enter the petition? It would be a reasonable assumption that they did it on behalf of the Company, of which they may by then have been senior and respected members, still serving the king, but members also of the Company and resident in the City. On the other hand, if this was the case, why was the Company not mentioned? It is a mystery which currently defies solution.

When considering the original Ordinances of 1500, we noted the exemptions under which minstrels of the royal household and some others were 'permitted to practise minstrelsy' in the City without being subject to the Ordinances,[34] and that the exemption was qualified by the words 'so long as they are not resident or continually conversant within the City'. This provision does not seem to have been effective in compelling minstrels in the royal household who resided in the City to join the Company, and one suspects that as a piece of legislation it was no more enforceable than the sweeping powers given to the King's Minstrels in Edward IV's Charter. However it may have coloured the relationship between the two groups; King's Minstrels who were English and City-based may have joined voluntarily in the early years. If it were not so one would expect to see more signs of friction, similar to what was to come in Nicholas Lanier's time. On the other hand it should be noted that in the year after the City Minstrels obtained their second set of Ordinances, the new Marshall of the King's Minstrels, John Gilmyn, obtained confirmation of the Edward IV Charter from the king, thereby perhaps strengthening his defences in case the Company became too demanding.

Not that the King's Minstrels had anything to fear from the new Ordinances, which were directed almost entirely to regulating relationships between members of the Company. Nor had the Company had much success so far in making its mark on City observances and orders of precedence. Among the records of the Founders' Company there is a copy of the 'order and direction' of the Court of Aldermen dated January 1515 for 'all the Crafts and Mysteries' processing, standing and riding, 'the said order and direction to be from henceforth firmly observed and kept'. Forty-eight Companies are listed, but the Minstrels are not on the list.[35]

It is time to take note of the 1519 Ordinances,[36] and to see how these follow the precedents set by other Livery Companies in tightening up the Master and Wardens' control of the Company and its members. Although in 1500 the Company appears to have had no Master, the new Ordinances recite the fact that in the mayoralty of Sir Nicholas Alwyn the Company was given power to choose three officers, the Master and two Wardens. Alwyn was Mayor in 1499/1550, so this must be a reference to the original Ordinances. It may be inaccurate; we do not know when the first Master of the Company was appointed.

---

[34] See p. 9.
[35] Meade, *History of the Founders' Company*, p. 213.
[36] The Ordinances are contained in CL Jor 11, fol. 320–1b.

For reasons unexplained the Master and Wardens, John Clyn, John Chambre and Robert Strachey, declare in the petition that the annual election as established in Sir Nicholas Alwyn's mayoralty is thought to be 'right chargeable and not convenient' and they therefore ask that the election shall be for a two-year period. The Master and Wardens are

> to Rule and Govern the fellowship of the same craft and to punish such as in time to come shall make default, misuse or offend in any Acts or ordinances belonging to the said mistery and approved by

the Court of Aldermen.

This second Act is phrased in altogether tougher language than the original Act of 1500. After prescribing the same fine as before (20 shillings) for refusal to accept office, it continues:

> Also it be ordained that it shall not be lawful to every freeman of the said mistery under the pain of forfeiture of vi s viii d . . . to sue or implead another freeman of the same mistery in any Court of Records spiritual or temporal for any cause or matter unto the time that the party grieved complain and shew first his grief unto the Master and Wardens of the said mistery for the time being to the intent that the same Master and Wardens of the said mistery for the honesty of the said fellowship shall charitably call the said parties afore them they to hear and examine the matter in variance between the said parties. And thereupon the said Master and Wardens if they can or may to settle the said parties at rest and peace. And if the said Master and Wardens cannot so do that then they to remit the matter And the party grieved in that behalf to take such remedy as he can obtain by the law the said penalty notwithstanding.

This form of internal arbitration was standard and approved practice amongst the guilds, and must have been seen as a way of drastically cutting down the waste of unprofitable time spent in court. The fact that an aggrieved party who refused to accept the Master and Wardens' award still had to pay the fine if he insisted on going to court must have acted as a further disincentive.

> Also be it ordained that no manner or person of the same occupation entice procure or counsel any man's servant or apprentice of the same occupation out or from the service of his master during the time of his retainer or as long as the master or servant be in covenant upon pain &c . . . [usual penalty] Except it be ordered by the Master and Wardens that the servant shall be cut and at liberty from the service of his master.

On the face of it this regulation is not limited to members of the Company or fellowship. It specifically refers to 'persons of the same occupation' and it was a well-established practice that minstrels might belong to another guild. Later ordinances gave explicit authority to the Master and Wardens to exercise control over minstrel/musicians of whatever guild,[37] and this may have been a deliberate attempt at a precedent.

---

[37] See for example the Ordinances of 14 June 1574.

The fact that the Master and Wardens could also release a servant from his contract, presumably in cases of harsh or unfair treatment, is indicative of the relatively liberal conditions prevailing at the time.

> Item be it ordained that if any person freeman of the said fellowship of minstrels be so misadvised to rebuke or revile with unfitting language or smite another person freeman of the same in the presence of the Master and Wardens or in any open audience that then upon a due proof thereof had before the said Master and Wardens the same person so being misadvised shall pay such reasonable fine . . . as shall be assessed thereupon by the Master and Wardens for the time being always regardant to the quality and quantity of the said misbehaviour

Worse was to come:

> Moreover be it ordained that if any person of the said fellowship within the City of London or liberties of the same of whatever condition soever he be hereafter be found disobedient much obstinate or contritious against the Master and Wardens of the said fellowship for the time being or against any of them so that they may not lawfully exercise their office according to their acts and ordinances upon a due proof thereof had the same Master and Wardens by the help assistance and consent of the Mayor of the City of London or of the Chamberlain of the same for the time being shall commit the same person unto ward there to abide such punishment as shall be thought reasonable to the said Mayor or Chamberlain and the said Master and Wardens for the time being.

Does this suggest that the membership of the Company were out of control or ungovernable? Were servants and apprentices of minstrels prone to causing trouble and giving the profession a bad name? It is quite possible. But there was also a much more forceful argument for giving the Master and his Wardens these draconian powers. Only two years before there had occurred in the City the 'Evil May Day Riots',[38] a flagrant and embarrassing act of xenophobia deliberately stimulated by a group of 'Little Englanders' who put the blame for all their discontents on the aliens in the City, of whom there were many. The French, it seems, were in particular disfavour. The riots humiliated the City authorities who were totally incapable of controlling them. Henry VIII, who had been forewarned of the trouble that was brewing, sent the Duke of Norfolk with 2,000 soldiers to restore order, and nearly three hundred rioters were tried for treason at a special court a few days later. All were sentenced to death, but only a few were actually executed. Nevertheless the reputation of the City was severely compromised, and there can be little doubt that the Court of Aldermen would have leaned heavily on the Livery Companies in its efforts to restore discipline throughout the City.

To complete the new set of Ordinances there is an express prohibition on any member of the Company having more than one apprentice at a time, except for present or past masters or wardens who could have two. Then there is a new pro-

---

[38] The Evil May Day Riots are described in detail in Ridley, pp. 104–7.

vision designed to ensure that members of the Company can have 'quiet enjoyment' of their contracts:

> Also be it ordained that it shall not be lawful to any Minstrel freeman of the said
> fellowship to supplant hire or get out another minstrel freeman of the same fellow-
> ship being hired or spoken to for to sue at any triumphs feasts dinners suppers
> marriage gilds or brotherhood or any other doing whereby any such minstrel
> should have perte of his living under the pain to every such supplanter as often as
> he so doth &c . . . [penalty]

And finally a qualification test for apprentices, which brought the Company
into line with City practice as it had generally been observed for many years in
the craft guilds:

> Also be it ordained that no Apprentice to any minstrel freeman of the said mistery
> shall use or occupy his instrument openly or privately within any Tavern hostelry
> or Alehouse within the City or at any feast gilds marriages dinners suppers or such
> other unto the time that the same Apprentice by the Master and the Wardens of the
> said mistery for the time being be first examined and apposed and by them abled
> to use his instrument in form aforesaid for honour of this City and honesty of the
> said mistery And that master that suffereth to do the contrary shall forfait &c . . .
> [penalty]

At this crucially interesting moment all records relating to the Company dry
up for thirty years. Like a young river in a limestone valley it disappears through
a hole in the valley floor, and re-emerges in a quite different environment. By the
time the records begin again, the first wave of the Reformation had swept
through London, leaving the churches in a disembowelled state, with no shrines,
no chantry chapels, no rood screens, no statue or image capable of being wor-
shipped, and therefore no more church holidays or feast days. There were no
more pageants in parish churches or religious play cycles presented by the Guild
of St Nicholas, all formerly given with musical accompaniment. The sacred precincts of the great abbeys and priories had become building sites; London was no
longer the fair and spacious city which it had been in 1500. During the 16th
century there was a fourfold increase in the population of London, so that by
1550 it would have grown at least to 100,000, with the inhabitants living in
denser and less hygienic conditions, even allowing for the huge amount of space
which had become newly available for building when the monasteries were dissolved. London had become a tougher environment, less tolerant, more difficult
to control and in consequence subject to more regulation. To add to the problems of its inhabitants the king and his ministers had identified the Livery Companies as the 'milch cows' for purposes of funding state expenditure,[39] mostly on
war with France. When this method of taxation was exhausted the king debased

---

[39] See Unwin, p. 239.

the currency, and a period of inflation began which continued for the rest of the century.

In musical terms one of the saddest casualties of the Reformation in London was the Guild of St Nicholas. The Guild was almost synonymous with the Parish Clerks' Company, which fought a hard battle to be classified as a trade guild and so to survive. But unfortunately it had never had a livery, and after much deliberation and legal argument the government decided that the Guild's objects were 'superstitious' and all its endowment was therefore forfeit to the State, while the Parish Clerks would have to reform themselves so that the clerical (in the modern sense) duties of the Parish Clerk would predominate at the expense of their former musical skills. A remarkable tradition created by a most distinguished succession of church musicians was lost, and we can be sure that the work of the composers who were St Nicholas men,[40] together with the support which it received from the gentlemen of the Chapel Royal, and the fact that the list of members from 1449 to 1521 contained more than 5,000 names, would have put the Guild, if it had survived, into a position of pre-eminence far above that of the Musicians' Company. The expertise which developed in the composition of secular music towards the end of the 16th century cannot have been unconnected with the demise of an ancient and powerful association of London church musicians. It was a shift from which the Company benefited greatly.

During the miseries of the last decade of Henry VIII's reign, music and musicians within the royal circle thrived. It is now well established that at the king's death the King's Music numbered over one hundred highly skilled performers on the royal payroll, and even allowing for the large number of aliens, these musicians did not exist in a vacuum. In many cases musical skills and know-how were passed from father to son, but there must also have been a pool of talent from which gaps could be filled. On the other hand there was a 'steep learning curve' for the native musicians if they were to have any chance of catching up with the Italians and other aliens in the techniques required for new instruments and in playing polyphonic music.

The evolution of the Waits from simple bandsmen, playing only on shawms or waitpipes, into the accomplished and many-faceted musicians worthy of Thomas Morley's praises occurred just at this time, and can be charted by the entries in the City Repertories relating to the purchase of new instruments. The Waits' first sackbut was bought in 1526, more in 1555 and 1559. 'Certain instruments called a set of vialles' were ordered by the Court of Aldermen in 1561, followed by a 'whole set of recorders' in 1568. More sackbuts (replacements?) were bought in 1581 and 1597, and a curtal (which was a type of bassoon) in 1597.[41] It

---

[40] The composers included, among many others, William Cornyshe the elder, Robert Fayrfax, John Taverner, John Shepherd, Nicholas Ludford, Thomas Tallis and William Mundy. The subject is dealt with fully by H. Baillie in 'A London Guild of Musicians 1460–1530', in *Proceedings of the Royal Musical Association* 83 (1956–57), pp. 15–28.

[41] Woodfill, p. 34.

would be unthinkable that City minstrels, some of whom by the end of the century, as we shall see, were men of standing and property, would not be following the Waits' example, and learning to use the new instruments as fast as their resources allowed. Would it not also be likely that they would seek tuition from the aliens who already had the expertise and lived close by?

One would expect that the aliens who lived in the City would have performed there from time to time, privately if not publicly, when not on duty at Court. Some of them, like the Bassanos, were instrument-makers and repairers,[42] and the City minstrels would have needed their services. There would have been an interface between the two groups; fraternisation must have taken place, and the natural propensity of professional musicians to get together and play for pleasure may have deepened such relationships.

There seems to have been no lack of City minstrels conforming to the Company's required standards (which must have been constantly rising). By tradition a new monarch rode through the City from London Bridge to Temple Bar on his accession, and on 17 October 1549, the young Edward VI processed in state along this route, which was lined all the way with Minstrels and Singing Men. The Order is set out in the Repertories:[43]

Bridgefoot	Minstrels
St Magnus Corner	Singingmen
St Margaret's Church	Minstrels
Gracechurch Conduit	Singingmen
The Falcon	Minstrels
Leadenhall Street	Singingmen
Cornhill Conduit	Minstrels
St Mildred's at the Stocks	Singingmen
Great Conduit in Cheap	Minstrels
Bow Church	Singingmen
St Peter's Church, Cheap	The Waits
Little Conduit, Cheap	Minstrels
Against St Paul's School	The children of Paul's
Ludgate	Minstrels
Fleet Street Conduit	Singingmen
St Dunstans Church	Minstrels
Temple Bar	Singingmen

'Every of the said places to be honestly garnished with Arras and other decent hangings.'

We do not know how many minstrels would have been performing at each station, but one might hazard a guess at a total number of seventy to one hundred, mostly playing shawms, sackbuts, trumpets and drums to make them-

---

42 Holman, p. 120.
43 CL Rep 12, fols 156r–156v.

selves heard above the roar of the crowd. It would have been a formidable parade.[44]

Only a few years later, in 1555, the City Corporation was issuing strict instructions forbidding the keeping of 'dancing houses' in the City on pain of imprisonment.[45] This was a new phenomenon, which was to play an increasingly important part in the affairs of the Company, but at this early date it simply demonstrates that, despite the express disapproval of the City authorities, the new style of dancing referred to earlier in the chapter, which the Flemish musicians had introduced to the Court thirty years before, had by now become a popular pastime in the City. Members of the Company would undoubtedly have been actively involved, whether or not they were the actual keepers of the dancing houses. As dancing masters they would have been among the first English executants of dance music played on the violin, an art which they could only have learnt from the Flemish or Italians.

By this time the Company had built up enough clout to be able to exercise some proper control, not only of its own members, but of minstrels in the City generally, especially by keeping out 'foreigners' (i.e. those who were not free of the City) and clamping down on buskers and other unqualified performers who might give the profession a bad name. Ordinances dated 2 March 1554, issued just at the end of the reign of Edward VI,[46] stated in the preamble the abuse which they were designed to prevent:

> Forasmuch as divers and many foreign minstrels from the liberties and freedom of this City of London have of late and yet do openly exercise use and practice their said science of minstrelsy within the same City and the liberties thereof as though they were free of the same City not only to the great loss and hindrance of the gains and profits of the poor minstrels being freemen of the same City but also directly in many points contrary to the good ancient allowed Acts and Laws and Ordinances heretofor taken made and established within the said City concerning the said minstrels being free of the same City Whereby much disorder will rule, vice and sin doth secretly spring grow and daily ensue within the said City and the liberties of the same . . .

There is very little evidence concerning these alleged 'foreigners', or of the 'vice and sin' which were secretly growing, but the Ordinance goes on to impose fines on any foreigner who, after being warned by the Master and Wardens of the

---

44 Did some of the minstrels do a double act, and dash from one staging to another? It is possible.

45 The Precept (in CL Jor 16, fol. 328) is set out in a modern translation, with some punctuation added, in Appendix 3. It dates from the first year of Mary's reign, and is surprisingly 'Calvinist' in tone, prohibiting all minstrels from performing in taverns, alehouses and eating houses, as well as clamping down on the dancing houses. Whether this was really issued at the queen's behest or is an over-run from the proto-puritanical attitudes of the previous reign is debatable.

46 CL Jor 16, fols 253–4.

3. Edward VI's Accession Procession through the City on 17th October 1549, showing Cheapside Cross where the Waits would have been playing on staging 'honestly garnished with Arras and other decent hangings'. Groups of Minstrels played at each end of Cheapside. A 19th century engraving from a contemporary painting now owned by the Society of Antiquaries.

Company, continued to 'exercise any minstrelsy' in any 'common hall tavern inn alehouse or any like place'. There is then a prohibition on any minstrel, whether free of the City or not, playing any instrument in the open street after 10 o'clock at night or before 5 o'clock in the morning, the Waits of course excepted. The total prohibition on keeping dancing schools in the City is repeated (London had reached its zenith of Reformism at this date). Finally the Company gets the right to fine the buskers:

> Item forasmuch as divers and many artifice and handy craftsmen as Tailors and Shoemakers and such other leaving the use and exercise of their crafts and manual occupations and giving themselves wholly to wandering abroad riot vice and idleness do commonly use nowadays to sing songs called 'three mens songs' in the Taverns Alehouses Inns and such other places of this City to the great loss prejudice and hinderment of the said poor fellowship of the minstrels of the said City. Be it therefore also ordained and enacted by the authority aforesaid that no manner of person or persons whether he or they be free of the said City or not free

using to sing any songs shall from henceforth sing in or at any Tavern Inn Alehouse weddings feasts or any like place or places within the said city or liberties thereof any manner of such song or songs (except the same be sung in a common play or interlude) upon pain of forfeiture &c . . .

There is a touch of inconsistency in this regulation. If there was to be a total ban on 'three mens songs'[47] it was not going to help the 'said poor fellowship' much if the tailors and shoemakers were silenced, unless we are to believe that the patrons of the taverns where these songs had been sung would be equally content with something less lewd and risqué.

Less than ten years later, when Queen Elizabeth was in the fourth year of her reign, the Court of Aldermen decided that it was no longer realistic to try to ban the teaching of dancing in the City, and the Aldermen therefore asked the Lord Mayor to call before him all Minstrels and Dancing Masters practising in the City and admonish them to be obedient to the Master and Wardens of the Fellowship of Minstrels.[48] This effectively set the seal on the Company's rights and responsibilities throughout the reign of Elizabeth. The final provisions of an Ordinance dated 14 June 1574 set out the extent of the Company's control more precisely:

It is also ordained and enacted that *all persons using the said art* shall keep obey and be subject unto all such good laws rules and ordinances for good rule and order and governance as the said company of the minstrels are bound to do Which shall be perused and allowed by the Lord Mayor and his brethren the Aldermen upon like pains and in like sort to be levied and employed as by the said good laws rules and ordinances it is appointed.

These powers were still further extended by the James I Charter of 1604 which we shall examine in the next chapter.

Among the 'good laws, rules and ordinances' set out in the 1574 Ordinance was the right of examination of apprentices, whether their master was free of the Company or not, to be reserved to the Master and Wardens of the Company:

No apprentice to any Citizen free of the said company of minstrels or of any other company of this City shall use the said feat of a minstrel during the time of his apprenticehood for gain to himself or his master until such time as the same apprentice by the Master and Wardens of the said mistery of minstrels for the time being be first examined and apposed and by them judged able and allowed to so use the said art on pain that the master of every such apprentice shall for every offence forfeit vis viiid Provided that for avoiding partiality that if any apprentice of any Citizen being free of any other company shall be refused or disallowed or upon request of his master be not allowed by the said Master and Wardens then

---

47 *The New Grove Dictionary of Music* (Vol. 17, p. 516) describes 'three mens songs' as a 'distinctive tradition' in early 16th century English secular polyphonic song – partsongs for three voices, 'all provided with the text in the sources'.

48 CL Rep 15, fol. 144.

such apprentice shall be apposed by one of the Master or Wardens of the Minstrels and by one other person skilful in music to be therefor appointed by the Lord Mayor for the time being by whose judgement the said apprentice shall be allowed or disallowed according to his skill and worthiness.

The 1574 Ordinance also addressed the chronic problem of the number of apprentices a freeman in another company who was a practising musician could have, the problem arising from the fact that many other companies did not restrict freemen to 'one master, one apprentice'. A committee of aldermen which had been set up the previous year to decide which members of the Company should be allowed to keep dancing schools considered this matter also,[49] recommending that if a practising musician had been a freemen of another company for fourteen years or more he should be allowed two apprentices. Otherwise the Minstrels' own rule of one apprentice only must apply universally.

One other interesting feature appears in this Ordinance and in the previous one. Under the earlier legislation the proceeds of fines were divided equally between the City and the Company. In 1554 and 1574 it was provided that half of the 'forfeitures' should go 'to the use of the poor of the said company of minstrels' and the other half to 'the relief of the poor in Christ's Hospital'.

The Hospital had been founded by Edward VI in 1552 on the site of the Greyfriars Priory as an orphanage and home for abandoned children. From the outset it was the Governors' policy to enable able-bodied children from the Hospital to learn a trade or craft through apprenticeship in the normal way, and the early records include numbers of children of minstrels who had been taken in, and others, presumably with an aptitude for music, who were apprenticed to minstrels. In 1560 (15 July) there is an entry:

John Osburne, 9, son William O. minstrel born at Newington (from Calice)[50]

(i.e. a refugee from Calais which was captured by the French in 1558).

On 16 March 1562, a complex entry:

Melcher Sampton, [no age given] one of the poor children of this Hospital delivered to one John Whitlock of Uxbridge musician to dwell with him for 8 years and he to have at the end of his years of his said master 20s in ready money and an instrument, for the performance whereof the said John Whitlock and John Edling musicians of Uxbridge with Nicholas Browne merchant taylor stand all bound by obligation to the Governors of this House as by the said bond doth and may appear.[51]

Two apprenticeships are recorded in the records for 10 April 1563, although the actual apprenticeship did not begin until later:

---

[49] CL Rep 18, fol. 232.
[50] *Christ's Hospital Admissions. Vol. 1, 1554–1599* (London: Council of Almoners of Christ's Hospital 1937), p. 14.
[51] *Christ's Hospital Admissions. Vol. 1*, p. 27.

1. Thomas Jones, 6, May 8 to Margerie Arnold of Hayes. 1565 April 21, Home. 1569 Dec 17, App to Thomas Styvy goldsmith master of the song school, 8 years, and put on by him to Thomas Foster a furrier.

Young Tom was fostered for 2 years and then returned 'home' to the Hospital. 5 years later at the age of 11 he was apprenticed to a goldsmith who was either a choirmaster in his spare time or one of the minstrels free of another company who would be brought under the Company's surveillance by the Ordinance of 1574. However Tom does not appear to have had the musical ability expected of him, so he was 'put on' to a furrier.

2. John Jackson, 9, 1564 May 6 App to Walter Holcroft of Lambeth minstrel.

It is interesting that in both the cases of Sampton and Jackson the apprenticeship was to a minstrel outside the City. Does this suggest that the ample supply of apprentices from City families to members of the Company precluded their acceptance of apprentices from the Hospital? If so, this may explain why in 1587 Christ's Hospital became one of the first schools in England to have its own music curriculum. In that year John Howes, who was on the staff of the Hospital, decided that the children were to

> learn to sing, to play upon all sorts of instruments, as to sound the trumpet, the cornett, the recorder or flute, to play upon sackbuts and all other instruments that are to be played upon either with wind or finger.[52]

Here in the City was a discrete education in music, in competition with and beyond the control of the Company, and there is no reason to suppose that Christ's Hospital children who matured into professional musicians would necessarily become freemen of the City or join the Company. Apart from the King's Music they had the opportunity of joining a nobleman's group of musicians or working with one of the troupes of 'Players', the professional actors who at this time were establishing companies under noble patronage. They could also become music teachers outside the City.

Girls at the Hospital seem to have had a better chance of staying in the City. The following entry appears for 29 April 1587:

> Frances Brightwell, 9, daughter John B. musician (St Benets Pauls Wharf) with 40s in ready money received of the churchwardens. To Robert Haunchet of Standon. 1594 Nov 11, put covenant servant to George Wolfe and Dionis his wife of St Stephens in Coleman Street lutemaker, 7 years.[53]

There is also perhaps the first female apprentice musician of whom we have a record (8 November 1595), apprenticed to one of the City Waits whose name appears in the 1604 Charter as a member of the Court of Assistants:

---

[52] P. Holman, p. 129.
[53] *Christ's Hospital Admissions. Vol. 1*, p. 206.

Ellin Gillet, 4. daughter of the said Ambrose [who was a salter of St Mildred Bread Street]. 1599 June 26 Appr to Walter Lowman musician of London and Margery his wife 10 years.[54]

Further competition for the minstrels and their apprentices (all of which helped to raise standards of teaching and performance) was coming from the choir schools attached to the cathedrals and major churches. Not only had they formed their own 'professional' acting troupes; they were also becoming proficient instrumental musicians. On his death in 1582 Sebastian Westcote, Organist and Master of the Children of St Paul's, in his will left his chest of violins and viols to the cathedral 'to exercise and learn the children there'.[55] Westcote, like his more famous contemporary, William Byrd, was a loyal subject who had refused to renounce the Catholic faith, at a time when draconian anti-Catholic legislation was in force and constantly being invoked. Not surprisingly the increasingly puritan authorities in the City regarded it as a scandal that their cathedral choirmaster should be a papist, but Westcote had the protection of a higher authority (although he spent some time in the Marshalsea), because under his sole direction the 'Children of Paul's' became the most highly regarded of the chorister dramatic troupes, and between 1558 and 1576 this company gave more performances at Court than any other.[56] Significantly it was in the following year, when the queen for the first time preferred the adult players for her Christmas entertainment, that Westcote suffered imprisonment. Fortunately for him the Children of Paul's were in demand at Court again the following Christmas.[57]

William Byrd was arrested no less than 5 times (his wife Juliana rather more frequently) and could have suffered lengthy periods of imprisonment; but by getting the proceedings against him transferred from the county sessions to the King's Bench, and through the queen's personal interest, he was spared all but the most trivial financial penalties.[58] At the same time he was allowed to retain the unique privilege of holding the monopoly of music publishing, which had been granted to him and Thomas Tallis for 21 years by the queen in 1575. After Tallis' death in 1585, Byrd assigned the publishing rights to Thomas East, who was a professional publisher, and who persevered through many difficulties in creating a permanent record of all that is best in late Elizabethan music. Although it is true that much of the best music might have survived also in manuscript, as in the Mulliner and the Fitzwilliam Virginal books, it is frightening to speculate on how much less we would now know about the Elizabethan repertoire if the

---

54 *Christ's Hospital Admissions. Vol. 1*, p. 243.
55 Holman, p. 129.
56 Edmund K. Chambers, *The Elizabethan Stage*, vol. II (Oxford: Oxford University Press 1923), p. 4.
57 M. Shapiro, *Children of the Revels: The Boy Companies of Shakespeare's Time and their Plays* (New York: Columbia University Press 1977), p. 13.
58 See David Mateer, 'William Byrd's Middlesex Recusancy', *Music and Letters*, vol. 78, no. 1 (February 1997), pp. 1–14.

monopoly had been exercised by its grantees, first Byrd and then Thomas Morley, in a selfish and exclusive manner. Fortunately, because so much was published, it was immediately available for performance in great profusion, as much by City professionals and amateurs as by many others up and down the country. As Ernest Walker put it *in A History of Music in England*:

> With the defeat of the Armada in 1588 the danger of religious upheaval passed away from England; and musicians turned with a curious suddenness, and with almost complete unanimity, to follow secular ideals. Since 1530 only one collection of non-ecclesiastical music had been printed – a book of songs for three, four, and five voices composed by Thomas Whythorne and issued in 1571; but between 1588 and 1630 well over eighty vocal collections, containing between 1500 and 2000 pieces, nearly all secular in character, were published in part-books, and many more still remain in manuscript.[59]

This massive proliferation, except in the last decade, occurred during the period covered by the publishing monopoly.

We have reached the last decade of the 16th century, and it was at this time, I believe, that the Company was about to make the final ascent to the most eminent level of fame and status that it ever achieved as a craft guild. As a livery company, it was still ranked among the poorest, but this was the result of its composition and the way in which musicians conducted their professional life, then as now. They gave generously of their services on appropriate occasions, but they did not have the surplus wealth which a City merchant who belonged to one of the Great Twelve could transfer to his company, either for charitable purposes or to enhance the company's hall or other property. There was no pyramid of partners, managers and labourers, the *sine qua non* for fortune-building, in the music profession. Outside the royal household, it was scarcely possible at this time to perform in groups of more than four or six. Comparisons with the prototype capitalist entrepreneurs who controlled London's trade are therefore quite unrealistic. The Company's achievement at this time has to be judged by the proximity of its most prominent members to the City Waits and the Queen's Music, and the evidence that this provides that at its best the Company could match the highest musical standards.

However it was not just professional standards that illustrate the excellence of the art or science of music during this first flowering of the 'English Renaissance'. At a time when so many intellects were brimming over with originality in the creative arts, gentlemen of education and leisure and their ladies were being encouraged, if not forced, to participate in artistic activities, music in particular. There was a general expectation that they possessed some such skills:

---

59 Ernest Walker, *A History of Music in England*, 3rd edn, ed. J.A. Westrup (Oxford: Clarendon Press 1951), p. 76.

Hamlet: O, the recorders: – let me see one – . . . [to Guildenstern] Will you play
     upon this pipe?
Guildenstern: My Lord, I cannot.
Hamlet: I pray you.
Guildenstern: Believe me, I cannot.
Hamlet: I do beseech you.
Guildenstern: I know no touch of it, my Lord.
Hamlet: 'Tis as easy as lying. Govern these ventages with your finger and thumb,
     give it breath with your mouth, and it will discourse most eloquent music.
     Look you, these are the stops.
Guildenstern: But these cannot I command to any utterance of harmony; I have
     not the skill.[60]

Before the last lines Guildenstern would surely have given the recorder a hearty
overblow to prove his incompetence.

In concept as well as in performance, art was moving into a new dimension.
Marlowe and Shakespeare and their contemporaries were challenging their audiences with depths of comprehension which would have been unattainable a
decade or two before. Even the madrigalists were following suit. 'Fair Phyllis' was
still very much in evidence, and 'Oriana' was *de rigueur*, but sometimes the
sophisticated amateur singers needed something more substantial to grapple
with, and Thomas Weelkes was one madrigalist who was ready to oblige:

Thule, the period of cosmography
Doth vaunt of Hecla, whose sulphurious fire
Doth melt the frozen clime and thaw the sky.
Trinacrian Aetna's flames ascend not higher.
These things seem wondrous, yet more wondrous I,
Whose heart with fear doth freeze, with love doth fry.

The Andalusian merchant, that returns
Laden with cochineal and China dishes
Reports in Spain how strangely Fogo burns
Amidst an ocean full of flying fishes.
These things seem wondrous, &c . . .

Contemporary English madrigal writing for amateurs was elaborate, if not
tortuous. How much more would have been expected of professionals! If further
evidence is sought, it can be found on the Continent, where either for religious
or commercial reasons, English troupes of musicians were to be found, usually in
association with the theatre companies which were touring Europe at this time.
The musicians were highly regarded. Noting that two such groups were
employed in succession after 1595 by the Landgrave of Hessen-Kassel, someone
commented that 'they have such musicians as can hardly be found anywhere'.

---

[60] Shakespeare, *Hamlet*, Act III, scene II.

Another disgruntled Kassel resident, giving grudging praise to their string-playing, refers to 'the damned Englishmen'.[61]

So far very little has been said about the individual City musicians who were flourishing at this time. This is not because their names have not survived, but because so little is known about them. The statutory requirement to keep Parish Registers, which actually dates from 1538 (although few registers go back that far) has provided a comprehensive record of births and deaths in many of the City parishes since the reign of Elizabeth. This has been and will continue to be the source of a great deal of basic information about the residents in each parish including 'minstrels', 'musicians', 'trumpeters', 'organists' and 'virginalmakers'.[62] A man's trade or calling was usually included in each entry, whether it related to his burial or that of his wife, or the christening or burial of his child. Such entries tell us that as with many crafts and trades there was a tendency for musicians to 'cluster' in certain parishes. The musicians were much more numerous in the parish of St Giles Cripplegate than in any other. This parish, although fully incorporated into the body of the City and neither a liberty nor a suburb, actually lay outside the City wall. It was necessary to pass through the Cripples' gate to reach the church, and the parish extended some distance beyond that. According to Stow, in 1597 'Golding Lane' (now Golden Lane), which was in the parish, 'on both the sides is replenished with many tenements of poor people'.[63] It was therefore recognised at this time as being a poor outlying parish, and it was natural for indigent minstrels to settle there earlier in the century. Other smaller clusters are to be found in St Michael Bassishaw (close to St Giles), St Helen's Bishopsgate, St Olave, Hart Street, where a group of royal musicians lived, St Botolph's Aldgate and St James Garlickhythe.

The bare statistics show that in a survey of twenty-six City parishes out of a total in excess of one hundred, there were 121 freemen who fell into one of the five categories quoted in the last paragraph in the 16th century (the earliest in 1544) or who have entries in the Register spanning the two centuries, and 207 in the 17th century up to 1666. The fact that they appeared in the Register under one of the five headings does not of course prove that they were freemen of the Company; organ-builders (but not organists) and virginal-makers in particular

---

61 See Holman, p. 156.
62 The information about individual musicians comes from two sources. The first is W. Ingram's article 'Minstrels in Elizabethan London: Who Were They and What Did They Do?' in *English Literary Renaissance*, vol. 14 (1984), pp. 29–54. The other is a valuable but hitherto unacknowledged piece of research undertaken on behalf of the Musicians Company by John Lynn Boston in 1952 who described himself as 'Scholar elect of Lincoln College, Oxford, and member of the Galpin Society'. The background to this research is unknown. It cannot have been in connection with the 'Short History' which had been completed in November 1949. Boston's research covered 12 City Parishes. Ingram's covered 14 in addition to some of those researched by Boston, and also five parishes outside the City and its liberties.
63 John Stow, *A Survey of London in 1598* (Stroud, Glos.: Alan Sutton edn 1994), p. 390.

had their own trade guilds, although they did not last very long. But there is at least a presumption that many of them would have been freemen of the Company.

Unfortunately the Registers tell us absolutely nothing about their careers. Any information that survives about what they did has to be found elsewhere.

Of special interest to the Company are those musicians who worked their way up to proficiency through apprenticeship and became freemen of the Company, and who were then appointed to a vacancy in the Waits, or in one or two cases selected for the King's Music. The ties between the Company and the Waits at this time were as close as they would ever be. Under the 1604 Charter, which will be examined in the next chapter, Thomas Carter, City Wait since 1593, was appointed one of the Wardens. Another City Wait, Walter Lowman (to whom the little girl from Christ's Hospital was apprenticed), and three former Waits, Arthur Norton (retired), Robert Baker (resigned to become queen's musician in 1594) and Anthony Tindall (resigned and pensioned), were among the fourteen members of the Company appointed Assistants (i.e. members of the Court) under the Charter. Robert Strachey, who was Master in 1596, and almost certainly a descendant of the Robert Strachey who had been Warden in 1518, was another Wait who should have been appointed, but there had been a major row in the Company shortly after he had taken office as Master in 1596. Apparently (with every justification) Strachey demanded to see the accounts and to have the cash balance handed to him in the usual way. This was objected to for reasons that are unexplained, and the objectors took the matter to the Lord Mayor who decided that Strachey should be relieved of his office. Strachey then demanded a rehearing, and a Committee which was appointed by the Lord Mayor to inquire into the matter decided that he had been unjustly treated and he was reinstated.[64] There must however have been blood on the carpet, as Strachey was not recognised as a suitable person for Court membership in 1604, in contrast to William Warren who appears to have been faced with the same problem two years before, when he took office as Master. Either Warren had acted with more tact, or had left the unknown *ad hoc* treasurer to his own devices.[65]

Two other members of the new Court of Assistants, William Warren and Rowland Rowbedge, were in the King's Music, without having served as Waits. Carter, Baker, Tindall and three other Waits, William Pine (or Pynne), John Robson and Stephen Thomas, were all resident in the Parish of St Giles.

To summarise, in 1604, the Master, Wardens and Court of Assistants of the Company included three members of the King's Music, two serving Waits and two retired Waits. Robert Strachey, another Wait, was a senior member of the Company, but not on the Court.

Having thus established the Company's closer-than-ever connections with the

---

[64] CL Rep 24, fols 72–3.
[65] *Analytical Index to the . . . remembrancia . . . 1579–1664*, ed. Overall (London 1878), p. 92, quoted by Woodfill, p. 10.

Waits and the musicians of the queen's household, it is appropriate that we should end the chapter by recalling the events of 6 January 1601, a date which was just seven months after the Company's first centenary.

For very many years it had been the established tradition of the Court to spend the time from early November until Shrove Tuesday each year in revels and dancing, with masques and plays, and the twelve days of Christmas were always the time when these festivities were at their peak. It seems that the queen towards the end of her reign had tired of masques, and as a result there was an increase in the number of romantic and satirical comedies, usually filled with topical allusions, which were performed for her entertainment at this time of year, written for three adult theatre companies, the Lord Chamberlain's Men, the Lord Admiral's and the Earl of Derby's (a less favoured group than the other two), and the chorister companies, the Children of Paul's and the Children of the Queen's Chapel.

In 1954, Dr Leslie Hotson, one of the most imaginative of twentieth century Shakespeare scholars, published a book entitled *The First Night of Twelfth Night*.[66] In it he achieves a truly remarkable reconstruction of the festivities which took place on Twelfth Night 1601, starting from three basic facts (i) that Shakespeare's company, the Lord Chamberlain's Men, were paid for presenting a play at Court on Twelfth Night 1601, (ii) that one of Shakespeare's comedies was called 'Twelfth Night', and that it is known to have been written in or about 1601, and (iii) that the queen entertained an Italian Duke, whose full name was Virginio Orsino, Duke of Bracciano, at Whitehall on 6 January 1601.

Using these clues, Hotson set about his reconstruction, which led him to the discovery that there was not just one foreign notable at Court during the Christmas season in 1600/1, but four; Wolfgang Wilhelm, the heir to the Count Palatine Duke of Zweibruck, Duc de Rohan from Brittany, the Russian Ambassador, Grigori Ivanovich Mikulin, and the Duke of Bracciano. Although the German and French visitors missed the Twelfth Night celebrations, the respective reports of their visit have survived, and provide valuable background material. So, more significantly, have those of the Ambassador and Don Virginio, who were both present on that day, but in rather different circumstances.

Proper courtesies were of course extended to the Russian Ambassador, a great bear of a man, whose survival on returning home to the Court of the Tsar Boris Godunov was known to depend on his being able to show that he had been received with dignity and honour during the eight months that he spent in London. This he was able to do, because on the 6 January a Treaty of Friendship with Russia was ratified by the somewhat outlandish practice of Mikulin and the queen eating bread and salt together.

It was however the young Italian Duke who benefited most from the queen's

---

66 Leslie Hotson, *The First Night of 'Twelfth Night'* (London: Rupert Hart-Davis 1954). The brief account which concludes this chapter is almost entirely derived from Hotson's book, and I have therefore been sparing with references.

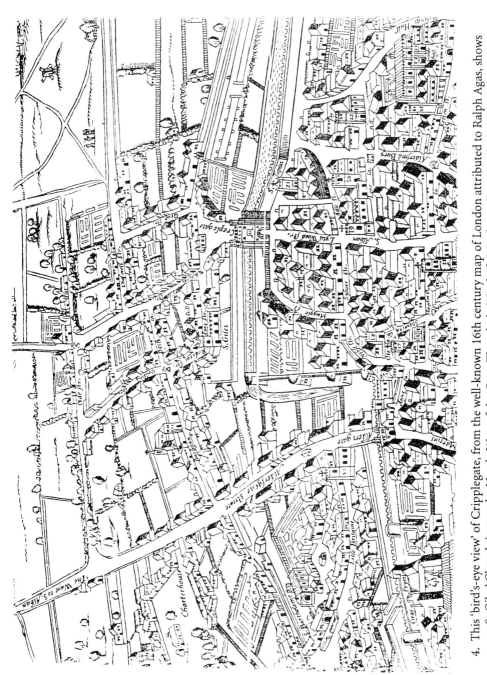

4. This 'bird's-eye view' of Cripplegate, from the well-known 16th century map of London attributed to Ralph Agas, shows St Giles' Church just to the North-West of the Gate. The whole Ward of Cripplegate lies outside the City Walls. It was where the greatest concentration of London musicians lived at the time.

attention. He was a nephew of Grand Duke Ferdinand de Medici, the ruler of Florence, as well as being a member of the old Roman Orsini family. Grand Duke Ferdinand had effectively adopted him when he became an orphan at an early age, and he was to spend the rest of his life in the service of Florence. His visit to England was an extension of a state journey to Paris, accompanying his cousin Maria de Medici to her marriage with King Henri IV of France, who, to Elizabeth's fury, had shortly before divorced his first wife and converted to Catholicism. Virginio's extended journey was unauthorised. He was in fact the first Catholic prince to visit England since the papal 'crusade' against England had begun, but he was no friend of the present Pope, Clement VIII, who belonged to the Aldobrandini family, enemies of the Medici, and this was partly the reason for his being in London. When the Pope's nephew, as papal legate, arrived in Florence in September 1600, to present the future queen of France on behalf of the Pope with a Golden Rose (shades of *Der Rosenkavalier!*), Don Virginio assumed for himself pride of place over the Cardinal (who had planned a public humiliation for him) at the formal ceremony of greetings. The legate threatened to return home. Harmony was restored by the Grand Duke, but it was Don Virginio's day. Whether it would be safe for him to stay in Italy thereafter was for the time being questionable.

In her palace at Whitehall, Elizabeth was aware of all these events. She also knew that Virginio had distinguished himself fighting against the Turks in Hungary in 1595, and that since that time he had offered his services to herself through a number of emissaries, and that he had graciously entertained William Cecil, nephew of Sir Robert, her chief minister, in Florence earlier in 1600. The omens were favourable for a very special visit.

At this point Dr Hotson's researches led him to some papers which shed light on the celebrations as nothing else except Virginio's own account of the day could have done; in the Collection of Historical Manuscripts belonging to the Duke of Northumberland there was a document dated 6 January 1601, and catalogued as 'a full narrative description of the reception and entertainment of the Muscovite Ambassador and of an Italian nobleman, the Duke of Brachiana . . . (much damaged at the edges by fire. 6pp)'.[67] Hotson discovered that the manuscript was not greatly damaged, and was in two parts, first the 'description', as catalogued, and secondly the 'original memoranda of Lord Chamberlain Hunsdon of things to be done to prepare the palace and to conduct the ceremonies in state'.[68]

It is at this point that the relevance of the story for the Company begins to emerge. The queen was determined that Don Virginio should be the guest of honour for the most important part of the evening's entertainment. Immediately after Christmas, Lord Hunsdon, the Lord Chamberlain, set out the protocol for 6

[67] The description comes from the Historical MSS Commission, *Third Report*, App., 51b.
[68] Hotson, p. 15.

January (which was designed to give appropriate precedence to the Russian Ambassador, but to remove him from the scene before the play began), and then made a note:

> To confer with my Lord Admiral and the Master of the Revels for taking order generally with the players to make choice of play that shall be furnished with rich apparel, have great variety and change of music and dances, and of a subject that shall be most pleasing to her Majesty.

The result of this conference was that the Lord Chamberlain's Men were chosen to present the play, and probably (there is no proof, but plenty of presumptive evidence) that Shakespeare was commissioned to write a play which would be in honour of the queen's principal guest, and that he then wrote *Twelfth Night or What You Will* and rehearsed it in eleven days.

Another note follows shortly afterwards in the Lord Chamberlain's memoranda:

> To Appoint Music severally for the Queen and some for the play in the Hall. And Hales[69] to have one place expressly to shew his own voice.
> To send for *the Musicians of the City* to be ready to attend.

On this great occasion, therefore, perhaps the last unclouded celebration in the great queen's reign,[70] the Musicians' Company participated in the festivities at Whitehall. Whether it was *in multo* or *in parvo* depends on the interpretation of the Lord Chamberlain's expression 'Musicians of the City'. It could mean a summons to the Master of the Company, in which case its members would have turned up in force. More likely it refers to the Waits. If so, the Company can still rejoice in the fact that, if they were all on duty, six members of the Company would have been playing, three in the Queen's Music and three among the Waits.

It is unlikely that any of them would have provided music for the play itself. This would have been performed by the musicians who were permanent members of the troupe. Extracts from Don Virginio's own account (from which a lot of important detail was unfortunately withheld because he wanted to keep the best for his wife, to be told face to face) may give some clues as to how they were deployed:

> Presently after her Majesty had sat down to table, the Muscovite Ambassador (of whose ridiculous manners I shall give an account) fell to dining; and I was conducted . . . into a hall where there was prepared for me a most noble banquet, at the end of which appeared a good music.
> As soon as the banquet was ended I rose from the table and went to her Majesty, who was already on her feet; and talking now with me and now with the Muscovite Ambassador, she tarried for a while, and then was attended by me to her room.

Don Virginio was conducted to his lodging to rest,

---

[69] This was Robert Hales, described by Hotson as 'England's leading singer': p. 181.
[70] See p. 62.

but after a little while the chief [of the acquaintances he had made] began coming to visit me; and then there was music, of some instruments to my belief never heard in Italy, but miraculous ones; so that with good entertainment we came to the hour of supper.

Hotson suggests that the 'instruments' were hautboys, but if one is really looking for instruments unknown in Italy, the most likely candidates would be the bandora and orpharion, both wire-stringed instruments developed in England in the latter half of the 16th century.

After supper Sir Robert Cecil took Virginio to the queen's lodgings where he was invited to greet all the ladies 'in the French fashion' (one kiss to the fingers, one kiss to the lips and then an embrace at the waist).[71] Then the queen came in and took him in conversation to the base of the stairs to the Hall:

Her Majesty mounted the stairs, amid such sounding of trumpets that methought I was on the field of war, and entered a public hall where all around were rising steps with ladies, and divers consorts of music. As soon as her Majesty was set at her place many ladies and knights began a Great Ball. When this came to an end, there was acted a mingled comedy, with pieces of music and dances, and this too I am keeping to tell by word of mouth.

Inasmuch as Virginio wished to keep for the personal telling the fact that the play featured a Duke Orsino who bore a more than passing resemblance to himself, we are the losers. One hopes that he enjoyed the English play, although he knew no English. He had however reported earlier that 'he found no more than two gentlemen who knew no other tongue than English'; those who greeted him had spoken to him in Italian, French or Spanish. It would not have been out of character for the queen herself to have acted as interpreter from time to time during the play.

After more conversation with the ladies in Italian and French, Don Virginio finally left the palace at about two in the morning. He returned through the night to his lodgings in the house of the rich Italian merchant Sgr Corsini in Gracechurch Street. It would be good to know whether the exhausted members of the Musicians Company arrived at their homes in the City before him, or were obliged to remain in attendance until the Duke had departed.

[71] Hotson, p. 202.

4

Royal Charter, Bearings (and Hall?)

JUST one month after the splendid festivities at Whitehall on Twelfth Night, the Earl of Essex, who had been banned from Court for his abject failure to tackle the crisis in Northern Ireland, charged through the streets of the City with 300 mounted men, shouting 'For the Queen! A plot is laid for my life!' While the City turned its back, with not a hand raised in his support, the queen's ministers took a serious view of what looked like an attempt by her disgraced favourite to raise a rebellion in the heart of the capital. What might have once been treated as a publicity stunt in bad taste led to a full-blown treason trial, and before the end of February the earl's charismatic but unbalanced head had been separated from his body on Tower Hill. Shakespeare, who had known Essex since the time when his patron, the Earl of Southampton, had become one of his party, is thought to have drawn on his complex character to develop the personality of Hamlet for the play, which was written the same year.[1]

So ended the romance of 'Gloriana's' reign. Up to this moment it had seemed as if the wondrous reign might continue indefinitely, but now the queen's ministers and her courtiers were forced to face up to her mortality. She continued to preside over her Court, as well as govern the nation, well into her seventieth year, but increasingly gloom and ill-health replaced joy and energy, and the queen died on 24 March 1603.

The Musicians' Company members would have played their full part in the majestic Funeral Procession and the street-lining, as the crowds flocked to pay their last respects to the great queen. But already, it seems, their collective mind was focused on securing the Company's future as the sole supervisory authority for the performance of secular music, not just in the City and its liberties, but throughout the new suburbs as well. With a population now approaching 200,000, London had had to expand beyond its walls, although no attempt was ever made by the City authorities to extend its municipal responsibility beyond its old boundaries (except in respect of the old 'liberties' which lay just outside

---

[1] See J. Dover Wilson, *The Essential Shakespeare* (Cambridge: Cambridge University Press 1945), pp. 106–7.

the walls). It was therefore left to the office-holders of the suburban parishes to take charge of the health, hygiene and good order of the large and growing population within their boundaries. By contrast it was natural for the City Livery Companies to want to extend their control over crafts and trades into these parishes. Without such control so-called 'Londoners' (although city-dwellers called them 'foreigns') could evade the quality control and the profitable restrictive practices in force within the City.

The only way that the controls could be extended was by royal concession, and this involved obtaining a royal charter. The 'Great Twelve' and the other companies which had retained the strongest hold over their respective 'misteries' had, since the 14th century, been obtaining royal charters and having them confirmed and updated, giving them rights of search and forfeiture in respect of their craft or 'art' throughout the kingdom. As the musical profession involved no manufacture or trade, what the Master and Wardens of the Company were now seeking was a right of examination of and control over all who claimed to exercise the art or science of music, or the teaching of music or dancing, within three miles of the City. Practical considerations ruled out any realistic extension of this authority to more remote parts of the kingdom. The Company would be content with bringing the 'foreigns' who lived in places such as Lambeth, Southwark, Bermondsey, Islington, Hackney and Whitechapel under its authority.

At the same time those members of the Company who had achieved their ultimate ambition of becoming City Waits or joining the royal household clearly felt the need for some outward show of status for the Company, and it was therefore decided not just to apply for a charter, but also for a grant of arms. With the charter would be a new set of bye-laws. These had to be approved by the Lord Chancellor.

Before applying for a charter it was obligatory for a livery company to ask the Court of Aldermen for their approval. This was more than just a formality, and in certain cases permission was refused, but the Company received a Licence to apply on 6 March 1603,[2] three weeks before the death of Queen Elizabeth. The change of dynasty does not therefore seem to have been a factor which was directly relevant to the Company's objectives.

Apart from the fact that it took over two years, there is nothing to suggest that the Company experienced any difficulty in achieving their triple objective. That the king's musicians raised no objection is very significant, and it must have been because there were, at the time, three of their own fraternity in the Company. It was also expressly stated in the new bye-laws that nothing contained therein was to infringe upon the rights of the 'King's Majesty's musicians in ordinary *being not free of the said commonalty of the musicians of London*'. The phraseology of this proviso is noteworthy, in the light of the violent assault on the Company and its charter by Nicholas Lanier thirty years later. It must mean that it was antici-

---

[2]   CL Reps 26 (2), fol. 307.

pated that the native-born king's musicians would naturally wish to join the Company, but that an exception would be made for those who did not.

The Charter was granted on the 8 July 1604, the Grant of Arms on the 15 October 1604 and the Bye-laws were issued on 25 August 1606. The text of the Charter and the Bye-laws makes for heavy reading, in marked contrast to the concise wording of the City Ordinances. No doubt the scriveners in the Lord Chancellor's Department charged their captive clients by the folio, and it was therefore advantageous to include as much synonymous repetition as possible. The documents are set out in full in Appendix 4, and a close study, particularly of the bye-laws, will show that they effectively consolidate what had been achieved during the previous one hundred years. There are however a few matters of real interest which deserve to be highlighted at this stage.

Looking first at the Charter, it recites that the king has received a petition from 'the freemen of the Society of Minstrels of our City of London', which suggests that the old word 'Minstrel' was used in the petition in order to provide a link with the older Ordinances. That it was not a title in current use is indicated by the words which appear a few lines down the page, almost in parenthesis, 'or by what other name or names the same Society is called or named'. Removing all future doubts the Charter then declares that the body corporate would have the title:

> Master, Wardens and commonalty of the Art or Science of the Musicians of London . . . and so from henceforth shall be named, called and accepted in our City of London and elsewhere, and not otherwise.

After dealing with the corporate powers of the Company and the principal Officers, the Master and Wardens, there appears the first mention, in any surviving Company document, of the Court of Assistants. The number of assistants, then as now, was to be not less than thirteen nor more than twenty, and their role was to aid and assist the Master and Wardens. The Court was to have power to make 'reasonable laws, statutes, constitutions, decrees and ordinances' as may from time to time be necessary for the good rule and government of the Company 'and of all other minstrels and musicians of the City of London, and within three miles of the same city'.

The Charter goes on to name the first Master and Wardens and fourteen Assistants. The first Court was composed of the following:

Master:	Phillip London
Wardens:	Isaac Thorpe
	Thomas Carter (City Wait)

Assistants:

Anthony Tindall (retired City Wait)	Rowland Rowbedge (King's Music)
James Sherman	Robert Baker (King's Music)
Walter Lowman (City Wait)	John Mitchell
William Warren (King's Music)	John Popson

Arthur Norton (retired City Wait)	Vincent Johnveryn
Tristram Waters	John Bickley
William Benton	Simon Hopper

Two years later, when the Bye-laws were issued, Tristram Waters had progressed to the office of Master, and William Benton and Vincent Johnveryn (now spelt Janvrin) were the Wardens. The Charter provided that the Court should elect at their discretion and from time to time such of the 'ancientist and most worthy freemen' as shall be thought meet, up to a maximum of twenty, with power likewise to remove and replace any assistant 'for any reasonable cause'. The Master and/or Wardens could also be removed by vote of the court 'for evil government' or for any other reasonable cause.

A long section follows, dealing with the holding, acquisition and disposal of land, the chief point of interest being the limit of £20 annual value placed on the aggregate holdings of property. It was relevant to the Company's right to own a Hall, which we shall be considering later in the Chapter.

Finally the charter sets out the vital extension of the Company's supervisory powers:

> For the better rule and government of all those which in our City of London, and within three miles of the said city, do profess and exercise and hereafter shall profess and exercise the art or science of music . . . the said master wardens and their successors, for the time being for all times to come shall have the survey, search, correction, and government of all and singular musicians and minstrels within our said City of London, or within the suburbs, liberties, and precincts of the said city, or within three miles of the same city.

Was it an oversight that the King's Music were not excluded from the scope of the charter in the document itself, or was it always intended that this exclusion should appear in the bye-laws (which, being an instrument intended to regulate the guild, is not the most obvious place to declare it)? If it was an oversight it was to prove a fatal mistake.

Two years were to elapse before the Bye-laws were officially approved and published. If in the meantime the new king's Whitehall Establishment had been shaken by the affair of the 'Gunpowder Plot', this would not necessarily have contributed to the delay, as it was the responsibility of the officers of the Company to draft the new bye-laws and to present them to the Lord Chancellor in the form of a petition.

A quick review of the new regulations (which appear in full in Appendix 4) reveals the aspirations of a group of professionals who are not only seeking to extend their control, but who are also looking for greater status and a higher standard of respectability. This is particularly evident in the last part of the document,[3] where there is a prohibition against any professional musician, whether a

---

[3] See p. 264.

freeman of the Company or not, from walking in the street or going from house to house with an *uncased* instrument 'to be seen by any passing by'. To play any instrument either night or morning 'under any nobleman, knight, or gentleman's window or lodging in the street, or the window or lodging of any other person whatsoever', without the Court's permission, is also forbidden. Both these rules could only have been intended to emphasise the fact that the Company now disowned and wished to put a stop to the old habits of street minstrelsy within the City and the wider area now under its jurisdiction.

The structure of the Company, as it has survived into the 20th century, can be seen taking shape in the bye-laws. Whereas the 16th century Ordinances were principally concerned with rights and obligations of freemen of the Company and with rules relating to apprenticeship, the 1606 bye-laws recognise the Court of Assistants as the governing body, and introduce the procedure for elections to the Livery 'and clothing'. On election, liverymen are required to pay a fine of £1; if they are elected and refuse to take up the livery they are to be fined £2. Quarterage on the other hand was to be levied on the whole fellowship, freemen as well as livery (and 'widows of the same art'), at the rate of sixpence a quarter.

The office of Steward makes its first appearance; two stewards were to be appointed annually to take responsibility for arranging and underwriting the quarterly Court Dinners (although the Master and Wardens had the right to nominate where the feasts were to be held). Every assistant attending a dinner was obliged to contribute twelve pence, but the stewards would have to make up the deficit if there was one.

The regulations were designed to give the Court as much control as possible over all musicians within the prescribed boundaries, and to deter any member of the Company from thinking of a transfer to another company. Not only did musicians who belonged to another company have to pay quarterage to the Musicians Company at the same rate as members, in addition to whatever charges might be due to their own company, but a swingeing fine of £10 was due to the Company from any of its own members who 'shall go out of the said fellowship' without the consent of the Court.

Further restrictions were placed on the solitary minstrel and on those who might formerly have played together in twos and threes by a bye-law which prohibited musicians performing on any public or semi-public occasion 'under the number of four, in consort or with violins'. The occasions to which this applied were described as 'weddings, feasts, banquest, revels, or other assemblies or meetings', and these, together with 'triumphs . . . guilds and brotherhoods', as mentioned in another bye-law, would have been the principal livelihood of the rank-and-file City musician. The other activity which had become the Company's responsibility early in the previous reign was the teaching of dancing, and the opportunity was now taken to introduce further supervisory powers. The master and wardens 'or such other discreet and skilful persons of the Company' as they should appoint had the right to call in all professional musicians, and all who taught music or dancing and to examine them 'for their sufficiency and skill'. Anyone who failed the examination would be disallowed and subject to fines if they continued to practise without further examination.

An additional restriction on dancing masters was re-enacted; there was to be no teaching or exercising of dancing on the Sabbath Day. In similar vein, reflecting the puritan tendency in the City at this time, it was the responsibility of the Company's officers to see that no person sang 'any ribaldry, wanton, or lascivious songs or ditties at any time' within the City and the three-mile limit 'whereby God may be dishonoured'. Bearing in mind that this was just the time when the writing of satirical comedies had reached its apogee, and the Inns of Court, where these plays thrived among the student population, were just down the road, this was bound to be an impossible task, and the Lord Mayor took matters into his own hands a few years later.[4]

The bye-laws end (although there was some confusion in the compiling of the 17th century copy in the Company's possession and the last pages are not in the right order[5]) with the wording of the respective Oaths of Master, Wardens and Freemen of the Company, which have survived almost unaltered to the present day.

The chartered Company now had its constitution. It had also received its grant of arms. These were granted soon after the date of the Charter, on 15 October 1604 and, like the Oaths just referred to, the Arms of the Company have survived and are well known to all members of the Company. Their symbolism is however less well known and is often indeed the subject of controversy if not puzzlement.

The Bearings are properly described as follows:[6]

> Azure a swan with wings expanded argent within a double tressure flory counter-flory or, on a chief gules a pale between two lions passant gardant or, thereon a rose gules barbed and seeded vert.
> *Crest:* On a wreath of the colours a lyre or.
> *Mantling:* Azure doubled or
> Granted by William Camden
Clarenceux
15th October 1604

Apart from the swan and lyre, all the emblems have royal associations. The lions and the rose need no comment, but one may ask why the rose is red. It has been suggested[7] that both these emblems reflect the fact that the Company in 1604

---

4 See CL Rep 32, fol. 75 (1615), containing an Aldermanic prohibition against the singing of any 'Latin, Italian or French song . . . till it be first read in English to the Lord Mayor . . . and by him allowed'. An early form of secular censorship, one wonders how effective it was. See also Woodfill, p. 16.

5 See pp. 263–6.

6 From J. Bromley and H. Child, *The Armorial Bearings of the Guilds of London* (London: Frederick Warne 1961), pp. 178–80.

7 Bromley and Child, p. 179.

claimed descent from the King's Minstrels chartered in 1469 by Edward IV, but if that were the case the rose should surely be the white rose of York. A more sensible assumption would be that the red rose is an allusion to the Company's origins in Tudor times in 1500, of which the Master and Wardens in 1604 would have been well aware.

The silver swan is described as being set 'within a double tressure flory counter-flory', in other words a double band decorated with a floral motif alternately the right way up and upside down. This appears to have been a feature of the ancient royal arms of Scotland[8] and would have been included in honour of the new king.

But what of the swan itself? The immediate reaction, with Orlando Gibbons' famous madrigal in mind, is to assume that a swan 'that living hath no note' but who sings at its death was thought to be a suitable symbol for the Company, notwithstanding that Gibbons had not yet written his piece at the time. The legend of the dying swan was of course part of the common currency of romantic literature, but more significant was the fact that the swan, like the lyre, was a symbol of Apollo, the God of Music. Apollo had a small menagerie of sacred animals and birds attributed to him, including the wolf, roe deer, hawk, crow, swan, snake, mouse, grasshopper and the griffin, but it was the swan and grasshopper which symbolised music and song. Song and the grasshopper were obviously associated, and there is no need therefore to linger over the notion of the dying, singing swan. It must have been the beauty and the power of the great white bird which connected it with music and Apollo, and because, like the swan, music flies straight through the air.

However there were two other special factors which may have influenced the Company's choice of the swan as the principal motif. The first was that the late Lord Chamberlain, George Carey, 2nd Baron Hunsdon, who had died the previous year, besides being the patron of the Lord Chamberlain's Men (Shakespeare's and Burbage's company, and the leading theatrical troupe), was also an eminent amateur musician. Lord Hunsdon's badge was the silver swan, and Hotson claims that it was this badge which was responsible for Shakespeare's nickname, 'Swan of Avon'.[9] The Company may have decided to pay tribute to the memory of this great patron of the arts by adopting the emblem from his badge.

There is also the rather mysterious link between the swan and mediaeval minstrelsy, the tradition of which would have survived into the early 17th century. The best illustration of this was the Knighting of Prince Edward in 1306, which was described in chapter 2.[10] The Prince and all the other new knights made their vows before a 'subtlety' or device consisting of 'two cygnets or swans, orna-

8   Bromley and Child, p. 179.
9   Hotson, p. 79.
10 See pp. 17–18.

mented with golden nets or gilded pipings'.[11] At the coronation feast of Henry V, the symbol of the great swan was once again used.[12] No precise explanation of the significance of the swan is available, but in mediaeval times it could perhaps have been symbolic of feasting (good to look at, good to eat), and therefore had some mystic force for minstrels whose livelihood depended on the feast.

With Charter, bye-laws and armorial bearings, the Company now had the status for which it had been aiming. It could take its place alongside the other City Livery Companies, collectively the most wealthy and powerful institutions in the realm. But a high price had to be paid to attain this position, and it was going to be expensive to live up to the standards set by the other companies and the obligations put upon them by the government, which was chronically short of money, and always looking to the City of London for financial support.

As there are no surviving Company records from this period, we have no means of knowing just what the Company had to pay to obtain its charter. But the Founders' Company also obtained a charter a few years later, in 1613, and a full account of its expenses is available,[13] and is reproduced here, as the figures cannot have differed greatly.

First of all the Court allocated £1 for suit in the Court of Aldermen, to obtain the Licence to apply for the charter. Thereafter the expenses payable in Westminster were as shown in this statement:

	£	s	d
Paid for writing our reasons and desires – what we desired to be granted for our Corporation	0	5	4
Given unto Sir H Montagu, Recorder, for his advice	2	4	0
Given to Mr Young, clerk to Sir Francis Bacon	0	11	0
Given to Mr Bassett, secretary to Sir Julius Caesar	0	11	0
Given to Mr Lock, clerk to the King's Commissioners	1	13	8
Paid unto Mr Diss for the procuring of a Corporation for the Company	100	0	0
	115	14	0 – [sic]

Sir Francis Bacon was Attorney-General in 1613; Sir Julius Caesar was Chancellor of the Exchequer, and about to be appointed Master of the Rolls.

By contrast to this great sum, the grant of arms to the Founders Company involved the payment of only £3 2s 8d to Clarenceux King of Arms.

The Founders Company did not have sufficient funds available to meet the full expense of obtaining the charter, and were dependent on a loan from one of their livery, a Mr Richard Rowdinge, who agreed to lend them £150. The yeo-

---

[11] From 'Flores Historiarum' by the 'monk of Westminster', quoted by Bullock-Davies, p. xxx (Introduction).

[12] Bullock-Davies, p. xxxiv (Introduction): 'one great swan sitting upon a green stock surrounded by six cygnets and twenty-four other swans with mottoes in their beaks'.

[13] See W.N. Hibbert, *History of the Worshipful Company of Founders, of the City of London* (London: privately printed 1925), p. 31.

manry also agreed to meet the interest charge for two years. It was noted that nine years later the Company was still in straitened circumstances.

How would the Musicians Company have coped with a similar financial burden in 1604–06? There is no doubt that £100 was a very large sum at that time. During the reign of Queen Elizabeth the whole procedure of obtaining royal charters had become a revenue-raising exercise connected with the grant of monopolies and, despite promises by James I at his accession that these would be abolished, they continued and the price was high, as the exchequer was permanently short of funds. It is difficult to assess what would be the equivalent in modern currency, because so many ratios were quite unlike those that now apply, and in particular the difference between rich and poor was much greater.[14] We know that at this time a member of the King's Music could expect to receive about £50 a year, not including fees for unofficial engagements.[15] For a musician near the top of the profession £100 would therefore represent something under two years' income, but any who were attached to the royal household might benefit from huge bonuses in the form of export or import licences or patents.[16] Special fees for special events were also sometimes paid; this was a tendency which would increase during James I's reign.[17]

City Waits were paid £20 per annum,[18] but would receive a substantial amount of extra fees for engagements outside their official duties. For them £100 might be the equivalent of three years' income. The ordinary rank and file of the fellowship would lag a long way behind, and might need between five and ten years to earn £100.

The conclusion must be that the greater part of the burden was borne by those members of the Company who were of the King's Music and the Waits, who were already well off and who would benefit most from the grant of the charter, but whether the money was provided in the form of a loan, as in the case of the Founders, or by voluntary contribution we may never know. As was noted in the last chapter, the City Parish records suggest that there were nearly twice as many (207) musicians living in the city in the first half of the 17th century as there had been in the previous half century. It seems therefore that many more professional musicians were now able to support themselves in or around the City. The figures given are almost certainly an under-estimate as they probably exclude musicians who belonged to other guilds. Some recent research carried out by Dr David Lasocki does, however, suggest that there were not so many of

---

[14] A multiple of 500 would give a figure of £50,000, and this would seem to be a fair comparison and in line with the salaries quoted.

[15] Woodfill, p. 179.

[16] Holman, pp. 48–9.

[17] Just to take two examples, the French Dancing Master Nicolas Confesse received £50 for his work on the masque 'Oberon'. In 1616 Nicholas Lanier was paid £200 by George Villiers for the Masque 'Gypsies Metamorphosed'.

[18] Woodfill, p. 37.

these during the period following the grant of the Charter as there would be in Charles I's reign. He has discovered only four in 1612, compared to seventeen or more in 1636.[19]

The opportunity to bring all City musicians 'under one roof' at a time when the Company was in a prosperous state and the number of stragglers was perhaps historically low may have been the reason for another petition which the Company presented to the Lord Mayor in November 1612.[20] It requested that all professional musicians in the City who were freemen of other companies should be translated into the Company. As this proposal cut across one of the most hallowed customs of the City, the Company must have had a pretty strong case to justify the presentation of the petition, and it appears that a Committee of the Court of Aldermen[21] set up to consider the matter were fully persuaded, because they recommended to their brother Aldermen that they should endorse it as 'a thing very well liked and approved by this Court' and pass it on to the Court of Common Council.[22] Unfortunately for the Company, that was as far as the initiative was allowed to go; City custom was too strong to allow a precedent of this sort to be created.

There was indeed a good case to be made on financial grounds in support of the petition. Although the Master and Wardens could freely exercise the power given them under the Charter to examine any one claiming to be a professional musician, whatever their company, and to adjudicate on their ability, there was no easy way to collect the quarterage which was due from musicians who were not free of the Company. Freemen of other companies were not obliged to attend the Company's quarterly assemblies when the levy would normally be payable. They had to pay their own company's quarterage, and would therefore plead poverty or ask for time to pay the Musicians' levy, making it difficult and time-consuming to collect. The system was ineffective.

Another reason why the Company needed to increase its revenue at this time was its involvement with the Londonderry Plantation.

This strange adventure, to which all the City livery companies found themselves unwillingly committed, resulted from a sort of fusion (in the minds of the king's ministers) between the political situation in Ulster, after what was known as 'the Flight of the Earls' in 1607, and the development of the first settlements in Virginia which was taking place at the same time.[23] In Ireland, after many years of rebellion, inter-tribal warfare, pardon and pacification, and abortive attempts

---

19 I am most grateful to Dr Lasocki for allowing me to use this information which will shortly be published in an article on 'Musicians in City of London Companies in the 17th Century'.

20 CL Rep 31, parts 1, 6 and 85b.

21 The members were Sir Clement Scudamore, Sir John Jolley, Alderman Stile and Alderman Harvey (Alderman Harvey does not appear to have been included at the reporting stage in April 1613).

22 CL Rep 32, part 2, fol. 203b.

23 The whole detailed history of the Londonderry Plantation has been most recently told in

to turn the Ulster chiefs into English-style landed gentry, the Earls of Tyrone and Tyrconnel were once again discovered to have been intriguing with the Spanish to raise another Catholic insurrection. To escape arrest and a fate similar to that of the Gunpowder Plot conspirators, the two earls with their whole households secretly took ship for Flanders, never to return, and the English government suddenly found itself with a vast expanse of Ulster on its hands, lordless and ungoverned. The suppression in the following year of a final revolt by Sir Cahir O'Doherty, Lord of Inishowen, left virtually the whole of the 'six counties' available for settlement.[24]

In seeking a solution the government saw no reason why they should not equate the wild Irish clans in Ulster with the native 'Indians' in Virginia. Whether they were this side of the Atlantic or that, they all had to be driven off the lands which they occupied by tribal custom alone, because it was necessary first to find places into which a rapidly growing English population could overflow and settle, and secondly to use the settlers to create a more or less civilised society to replace the lawlessness of the clans and tribes. An earlier attempt at an Irish Plantation had been attempted in Munster and had ended with a disastrous massacre of the settlers in 1598; this time civilisation would have to be sustained by fortification and soldiery.[25] Where could sufficient resources in terms of personnel and finance come from? For the government there was only one answer – the City of London.

The Lord Mayor and Aldermen were deputed by the king and Lord Salisbury to present to the livery companies a document entitled 'Motives and Reasons to induce the City of London to undertake the Plantation in the North of Ireland'. Despite their strenuous efforts initial reaction, even from the Great Twelve, was unenthusiastic, but eventually agreement was reached in January 1610 to undertake this great project.[26] The City companies were to raise £20,000 immediately, and each company was to be assessed according to the corn-rate scale. For this purpose each of the lesser companies was grouped with one of the Great Twelve, in whose name alone the land-grants or 'Proportions' were made, with a fiduciary responsibility for the investment of the lesser companies in their group. The Musicians were in the Fishmongers' group.

The first levy of £20,000, as some pessimists had anticipated, proved to be quite inadequate, and by the end of 1613, the total amount of the precept had reached £45,000. Another £15,000 would be demanded in the next three years, but before this became due the Musicians Company, whose contribution had grown to the not inconsiderable sum of £30,[27] had had enough.

James Steven Curl, *The Londonderry Plantation, 1609–1914* (Chichester: Phillimore & Co. 1986).

[24] Curl, p. 20.

[25] Curl, p. 22.

[26] Curl, p. 33.

[27] Curl, p. 69. £30 was the smallest assessment, applied also to the Woolmen, Bowyers and

It must have become obvious by this time that the over-optimistic assumptions made by the promoters of the Settlement were placing an intolerable strain on the resources of the poorer companies, and also that only the Great Twelve were really going to benefit from the project in the long run. The lesser companies were therefore allowed to make whatever composition they could with the company in the Great Twelve in whose 'group' they had been put, and the Musicians' Company assigned its interest to the Fishmongers in 1614.[28] It is not known whether any consideration was passed back to them for the assignment, but as they were being released from an ongoing onerous obligation that would seem to be unlikely. More precious resources had therefore been wasted, and from the Company's point of view nothing whatever had been achieved, except to extricate itself from a position which was to deteriorate dramatically in the next reign.

There is no reason however to suppose that the Company was seriously affected financially by the Londonderry affair. It is true there was poverty in the Company at the time, and some of the members would have needed help from the poor box, like the Assistant John Mitchell who died worth 32s 8d.[29] But there were also very wealthy members, some of whom made bequests to the Company or its officers in their wills. These documents invite comparison with the dispositions made by senior members of the Company in the Edwardian era, which are described in Chapter 12, and in terms of general wealth and prosperity there is a similarity between the two periods. The principal source of wealth in the early 17th century was property ownership, both in town and country, following a massive shift in land tenure in the previous century, and this seems to be the way in which some of the musicians whose wills have survived made their money.

The most famous example was Henry Walker, who in 1604 bought a 'dwelling-house or tenement' within the old precincts of Blackfriars, including part which extended over a 'great gate' leading to a capital messuage later occupied by the Earl of Northumberland. The purchase also included a plot of land on the West side of the house which was used as a garden. Having bought the house Walker let it to William Shakespeare, William Johnson, John Jackson and John Hemmyng, and subsequently sold the freehold to the same parties on 10 March 1613. It must therefore have been used as an integral part of the Blackfriars Theatre where the King's Men (formerly the Lord Chamberlain's Men) performed during the winter seasons. The original deed of conveyance bearing Shakespeare's signature is held in the Guildhall Library.[30] The consideration for the sale was £140, but Walker's estate was worth considerably more than that at his death in 1616.

Fletchers, but it was still a heavy charge. On a multiple of 500, it would have been the equivalent of £15,000 in modern currency.

[28] Curl, p. 232.

[29] Mentioned in a letter from J.L. Boston to H.A.F. Crewdson, without date or reference.

[30] Guildhall Library MS 3738.

The wills are interesting for many reasons, for example they often mention the instruments owned by the testator, and miscellaneous legatees include two Beadles and one Clerk, whose names would otherwise be unknown. At the time of Robert Bateman's will in 1618 the Beadle was James Smyth, who received £3. Eleven years later, Simon Hopper gave a legacy of £3 to James Brook, the Clerk, and £2 to Philip Richman, the Beadle. But the chief fascination is the evidence (albeit mostly circumstantial) that the wills provide in support of the notion that for some years during the early 17th century the Company was actually in possession of a hall. Let it be said at once that, like so much in the early history of the Company, this presumption is incapable of proof, but there are sufficient 'arrows' pointing towards a Company hall at this time that it is right to mention them all, and then let each reader come to his or her own conclusion.

First, one must dispose of some evidence to the contrary. In December 1642, the livery companies were subjected to an inquisition as to why they were in arrears in contributing to the fund to suppress the rebellion in Ireland. The report on the Musicians Company stated briefly: 'Poor. Never a Hall; only a brotherhood'.[31] This information seems to have convinced the late Arthur Hill that his research into the existence of a hall was a waste of time. But it was perhaps a clever, disingenuous response, based on the fact that if ever there was a break in continuity of the Company, it occurred between the forfeiture of the Charter in 1635 and the reinstatement of the 'brotherhood' under City custom in 1638, as described in the next chapter. The reply to the inquisition would then have referred only to the reinstated Company. What better way to escape an unwanted fiscal liability?

Our positive evidence begins with the bye-laws of 1606, which contained no fewer than nine references to 'the common hall of the fellowship' and the 'hall book'. The Master and Wardens were to hold meetings every quarter 'at their common hall or other convenient place of meeting' to hear complaints and to receive quarterage payments; they were to hold their examinations, discipline offenders, and receive payment of fines in the same way, and apprentices were to be presented 'at their common hall or meeting place' for examination on completion of their apprenticeship.

The fact that in each of these examples there was always an alternative venue allowed for indicates that, in 1606, the Hall did not yet exist or was still in negotiation. Stronger evidence is therefore required, and for this one turns once more to Henry Walker, who left a long and very complex will[32] which effectively appointed the Musicians' Company as trustees of a charitable trust which he established for the benefit of the little town of Kington in Herefordshire. The will was dated 17 April 1615, and the trust money (£120) was given and bequeathed to:

---

[31] This note, among Arthur Hill's papers, bears no reference, and I have not been able to trace the source.

[32] Public Record Office, PROB 11/128 q94.

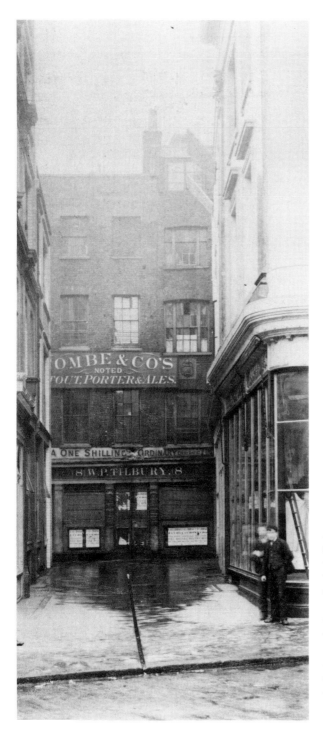

5. The derelict 'Goose and Gridiron' just prior to demolition about 100 years ago. Facing St Paul's Cathedral down London House Yard, it stood on the site where until 1666 the 'Mitre' Inn had been, next to which the Company may for some years in the first part of the 17th century have had its Hall.

> the Master Wardens and Assistants of the Company of Musicians (of which company I am a member) . . . to be paid unto them at a Court to be holden *within their hall* within the space of one year after my decease.

Walker also included a legacy to the Company of a piece of plate of the value of £8, but this was subsequently revoked by a codicil made shortly before his death in the following year, for the very good reason that he had in the meantime presented the Company with a piece of plate of a greater value. Other members of the Company were also leaving money in their wills to enable the Company to buy silver plate. One of these was Robert Bateman, the only 17th century composer whom the Company can positively claim as a member, who by his will dated 11 February 1618 left £10 to the Company 'to buy them a cup withall'.[33] Some years later Vincent Janvrin in his will dated 28 July 1630 left the Company a piece of plate of the value of £8.

It is tempting to deduce that members of the Company would not be interested in building up a collection of plate for the Company unless there was somewhere where it could be housed. The investigation therefore needs to be taken one stage further, and a search made for a likely site for the Hall. It does not, of course, have to be a freehold. Lacking the necessary capital to invest in freehold property in the City, a poor company would be in a better position to take a lease, with the rent being serviced from the quarterage.

There is only one known 'candidate', and the evidence is still slender. Next door to the Mitre Tavern, which stood on the north-west corner of St Paul's Churchyard, there was a 'Music Room'. After the Restoration it was owned by William Paget, a taverner and possibly one of the king's violins from 1662. In 1664 the Music Room was taken over by Robert Aubert or Forges for an 'exhibition of rarities' which were subsequently acquired by Sir Hans Sloane and formed part of the original British Museum collection.[34] It must have been removed from the Music Room before 1666, because the latter was then totally destroyed in the Great Fire. In the rebuilding the new tenant abandoned the tavern's old name, and called it instead 'The Goose and Gridiron', under which title the public house survived for over 200 years. The name was a contemptuous allusion to the coat of arms which hung or was carved on an escutcheon over the main door before 'the general devastation of the City'. The arms were of course the swan and lyre of the Company.

This could therefore have been the Company's hall, held on lease for a period of not more than 30 years from 1606 or shortly after. A few more scraps of evidence would help to determine whether the possession of this hall was a fact in the Company's history or just wishful thinking.

---

[33] Public Record Office, PROB 11/131 q18.

[34] See Leopold Wagner, *London Inns and Taverns* (London: George Allen & Unwin 1924), p. 77.

5

Nicholas Lanier

There is a tide in the affairs of men,
Which taken at the flood, leads on to fortune:
Omitted, all the voyage of their life,
Is bound in shallows, and in miseries.
(Julius Caesar, Act IV scene III)

SO wrote Shakespeare in 1600. Thirteen years later the tide turned for the Musicians' Company and continued to ebb for a very, very long time. At the peak of its prosperity and good-standing, the Company suffered its first set-back in 1613 when it failed to persuade the City Corporation to make the Company a 'closed shop', every practising musician having to belong. Two years later the Court of Aldermen showed their mistrust in how the Company was controlling the city musicians by imposing their own censorship on foreign songs:

> No Latin, Italian or French song whatsoever shall be sung by the musicians of this city or any other till it first be read in English to the Lord Mayor . . . and by him allowed.[1]

It was a small symbol of the clash between Pleasure and Damnation which was to dominate the first half of the 17th century.

In 1612 two men had died who could have calmed the seas and subdued the political storms which were shortly to engulf the nation and lead eventually to the execution of one monarch and the expulsion of another. The two men were Robert Cecil, Earl of Salisbury, the king's chief minister, who died aged 49, worn out with the cares of office. The other was the brightest star in the English firmament, Henry, Prince of Wales, a tall, extrovert and intelligent young man of 18, who suddenly contracted typhoid fever and died on 6 November 1612. This is not the place to speculate at length about what might have been the history of the Stuart dynasty if the prince had succeeded his father as King Henry IX. What can be stated with some certainty is that there would have been no Civil War, no ritual sacrifice of chief ministers and king, and no flirtation with Catholicism.

---

[1] CL Rep 32, fol. 75v.

Henry was a staunch protestant and saw himself primarily as a soldier, unlike either his father or his brother. He would therefore have involved the nation more directly in the turmoil in Europe known as the Thirty Years War. He might have entered into a historic partnership on the battlefield with his 'twin', the Swedish king Gustavus Adolphus (they were both born in 1594), and the armies of Sweden and England might then have held the line for the protestant states of Northern Europe. In so doing he would have had strong support from the puritan City of London. Money which neither James nor Charles could extract from the wealthy city would have been provided, even to the point of sacrifice, to support the cause of the reformed religion in the European war, and the armies which finally destroyed royalist power in the 1640s would have exhausted themselves instead on the desolate battlefields of Germany in the 1630s.

It was not to be. After the death of the Prince and the Earl of Salisbury, the king chose his ministers more by their looks than their ability, and Charles, the new Prince of Wales, although he himself was a serious young man, came to maturity in an atmosphere of flattery and frippery. The Palace of Whitehall was becoming an Ivory Tower. It was as if the staging erected in Yuletide each year for the annual masque served as a stockade to keep the common people out of the sacred precincts of the palace.

The high hopes of the promoters of the 1604 Charter that the Musicians' Company would be able to embrace the majority of the King's Music were therefore dashed. Those members of the Company who already held appointments continued until death or retirement, but no new appointments were made (unless John Adson, the City Wait, who was one of the King's Music from 1633 to 1640, was a member of the Company, and this is doubtful[2]).

It is arguable that the masque-culture at Court was primarily responsible for this break. To be a masque-musician one had to be ready to make oneself ridiculous, to play the fool, and to embrace the exhibitionism more normally attributed to actors than instrument-players. The musicians were often dressed in fantastic costumes, and might be set on top of a rickety tower or hung from the ceiling in a swaying 'cloud', playing in time and tune all the while. There had to be a prize for this absurdity, and it was to be one of a closed circle, and as a gentleman of the royal household to perform with members of the royal family and their courtiers in the grandest and the most intimate dramatics in the land.

Those musicians who took part in these productions therefore acquired skills and manners which no common musician could or would even wish to emulate. They were a caste apart; if the courtiers were the worshippers of the masque-culture, they were the priests. They were the masters of an art so esoteric that nearly all the specially composed music was thrown away as soon as the per-

---

[2] Adson was a City Wait, but there is no evidence to show that he was a member of the Company. After his death, his widow appointed Allen Johnson, citizen and fletcher, her attorney to receive Adson's arrears of wages from the treasury chamber (see Ashbee, vol. III, p. 106). Adson may therefore have been a fletcher.

II. The Company's portrait of King James I and VI, grantor of the Company's first Royal Charter in 1604. The king attached great symbolic importance to the jewels which he wore in his hat. In this portrait he is wearing a setting of three diamonds and one huge ruby which he commissioned in 1604 and which was known as 'the Mirror of Great Britain'. Another great diamond known as the 'Sancy' diamond hangs as a pendant. The portrait's artist has not been identified.

formance was concluded. 'No court masque', wrote Peter Walls,[3] 'was ever intended to have a life beyond the situation which formed it.' Not surprisingly the writers of the texts, in particular Ben Jonson, took great trouble to see that these were printed as soon as possible after the performance, not for the purpose of revived production but as a record of a presentation already made.[4] Most seem terribly humourless, pompous and contrived. The music must have been their saving grace, but what a waste of unique national genius! The English music Renaissance ended up not simply shunted into a siding, but lost down a tunnel.

The arch-priest of the masque in its finally evolved form was Nicholas Lanier. He was a man of many parts, a great and versatile musician, who could sing, dance, play the lute, compose and arrange the music of others and design the settings. He was also the only real enemy the Company ever had.

A man who is set on destroying an existing institution usually falls into one of two categories. Either he has viewed it from afar, with envy and perhaps fear, or he has grown up under its shadow, too close for comfort, and has become contemptuous and impatient. Nicholas Lanier fell into the second category. He was born in the City, in the parish of St Olave, Hart Street, where half a century previously the Italian musicians had made their home and some, like the Bassanos, still lived. It is thought that his date of birth was 9 September 1588, as he was baptised the following day.[5] His grandfather, another Nicholas, was the first member of the family to migrate from Rouen in Normandy to London, where at an early age he was appointed one of the queen's flautists in 1561.[6] Two years later another Lanier, John, arrived from Rouen and entered the royal service as a sackbut player. In 1570 the grandfather married for the second time. The wedding took place in London, and his bride was a Bassano, Lucretia, youngest daughter of Anthony, who was the fifth of the Bassano brothers of the first generation.[7] Nicholas already had three sons by his first wife, and now proceeded to have seven more. The second generation of Laniers in turn contributed to the increasing population of London to the tune of forty-three,[8] although some may have died in infancy. Like the Bassanos, the Laniers were a prolific family.

Young Nicholas' mother was a Galliardello, the daughter of Mark Anthony.[9] His father John was another sackbut player and had become one of the queen's musicians in 1582. Nicholas was therefore surrounded by music and musicians

---

3   Peter Walls, *Music in the English Courtly Masque 1604–1640* (Oxford: Clarendon Press 1996), p. 15.

4   Walls, p. 18.

5   Almost all the information on Nicholas Lanier contained in the rest of the chapter is derived from Michael Wilson's biography *Nicholas Lanier, Master of the King's Musick* (Aldershot: Scolar Press 1994), a most useful and valuable book of reference.

6   Wilson, p. 4.

7   Lasocki, p. 45.

8   Wilson, p. 6.

9   Wilson, p. 10.

from the earliest age, and would have been introduced as of right to the standard of living and standard of performance of those in the royal household who enjoyed the status of gentlemen by reason of their office. As a member of a very large family recently arrived in London and not wholly accepted as native, he would have shared the sensitivity, and the readiness to overreact to real or imagined slights, that is typical of such circles, and with such a numerous peer group in his own family he would have become naturally ambitious and keen to dominate those of his own generation.

About the age of 13, or perhaps a year or two earlier, Nicholas became an indentured servant to Lord Salisbury, who still maintained his own private band of musicians.[10] This meant that the boy would be educated in music and other more general subjects for seven years at his master's expense, singing and playing for his master's pleasure as required. Four years later he took on the responsibility for the care of the stringed instruments in the household, and was acquiring the professional skills needed for what was to be his principal instrument, the lute. Soon after, Lord Salisbury entrusted Lanier with the musical instruction of his son William, Lord Cranborne, and the two young men became good friends, an early sign of Lanier's ability to associate on equal terms with people in high places. Cranborne was sent to Paris; Lanier joined him. Cranborne was then ordered to travel to Italy and asked his father to allow Lanier to accompany him; this too was agreed. At the early age of 21 therefore, Lanier was experiencing the world at an elevated social level, in a way that very few young people from his background could have enjoyed.

In 1613 Lanier was involved as singer and assistant composer in a Whitehall masque.[11] The older generation of Laniers had been committed to the performance of music for masques since the accession of James (even including grandfather Nicholas, who survived until 1612), and young Nicholas, when not on his travels, would have been studying the art form, and in the process acquiring an understanding of its visual as well as its musical aspects.

Early in 1616 Lanier was given a place in the King's Music, the seventh member of the family to hold such a position. A year later he provided much of the music for the Twelfth Night Whitehall masque, 'The Vision of Delight', and a month afterwards was employed by one of the king's favourite courtiers, Lord Hay, in connection with another masque entitled 'Lovers Made Men', for which it was noted that Lanier 'ordered and made both the Scene and the music'.[12] This was a unique talent, with which no other contributor to the masque genre could compete, and was to bring Lanier to the notice of George Villiers, later Duke of

---

[10] Wilson, p. 12.

[11] Wilson, p. 22. The piece was 'The Squire's Masque' by Thomas Campion. Campion was a composer in his own right, but on this occasion he appears only to have written the text.

[12] Wilson, p. 58.

Buckingham, and then to the Prince of Wales. It was to be the source of great wealth for Lanier.[13]

Although his name does not appear in the list of the Prince of Wales' musicians, it is suggested[14] that this was due to the fact that the king never agreed to release Lanier from his own service, not to any lack of appreciation on Charles' part. At his accession, at a moment when two large musical households (the late king's and his own) had to be consolidated, it appears that Charles had already appointed Lanier to be Master of the King's Music, the first royal musician ever to hold this position. It happened so quickly that one must assume that the king and Lanier had been planning the move for some time and it seems likely that the appointment resulted from private discussions between Charles and Lanier on the subject of merging the two households. One suspects too that Lanier may have highlighted inefficiencies and indiscipline within the extended ranks of King James's household musicians, and that he held himself out as the man to bring everything into good order. That he was not able to introduce reforms to the regime immediately was due to the fact that the king had another mission for him, but in 1630 the order went out from the Lord Chamberlain that all the players of wind instruments in the royal household were to be divided into two bands, to be on duty in alternate weeks, with a separate schedule for 'Sundays and holidays'. The order named the members of each band.[15] Lanier tried to extend his authority to the string section as well,[16] but in this he was less successful.

During the previous five years Lanier had been given by King Charles a most important and exceptional assignment. Tudor interest in the visual arts had never progressed much beyond portraiture, and James I had not much interest in it either. And yet the Renaissance Courts of Europe were now filled with the finest paintings and sculpture. Prince Henry had begun to amass a splendid collection of bronzes,[17] and as his father's life drew to a close, it became Charles' ambition to create an art collection that would be the match of any in Europe. The news reached him, possibly through Aletheia Howard, Countess of Arundel, who had been travelling in Italy, that the notable collection of Ferdinando Gonzaga, Duke of Mantua, might be for sale. Within three months after his accession the king took action, and it was Nicholas Lanier whom he selected to carry out the delicate negotiations, and to investigate what other paintings he might be able to acquire at the same time. It was as if Lanier was reverting, con-

[13] Wilson, p. 66.

[14] Wilson, p. 67.

[15] H.C. de Lafontaine, ed., *The King's Musick: A Transcript of Records Relating to Music and Musicians, 1460–1700* (London: Novello & Co. 1909), p. 72. De Lafontaine was a member of the Court of Assistants and Master in 1920–21.

[16] Ashbee, vol. III, p. 53.

[17] See the chapter on 'The Prince's Collections' in R. Strong, *Henry Prince of Wales and England's Lost Renaissance* (London: Thames & Hudson 1986), pp. 184–219.

6. Nicholas Lanier, first Master of the King's Music. An engraving from a lost portrait (probably dated 1633) by Jan Lievens.

sciously or unconsciously, to the ancient role of 'minstrel', in the sense of the king's confidential servant; his master would have certainly been impressed by Lanier's fluency in French and Italian as well as by his artistic abilities and knowledge.

Lanier left London at the beginning of June 1625.[18] After two visits to Italy he returned to London in July 1628, having successfully completed his task, and having acquired a substantial number of paintings from the Mantuan collection on the king's behalf.[19] Greater honour and public appreciation might have been accorded him if the Court had not been shaken by a terrible event within a few weeks of his return; this was the assassination on 23 August of the Duke of Buckingham, who was one of his patrons. Nevertheless his achievement was a remarkable one, and one may assume, despite the lack of evidence, that he was consulted about the purchase of the rest of the Mantua collection, and would have been involved in the entertainment of Rubens when he visited London in the following year.

While in Venice in 1627, it is likely that he met Monteverdi, who had been engaged to entertain the Count Palatine (King Charles' brother-in-law) at the English ambassador's residence on 17 July.[20] He would certainly have used every opportunity to inform himself about the latest developments in Venetian music at first hand at that time.

On his return to London therefore, he may have felt that he had the world at his feet. Master of the King's Music, a respected Composer in his own right, and proficient on a number of instruments as well as the lute; singer, administrator, painter and stage designer, connoisseur and art dealer, linguist, traveller and courtier, a tall wealthy man of robust constitution in the prime of his life at 40, Nicholas Lanier must have been looking for new fields for conquest. The last thing that so grand a person would have wished for or expected was to find himself, early the following year, cooling his heels in a City jail. But this is what happened on 6 February 1629, after an affray which ended with Lanier and other members of his family (three uncles and a brother) assaulting a constable. The constable, whose name is unknown (but one wishes it was Dogberry), had tried to intervene in a fight between the Laniers and a man called Allen who they alleged was following them around with the object of robbing them.

The imprisonment must have been short, because it was not his confinement that Lanier complained of but the fact that he had not been brought before a magistrate before being locked up. A ferocious letter relating to the incident was sent by the Privy Council to the Lord Mayor:

---

18 Wilson, p. 84.
19 There were inevitably many problems before the deal could be completed. These are described in detail in Chapter 5 of Mr Wilson's book.
20 Wilson, p. 123.

If you understood of the miscarriage of the said officers and passed it without reproof, you have wilfully failed both in discretion and duty, for that you cannot be ignorant that the proper and usual way of proceeding in a case of this nature against his Majesty's Servants had been not by committing them to Prisons, but by an address or Appeal to the Lord Chamberlain.[21]

If Lanier was expecting a grovelling response from the Lord Mayor he was to be disappointed. The Domestic State Papers report on 26 February that a letter to the Privy Council was received from Richard Deane, Lord Mayor, confirming that he had 'taken examinations respecting the business'. The summary of the affair was noted as follows:

> *Relation of the tumult raised at the exchange in London on the 6th instant by Nicholas Lanier and others, his Majesty's servants, collected out of several examinations.* Lanier and others quarrelled with one Allen and beat him with their fists. He appealed to a constable, whose interference was answered with words and blows, and Lanier and his companions went forth in a ruffling manner into Cornhill, flourishing their swords, whereupon the people began to throw stones. After considerable tumult Lanier and his companions were reduced to reason by restraint of their persons.[22]

Even the Privy Council would have had difficulty in insisting that the appropriate remedy in such a situation was to 'appeal to the Lord Chamberlain', and nothing more was heard of the matter. Lanier's pride was undoubtedly severely bruised, and the desire for revenge for his humiliation in the very centre of the City must have started to fester.

There is one curious sequel to this affair. Although we shall never discover much about Allen, the suspected assailant or thief, it would be surprising if someone with criminal intent would actually cry out to an officer of the law for protection from the Lanier party. It would seem much more likely that he was trying to collect a debt or had some other complaint against one of the Laniers. This may be confirmed by an entry in the Privy Council papers just two days after the letter to the Lord Mayor:

> 18 February. A warrant to the Keeper of the Marshallsea to enlarge and set at liberty the person of James Allen.[23]

Of course this Allen may have been some quite different person.

Nicholas Lanier's anger against the City was given yet more provocation the following year. At the time he was living in Deptford, and wished to move into London. Because of an outbreak of the plague in Greenwich, the City authorities were prohibiting anyone in Greenwich from coming to London. Deptford was the next parish upstream and the authorities decided that Lanier was within the

---

21 *Acts of the Privy Council of England 1628 July–1629 April* (London: 1958) p. 333.
22 *Calendar of State Papers (Domestic)*, p. 479.
23 *Acts of the Privy Council*, p. 334.

banned area. Once again he complained to the Privy Council, who wrote to the Lord Mayor requiring him to give the necessary permission to 'his Majesty's servant'. As Lanier's household at the time consisted of 'twelve to fourteen persons', all probably servants apart from Nicholas and his wife,[24] the City authorities had good cause to suspect some degree of contact with the plague, even though Deptford was not part of Greenwich. The Lanier family certainly owned property in East Greenwich, which is where Nicholas died in 1666.

Whatever the outcome of this 'spat', it cannot have increased his affection for the City and its institutions, but it was four years before Lanier's mailed fist was to strike at the Company. At some stage in the intervening period, he must have retained a clerk in the royal household to search for Edward IV's Charter, and then consulted an attorney (perhaps the Attorney-General himself) to see whether there was a conflict between that Charter, which had last been confirmed in 1520, and the Musicians' Company Charter. Lanier evidently received the advice he was looking for, and whoever did the research clearly overlooked (or turned a blind eye to) the 'saving' for the King's Musicians contained in the Bye-laws of 1606. The 1604 Charter failed to include this, as we have seen.[25]

Despite the fact that the writ of *scire facias* was issued in the name of fourteen members of the King's Music, it is my belief that the initiative in taking this action and the effective underwriting of the case remained entirely with Lanier. If one looks at the co-plaintiffs, four of them (not including Nicholas) are Laniers, there are two Ferraboscos, lifelong companions of the Lanier family, and all the other seven (with one exception) were in Lanier's own section, the 'lutes and voices'.[26] The only plaintiff who could be described as independent was Daniel Farrant, the most senior member of the viol consort, and like Lanier, one who was entitled to an enhanced 'livery' allowance as well as salary.

The writ was dated 28 November 1633. It alleged that the Charter of James I had been obtained without any mention of the Edward IV Charter and that no enquiries were made before the grant of the new charter as to the prejudice which might be caused. James I was therefore left in ignorance that the earlier charter was still in force and was deceived into granting a new one. Then it specifically alleged that under their invalid charter Thomas Chamberlain, Master, and John Baker and Samuel Pickering, Wardens, were now claiming authority over every minstrel in the City of London and within three miles thereof, including the musicians serving in the choirs of all the cathedral and collegiate churches within two miles of the City, which were the special care of the King's Minstrels under the earlier charter, they being accustomed to appoint musicians there to assemble together and 'to the sound of the organ exercise themselves in symphony'. The City musicians are further accused of preventing the King's Musicians from exercising their power under King Edward's Charter, and of

[24] Wilson, pp. 165–6.
[25] See p. 65.
[26] Woodfill, pp. 304–5.

admitting very many persons not sufficiently learned in the art or science of music and using various trades, occupations and misteries, and a number of others not exercising the art of music but wholly unlearned into their society.[27]

It was a well-formulated series of charges, some of which would be difficult to deny or refute. The error made in not reserving the rights of the King's Musicians in the Charter instead of the bye-laws removed any defence to the allegation that that the king had been 'left in ignorance'. The right to claim authority over London minstrels up to the three-mile limit stood or fell with the Charter itself. The reference to 'the musicians serving in the cathedral and collegiate choirs' is more puzzling, as there is no other known reference to any involvement of this sort by the Company. The most likely explanation is that Lanier, who would have been closely associated with William Laud, then Bishop of London and shortly to become Archbishop, because they were both protégés of the late Duke of Buckingham, was attempting to entangle the Company in the 'Arminian' struggle, one feature of which was the reintroduction of organs into cathedrals and collegiate churches. Where this happened the sackbuts, hautboys and other instruments which had been used to support the choral music since the first destruction of church organs in Edward VI's reign would become redundant, and this could have led to complaints from those church musicians, backed perhaps by the officers of the Company. It is difficult to think what other grounds there may be for this charge.

The case was initially adjourned until the Easter Term. A letter written by Lanier during the adjournment may have been written to increase the pressure on the Company, but this depends to some extent on whether or not John Adson was a member; but even if he was a member of the Fletchers or some other Company his letter was still an attack on City Musicians. The annual Twelfth Night masque had been abandoned since James I's death,[28] but in 1634 the Inns of Court were prevailed upon by the king, in his defiance of recent public criticism of the Court's extravagance, to present a lavish new masque, entitled 'The Triumph of Peace', at two separate performances. The first performance for the king took place at Whitehall on 3 February. The second performance broke new ground and was presented at the Merchant Taylors' Hall in the City on 13 February. Both performances were preceded by a procession from the Inns of Court to the place of performance. For the first procession, the promoter of the entertainment, the music-loving lawyer Bulstrode Whitelocke, had allowed John Adson, who had just been appointed to the flutes in the royal band, to select some of his colleagues to play in the procession. On the face of it there were no grounds for complaint. The masque was not produced by the royal household,

---

27 The papers are preserved in the Public Record Office, I believe under reference C206/1, but time constraints did not allow me to locate them.

28 See *Court Masques, Jacobean and Caroline Entertainments*, ed. David Lindley (Oxford: Clarendon Press 1995), p. xxviii.

nor was the procession part of the masque, and the music within the palace at Whitehall would be provided by the King's Music anyway.

Lanier saw this incident as an interference with his musicians' prerogative. Notwithstanding the fact that the procession to the second performance would pass almost entirely through the City, from the Inns of Court to the Merchant Taylors' Hall, he wrote to Whitelocke in the following terms:

> Worthy Sir,
>
> I am bold to let you know that I understand by some, that one Adson of the King's Musicians (who is an unworthy fellow) hath prevailed with you to exclude the King's servants, that by my Lord Chamberlain's appointment and by my choice of them, did you service at Court. I thought good to let you know that you are abused, as well myself, or them, whose ableness to serve you cannot be equalled by any men now living. Not further troubling you, I remain
>
> Your humble servant
Nich. Lanier

On this occasion Lanier did receive a humble apology, and a promise to reinstate his musicians, who had not been retained for the procession on the first occasion because Whitelocke thought that it would be demeaning.[29] If Lanier's complaint did have some connection with his dispute with the Company the fact that the Company made no apparent objection must have encouraged Lanier to pursue his action in the Chancery Court to the uttermost.

After four adjournments, so that the case was finally brought before the court early in 1635, the Company offered no defence of its Charter, and it was ordered to be forfeited. Flushed with success, Lanier immediately obtained a charter from the king for a new corporation, whose full title was 'The Marshall, Wardens, and Cominalty of the art and science of Music in Westminster in the County of Middlesex', with powers remarkably similar to those granted to the City Company in 1604 (the earlier Charter must have been used as a precedent) except that they now extended to the whole realm, the City of London not excepted. The only exclusion was the County of Chester, for arcane reasons briefly explained in Appendix 5.

The Charter was dated 15 July 1635. It was a Lanier 'ego-trip'. Nicholas himself was to be Marshal for life. The Wardens, appointed not 'for life' but only until next Midsummer Day, would be Thomas Ford and Jerome Lanier. The three other Laniers and the others named as plaintiffs in the writ made up the Court of Assistants. The Westminster Company almost immediately attempted to enforce its authority in the City, but for the first time in its history the musicians of the City who were not members of the Company came to its aid, and all the City musicians united in petitioning the Court of Aldermen to protect them from their royal enemies.[30]

---

[29] This incident is recorded by Wilson on p. 187 of his book, from the Whitelocke papers held at Longleat House.

[30] CL Rep 49, fol. 253.

At that point, so far as the Westminster Company is concerned, the fog descends. Sir John Hawkins, in his famous eighteenth century 'General History of Music', took this very much in his stride. After quoting at length the text of the 1635 Charter, he then calmly stated that the Company held its first meeting on 2 October 1661, twenty-six years later! On the basis of surviving records this appears to be an accurate statement, but what had happened to the Company during the six years before the outbreak of the Civil War? Did the new Company meet regularly, and keep records which were lost or destroyed during the war? No evidence currently exists, but could still come to light in the course of further research.

The entries relating to the King's Music taken from the Lord Chamberlain's records and first recorded by de Lafontaine[31] give ample proof that from 1635 until the very end of 1641, everything proceeded as normal at Whitehall, and the total head-count for 'his Majesty's musicians' in 1641 was shown as sixty-one, plus twenty-seven trumpeters and drummers, the largest number in Charles I's reign. After January 1642, as one would expect, there is nothing relevant in the records until 1660. But during the previous six years, when the household appears to have been functioning normally, one might have expected to see signs that Nicholas Lanier was continuing to persecute the City musicians and throw his weight about as far from Westminster as he could reach, just as he did after the Restoration. It did not happen, and an explanation is needed. Was Lanier content to sit back, carrying on his routine duties as Master of the King's Music? Had he temporarily lost interest in music, preferring to fraternise when the occasion arose with the great painters who were residing in London at this time?[32] Or had relations between Court and City deteriorated to such an extent that it was impracticable or unsafe for Lanier to threaten the City with the Lord Chamberlain's power and authority? It is interesting to note that, coincidentally with the attack on the Company's Charter which occurred during the period of the king's 'personal rule', when Parliament was prorogued and did not meet for ten years, City interests suffered a much bigger attack. Sir Thomas Wentworth, Earl of Strafford, commenced proceedings against the Irish Society and 'the Great Twelve' Companies in relation to the Londonderry Plantation. The allegations made were based on supposed breaches of the terms of the Charter, but it would have been clear to any impartial observer at the time that the claims were specious and that the sole object was to extort money to reduce the king's debts. The case went to the Court of Star Chamber, where the likelihood of a fair hearing at that time was remote, and the Irish Society was condemned to a massive fine of £70,000, and its Charter confiscated. The Great Twelve were also fined and lost their land grants in 1638.

Shortly afterwards the king demanded 'Ship Money' to rebuild the decayed

---

31 See de Lafontaine (1st edn), pp. 92–112.
32 The most distinguished was Sir Anthony Vandyke who had painted Lanier's portrait some years before (Wilson, pp. 94, 174).

fleet, and then tried to levy huge war loans in the City. When these were refused, the king trebled his demands and threatened to confiscate the City's Charter. The City was still defiant and only the promise of an end to the Scottish war and the calling of a Parliament (which became the 'Long' Parliament) persuaded the Common Council in 1640 to raise one more loan of £50,000.[33]

In the absence of Parliament, prior to November 1640, resistance to the royal authority in the City was sullen and subdued, but beneath the surface it was seething. Nicholas Lanier would have been acutely aware of the increasing difficulties which he would face in attempting to make his writ under the new Westminster charter run within the City and its liberties. He may have decided to bide his time and wait for the crisis to pass. In the event he had to wait a long time, because the Civil War and the Protectorate intervened before another opportunity arose.

The complete list of the musicians of the royal household compiled in 1641 and referred to above has an almost spectral feel about it. There had been regular 'accounts for liveries' for all or most of the musicians before this date, but this was a list made without an explanation; it was simply a list *per se*. It was as though the clerk was conveying the message 'The Royal Household is closing down. These are the artists who will now be dispersing. If the Household is ever reconstituted those surviving should be re-engaged.'

Nicholas Lanier spent an uncomfortable year or so with the king in Oxford, but is known to have left the country at about the beginning of 1645. During the Interregnum he spent most of his time in Antwerp or Paris, but was allowed to make visits to England during the Protectorate.[34] It is not known whether he returned to England before Charles II's arrival in London on 29 May 1660; if not he would have been in the royal party. On that day London was *en fête* to greet the king, but among the City musicians there would have been heard a concerted and anxious murmur: 'Lanier's back.'

---

[33] Johnson, vol. III, pp. 134–48.
[34] See Wilson, chapter 8.

6

A Lost Opportunity

TRUTH was the principal casualty of the Company's surrender in 1635. Its failure to defend its right to the James I Charter encouraged Sir John Hawkins to believe that the Company had had no previous existence, and this was duly noted in his 'General History of Music':

> There can be no doubt that [the Westminster Company] is extinct, and there is good ground to suppose that the London company of musicians are in a condition but little better; their charter appearing to have been obtained by untrue suggestions, and to have been vacated by a judgement of the court of chancery. The law it is true recognizes as corporations those fraternities that subsist by prescription, but it requires as a condition to this title that their exercise of corporate functions shall have been from time immemorial; but as to that of London, its origin may be traced to the time of Ja. I which in a legal sense is within time of memory.[1]

The effects of this misinformation, when first published in 1776, will be revealed in due course.[2] Here it is sufficient to observe that the falsehood was not finally exorcised until the 20th century, as the closing paragraphs of this chapter relate.

What actually happened in 1634–35, so far as the Company's inner counsels were concerned, is a matter for speculation, but it can perhaps be assumed, from the fact that the action was adjourned no less than four times at the Company's request, that the Master and his Wardens and Assistants were divided in their opinion as to how to react. On the one hand it would not have been difficult to demonstrate that no prejudice had been intended or given to the king's musicians by the 1604 Charter, and all the prior City Ordinances relating to the establishment and governance of the Company could have been recited and produced in court. On the other hand the members of the Court would have been well aware that the case had been brought and was being maintained by one of the wealthiest commoners in the kingdom, who enjoyed the king's full confidence.

---

[1] J. Hawkins, *A History of the Science and Practice of Music* (London: Novello & Co. 1875 edn), vol. II, p. 698n.
[2] See pp. 157–8.

The helplessness of the Irish Society and the Great Twelve in the concurrent case concerning the Irish Estates was proof enough that a fair hearing in the Court of Chancery, operating under the shadow of the Court of Star Chamber, would be a forlorn hope. To attempt to defend would therefore be 'money down the drain'. As a separate argument in favour of a surrender members of the Court may have been reminded that the Company in the thirty years of the charter's existence had never actually made use of its powers. Unless there was anything of sub-stance in the charge relating to church musicians, there is nothing to indicate that the Company had ever exercised its supervision within the three-mile band around London. If the Company now withdrew into the City itself, there must have been a reasonable expectation that it could continue to operate under the protection of the City authorities as it had done since 1500, regardless of the charter.

We cannot be sure that the Company knew of Nicholas Lanier's plan to set up a rival company in Westminster, but it certainly recognised the urgent need, having lost its charter, to re-establish its old credentials in the City. In July 1635, the same month in which the Westminster Company received its charter from the king, the City musicians, describing themselves as 'the *late* Master Wardens and Assistants of the Company of Musicians London' petitioned the Court of Aldermen for permission to be made a brotherhood by the name of 'The Master Wardens and Society of the Company of Musicians London'. A Committee was established[3] and, as we have noted,[4] the Aldermen were presented with another petition in the following year by all the City musicians, not just the former members of the Company, which lent support to their request to be allowed to set themselves up once more as an unchartered City Company.

The original Committee either failed to report or gave outline approval which was not minuted. In April 1638 another Committee was instructed to examine the petition, this time with the new draft Ordinances attached. On 24 July the Committee reported in favour, and the Court of Aldermen authorised the re-establishment of the Company in this form. The threat from the Westminster Company was totally ignored, but any reference to supervision over musicians who were free of another company was also omitted. So far as the structure and internal regulation of the Company was concerned, little was changed, although the number of Assistants was increased to seventeen from the minimum in 1604 of thirteen , and for the first time there is a reference to 'journeymen', who would normally be in the service of certain of the freemen or the livery. Journeymen were required to pay quarterage at the rate of one shilling per annum, half the rate applicable to freemen. The Ordinances are set out in Appendix 6.

The Master of the Company under the Ordinances was to be Robert Gill, and the Wardens Samuel Pickering and John Starling. They were to hold office 'until

---

3   CL Rep 49, fol. 253.
4   See p. 87.

Michaelmas day next *and so until others shall be duly admitted and sworn in their several places'* (italics added).

This term-of-office formula seems simple enough, but from the few shreds of evidence that are available to us, and probably as a direct consequence of the events of the 1640s, they may have been given an unintended interpretation which brings into question the whole state of the Company at this momentous time. We shall be shortly looking at a document which suggests that Gill was still Master in 1649, and Pickering hovering around the office-bearers. Whether this means that the burden of office was circulating between a small number of Court members, as was to happen in the 19th century, or that Robert Gill remained in office throughout the war is unclear, but there can be little doubt that the Company was in a weakened state. One would have thought that the parliamentary victory over the royal power, which of course meant that the royal household was dissolved, would have enabled the City musicians to claw back the right to control music in suburban London which it had lost in 1635. No better opportunity could have existed for the Company to achieve a pre-eminent position and to replace the now suspended, dormant Westminster company. At the end of the last chapter we were looking for reasons for the failure of the Westminster company to press home its advantage while Charles I was still the effective monarch. Now it is the Company's turn to be scrutinised, when the advantage was with them and they too failed to make any progress.

The failure to make any progress was due to the almost complete suspension of festivities and ceremonies during the Civil War, a misfortune which the Company shared with all other luxury trades during the 1640s. This was not a deliberate 'puritan' policy. It is true that the theatres were closed by Parliament in 1642, and this may have been for dogmatic reasons, but public theatres had been banned from the City since the 16th century, so their closure would have affected the livelihood of City musicians only peripherally. The decision to clamp down on festivities, and the pomp and show associated with them, was taken by individual city companies because of the desperate financial position in which they found themselves, having paid out so much in taxes and loans to the king before the war began, and now carrying the burden of maintaining the Parliamentary forces. From autumn 1642 until the close of the first Civil War in the spring of 1646, the records of the Drapers' Company refer to little else but 'loans and taxes, the provision of arms and corn, and the dispensing with dinners'.[5] In June 1643 a Court minute of the Grocers' Company recorded that:

> This Court, entering into a sad and serious consideration of the miserable distractions and calamities of this kingdom, threatening the ruin thereof by sickness and famine, the certain attendants of an unnatural and bloody war which now reigneth in this kingdom, agree and order that the election feast shall be omitted.[6]

5 Johnson, III, p. 159.
6 Heath, p. 113.

Two months later, to meet the insatiable demands for war loans, the Grocers felt obliged to sell all the company's plate ('save the value of £300 for necessary use and service').[7]

This was no climate for music-making, in a distressed and impoverished society. A limited amount of private teaching would no doubt have continued, but even this would have been the subject of intense competition between the members of the Company, the displaced church musicians who had lost their appointments by decree of Parliament, and former members of the King's Music.

It is probable that many members of the Company enrolled in the army. In just the same way as in the Thirty Years War, now reaching its final stages in continental Europe, whole populations of villages which were pillaged and destroyed attached themselves to their destroyers as camp followers, because it was the only way to stay alive, so the London musicians would have seen the army as the sole source of subsistence, whether they served as trumpeters and drummers or as ordinary infantry soldiers. We know of some members of the King's Music and Chapel who enrolled, not always on the royalist side. The most celebrated was William Lawes, brother of Henry, and a composer of great promise, who was shot dead at the siege of Chester in 1645. William Howes of St George's Chapel, Windsor, joined the Roundheads. Henry Cooke was commissioned in the Royalist army. He subsequently became Master of the children of the Chapel Royal and succeeded Nicholas Lanier as Marshal of the Westminster Company, always being known as 'Captain Cooke'. Dr Christopher Gibbons, Orlando's second son, also served in the Royalist army.[8]

The London Company may therefore have been as dormant during the war as the Westminster Company. The City Waits suffered a similar fate although their office was not suspended. But they formally complained in 1644 that they had received no remuneration for two years,[9] and were perhaps fortunate in getting back to normal rather sooner than their colleagues, who appear to have been in a state of 'suspended animation' to the very end of the decade, and perhaps beyond.

Some idea of the state of the Company at the end of the Civil War can be found in a manuscript (Rawlinson D24) in the Bodleian Library.[10] It is (to use a legal term) an inchoate document, whose purpose is not self-explanatory. It consists of about forty folio pages, all but two of which contain the signatures of officers and liverymen of twenty-nine City companies, including the Great Twelve, and including the Musicians. There is no obvious common factor linking the lesser companies represented in the folio. Each page is headed with the name

---

[7] Heath, p. 114.

[8] Percy Scholes, *The Puritans and Music in England and New England* (Oxford: Oxford University Press 1934), pp. 287–8.

[9] See Alan Warwick, *A Noise of Music* (London: Queen Anne Press 1968), p. 51.

[10] This was noted in the Bibliography of Woodfill's book, but not otherwise referred to by him.

of the company, except in a few cases where the signatures run on to a second page. The first page contains the signatures of the Mercers, and there is no front-sheet explaining what the signatories were subscribing to, nor any date anywhere on the document. Fortunately it is possible to date the document with a fair degree of accuracy. The Haberdashers' page is headed 'Hillarie Mempris, Master', and the company's own records show that he was Master in 1649. The Fishmongers' page includes the signature of Thomas Andrews, 'Maior'. Andrews took over the mayoralty in April 1649 after Sir Abraham Reynoldson, a Merchant Taylor, had been sent to the Tower by order of Parliament because of his royalist sympathies. The date of the document should therefore be in the latter half of 1649.

An edited transcript of a similar document dating from 1651 can be found in the Guildhall Library. Under the title 'London Citizens of 1651' the editor, J.C. Whitebrook, has transcribed a Harleian manuscript[11] which closely resembles the Rawlinson one, although the Companies listed there do not include the Musicians. In his brief introduction, Whitebrook wrote:

> The fashion of applying the principle of the round robin to the government of religion reached its utmost popularity in 1649, when the 'Agreement of the People of England' and the 'Essex Watchmen's Watchword' respectively asserted, as of the common right, and denounced as Antichristian and anarch, the principle of religious toleration.

It was not only 'the government of religion' that became the subject of numerous petitions and counter-petitions at this time. The petition, as a means to obtain something from a governing body, is as old as government itself, but after the collapse of the monarchy in the mid 1640s it underwent a significant change. Petitions subscribed by a substantial number of persons in good standing were charged with an almost imperative force, like a primitive form of referendum.[12]

The last two pages of the Rawlinson manuscript are 18th century additions. One of them is a copy of the 1650 Livery list of the Leathersellers Company made in 1782, which indicates that all the signatories in the manuscript were liverymen. The other is a letter from an unidentified antiquarian whose opinion the owner of the manuscript had evidently sought as to the date and nature of the document. The writer gave the date as either 1649 or 1651 and suggested that it had something to do with the huge amounts of subsidy (£9,000 per month) which Parliament was demanding from the City to keep its army in the field. This does not seem very likely. Why would this require autograph signatures, and

---

[11] Harleian MS 4778. Whitebrook's book was published in London by Hutching & Power, but no publication date is given.

[12] For a more detailed analysis of London petitions at this time see Keith Lindley, 'London's Citizenry in the English Revolution' in *Town and Countryside in the English Revolution*, ed. R.C. Richardson (Manchester 1972), pp. 20–32.

if it was a straightforward protest against the exactions, would there not have been a much bigger response?

So what were the Musicians signing up to, and who were they? Unfortunately we do not yet know the answer to the first question, except that it seems to have been a petition of some sort, probably nothing to do with religious toleration. But it is the state of the Company at that date which is our primary interest, and the manuscript provides some useful information on this.

On the Musicians' page (which currently enjoys the distinction of being the earliest known autograph document of the Company still in existence) there are thirteen names, about the smallest number in the manuscript. In order of signing they appear as follows:

> Robert Gill
> Stephen Strong
> John Williams
> Samuel Pickering
> Thomas Fawron (?)
> William Saunders
> Christopher Fox   (Mark)
> John Evans
> Richard Layton
> John Beardwell
> Richard Nicholls
> Thomas Challenor   (Mark)
> Roger Rogers   (Mark)

The signatories may have been Liverymen, or members of the Court of Assistants who happened to be present at a particular meeting. Three members have signed by making their mark, which puts the Company on a par with the Bakers, Blacksmiths, Fruiterers, Joiners, Plasterers, Weavers and Woodmongers, all of whom have a few illiterate subscribers. The group of names at the top of the list is interesting. In the 1638 Ordinances it was provided that Robert Gill would be Master, and Samuel Pickering, who had already been named as one of the Wardens in the 1633 Writ, was to be Warden once again. The Musicians' page in the 1649 manuscript does not give the office of the signatories, but Robert Gill is still at the top of the list and Samuel Pickering's name is among the first four. A reference to Robert Gill is first found in Henry Walker's will,[13] where he is named as one of Walker's apprentices and given £5 and a mourning cloak. Pickering's name comes fourth, which could mean that he was now the senior member of the Court, but not at the time holding any office. Stephen Strong, who may have been Senior Warden, as he signed second, reappears in a Commonwealth manuscript of 1656 entitled 'Appearances of Persons coming from foreign parts'.[14] The

---

[13] See p. 74. I am grateful to Dr Ashbee for drawing this to my attention.
[14] British Library, Add. MS 34015, fol. 73, quoted in Ashbee, vol. III, p. 128.

entry relates to Robert Strong, of the parish of 'James, Clerkenwell' (saints were of course not recognised as such at the time), who was lodging at the house of Stephen Strong, his brother, of the same parish. Robert had been a wind instrument player in the King's Music who was reappointed at the Restoration, together with another brother, John.[15] John Beardwell became the 'great survivor' of this group. He was a City Wait from 1662 to 1688 and his name appears on a list of liverymen of the Musicians Company who are recorded as voting in a shrieval election in the 1680s. According to a subsequent case in the Court of Chancery[16] he died 'seized in fee of and in a considerable real estate'. The last name on the list, Roger Rogers, is also of interest, as it is possible that Roger was closely related to John Rogers of Aldersgate, who was one of Cromwell's musicians, a lutenist who joined the King's Music in 1660.

As there are thirteen names on the list, and under the 1604 Charter this was the minimum number of Assistants required for the Court, it might be thought that the signatures were taken at a full Court meeting. But it is not safe to make this assumption, because the 1638 Ordinances had increased the minimum to seventeen, although there is nothing to show that the increase had been put into effect. If however one looks at lists of the Livery relating to the next sixty years or so, which have been preserved in a haphazard way, as we shall see, the 1649 list of thirteen names corresponds numerically with some of the later ones, and we are left with the impression that during this last period of the Company's existence as an active craft guild, the members of the Court made up at least half the total Livery and sometimes more. Not many City musicians, it seems, were prepared to get involved with the supervisory activities of the Company, or with the expense of joining the Livery, and this must have left the Company debilitated and unadventurous.

It is often suggested that after peace had been restored under Oliver Cromwell, puritanical sentiment effectively put a clamp on all musical activity, and much misunderstanding still exists about the effect of a puritan government on the musical profession, despite Percy Scholes' lively rehabilitation exercise in his book 'The Puritans and Music'. When one recalls how the discouraging attitude of Queen Elizabeth (who loved music) and her ministers and clergy towards the old pre-Reformation liturgy resulted in a sudden outpouring of secular music, and one recognises that the puritan attitude in the Interregnum was not very different, one might assume that the opportunities awaiting secular musicians were much as they had been fifty or sixty years before. The love of music and dance was as evident in the 1650s as it was in 1600 and would be after the Restoration. The 'taboos' of the puritans were limited to the public performance of plays, 'profane' activities on the Sabbath day, and the use of instruments, especially the organ, in divine service. There should therefore have been plenty of work for the

---

[15] See p. 104.
[16] *Chancery Proceedings 1714–58*, Bundle 1309.

City musicians during the Protectorate, and there probably was. What was lacking was a sense of initiative, and perhaps certain skills or 'Science', which may have been partly lost as a result of the war. Although Cromwell made a point of selecting musicians for his Court who had not been associated with the King's Music, some of the former musicians of the royal household enjoyed great prominence as teachers and performers during the Protectorate, and were well placed to keep their seats warm in hopeful anticipation of the young king's return.

There was no new 'golden age' of English secular music composition when the Civil War ended. What we find instead is a sudden upsurge in the publication of popular music. One cannot quite describe it as 'pop music', but it was music (and dances) and 'tutors' for all the educated and literate. Within the limits of 17th century England 'music for the masses' had arrived. Things were moving fast, because the first book to be published, in 1651 when Cromwell and Charles II still had armies in the field, was John Playford's *The English Dancing Master: or plain and easy rules for the dancing of Country Dances, with the tune to each dance.* It contained 104 dances, and was so popular that it was reprinted the following year, and many times thereafter throughout the rest of the century. No sooner was this book off the press than it was followed by another, *A Musical Banquet,* the final page of which may explain why both books were published when they were. Scholes and others have laid great stress on the fact that these books demonstrate the great love of music and the lack of restriction on the practice and performance of secular music at the time, contrary to the myth of the dour killjoy puritan ethic perpetrated by Hawkins and Burney. What perhaps seems equally likely is that Playford was pressured into creating a public demand for musical self-entertainment by the more active and adventurous survivors from the royal household. This would explain why the final page of *A Musical Banquet* is little more than an advertisement for the best music-teachers.[17] Eighteen names are given under the heading 'voice or viol' and nine for 'organ or virginal'. In the first list eleven had come from the King's Music, and two in the second, which also includes Richard Portman, former organist of Westminster Abbey, and Randall Jewet, from Chester Cathedral.

In introducing the lists Playford wrote:

> I shall wish you good success in the practick part, which will soon be obtained by the help of an able Master, this City being at present furnished with many excellent and able Masters in this Art or Science . . .

The list of teachers contains the names of six musicians who do not appear to have any connection with the former royal establishments, sacred or secular. These are John Birtenshaw, Thomas Mayland (a violist and later to be a drinking companion of Samuel Pepys),[18] Jeremy Savile, John Cobb, 'Mr' Farmelow and

---

[17] See Scholes, p. 166.
[18] Robert Latham, *The Shorter Pepys* (London: Bell & Hyman 1985), p. 8.

Benjamin Sandley. It is possible that some of them may have had connections with the Company, but one suspects that the members of the Company who were giving music lessons at this time were mostly buried within the sweep-up expression 'cum multis aliis' with which Playford ended his book.

Playford actively continued his music publishing throughout the Protectorate. After the *Dancing Master* and the *Banquet* the best known book was John Hilton's *Catch that Catch Can, or a Choice Collection of Catches, Rounds & Canons* published in 1652. This was the amateur singer's delight, and sufficiently bawdy to cause offence to the stricter puritans, but its success caused it to be republished in 1658, the year after John Hilton's death when he, according to the contemporary diarist Anthony Wood:

> was buried in the Great Cloisters at Westminster, at which time the singing at burials being silenced, as popish, the Fraternity of Musicians who intended to sing him to his grave, sang the anthem in the house over the corpse before it went to the church, and kept time on his coffin.[19]

Hilton was Parish Clerk of St Margaret's Westminster, so 'the Fraternity of Musicians' were probably the Parish Clerks who furtively provided the music for his funeral. Or it could have been the Westminster Company, surreptitiously ticking over, despite the exile of its Marshal-for-life.

Another feature of the Interregnum, with which the Company ought perhaps to have been concerned, but clearly was not, was the attempt to reform musical education in London. The initiative for this appears to have come from John Hingston, who although he had no official title was effectively Master of the Lord Protector's Music. Hingston had not been one of Charles I's household, but he was engaged as tutor to Oliver Cromwell's daughter almost as soon as he arrived in London in 1650, having begun his musical career in the Yorkshire household of the Earl of Clifford. His name is included in Playford's list of teachers in the 'Musical Banquet'. After the Restoration he was given a place in the King's Music, and soon took on the appointment of repairer of the organs in the royal palaces and chapels, which he held until 1684 when he was succeeded by Henry Purcell.

In 1657, John Hingston was involved, and may have been the prime mover, in an attempt to set up a new corporation in London to control the music profession, to provide educational facilities to replace the defunct choir schools, and to regulate the manufacture of musical instruments. A petition was drawn up to this effect, and probably by pre-arrangement between Hingston and the Protector, a Government Committee was conveniently appointed to receive the petition, which read as follows:

> To the Right Honourable the Committee of the Council for Advancement of Music.
> The humble petition of John Hingston, Davis Mell, William Howes, Richard

---

[19] Scholes, p. 135.

Hudson and William Gregory, Gentlemen, on behalf of themselves and others the Professors of Music.   Sheweth

That by reason of the late dissolution of the Quires in the Cathedrals where the study and practice of the Science of Music was especially cherished, many of the skilful Professors of the said Science have during the late wars and troubles died in want, and there being now no preferment or encouragement in the way of music, no man will breed his child in it, so that it must needs be that the Science itself must die in this nation, with those few Professors of it now living, or at least it will degenerate much from that perfection lately attained unto. Except some present maintenance and encouragement be given for educating of some youth in the study and practice of the said Science.

Wherefore your petitioners most humbly pray, that there be a Corporation or College of Musicians erected in London, with reasonable powers to read and practise publicly all sorts of Music, and to suppress the singing of obscene scandalous and defamatory Songs and Ballads, and to reform the abuses in making all sorts of Instruments of Music, with other reasonable powers of purchasing lands and having a Common Seal and the like, as were heretofore granted to the professors of the said Science. And also that whatever lands, rents, moneys, or other effects or revenues shall be found to have been heretofore given or employed for maintenance of professors of Music in any way, may be restored settled and employed for future maintenance and encouragement of the said Science.[20]

Nothing came of the petition, or of the Council for the Advancement of Music. No money could be spared, the cathedral endowments having already been allocated elsewhere. But it is worth spending a moment on the petition and the motivation that lay behind it, and to decide whether to take a cynical or a visionary view of its presentation.

The sceptics would say that the petitioners, none of whom belonged to Nicholas Lanier's inner group (which had become the Court of Assistants of the Westminster Company), were actually trying to do what the City musicians should have done if they had been more active. At an opportune time they were aiming to set up a new monopoly to replace both the Westminster and the City Companies. The state of the musical profession was nothing like as bad as the petitioners had painted it. What about the first real performance of an Opera in England the previous year, William Davenant's *The Siege of Rhodes*? And the continued popularity of John Playford's publications? As regards education, the two Universities were continuing to award degrees in music by examination (although these had nothing to do with performance, only with theory), and in the previous year at Oxford Dr John Wilson, said by Anthony Wood to have been 'much admired by all that understood that faculty', had been appointed Heather Professor of Music by Cromwell.[21] Was the continued existence of the Science really in danger?

20 PRO State Papers 18, vol. 153 (No. 123, fol. 354) quoted in Scholes, pp. 284–5.
21 Scholes, pp. 138–9.

The visionaries would invite the reader to put himself or herself in the position of the most eminent 'professors' early in 1657. Oliver Cromwell was at the peak of his 'reign', in reasonably good health. At the age of 58 he had the power of a dictator, and it could fairly be assumed that some years would elapse before the problem of the succession would need to be considered, and that Cromwell would devote himself to finding a solution which would be best for the Commonwealth and its perpetuation. The fact that he died the following year of a 'tertian ague' (which was a sudden sickness and may have been malaria) could not have been foreseen. In this situation, the visionaries would argue, it was natural that the professors would be keen to introduce a radical change by setting up a 'college' in London which would have an educational role, as well as supervising professional standards. They may have observed and assessed the apprenticeship system as practised in the City and found it wanting as applied to the teaching of music, putting more faith in the quality of musicianship achieved by those who had been taught in the cathedral schools. They would probably have been aware of the schools in Naples and Venice where children received an intensive musical education. Nothing as good as those schools, or the former English cathedral schools, now existed in England. Under these circumstances it was natural for Hingston, who would have enjoyed Cromwell's support, to take the first steps towards the realisation of a grand and original project.

The votes in this imaginary debate would no doubt be close, but looking ahead to the next hundred years, the visionaries perhaps deserve the greater support. While it is true that the reign of Charles II saw a revival of music on a grand scale and some innovation, it lacked the stamina and the educational base which could have ensured the survival of a musical tradition equal to that of France, Italy and the German states in the 18th century. If John Hingston and his colleagues had been able to achieve what they appear to have been planning (and there would have been many difficulties, not just financial, which they would have had to contend with) the foundations for a strong and lasting 'exportable' English musical culture might have then been laid.

After Oliver Cromwell died and the Protectorate effectively collapsed. 1659 was one of the most anarchic years in English history. By the end of the year the City of London had turned royalist,[22] General Monck had re-established the Long Parliament (or those of its members who had survived from 1648) and a pro-monarchist Council of State had been appointed. From then on it was only a matter of time and skilful negotiation before the monarchy was restored. Charles II landed at Dover on 25 May 1660, and Nicholas Lanier was reappointed Master of the King's Music on 28 August. The Interregnum was over, and one fears that the Company had progressed not one whit.

It would be a pity to bid farewell to Percy Scholes and his special subject, puritans and music, without transcribing in his memory a much more recent occur-

---

[22] G.E. Aylmer, *Rebellion or Revolution* (Oxford 1986), p. 196.

rence which he describes in his book. The date would have been about 1932/3 when Scholes was researching for his book, and had discovered the forfeiture of the Company's charter (which he mistakenly dated 1606). 'Yet' he says, 'it is the charter upon which the present Musicians' Company is operating, printed in its handbook as the basis of its existence! See the Company's Handbook, last published in 1915; the cancellation of the 1606 charter is absolutely ignored. . . . All this is extremely perplexing!'

With his usual pawky sense of humour, and unable to resist twisting a few tails, Scholes continues:

> I have naturally referred my difficulties to the Company itself, but with little satisfaction. The Clerk to the Company writes to me:
> 'My Court carefully considered the whole matter and I was finally instructed to write to you that the Company were quite satisfied as to the validity of their Charter, about which there has been no question raised for at least two hundred years. They must leave you to make such use of the passage in Hawkins' History to which you refer as you think fit at your own risk.'
> What risk there can be in quoting a King on a Company I do not know, but whatever it is I cheerfully take it.[23]

Alastair Crewdson would at that time have been Clerk to the Company for about two years. His letter typically bears the imprint both of his legal training and the breadth of his interests. He was clearly under instructions from the Court to defend the 1604 Charter, but he is careful not to associate himself with their collective opinion. I have no doubt that this little contretemps helped to stimulate, and indeed may have been the catalyst for, his own researches into the Company's origins.

[23] Scholes, p. 286.

7

The Shift to the West

THE king was on the throne, and the cork was out of the bottle. All the Bible-based inhibitions and repressions which underpinned the Rebellion and the Interregnum seemed to evaporate, or became a burden which only the Quakers and Dissenters, who suffered dearly for their nonconformity, would continue to bear.

The City of London, which had been the seat of puritanism, had been shocked and frightened out of its defiance of the royal power. Better that sovereignty should be exercised within some form of a constitution established by long custom than by the wild extremists in the puritan movement, or by the army. It was one thing to pay for a republican army; quite another to be ruled by it.

John Evelyn describes Charles II's triumphal entry into London on 29 May 1660:

> This day came in his Majesty Charles the 2nd to London. . . . This was also his Birthday, and with a triumph of above 20000 horse and foot, brandishing their swords and shouting with inexpressible joy: the ways strawed with flowers, the bells ringing, the streets hung with tapissery, fountains running with wine; The Mayor, Aldermen and all the Companies in their liveries, Chains of Gold, banners; Lords and nobles, Cloth of Silver, gold and velvet everybody clad in, the windows and balconies all set with Ladies, Trumpets, Music and myriads of people flocking the streets, and was as far as Rochester, so as they were 7 hours in passing the City, even from 2 in the afternoon till 9 at night.[1]

Behind the scenes the officers of the Great Twelve were grumbling at the amount of money which they were having to find for the celebrations.[2] Following the king's arrival the Lord Mayor and Aldermen entertained the king and his two brothers to a feast at Guildhall on 5 July 1660. It was the most lavish event for

---

[1] *The Diary of John Evelyn*, ed. Guy de la Bédoyère (Woodbridge: The Boydell Press 1995), p. 113.

[2] See the references in the Drapers and Grocers Histories (Johnson, vol. III, pp. 261–2, and Heath, p. 120).

7. The Restoration Procession from Whitehall to the Guildhall on 29th May 1660. Note the trumpets and drums beyond the coaches. An anonymous engraving in the Guildhall Library.

twenty years at least, with a grand procession to Whitehall to fetch the king in state to the City, accompanied by the Privy Councillors, the Lords and Commons. The City's own procession consisted of more than 800 persons, and there would have been half as many again when the procession returned with the king. According to a contemporary account there were 108 trumpeters deployed through the City's procession with several kettle drums. Preceding the Lord Mayor's escort, in the City Marshal's contingent, there were 'eight waits in scarlet jackets' and badges on their sleeves, wearing cloaks with silver lace. These were not the City Waits, who are separately described in attendance on the Lord Mayor and Aldermen, so they would probably have been provided by the Company. At dinner in Guildhall, the service of the meal began (in three separate chambers) at the sound of the 'loud music', and 'during Dinner time' the king 'hath several musical complisances both instrumental and vocal'.[3]

Then in the following year there were two days of celebration to mark the Coronation; on 22 April the king processed from Whitehall to the Tower, and on the 23rd the Coronation procession passed the other way *en route* for Westminster Abbey. The music provided is said to have consisted of 'three lots of waits, groups of singers, a band of wind instruments at the Stocks'; also '8 nymphs and 8 musicians' at Cheap Conduit.[4] This seems to have been a rather poor turnout compared with the mass of music provided for Edward VI at his accession,[5] but once again austerity and lack of resources may have been the cause.

No such financial constraints deterred Nicholas Lanier from recreating the music for the royal household with as much energy as he had shown at the accession of the king's father thirty-five years previously. The Lord Chamberlain's records for the period from mid-1660 to the end of 1661 are packed with appointments, substitutions, grants of livery, rates of pay and lists of the various groups of musicians.[6] A comparison with the 1641 list shows a fair number of survivals; of the wind instruments there were six out of eighteen, plus two brothers, Robert and John Strong, who were given places also in the violins. Only three of the original twelve violins appear on the list, although there were many new appointments to satisfy the king's ambition to have a string band equal in strength to that of his cousin Louis XIV. The 'lutes viols and voices' section (which included one or two harpers) had seven survivors out of twenty-three, not counting Lanier himself. This gives a total of nineteen out of fifty-three, or just over a third.

Some of the younger and newly appointed musicians must have found it a

---

3 The detail is taken from *London's Glory Represented by Time Truth and Fame: at the Magnificent Triumphs and Entertainment of his most Sacred Majesty Charles the II &c*, a contemporary account of the procession and feast by J. Tatham, printed by William Godbid in 1660.

4 Warwick, p. 27.

5 See p. 46.

6 See de Lafontaine, pp. 113–37.

little difficult to take seriously this extraordinary old man of seventy-three who was so busily reorganising them, because the Lord Chamberlain felt obliged to issue a 'certificate' to all his Majesty's musicians in March 1661 that:

> Nicholas Lanier is sworn master of his Majesty's music, and hath power to order and convocate the same at fit time of practice and service as is expressed in his privy seal given him by his late Majesty when he was Prince of Wales, and that if any of them refuse to wait at such convenient times of practice and service as he shall appoint, and for such instruments, voices and music, as he in reason shall think them fitted to serve in, upon his just complaint, I shall punish them either in their person or their wages as I shall think the offence deserves.[7]

The wording of the certificate appears to confirm the view that Charles I appointed Nicholas Lanier Master of the King's Music in advance of his accession, to take immediate effect on his accession day.

Not content with all that had to be done to get the King's Music back to its former quality and strength, Lanier was also active in reviving the Westminster Company which, as noted by Hawkins, held its first meeting after the Restoration on 22 October 1661. The Company had leased a meeting-room in Durham Yard off the Strand, and seems to have had all its meetings there at least until 1670. The Minute Book, covering the period from 1661 to 1679, when the Company became inactive, survives in the British Library.[8] It shows that the frequency of meetings was wildly inconsistent. As one would expect with Lanier fanning the flames, the regularity of meetings was most apparent in the early years; twelve were held in 1662, seven in 1663 and ten in 1664. There were then no meetings minuted until 1668. 'Captain' Henry Cooke had been appointed Deputy Marshal in 1663, and was signing minutes as chairman of meetings during that year, although Lanier returns for the November meeting and was certainly most active in 1664. He obtained confirmation of the Company's charter (in the name of the 'Corporation of the Art and Science of Music') on 18 March 1664.

At the end of that year, although hitherto amazingly robust, the Marshal at the age of seventy-six may have found his health threatened. A letter from him to his niece survives and is quoted by Michael Wilson in his biography.[9] It is dated, maddeningly, 'St Valentine's Day', without a year, and could therefore have been written at any time from 1662 to 1665. Lanier begins the letter: 'Ever since your kind entertainment I have been in torment with my infirmity, and am yet stark lame.' It may date from 1663, which could explain why Cooke was then deputising for him. Or the date may be 1665, which might account for the lack of minutes from 1664 until 1668. In any event Lanier appears to have retired to his property in East Greenwich in 1665, where, although safe from the notorious

7 De Lafontaine, p. 130.
8 Harleian MS 1911.
9 Wilson, p. 228.

plague epidemic, he died in February 1666. Just one month before his death, he had been entertained in Greenwich by Samuel Pepys and his wife to an evening of good music and company.[10]

The Westminster Company Minutes for 1664 record a build-up of aggression against the City Company. They indicate that through his many years of exile Lanier had been planning to deliver a decisive blow which would finish off the City Company for good. The fact that not much occurred during the previous year may reflect Lanier's absence through illness, and a 1663 date for the 'Valentine's Day' letter may therefore be the more likely. In the Lord Chamberlain's records he is shown as being active at Windsor in July 1663.[11] No further mention is made of him that year, but suddenly on 12 November the Lord Chamberlain issued an Order:

> for the apprehension of all musicians playing at any dumb shows, modells,[12] gamehouses, taverns or any other places, in the city of London and Westminster without leave or licence from the Corporation of the Art and Science of Music [i.e. the Westminster Company].[13]

The only relevant record that survives in the City archives dates from 1665, so we can only guess what was the immediate reaction to this attack on city liberties. It must to some extent have been a forceful one, because there is a Westminster minute dated 13 May 1664 ordering Henry Cooke, George Hudson, John Hingston and John Lilly 'to meet four of the music of the City of London, to treat upon such matters and things as concern the good of the said corporation'. The meeting, if it took place at all, cannot have been productive, because only a month later, on 14 June, another minute authorised proceedings at law 'against all such persons that make any benefit or advantage of music in England and Wales, and that do not obey the grant under the great seal to the corporation'. On 21 June the Westminster Waits were required to appear before the corporation, and on 28 June there was a peremptory order for 'John Spicer and his Company' to do likewise. We do not know whether this was a reference to the City Company or not. Finally on 16 July the Lord Chamberlain issued a Warrant for the arrest of all who were practising the art and science of music in the City of London and Westminster without licence. There is no mention this time of 'dumb shows' or 'modells'; the word 'playhouses' is substituted.

Twelve months passed before the opening shots were fired in the form of a *Quo Warranto* writ. The delay in issuing legal proceedings may have been because Nicholas Lanier was by this time in retirement in Greenwich, and there

---

[10] Latham, p. 560.

[11] De Lafontaine, p. 159.

[12] One of the meanings of the word 'model', according to Dr Johnson in his Dictionary, was 'a representation in little of something done'. Perhaps this refers therefore to a musical entertainment such as the 'Siege of Rhodes' where the historical event was retold in recitative form.

[13] De Lafontaine, p. 162.

were many other matters to engage the attention of the royal musicians. The City Company appealed to the Court of Aldermen for help on 11 July 1665. The Aldermen rapidly responded, and made the following order:

> Upon the humble petition of the Master Wardens & Assistants of the Company of Musicians London Shewing that the petitioners have been exposed to great charge and troubles by the persecution of his Majesty's Musicians for using their profession and the privileges of their Company within this City and Liberties and now at last have sued a Quo Warranto against them aiming wholly to destroy their Society and government and to subject them to their own rule and authority, Forasmuch as the said Company of Musicians are an Ancient Member of this City and have all the qualifications and do bear and perform all common Charges and Services as other Companies of this City, and are therefore to be owned and maintained in all their just rights and liberties, It is Ordered by this Court that the City Counsellors and Solicitors of this City be advising and assistant to the petitioners for their defence in the said cause, And that any thing further be done or declared by this Court which shall be fit and advisable in this behalf.[14]

This magnificent declaration of solidarity by the Court of Aldermen must have brought great comfort to the hard-pressed and indigent members of the City Company. The Aldermen had recognised that the threat to the Musicians was a threat to the whole guild system in the City, and that it had been made by an upstart thirty-year old Westminster guild which was relying entirely on its royal patronage. The whole weight of City custom, precedent and history was put in array in defence of the Musicians.

Six months later Lanier had died, and the case was dropped. Never again was the status of the Musicians Company to be legally challenged, either by the Westminster Company or by anyone else. In 1665 the officers of the Westminster Company would have been pulled up sharply on realising that if they pursued the case they would be taking on not just the livery company but the whole City Corporation. The situation was now quite different to that which existed in the 1630s. Seen from the viewpoint of a member of the King's Music, the monarch, his lord and master, was no longer invincible. Whereas in 1635 it was thought to be inconceivable that the king could be overthrown by rebellious subjects, in 1665 musicians in the royal household could not fail to recall the awful events of 1648–49, and could not be totally confident that they would not happen again. Lanier's arrogance of thirty years before was now quite out of place. In addition it was only too apparent that the royal household was short of funds, and the lavish generosity which enabled James I and Charles I to reward their most notable servants with leases, grants and monopolies, when their remuneration was in arrears, was no longer on offer. The Lord Chamberlain's records show that the payment of livery allowance to the King's Music was nearly always in arrear, often for three or four years. The new Marshal, Henry Cooke, and his Court

---

14 CL Rep 70, fol. 145b.

therefore lacked the resources and the will to take any further action against the City Company.

They did however realise that the powers given them under the 1635 charter entitled them to collect fines from any musician 'teaching, practising or exercising music without the licence or approbation of the Marshal and Corporation of Music'. During the four years from 1669 to 1673 warrants were issued against no fewer than fifty-seven named musicians. Some names appear more than once, like that of Francis Pendleton whom we shall follow more closely in the next chapter. Pendleton was a Liveryman of the Company, so the Westminster Company may have decided to continue their campaign against the City Musicians by attacking them individually, although it is perhaps more likely that the playing complained of 'in companies and at public meetings' occurred outside the City boundaries, especially as there would have been little work in the City at this time because of the reconstruction after the Fire. If freemen of the City Company were the principal target, then the names as recorded may provide a useful guide to the membership of the Company at that time, information which is not available from any other source.[15]

Whether the fines were paid and what happened to the money is not apparent from the records. If they were paid, it is tempting to assume that the proceeds were shared out among the royal musicians who were undergoing hardship through non-payment of their allowances. Clearly there were no loftier projects such as a national education programme in prospect, although the following notice appeared in the *London Gazette* in August 1670:

> From Monday, August 22nd, to Thursday August 25. Whereas His Sacred Majesty hath been pleased, after the example of his Royal Ancestors, to incorporate the Musicians of England for its encouragement of that excellent science, and the said corporation to have power over all that profess the same, and to allow and make free all such as they shall think fit: This is to give notice to all persons concerned in Music that the Corporation sits the Saturday in every week at their Hall in Durham-yard in the Strand, in pursuance of the trust and authority to them committed by his Most Gracious Majesty, and that they have granted several deputations into several counties to execute the same.[16]

This seems to be little more than an open invitation to roll up and buy a licence, but perhaps it had a greater significance. It would be interesting to know whether a visitation by one of the 'several deputations' is recorded elsewhere. There is no mention whatever of this initiative in the Minute Book.

After 1673 no further warrants against unlicensed musicians were issued, and the number of meetings of the Court were reduced to an average of two a year. The minutes at this time relate only to internal matters. Henry Cooke died in

---

[15] Following publication of this book, a consolidated list of the fifty-seven names will be held in the office of the Clerk to the Musicians Company for the use of researchers.

[16] *London Gazette*, no. 498, p. 173, as quoted by Hawkins, p. 698.

1672, and Thomas Purcell succeeded him. Pelham Humphreys and John Blow were both members of the Court of Assistants. The last entry in the Minute Book was on 2 July 1679.

Two years previously the City Company had been confirmed in its duties and functions in the City by a precept issued by the Lord Mayor against unlicensed and 'foreign' musicians which follows traditional precedents and gives the impression that the clock had stopped since the Ordinance of a century before. A petition had been presented by 'the Common Waits and other Musicians freemen of this city'. It complained that 'divers fiddlers, pipers, waits and others' were ignoring the former Ordinances, thereby giving 'great and continual disturbance to the Citizens and Inhabitants'. Persons who were not freemen must not therefore 'use or exercise singing or playing upon any instrument in any common hall, tavern, inn, alehouse or other like place', and no one except the City Waits must play 'in any open street or public passage' between ten at night and five in the morning. The Master and Wardens of the Company of Musicians and the City Waits were made responsible for the observance of this Order, and the City Constables and 'other Officers and Ministers' must use all due endeavours:

> that all persons who shall presume to go about to play upon any instrument within this City or Liberties contrary to the said ancient constitutions and the direction of this Court may be hindered and suppressed and that such of them as they shall find refractory they bring before the Right Honourable the Lord Mayor to be dealt withall as their offence shall require.[17]

In 1665 the City Company had forced their 'persecutors' to withdraw, but it was a Pyrrhic (or perhaps one should write 'pyral') victory. The terrible visitation of the plague in 1665 would have led to the cancellation of many normal engagements, but that was as nothing compared to the utter disaster of the Great Fire in September 1666. When considering this famous event, there is a natural tendency to focus on the four-day saga of the fire itself, how it started and spread, and how it was eventually contained. The various brilliant and idealistic schemes for rebuilding the City also come in for close scrutiny, together with Sir Christopher Wren's successive designs for the new St Paul's Cathedral. Less attention is paid to the much more immediate question of what effect the fire had on the social and economic life of the City. For the Musicians whose former places of performance were now part of one vast wasteland, this was a very important issue indeed.

The profile of the area destroyed by the fire is like a shadow cast in a westerly direction by the walled City. The immediate surroundings of the Tower, and the City's North East corner lying within the Walls between Aldgate and Bishopsgate, and a narrowing strip between Bishopsgate and Cripplegate, survived the fire. The whole of the rest of the City within the walls was devastated, and to the

---

17 CL Rep 82, fol. 247b.

8. The devastation around St Paul's after the Great Fire, as recorded by Wenceslas Hollar. Compare this with photographs of the effects of the Blitz in 1940–1; the damage was far greater in 1666; not a performance venue in sight.

west, because of the direction of the wind at the time, the flames vaulted over the walls and the Fleet River into the Ward of Farringdon Without, being stopped only at the perimeter wall of the Inner Temple and at Fetter Lane. 13,200 houses were destroyed, together with eighty-seven churches and fifty-two Livery Halls.[18] The actual number of citizens and their families rendered homeless was never recorded, but it can hardly have been less than 50,000. On 6 September, when the worst was over, the king addressed the refugees in Moorfields, and one can imagine Moorfields and the Artillery Ground and Finsbury Fields being turned into a 'city of canvas'. It is however strange that so little was written at the time about the dispossessed Londoners, and how they coped with their predicament. Pepys and Evelyn show curiosity but little more about the destruction and rebuilding, virtually none about the homeless. Perhaps most of them had relatives or friends in other parts of London who took them in. Pepys noted on 8 December 1666, three months after the fire, 'I saw smoke in the ruins this very day.'[19] On 23 March 1668 he made an expedition to Bishopsgate 'thinking to find a Harpsicon-maker that used to live there before the fire, but he is gone'.[20]

If as a resident in the parish of Cripplegate, outside the North Wall of the City, a member of the Company had climbed the tower of St Giles' Church one day in the middle of September, 1666, his first thought would have been to say a thankful prayer that his own house had been spared (with special thanks for the king who had personally helped to save Cripplegate from the flames[21]), followed immediately, as he looked over the smoking ruins, by a sense of despair as he realised that all his performance venues had been obliterated, and his means of livelihood had gone. There was nowhere left to play; no halls, churches, taverns or gaming-houses. It would take five years for the City to return even to a superficiality of normality, and musicians could not afford to do nothing for five years. Reddaway quotes Rolle in his 'London Resurrection' (1668) as saying that in July of that year a 'major part of the houses were let out to alehouse keepers and victuallers to entertain workmen employed about the City'.[22] These rough and ready establishments would have needed plenty of popular music – what Hawkins described as 'concerts in the unison, if they may be so called, of fiddles, of hautboys, trumpets &c'. The provision of this sort of music would hardly have satisfied the more expert among the City musicians. In the short term the prospect of trying to find suitable work and then, having been engaged, to make oneself heard amidst the roar and rattle of one vast demolition and building-site would have been repugnant. Looking further ahead, the development of the suburbs all

---

18 See T.F. Reddaway, *The Rebuilding of London after the Great Fire* (London: Jonathan Cape 1940).
19 Latham, p. 701.
20 Latham, p. 892.
21 Antonia Fraser, *King Charles II* (London: Weidenfeld & Nicolson 1979), p. 245.
22 Reddaway, p. 279.

round London as part of an elegant new city in which the nobility and gentry would reside, coupled with the opportunity to escape the ancient and customary restrictions to which all the performing arts had been subjected in the City since the early 16th century, pointed to a move out of the City in almost any direction, but more particularly westward. It is of course possible, and new research may show, that the musicians who made up the next generation of concert performers (not counting the many aliens who came to seek their fortune in London) had moved away already or had never been City residents in the first place. But how many of the fifty-seven who had fines imposed on them by the Westminster Company were still City residents? The dates when the fines were imposed, 1669–73, are suggestive. If, as seems most likely, the offence to which the warrants related was making music in Westminster and further afield, but not in the City, this would have been just the time when the uprooted City Musicians would have been establishing themselves and securing engagements elsewhere.

What is indisputable is that with very few exceptions the concert rooms and music houses which were to feature so significantly in London musical life over the next century were all located outside the City. Taking the metropolis as a whole, from the late 17th century onwards music-making within the City became an increasingly unimportant part of the greater musical scene, and the Company's role as a controlling body, which it had tried but failed to extend beyond the City boundary, was redundant. On the other hand the Company could take comfort from the fact that during the second half of the 17th century its members were selected to fill most of the vacancies in the City Waits. Out of twenty-three appointments, eighteen were of members of the Company, and this would have helped to sustain the morale of the Company during some difficult years.

There was of course no lack of secular music in the City during normal times in Charles II's reign, falling into four categories. The first and most extensive use would be at private or family gatherings, which if Pepys's example was being followed all over the City would have meant that in the evenings the sound of indoor music-making would be commonly heard by passers-by in the streets. Then there would be the music provided by City Companies at their feasts, and the ceremonial music associated with the Lord Mayor, provided mainly by the City Waits, except on Lord Mayor's Day, when every City musician would have had a part. Finally there would be the heavily regulated and closely watched music in taverns and gaming-houses. Most of the musicians who resisted the temptation to move westwards would therefore have had enough work to make a living.

Nevertheless one cannot help experiencing a sense of disappointment that so much effort, time and money was being spent in the years after the Great Fire 'putting back the clock'. Apart from the notable improvement in building regulations, everything else that was done seemed to be designed to restore the City to its old shape, form and manners. So far as the musicians were concerned, forward thinking such as, for example, asking the Corporation to provide a large music-room as a platform for City performers, or of setting up an educational Academy, appears never to have entered their heads. This is all the more surprising when one finds that the Livery Companies as a whole were placed in considerable financial difficulties by their property losses in the Fire, and were unable to proceed speedily with the rebuilding of their Halls, thereby placing constraints on the number of venues where music could traditionally be heard. Most companies were obliged to grant their city tenants long rebuilding leases at a premium and a very favourable rent, in order to find the capital required to rebuild the Hall. The Merchant Taylors were the first to complete the rebuilding, in 1673 (although the Court Room was not finished until ten years later), followed by the Stationers in 1675 and the Mercers in 1676. The Drapers' Hall was ready in 1678 and the Grocers' in 1680. Reddaway summed up the undertaking by saying 'By 1685 Companies were housed in all their old state.'[23]

There seems to be a consensus nevertheless that 1671 was the year when things began to get back to normal. By that time 7,359 houses (well over half the number destroyed) had been 'set out', that is completed or in process of being built, and the 'ancient shows and formalities' associated with Lord Mayor's Day were reinstated.

The 'shows and formalities' would have included the River Pageant, during which the Livery Companies escorted the Lord Mayor in their barges from the City to Westminster, which was as much a musical feast as a spectacle. The musicians traditionally played in the stern of the barges, and because the impact of massed violins was still a novelty and beyond the resources of the City musicians, the music consisted of the long-established 'loud music' of trumpets, drums, sackbuts, hautboys, flutes and cornets.[24] There was great competition among the companies to obtain the services of the City Waits, the Royal Musicians usually being retained for the Lord Mayor's own barge. The Clothworkers complained in 1682 that they were 'generally ill-served' with trumpets, and the music of the Waits might 'do as well' and 'may be procured for half the money'. There were usually five or six players in each barge, but the number was sometimes increased to nine. An observer in 1686 described the procession of barges:

> with drums beating, Trumpets sounding, Music playing, which is echoed from the several Pleasure boats and others that are plying from each side with Pattararas, and other small pieces, to compliment them as they pass, insomuch that the Thames is nothing but a continual flowing Harmony, which never ebbs till his Lordship is landed.[25]

On 21 September 1671 Evelyn dined at Ironmongers Hall, which had survived the Fire because it was then in Fenchurch Street, east of the devastation. It was the Stewards Feast:

---

[23] Reddaway, p. 256.
[24] See Julia K. Wood, ' "A Flowing Harmony", Music on the Thames in Restoration London', *Early Music* (November 1995), p. 561
[25] M. Taubman, *London's Yearly Jubilee*, quoted in J.K. Wood.

9. An 18th century drawing of the Lord Mayor's River Procession to Westminster. In the background is the first Westminster Bridge, completed in 1750. Southwark Cathedral (then St Mary Overie) is to the left. The builders' wharf in the centre of the picture is roughly on the site of the National Theatre.

10. Detail of the previous illustration. There are groups of musicians at the stern of each of the four barges.

where the four stewards chose their successors of the next year with a solemn procession, garlands upon their heads and music playing before them.[26]

It might be thought that from 1666 until 1697, when the new building was
officially opened and consecrated, St Paul's Cathedral would have had its own
'intermission', and would have had to disband its choir. However this was not the
case, and under the energetic leadership of Dean Sancroft, later to become Archbishop of Canterbury in William and Mary's reign, temporary arrangements for
the continuation of the daily observance and the choral tradition continued for
twenty years from 1668, after which a part of the new cathedral could be used.
The Dean and Chapter managed to find a small part of the nave at the extreme
west end of the cathedral which could be used as a temporary church, and something in the right place and of the right size, although rather bigger than one
would expect, is shown in the Wenceslas Hollar engraving (see Plate 8). In the
Cathedral Archives for 1668 the following instruction is recorded:

> A Choir and Auditory for present use be forthwith set out, repaired and finished
> . . . in the body of the church between the West end and the second pillars after the
> little North and South doors.[27]

The cathedral receipt books show that the members of the choir continued to be
paid for their duties throughout this period.

The exodus from the City was associated with the evolution of the concert,
from the earlier practice of providing tavern music for patrons as they drank and
ate. The first stage in the process had been the provision of a separate room for
listening to music, which was probably no more remarkable than the 20th
century practice of having smoking and non-smoking bars. The second stage
came when the music in the music-room became more important than the food
and drink. The final stage arrived when the music room was physically divided
from the tavern. Just when this happened is somewhat uncertain. The formally
advertised concert series almost certainly began with John Banister, but informal
performances for the regular patrons of taverns probably began during the Interregnum, despite a new law designed to reinforce the illegality of music in taverns.
It was a law passed by Parliament on 20 January 1657 whose members were then
entertained after dinner by Oliver Cromwell to a concert of 'rare music' at the
Cockpit Theatre in Whitehall, 'his Highness being very fond of music'.[28] On 18
February 1660, Pepys made an entry in his diary about a visit to 'the Mitre
Tavern in Fleet Street' with Captain Holland, his naval friend, where they sat in a
room 'above the music-room' and 'heard very plainly through the ceiling'.[29]

Another reference to the tavern 'concert' appears in a well-known passage
from John Evelyn's diary for 21 December 1662. Describing a service in the

26 Evelyn, *Diary*, p. 185.
27 See Sir Simon Dugdale, *The History of St Paul's Cathedral* (London 1818), p. 127.
28 Scholes, p. 49.
29 Latham, p. 18.

Chapel Royal at St James's on that day, and the king's foreign taste in the matter of sacred music, Evelyn wrote in disgust:

> Instead of the ancient and grave solemn wind music accompanying the Organ, was introduced a Consort of 24 Violins between every pause, after the French fantastical light way, better suiting a Tavern or Play-house than a Church.

One last example of a tavern with a room set aside for music: in 1658 there was a Music House at the Blue Bell 'by the postern gate of London Wall' (probably the little gate constructed at the time of Edward VI to provide access between Christ's Hospital and St Bartholomew's Hospital). The proprietor, Thomas Smith, was prosecuted, not under the new law of 1657 'for making music in a tavern', but for serving 'one puncheon of compounded and adulterated unwholesome Drink fit to have the head beaten out'.[30]

On the very edge of the City, John Banister inaugurated a series of regular afternoon concerts on 30 December 1672 in a house 'now called the Music School over against the George Tavern in White Friars'. It was an interesting choice of venue, because White Friars, between the Fleet River and the Inner Temple, was one of the ancient 'liberties' which had originally been outside the jurisdiction of the City. Even now it was an asylum for debtors; perhaps therefore a 'no-go area' for city enforcement officers. It cannot have been wholly satisfactory. Access would have been inconvenient, and the neighbourhood had a bad reputation. Four years later, therefore, Banister moved his concerts to a more salubrious venue, the 'Academy' in Lincoln's Inn Fields. From that moment there would be hardly any programmed public concerts within the city boundaries until the 19th century.[31]

John Banister was particularly well-equipped to organise the first proper concerts. Having been first a City Wait and then appointed to the King's Music in 1660, he became responsible in the years following, after a visit to the French Court, not only for the marshalling of the Twenty-Four Violins (the king's favourite ensemble), but also for much of the music (performed by his violinists) for the productions of the two licensed theatre companies, the king's and the Duke of York's.[32] If, after Lanier's death, Banister had been appointed Master of the King's Music, as he had hoped, the initiative for devising the organised concert would have passed to some other person. As it was, Nicholas Lanier's successor was the Spaniard violinist, Louis Grabu, who was probably more fully acclimatised to the manners and affectations of the French Court which Charles II desired to emulate. The disappointed Banister continued to serve in the violin band, but his principal interest was once more directed towards the stage.[33]

In extending this interest to the non-dramatised public concert Banister could

---

30 Elkin, p. 14.
31 Elkin, pp. 14–22.
32 For a detailed description of John Banister's career, see Holman, chapter 14.
33 Holman, p. 336.

11. Thomas Britton, 'the Small Coal Man', historically one of the least likely and yet most successful concert promoters.

perhaps be justly described as the first English impresario. He 'composed' the music for the concerts, which seems to have had the additional meaning that he put together the programme in advance, a definite progression from the tavern music in which each artist, if there were more than one, would play pieces of his own choice in an uncoordinated way. It was the beginning of 'programme building'. Banister also brought back from France the code of 'ensemble discipline' attributed to Lully, which introduced to London the habit of beginning a performance from silence, and the science of synchronised bowing, both now so automatic on the concert platform that it is hard to imagine how different things once were.[34]

In a totally different environment, but equally close to the City, the phenomenal Thomas Britton began his thirty-six-year run of concerts in Clerkenwell in 1678. His relevance to the Company and to this book is not because he was a City man, much less a freeman or liveryman (so far as we know) of the Company, but because his working life was spent in the City, and also because he was an ordinary (but remarkably accomplished) man who had no connection with or dependence on the Court and its musicians. Coming from plain yeoman stock in Northamptonshire, his achievement was uniquely possible in the 17th century, after the great levelling of the Interregnum and the relaxation of social barriers during the reign of Charles II. The stratification of society which ensued in the 18th century would have made it quite impossible for a person of Britton's humble origin, plying his trade each morning as a retail coal merchant, to have given regular weekly concerts for thirty-six years in a long narrow upstairs room over a coal store in Clerkenwell, which could only be reached by an outside stair, and to have attracted performers of the quality of Handel and Pepusch and a regular audience from the upper reaches of society. Sir John Hawkins, who wrote at length about the Britton concerts, commented:

> A lady of the first rank in this kingdom, the duchess of Queensbury, now living, one of the most celebrated beauties of her time, may yet remember that in the pleasure which she manifested at hearing Mr Britton's concert, she seemed to have forgotten the difficulty with which she ascended the steps that led to it.[35]

Hawkins added that the stairs 'could scarce be ascended without crawling', and that the concert room 'had a ceiling so low that a tall man could but just stand upright in it'.

It seems that Thomas Britton's personality was such that he was loved by all. 'He was a plain, simple, honest man, perfectly inoffensive, and highly esteemed by all who knew him,' was Hawkins' epitaph. He made many friends on his coalround through the City streets, and in Clerkenwell, where he lived. One near neighbour was Dick Sadler, the Highway Surveyor, who rediscovered the bricked-up wells ('Sadler's Wells') in Islington after he too had built a music-

[34] Holman, p. 293.
[35] Hawkins, p. 790.

house on the path by the New River, leading from Clerkenwell to Islington. This was in 1683. Was there perhaps some collaboration between Britton and Sadler, with their music-houses in close proximity? According to Hawkins, the person most responsible for getting Britton's concerts established was Sir Robert L'Estrange, 'a very musical gentleman, who had a tolerable perfection on the bass viol'. This sounds like a contradiction in terms; it may reflect the fact that L'Estrange was a prominent politician and had many other accomplishments. His relationship with the 'small-coal man' appears to have been cemented by Britton's remarkable knowledge of literature and his extensive library. Britton had also interested himself in chemistry and philosophy. But still every morning, in his 'blue frock', he heaved the sacks of coal on his back around the City.

Our knowledge of the performers who provided the music for Britton's concerts is extremely sketchy; from the small number of names given by Hawkins it would appear that some of them were gifted amateurs. But thirty-six years is a very long time to be presenting weekly concerts, and it would be a reasonable assumption that as Clerkenwell lay just across Smithfield from the City, there would have been City Musicians participating from time to time.

During the long years, Thomas Britton had accumulated a huge music library, much of it 'pricked' by himself 'very neatly and accurately', and the catalogue of this music when sold after his death is set out in full in Hawkins's General History.[36] It is an almost complete repertoire of music known in London at the time, going back to Tallis, and including many Italians, but no French composers other than Lully. As one would expect, there are works by Purcell in great variety and quantity, but only vocal music by Blow. In chronological terms the list ends with Corelli, Croft and Vivaldi. Britton died in September 1714, and his music sold at auction for about one hundred pounds. His collection of musical instruments, including about twenty fine stringed instruments, and a 'Rucker's virginal thought to be the best in Europe', sold for eighty pounds. The preamble to the catalogue reads as follows:

> A catalogue of extraordinary musical instruments made by the most eminent workmen both at home and abroad. Also divers valuable compositions, ancient and modern, by the best masters in Europe; a great many of which are finely engraved, neatly bound, and the whole carefully preserved in admirable order; being the entire collection of Mr Thomas Britton of Clerkenwell, small-coal man, lately deceased, who at his own charge kept up so excellent a consort forty odd years at his dwelling-house, that the best masters were at all times proud to exert themselves therein; and persons of the highest quality desirous of honouring his humble cottage with their presence and attention.

At the same time as the Britton concerts continued, other concert series were coming into existence. There were the York Buildings concerts, presented by professional musicians from 1680. Roger North suggests that these concerts devel-

---

36 Hawkins, pp. 792–3.

oped from a private club of amateurs (including himself) who originally met in private rooms, but then moved to a permanent venue at the Castle Tavern in Fleet Street. Unfortunately for the amateurs the taverner realised that there was money to be made out of these excellent performers, and he encouraged 'divers gentlemen and ladies' to come and hear them play, taking 'seats of distinction for price'. Roger North wrote:

> The gentlemen, being under the *fastidium* of losing the freedom of a private meeting . . . dropped off by degrees, and masters of music entered and filled the consort, which they carried on directly for money collected as at other public entertainments. Then this was called the Music Meeting, and was a night resort (for the consort began not till some time after the play was done) of most of the gay idle people of the town.[37]

Thus the concert continued to evolve as a non-participating sport. Professional persistence and stamina replaced amateur enthusiasm, while the amateurs contributed their expertise to promote concerts, choosing the artists and the programme, and commissioning new works. This was the basis on which the St Cecilia Celebration was organised from 1683 to 1703, in all but the first year at the recently rebuilt Stationers Hall. It has been suggested that the amateurs who played at the Castle Tavern, having made way for the professionals who moved to York Buildings, then occupied themselves with promoting the St Cecilia Celebrations.[38] However if Roger North was one of the group it is surprising that he does not refer to the annual events at Stationers Hall. The Stewards at the inception of the festival included the barrister, Gilbert Dolben, son of the Archbishop of York, William Bridgman, a distinguished amateur musician later to become Secretary to the Admiralty, Francis Forcer who was Dick Sadler's partner and successor at Sadler's Wells, and Nicholas Staggins, Master of the King's Music after Grabu. They were therefore a mix of amateur and professional. The patrons called themselves 'the Musical Society' and each year commissioned a poet and composer to provide an Ode in praise of music. This was performed after a fine banquet; from 1693 there was also a service at St Bride's Fleet Street with special music and sermon.

Some twenty years after the demise of the St Cecilia Celebration, the name of the Castle Tavern recurs, but on this occasion it is the Castle in Paternoster Row, by St Paul's. Again it is the venue for an amateur music society, which continued, with its own bye-laws, until towards the end of the 18th century.[39]

The knowledge, influence, skill and financial resources of the musical amateur was becoming a dominant factor in the presentation of secular music in London.

---

[37] John Wilson, ed., *Roger North on Music* (London: Novello & Co. 1959), p. 305 n. 52.

[38] Maureen Duffy, *Henry Purcell* (London: Fourth Estate 1994), p. 84.

[39] *The Blackwell History of Music in Britain: The Eighteenth Century*, ed. H. Diack Johnstone and Roger Fiske (Oxford: Basil Blackwell 1990), chapter 2 (Rosamond McGuinness and H. Diack Johnstone), pp. 36–7.

It was now the promoters who chose the artists, without any reference to any qualifications or standards which the Musicians' Company might attempt to lay down. He who was paying the piper was really calling the tune, and it was difficult to see what ongoing role the Company could have as a regulatory body. There was however one musical activity which still provided an opportunity for supervision, and, some would say, definitely needed it. This was the profession of Dancing-Masters, who were already well-represented within the Company. The attempt to bring them all under the Company's jurisdiction was to be the last round in its fight to remain an active craft guild.

8

Devil's Grasshoppers

Except that they appear to have virtually taken over the Company, there was nothing new about Dancing Masters in the 1690s. The earliest Court records of dancing go back at least to the 14th century, and the chronicles tell of dancing minstrels who did their solo turn long before that. In 1296, three household minstrels performed a mime in mask at the wedding of Edward I's daughter Elizabeth to the Count of Holland.[1] Edward II was entertained in France in 1312 by 'Bernard le fol' and his fifty-four companions dancing naked for his amusement.[2] And one of the activities of Edward III's Order of the Garter which attracted most notice in its earliest days was to go masquerading in various ways, such as galloping through the City dressed as Moors, and to participate in dances and masques which were a precursor of those produced in the 17th century.[3] The first record in the royal accounts of a payment being made to a Dancing Master appears to have been in 1380, when ten marks were paid to a Venetian named John 'Katherine' or Caterina.[4]

After that there was little change or development until Tudor times, when the Courts of Henry VIII and Elizabeth were eager to learn and copy what had been happening on the Continent in the way of new dances; it was from this time that the reputation of the English Court for its dancing prowess spread through Europe.[5] Dancing Masters became a permanent fixture in the royal household in the reign of Elizabeth, but it is a little curious that the authority given to the Master and Wardens of the Company by the Court of Aldermen, to control 'all those that keep dancing schools' in the City, predated the first official appoint-

---

[1] Southworth, p. 81.
[2] Southworth, p. 86.
[3] Southworth, p. 108.
[4] A great deal of information in this chapter has come from an unpublished dissertation entitled 'The English Dancing Master 1660–1728, His Role at Court, in Society and on the Public Stage' by Jennifer Martin (University of Michigan 1977), and this assistance is gratefully acknowledged. Martin noted the information regarding 'Katherine' as having been recorded in an earlier dissertation by Shirley Wynne: 'The Charms of Complaisance: Dance in England, 1660–1700' (Ohio State University 1967).
[5] Holman, p. 113.

ment of a Court Dancing Master by over ten years. The Company's authority dates from 12 November 1561; the appointment of Thomas Cardell, the first Court Dancing Master, was made on 8 December 1575.[6] Not too much weight should be given to this time-lag. The alien musicians imported by Henry VIII had brought the new dances with them, and the violinists in particular would have been teachers as well as dance accompanists. Nevertheless it does show that the popularity of dancing in Tudor London should not be underestimated. It will be remembered that an attempt had been made in 1554 to outlaw dancing schools in London completely (see Appendix 3). This had failed; no one could stop people dancing, so control of the teaching establishments was the only practical answer, although the nagging disapproval of the reformed church was having some effect in damping down the enthusiasm.

One hundred years later, the situation was not very different. During the first half of the 17th century, prior to the Civil War, there had been a succession of distinguished Dancing-Masters, French and English, at Court, doing their duty as teachers, choreographers and soloists, with particular reference to the masques. But dancing remained a popular sport as well, despite the puritan restraints imposed on Sunday entertainment. Until the Restoration this was mostly traditional English 'country' dancing, and the widespread circulation of John Playford's 'The English Dancing-Master' from 1651 onwards shows how much demand there was for a manual which contained both the steps and the music, and which could be used in any literate group or household. However, even during the Interregnum changes were taking place, particularly in the establishment of girls' boarding schools, where the more formal Court dances were taught. Although the first of these was opened in Hackney by a Mrs Perwich in 1643 for 'upper-class girls', the rapid spread of these schools during the Interregnum owed nothing to royal encouragement or example, and there seem to have been no religious objections to the inclusion of dancing in the curriculum. But when the Restoration came, business boomed.

Dancing Masters had a new and demanding role to play in post-Restoration society, which was adapting itself as fast as it could to the niceties and artificialities of daily life *à la mode* imported from across the Channel. Courtly dancing was only the central activity around which to erect a whole structure of deportment and manners, the more unnatural the better. But in the acquisition of this artifice it was all too easy to be grotesque instead of gracious, and the Dancing Master's teaching was essential for the avoidance of ridicule. How to greet people of differing social degrees, how to bow and curtsey, how to smile, whether to laugh, how to deploy a fan, how to handle a cane or a hat or a sword, or take snuff – all these things were important in an upwardly mobile society, and there was no shame attached to having private or public tuition in the social graces

6   Holman, p. 115.

from an established Master, while pausing for breath in the middle of the dancing lesson.

The profession of Dancing Masters therefore multiplied. The satirist Thomas Brown wrote:

> Dancing masters are also as numerous in every street as posts in Cheapside, there is no walking but we stumble upon them; they are held here but in very slight esteem, for the gentry call them leg-levers, and the mob, from their mighty number and their nimbleness, call them the devil's grasshoppers.[7]

Brown's remarks, ostensibly in a letter from the 'dead' Purcell to the 'living' John Blow, illustrate the ambivalence with which many contemporary men regarded these intruders into domestic life who threatened their traditional status. The master of the household needed them to maintain his status in society; he mistrusted them when obliged to leave his wife and daughters in their charge.

These were the men, articulate in mind and body, who for a short period of about thirty years came to dominate the Company and use it for their own purposes.

Even at this late stage in the Company's history, which just overlaps the Company's own first surviving records, we are handicapped by a lack of information as to just how much control the Dancing Masters exercised, and we are forced once again to make assumptions which future research may prove to be mistaken. The evidence that is available is threefold; first, a short list of Liverymen of the Company, dated to about 1690, which includes two of the best-known City Dancing Masters among its ten names; secondly, a petition of 1694, which stated that 'the present Master, several of the Assistants and divers of the freemen' were Dancing Masters; lastly, in January 1718, an official from the Lord Chancellor's Department attended on the Court of Aldermen and informed them that 'the Dancing Masters and the Musicians are endeavouring to obtain a charter to be joined together'.

It will be instructive to look at each of these strands of evidence.

The Livery list is not complete because it comes from a polling list for two shrieval candidates, a Mr North and a Mr Boxx. Other livery members may have polled for other candidates or not at all. John Dyer was Master, and his name heads the list, followed by the two wardens, Richard Hill and Robert Povvy or Povey. Included in the remaining seven names is Thomas Looe, who was organist of St Martin, Ludgate, and the two Dancing Masters, Francis Pendleton and Walter Holt. Pendleton's name has become well-known because he was employed by Samuel Pepys to teach his wife to dance and acquire the social graces. Through the lucky chance of his relationship with the Pepys' household he is the first member of the Company of whom we can construct a 'flesh and blood' impression. Walter Holt was Master of the Company at the time of the

---

7   See Arthur L. Hayward, ed., *Amusements Serious and Comical and other works by Tom Brown* (London: George Routledge 1927), p. 433.

1694 petition. The Holts were a large family, and there may have been five of them at least engaged in teaching dancing. There were two Walters, father and son, and the one in the list is probably the senior, who is recorded as keeping a dancing school in Bartholomew Lane, behind the Royal Exchange.

The 1694 petition is dated 26 February and deals almost exclusively with dancing and Dancing Masters. It begins with the usual protestation that the members of the Company are all good citizens and tax-payers, and refers to the many ordinances of the City protecting the rights of the citizens (but not specifically the rights of musicians who are free of the City – one wonders why these were not stressed) before going on to complain that:

> Many Dancing Masters that are foreigners papists and aliens (most of whom are lodgers and pay no scott nor lott) come within the freedom of the said City of London and not only teach in private houses but also keep public schools in halls and other houses and some do keep rude and disorderly Schools and some from tradesmen turn unskilful dancing masters not only to the prejudice of young Gentlemen and Ladies in their education but also to the abuse and dishonour of this City and of your petitioners because the name of dancing Masters is not particularly named in the said Acts of Common Council although by their Bye-laws your petitioners have the oversight and rule of all persons using the said art of Dancing within the said City and within three miles of the same.[8]

We should note in passing that the Master and Wardens were still taking for granted the fact that the 1606 Bye-laws remained in force, despite the loss of the charter in 1635. The reference to 'papists and aliens' probably refers to the French Dancing Masters who were greatly in demand in London, but may also relate to the Italian instrumentalists who were flocking to London at this time.

The petition goes on to ask for a new Act prohibiting foreigners from exercising for profit the arts and misteries of music and dancing within the City and its liberties, and allowing only those to do so who have served a seven-year apprenticeship and have been licensed by the Master and Wardens:

> whereupon your petitioners and their successors shall be able and will take particular care that all irregularities shall be prevented for the future for the honour and advantage of youth of both sexes and that none shall be permitted to teach the said arts and misteries of music and dancing (for lucre and gain) for the future but such as are civilised persons, nor any keep schools but artists.

Yet again and, as it happens, for the last time, the Company showed its fatal attraction to the system of apprenticeship. It was the only form of education that it understood, and it could not conceive of any alternative, not even a form of honorary status for the highly trained aliens who were poised to wipe out the native competition. It is only fair to add that the Court of Aldermen might have

---

[8] CL Rep 51, fol. 300b–301.

rejected any such proposal, although they had been very generous to the refugee Huguenots at about this time.

The Company's petition was referred to the Gresham Committee, and was then referred back to the Court of Aldermen on 4 June 1694, who recommended that the Bill be read a second time at the next meeting of the Court of Common Council. However at that meeting on 15 June, the Bill was referred back to the Committee, and it was not until 11 September 1699 that an amended Bill was finally enacted.

Even then, the Company failed to win the powers they were seeking, because on the strength of the Act of 1699 they had taken legal proceedings against John Groscourt, a well-known Dancing Master who had persisted in defying the Company by keeping a dancing school in the City without the Company's permission (one suspects that his resistance may have been one of the principal factors which were responsible for the petition and the new Act), and unfortunately for the Company, judgment had been given in his favour. The court had decided that the Act was not obligatory on Dancing Masters, and that earlier regulations such as the 1606 Bye-laws were no longer effective.

With yet another petition and further amendments to the draft Bill, the Musicians went back once more to the Court of Aldermen, and finally obtained their Act on 11 December 1700 (see Appendix 7). The cost of five years' work struggling to get the new Act, followed by the litigation against Groscourt and then yet another petition and an amended Act, must have been immense, but it helps to put into context the massive earnings of the Dancing Masters, especially those with schools, in comparison with the meagre returns now available to the musicians still working in the City. The satirist, Edward Ward, damned the Dancing Masters for their mercenary ways:

> The Quarterages flowed so fast into the Master's pocket, that the Money chinked as he capered.[9]

Almost as an afterthought the new Act provided that any musician working in the City who was not then free of another Company would in future be obliged to join the Company; a law for which the Company had been fighting since the beginning of the Century. Applied to the Dancing Masters with schools in the City, it should have been effective and beneficial to the Company, but from the point of view of the instrumentalists it was probably too late. The new locations for music performance had taken most of them westwards.

The last of the three strands of evidence for the Dancing Masters' 'supremacy' arose in January 1718, when the City authorities were alerted by Westminster that steps were being taken to obtain a new charter whereby the Dancing Masters and the Musicians would be 'joined together'.[10] The attempt must have reached a

---

9 Edward Ward, *The Dancing School with the Adventures of the Easter Holy Days* (London: J. How 1700), p. 5.
10 CL Rep 122, fol. 97–8.

fairly advanced stage, because in February the Remembrancer was instructed to retain Counsel on the Corporation's behalf to oppose the granting of a charter.[11] One wonders just what was going on. In the first place the Lord Chancellor's clerk, Mr Woodford, must have been under some misunderstanding about an amalgamation, because the Dancing Masters had never had a livery of their own. The misapprehension probably arose from the fact that all the activity was coming not from the musicians but from the dancing masters. Was it not the Dancing Masters who wanted the charter, so that they could claim back the lost three mile radius granted in the King James charter? Then they could control all the Dancing Masters (control of musicians was incidental to them), in London, whether they be in Westminster, Holborn, Covent Garden, Mayfair, Hackney or Chelsea.

Unfortunately they had failed to obtain the best advice, like the status-seeking members of the Company in 1604 who allowed the 'saving clause' for the King's Music to be written into the Bye-laws instead of the Charter. Everyone knew, except apparently the Dancing Masters, that a City Livery Company could not apply for a Royal Charter without the licence of the Court of Aldermen; and that any company that ignored this requirement was bound to end up facing a lot of irate and antagonistic Aldermen. The project for a new charter was doomed. Whether it could ever have been applied effectively is very doubtful. The Westminster Company had failed, and a new and almost insuperable problem was being created by the steady trickle of foreign musicians arriving in London in the early years of the 18th century, which soon became a flood, and included a formidable influx of French dancing masters. How could the Company have controlled all these foreigners? What possible control could it have exercised over Handel and his circle? A certain scepticism will always hang over the aspirations of those Dancing Masters, even if they had the best interests of the Company at heart.

There were three ways in which Dancing Masters taught their pupils during this 'peak period' of their activity. There were the girls' boarding schools, the public dancing classes, which attracted so much attention from the satirists and, for those who could afford the luxury, there were private lessons at home. The information contained in Pepys' diary relating to Francis Pendleton gives a unique description of how a Dancing Master at that time set about teaching a client privately. Although he gave Pepys, who described him as 'a pretty neat blackman', four of the worst months of his married life, during the time that his wife Elizabeth's dancing lessons continued, one can deduce that Pendleton was a man of considerable discretion and sensitivity, because Pepys is honest enough to admit to his diary that the hell that he went through was entirely due to his own jealousy.

The first lesson was on 4 May 1663. On the 12 May he wrote that Pendleton

---

[11] CL Rep 122, fol. 186.

was now coming twice a day and Elizabeth could think of nothing else. On the 15th he went home and found them alone together, 'not dancing but walking'. On Sunday 24th at church he 'espied Pembleton [as he always described him] and saw him leer upon my wife all the sermon . . . and my wife upon him; and I observed she made a curtsey to him at coming out'. On 26th, when he discovered that Pendleton had spent most of the day alone with Elizabeth 'he went softly up to see whether any of the beds were out of order or no, which I found not'. There was a quarrel with his wife in the small hours of that night, after which Elizabeth said that unless Samuel was there she would not allow Pendleton to come to the house. He was due to come next day; when he arrived Elizabeth sent for her husband to come home. He told her to carry on with the lesson, and eventually went home with a colleague from work. Quite late he joined the dancers,

and there we danced country dances and single, my wife and I, and my wife paid him off for this month also, and so he is cleared. After dancing, we took him down to supper and were very merry; and I made myself so and kind to him as much as I could, to prevent his discourse; though I perceive to my trouble that he knows all, and my doty doth me the disgrace to publish it as much as she can.

Pepys' suspicions continued, because a week later Elizabeth sent the boy, Will Hewer, on an errand and would not say where she had sent him. Pepys was sure that it was to take a secret message to Pendleton. The following day he discovered that she had sent him out to buy some starch! On 9 June he was surprised and angry to find Pendleton at home and dancing, despite the series of lessons having finished, but Mary Ashwell was chaperoning his wife on this occasion. After that the Pepys' went to the country for the summer, but on 30th August Samuel, having gone to church alone in the afternoon,

there saw Pembleton come in and look up, which put me in a sweat, and seeing not my wife there, went out again. But Lord – how I was afeared that he might, seeing me at church, go home to my wife; so much is it out of my power to preserve myself from jealousy – and so sat impatient all the sermon. Home and find all well and no sign of anybody being there.

Pendleton fades out of the diary at that point, innocent, surely, of all that Samuel had suspected him of, as he later reappears for two social occasions, the first of which was on 24 January 1667 when there seems to have been an all-night session of music and dancing. Pepys summed it up by writing:

my mind mightily satisfied with all this evening's work, and thinking it to be one of the merriest enjoyments I must look for in the world, and did content myself therefore with the thoughts of it, and so to bed . . . Only, the Music did not please me, they not being contented with less than 30s.

It is extraordinary that Pepys could write in such terms when just a few yards away from the festivities, the total devastation caused by the Great Fire stretched westwards as far as the eye could see.

The last record in the diary was in respect of a Twelfth Night supper party which the Pepyses gave a year later in 1668. After watching a performance of *The Tempest* at the Duke of York's, Samuel took the principal actor, Henry Harris, home where there were Pendleton, his wine merchant friend Batelier, and three others besides the theatre party:

> and there fell to dancing, having extraordinary music, two violins and a bass viallin and Theorbo,[12] the Duke of Buckingham's Music, the best in town, sent to me by Greeting; and there we set in to dancing. By and by . . . to a very good supper, and mighty merry and good music playing; and after supper to dancing and singing till about 12 at night; and then we had a good sackposset for them and an excellent cake, cost me near 20s of our Jane's making, which was cut into twenty pieces, there being by this time so many of our company by the coming in of young Goodyer and some others of our neighbours, young men who could dance, hearing of our dancing.

The party broke up about 2 o'clock, and Pepys gave the fiddler £3 for the four players.[13] There is no reason to suppose that that was the end of the friendship between Pendleton and Pepys, although Elizabeth died tragically of a fever in 1669. Pepys gave up his diary at the end of May 1669, because he was convinced that he was going blind. It was a false alarm, but he never resumed his detailed diary-writing.

In the same year, on 28 June, Pendleton and Josiah Priest were arrested and fined by the Westminster Company because they were practising music without the Company's licence. Priest was clearly undeterred by the fine, and a few years later was involved in the choreography for *Calisto*, the opera/masque performed in Whitehall in 1675. He is best known for his girls' boarding school in Chelsea, where Purcell's *Dido and Aeneas* was first performed in May 1689, but twenty years earlier he had his school at Leicester Fields. It seems more than likely that Pendleton and Priest had been targeted for arrest because they were both members of the City Company. Pendleton, as we have seen, was included in the 1690 list of liverymen, and Priest is listed as a liveryman in 1700.[14] (Pendleton is not included in this comprehensive list so must be assumed to have died before the turn of the century.) At the date of their arrest they were probably both freemen.

By 1672 the Dancing Master was sufficiently recognised as an everyday part of social life to be the focus of a Restoration comedy – although the hero's role was to try to pretend to be one. William Wycherley's *The Gentleman Dancing Master*

---

[12] After the word 'Theorbo' Pepys wrote in parenthesis 'four hands', which is rather baffling. It cannot mean that it required two persons to play, because there were only four musicians altogether. Was it a humorous reference to the number of strings?

[13] This summary of the Pepys/Pendleton relationship is taken from Robert Latham's *The Shorter Pepys* at pp. 271, 274, 275, 278–81, 285, 718, 861–2.

[14] A unique typescript held in the Guildhall Library contains an alphabetical list of names of the Liverymen of all the City Companies in 1700. It is entitled 'An Index to the Liverymen of London in 1700', and was transcribed and compiled in 1933 by T.C. Dale.

scores a few points at the expense of Dancing Masters as a type, but the real butt of his satire are the new rich who seek to impress by aping foreign habits and costume and taking French and Spanish names. The hero, Gerrard, is a plain Englishman; his heroine, Hippolita, is presented as a girl of fourteen who has just left her boarding school in Hackney, although she has the composure and sophistication of a girl twice that age. Her foolish 'Spanish' father, whose real name is James Formal, but who likes to be called Don Diego, has returned home to marry Hippolita to the French-besotted 'Monsieur de' Paris. The Don, having tried to kill Gerrard before being persuaded that he is a Dancing Master, utters the conventional sentiments that the audience were no doubt waiting for:

> I hope he does not use the dancing-master's tricks, of squeezing your hands, setting your legs and feet, by handling your thighs and seeing your legs.

Hippolita replies that she would give him a box on the ear if he did. The play is light-hearted and gently satirical, and no professional Dancing Master could complain that it was damaging to his reputation. Gerrard and Hippolita are left alone on stage on several occasions in the play, even though Hippolita's aunt and chaperone, the terrible Mrs Caution, has grave doubts about Gerrard's profession. Relating this to Pepys's suspicions about Pendleton, it does indicate that the conventions of the time were not too strict, and that a Dancing Master might be left with a female pupil to get on with their lesson unchaperoned.

As time went on, satire and criticism grew stronger and more vicious. Thomas D'Urfey wrote a play in 1691 called 'Love for Money' about a girls' school with three lustful schoolmasters: a music teacher, a Dancing Master and a French teacher. As D'Urfey had just been staying at the Priest's school in Chelsea it was popularly believed that the play reflected life at the school, although in the preface to the play the author denied that this was the case. Relations between the Priests and D'Urfey were severely strained, and for a time Purcell refused to work with him either, although he had provided the text for several of Purcell's Odes and the Epilogue for *Dido and Aeneas*.[15]

Edward Ward in the 1722 satire, *The Dancing Master* was the most savage:

> Of all the plagues with which poor England's curst
> Or ever was, the Dancing Tribe's the worst.
> From France arrive, with fluttering Airs and Hopes
> Others, who'll teach you how to stand on Ropes,
> Fly in the air or stand upon your Head.
> And can you, Ladies, e'er be better bred?
>
> Ign'rant of Nature, they would give her Law
> And Lines and Marks, to circumscribe her, draw.
> Large is their Boast, and Mighty their Pretence
> To mend your Manners, and direct your Sense

---

15 Duffy, pp. 182–3.

Their Education's vile, and so's their Birth
And they the dregs and scum of all the earth.[16]

Ward's reputation matched the coarseness of his prolific verse. In 1705 he had stood in the pillory for an attack on the government.

It was always going to be difficult, if not impossible, for Dancing Masters to enjoy the same reputation, let alone adulation, as the great musicians, particularly those from Italy, who were now drawing the crowds into the Music Rooms. Dancing Masters were as necessary as a barber or a dentist, but many people must have been reluctant dancers and would have been happier without them. This was perhaps the reason why in the early 1700s some Dancing Masters went to great trouble to write lengthy apologia for their art and work, linking their practice with that of the ancient Greeks, and emphasising that dancing was a social activity of high civilisations.[17] John Weaver was the foremost apologist, although he spent more time in Shrewsbury than London. His 'Essay Towards a History of Dancing' of 1712 concentrated on links with ancient times and writers. Then in his 'Anatomical and Mechanical Lectures upon Dancing' of 1721, he attempted 'to place the Art of Dancing among the liberal Arts and Sciences; by laying down Fundamentals, and Rudiments explaining the Laws of Motion, Mechanical and Natural'. There were many other writers of treatises on dancing during this period, among which perhaps the most singular was the first book of notational signs for social dancing, written at about this time by the Frenchman Raoul Feuillet, and translated into English by the Dancing Master John Essex in 1710.

One special achievement should not be forgotten, because it gave the English Dancing Masters at the end of the 17th century a claim to immortality which those who wrote about them so scurrilously cannot take away. While every London household of pretension was striving to collect the last drop of French manners and etiquette from French and French-trained teachers, French Dancing Masters were coming to London, not just to teach the ignorant Londoners, but to be taught the English country dances in order to take them back to Versailles. The reason for this was that in the creation of his glittering but artificial court Louis XIV, first in St Germain and then Versailles, had effectively sterilised French Dance. It had become a weapon of oppression, and was incapable of metamorphosis into something different.

The Sun King's weapon of exquisite torture was the Minuet, which seems to have been introduced in the French Court at about the time of the king's marriage in 1660, the king himself being an incomparable dancer. In his book *Music and Image*, Richard Leppert explains:

---

[16] Edward Ward, *The Dancing Master, A Satyr* (London: A. Moore 1722), p. 3.
[17] See Richard Leppert, *Music and Image: Domesticity, Ideology and Socio-cultural Formation in Eighteenth Century England* (Cambridge: Cambridge University Press 1988), p. 75.

The minuet was a ritualized microcosmic social order, exactly replicating a real one. It demanded an exactingly prescribed behaviour. The dance was extraordinarily complicated, not because its steps in themselves were so difficult, but because it involved precise control over the whole body, from the carriage and turn of the head to the position of the arms, wrists, hands, legs and feet. By dancing the minuet in the prescribed manner (the only way permissible), the French aristocracy nightly affirmed *visually and formally* their submission to the King – and, equally important, they did so *silently*, moving without speech in time to the music and under the King's watchful eye.[18]

The ritual devised by the king provided for him to open the dance. He then went to his throne and watched. Any dancer who failed to perform the minuet to his satisfaction was banished from Court and lost his or her allowance.

By the time Louis took up residence at Versailles, in 1682, and probably under the influence of the Dauphin, a young man in his early twenties, he was willing to relax the regime a little and consider the introduction of dances from other cultures to complement but not to replace the stifling minuet. Noble visitors to the Court of his cousin Charles in London must have commented on the variety and liveliness of English dance. In 1684 an invitation was received by Isaac, one of the most respected English Dancing Masters, to visit the French Court and teach English country dances to the ladies of the court. In the following year, the French Dancing Master André Lorin was sent to London to study the English dances. He produced a book three years later entitled *Livre de contredance du Roy*, in which he refers to Isaac as 'Isaac d'Orléans', and says that he studied the dances in the same school where Isaac had learnt them. There is considerable confusion about this Isaac, as there were several persons attached to the royal household with that name, including two Children of the Chapel Royal, Peter and Bartholomew, whose voices broke in 1672 and 1677 respectively, and another much earlier Isaac who was apprenticed to the eccentric John Ogilby, who was a Dancing Master in Charles I's time. The distinguished Isaac became Queen Anne's Dancing Master, but seems to have been known by various titles, Monsieur Isaac, Mr Isaac, and Isaac d'Orléans. This last version seems akin to that of the foolish Mr Paris in Wycherley's play, the character who insisted on being addressed as 'Monsieur de Paris'. Like the fictional Paris, Isaac has no second name. He may of course have been the former chorister Peter, who would have been about twenty-six in 1684, and Peter and Bartholomew may both have been sons of John Ogilby's apprentice.

The school where Lorin studied is thought to have been in Holborn and to have been kept by Thomas Caverley, who enjoyed an exceptional reputation among his peers and former pupils. Lorin produced two books of *contredanse*, and no doubt other French Dancing Masters followed his example, as there was money to be made from the two-way traffic. The English dances were naturally

---

18 Leppert, p. 89.

subjected to French refinement in the process of transfer, and the *contredanse*, based on English country dance with its addictive rhythms, thus began to develop into the glory of baroque dance. Rameau, some would say, should have been an honorary Englishman.

'Monsieur' Isaac (which is how he was described by John Evelyn, whose daughter was his pupil) shared too in the benefit of the two-way traffic, because in London he was known as a specialist in French Court dance, and in his choreography of what were known as 'ball dances' he became a pioneer in the field of classical ballet technique.[19] It was Isaac and his younger contemporaries who introduced the minuet to the London dancing classes, thereby bringing into fashion in London the artificiality of the French style, although as Richard Steele reported in the following extract from *The Spectator*, it was the practice at balls in 1711 to begin with the formal dances and then relax into the informality of the traditional English dances. Steele wrote:

> The following letter is sent me by some substantial tradesman about Change
>
> SIR
>
> I am a man in years, and by an honest industry in the world have acquired enough to give my children a liberal education, though I was an utter stranger to it myself. My eldest daughter, a girl of sixteen, has for some time been under the tuition of Monsieur Rigadoon, a dancing-master in the city; and I was prevailed upon by her and her mother to go last night to one of his balls. I must own to you, Sir, that having never been at any such place before, I was very much pleased and surprised with that part of his entertainment which he called *French Dancing*. There were several young men and women, whose limbs seemed to have no other motion, but purely what the music gave them. After this part was over, they began a diversion which they call *country dancing*, and wherein there were also some things not disagreeable, and divers *emblematical figures*, composed, as I guess, by wise men, for the instruction of youth.
>
> Among the rest I observed one, which, I think, they call *Hunt the Squirrel*, in which while the woman flies, the man pursues her; but as soon as she turns, he runs away, and she is obliged to follow. The moral of this dance does, I think, very aptly recommend modesty and discretion to the female sex.
>
> But as the best institutions are liable to corruptions, so, Sir, I must acquaint you that very great abuses are crept in to this entertainment. I was amazed to see my girl handed by, and handing young fellows with so much

---

[19] A detailed study of 'Isaac' appears in Jennifer Martin's dissertation referred to above. She does however test one's credulity somewhat by suggesting that the well-known Isaac can be identified with the Isaac who was apprenticed to John Ogilby in or by 1631. In contradiction to this she quotes a remark by Edmund Pemberton, another well-known Dancing Master and apologist, writing in 1711, to the effect that a dancing master named Gorée 'had the honour to teach eight or nine Crown'd heads . . . during the Minority of Mr Isaac'. Jerome Gohorri was active in the 1670s and 1680s.

familiarity; and I could not have thought it had been in the child. . . . At last an impudent young dog bid the fiddlers play a dance called *Mol Pately*, and after having made two or three capers, ran to his partner, locked his arms in hers, and whisked her round cleverly above ground in such manner, that I who sat on one of the lowest benches, saw farther above her shoe than I can think fit to acquaint you of. I could no longer endure these enormities; wherefore just as my girl was going to be made a whirligig, I ran in, seized on the child, and carried her home.

I know not what you will say to this case at present, but am sure that had you been with me, you would have seen matter of great speculation.

I am

Yours, &c

I must confess I am afraid [Steele continues] that my correspondent had too much reason to be a little out of humour at the treatment of his daughter; but I conclude that he would have been much more so, had he seen one of those kissing dances, in which Will Honeycomb assures me they are obliged to dwell almost a minute on the fair one's lips, or they will be too quick for the music, and dance quite out of time.

I am not able however to give my final sentence against this diversion; and am of Mr Crowley's opinion, that so much of dancing, at least, as belongs to the behaviour and an handsome carriage of the body, is extremely useful, if not absolutely necessary.

As for country-dancing, it must indeed be confessed that the great familiarities between the two sexes on this occasion may sometimes produce very dangerous consequences; and I have thought that few ladies' hearts are so obdurate as not to be melted by the charms of music, the force of motion, and an handsome young fellow who is continually playing before their eyes, and convincing them that he has the perfect use of all his limbs. But as this kind of dance is the particular invention of our own country, and as every one is more or less a proficient in it, I would not discountenance it; but rather suppose it may be practised innocently by others, as well as myself, who am often partner to my landlady's eldest daughter.

This slightly abridged extract from *The Spectator* of 17 May 1711 summarises the problem of acceptance which faced the Dancing Masters and their way of life throughout their period of prominence, and the dilemma of the average Londoner, brought up in an age and environment of 'Middle-class Morality'. It also shows that in Steele the Dancing Masters had a fair and even-handed supporter.

After the Company's failure to obtain the new charter, the involvement of Dancing Masters in its activities seems to have waned fairly rapidly. Those who had their schools or gave private lessons in Holborn, Covent Garden, Mayfair and other fashionable new suburbs continued in a self-employed and unregulated fashion throughout the 18th century, becoming a favourite subject for caricature by Rowlandson and many of his contemporaries. Others were attracted to the theatre, and by necessity would have lived close to their place of work. In the City, as we shall see in the next chapter, there are signs of some professional training continuing, as young people of both sexes were still taught to dance through the system of apprenticeship in the Company. The girls were probably training to become professional dancers, the boys either to dance or to teach. And City-dwellers went on dancing, graciously or grotesquely, according to their ability and teaching, or their lack of it.

9

Metamorphosis

The first two Hanoverian kings, George I and George II, brought as their gift to England the political stability (one might almost say 'serenity' except that politics are never serene) which had been hoped for during the reigns of William and Mary, and Anne, but had never materialised. By 1715 the country was politically exhausted, after nearly two centuries of war and stratagem, between pope and monarch, between monarch and parliament (with the municipal corporations dragged in too, especially the City of London), and finally between Whig and Tory. Even after the 'Glorious Revolution' of 1688 hope of a permanent peace was deferred, owing to the nation's involvement in the continental land-war, involving movement and logistics unheard of in England since the Crusades. The great victory of Blenheim in 1704 was won by John Churchill, Duke of Marlborough, on the banks of the Danube, many hundreds of miles from home, with 9,000 British troops in his army of 56,000 men. At last, nine years later, with the Treaty of Utrecht, and with Louis XIV reaching the end of his devastating reign, there was peace in Europe for a time, and England was in a much better state economically than either its allies or its former enemies. The City of London had taken over the management of the government's war finance, and had not suffered economically as a result. Nor was there any noticeable interruption in the normal round of cultural diversions while the war continued. The Italian Opera thrived, there was a great variety of musical entertainment on offer,[1] and dancing was enjoying a tremendous vogue.

In some ways the political situation was very similar to that which preceded the 1590s, which was a golden decade for music, stimulated by loyalty to the Virgin Queen and relief at the ending of the threat from Spain. However in 1714 the death of Queen Anne and the change of dynasty seemed to eliminate any creative impetus of a celebratory nature which might otherwise have existed. Whether the situation would have been different if 'the immortal' Henry Purcell had not died in 1696 at the tragically early age of thirty-seven, is a speculative issue. During his life he had many friends and colleagues, but no real 'circle' or

---

[1]   See Michael Tilmouth, in *Royal Musical Association Research Chronicle*, no. 1 (1961).

prize pupils, who might have gathered round him and been nourished by his genius if he had enjoyed a full life-span. After his death there were of course many contemporary English composers of merit, but not of sufficient distinction to resist the invasion of Italian musicians and their repertoire (by which Purcell himself was influenced),[2] which had begun in the 1680s. But the epithet 'immortal' must have been attributed to Purcell because his music continued to feature strongly in the repertoire during the early years of the century.[3]

The interest excited by the Italians may help to explain why the view prevalent during the 20th century, that 'after Purcell there was nothing', would not have been shared by the musical *cognoscenti* of the time. The Italian musicians who flocked into London, bringing their new music with them, were enthusiastically received. In the early 18th century there was almost an Arcangelo Corelli cult, although Corelli never visited London himself. His compatriots became his evangelists, especially those who could teach the violin technique as practised by the maestro. Roger North wrote that the people are 'wedded to the solos airs and sonatas of Corelli', bitterly regretting what he called 'the improvement of music'. North, the frustrated amateur, was comfortable with his gentle viol consort music, and quite unable to cope with the complexity of the Italian import:

> Since it is arrived at such a pitch of perfection that even masters, unless of the prime cannot entertain us, the plain way becomes contemptible and ridiculous, therefore must need be laid aside. By this you may judge what profit the public hath from the improvement of music.[4]

Where North failed, many others succeeded, up to a level of competence good enough to enable them to participate as amateurs in ensemble playing whenever the opportunity arose. In addition there was a huge corpus of published music available to satisfy the amateur musicians, many of them self-taught from 'Tutor' books.[5]

With the end of the Stuart dynasty, the professional musicians found themselves in a new environment. The massive concentration of musical talent within the royal household of Charles II and his brother, and the financial outlay it had involved, had already been discouraged by William III, and in 1714 the King's Music was a pale shadow of its former glory. The Household music consisted of the Chapel Royal, the King's Trumpeters and Drums, and the King's and Queen's Bands, on a much reduced scale. The former Royal patronage was now either replaced by that of the nobility or institutionalised, and instead of the generous salaries paid (somewhat irregularly) to the royal musicians, the takings from

---

2 Duffy, p. 123.
3 Tilmouth. There is hardly a page relating to the period 1700–15 that does not contain one or more announcements of a concert including Purcell's music.
4 Wilson, ed., *Roger North on Music*, p. 12.
5 Roger Fiske, Chapter 1 of *The Blackwell History of Music in Britain: The Eighteenth Century*, p. 4.

public or subscription concerts or theatre performance (together with tuition fees) became the principal source of revenue.

While the switch of patronage was, in a sense, a natural development in a more open society, it was one of the reasons, together with the lack of a proper system of advanced musical education, why the work of English composers disappeared from the international repertoire for the next two hundred years. For most of the 18th century in continental Europe there was still a role for the 'Court Composer', who was of course a servant of his royal or grand-ducal patron, and subject to the relentless discipline associated with the office of *Kapellmeister*. It was surely no coincidence that each of the four great 18th century German and Austrian composers had to conform, at some time in their lives, to the same exacting regime under which the *Kapellmeister* was expected to work, forcing their creative genius into a state of sleepless invention, and fully extending, and thereby improving, the resources available to them for performance. George Frideric Handel was one of them, and although no such pressure existed in London, the intense productivity as shown by his London compositions may owe something to the discipline acquired at the Elector's Court in Hanover.

The fact that Handel was part of London life for more than forty years, and polite society could claim him as their own, was bound to have an adverse effect on 'the home product'. What scope was there for native talent when Handel was there? English composers throughout the 18th century had to stand in the shadow first of Handel and then of J.C. Bach and Haydn. Many of their works, long forgotten, are now being rediscovered and analysed, but still infrequently performed. For their contemporaries, the concert patrons and theatregoers, their music was pleasant and cultivated, but seldom to be compared with the great foreign masters who had chosen to live and work in London, and for whom the snobbery of society demanded uncritical adulation.

The musical taste of Georgian society in London, which now replaced the royal preferences of Stuart kings, was defined by the dilettanti groups who formed themselves into 'Academies' and similar bodies, in order to patronise and promote, and often to practise, the type of music to which they were principally devoted. Although the founders in each case tended to be purist, and therefore resistant to what was taking place elsewhere, one suspects that the majority of members and subscribers were very happy to take their pick of concerts or theatrical entertainments according to their fancy, which meant that for them there was a great range of 'attractions' on offer. Of the Academies the first in time was the 'Royal Academy of Music' established in 1719 by fifty 'notables', under the governorship of the Duke of Newcastle, specifically to establish Italian Opera as a regular feature of London cultural life.[6] It achieved nine seasons at the King's

6   Rosamund McGuinness and H. Diack Johnstone, in *The Blackwell History of Music in Britain: The Eighteenth Century*, p. 119.

12. 'The Anacreontic Society', a harsh caricature by Gilray. The member on the left has the music for the Society's 'Ode' in front of him, which was transformed into the National Anthem of the United States of America.

Theatre Haymarket, with operas by Handel, Bononcini and Ariosti, before being upstaged and bankrupted by the runaway success of John Rich's first production of *The Beggar's Opera* at the Lincoln's Inn Fields Theatre in 1728.

The Castle Society was formally constituted in 1724, having previously been an informal group, and it continued in existence for about sixty years, meeting originally at the Castle Tavern in St Paul's Churchyard, then in the 1750s in Haberdashers Hall, and finally from 1764 at the King's Arms in Cornhill, a well-known musical venue.[7] According to Hawkins it was a society where young men had to be seen if they wanted to get on in the world. He remarked that:

> many young persons of professions and trades that depended on a numerous acquaintance were induced by motives of interest to become members.[8]

7   McGuinness and Johnstone, p. 37.
8   Elkin, p. 50.

This sounds like the distinguishing mark of a City-based club.

In 1726 the 'Academy of Vocal Music' was founded, very soon changing its name to the 'Academy of Ancient Music', and dedicated, in sharp contrast to the 'Royal Academy', to the preservation of old music, originally looking back as far as the 16th century, but arriving gradually at a compromise with the recent past, so that by the end of the century in its last years the work of Handel and his contemporaries was quite acceptable.[9] The Academy distinguished itself from the other societies by setting up a true academy in the modern sense; in 1735 it opened a music school for boys under Dr Pepusch, offering them an education which 'would fit them as well for trades and businesses as the profession of music'. Hawkins says that many of those pupils became afterwards 'eminent professors in the science'.[10]

Even more narrowly selective was the 'Madrigal Society' formed in 1741 by John Immyns, a lawyer whose youthful indiscretions caused him to be disbarred. Immyns was a member of the Academy of Ancient Music, and had a strong counter-tenor voice, but his principal attribute was his ability to copy music 'with amazing speed and correctness'.[11] The society's original members being mostly city workers, it was established, and has faithfully continued, to sing madrigals and motets of the 16th and 17th centuries and virtually nothing else.

From 1730 there was the 'Philharmonic Society' or 'Society of Gentlemen Performers of Music', composed entirely of amateur players (except for its leader Michael Festing), which met weekly at the Crown and Anchor Tavern in the Strand during the winter. And for other amateurs there were the informal glee and catch clubs, some of which used the Crown and Anchor also.

After the huge popular impact of *The Beggars Opera*, another group of aristocratic patrons tried, not very successfully, to revive the Italian Opera with Handel as their principal composer. These called themselves 'The Opera of the Nobility', and survived four seasons at the King's Theatre Haymarket from 1733 to 1737.

The most important society, because it was open only to professionals, and had a benevolent purpose, was the 'Society of Musicians' (from 1790 'the Royal Society of Musicians') which came into existence through the efforts of Michael Festing and others[12] in 1738, and immediately enjoyed not only the generous patronage of Handel, but also that of Dr Pepusch, Thomas Arne and William Boyce. The first London performance of *Messiah* in 1743 was presented by Handel in aid of the society. The 'RSM' and the Madrigal Society are the only survivors from this proliferation of 18th century academies.

Later in the century, the 'Anacreontic Society' was established in 1766; it was a private club of amateur performers which included merchants and bankers

---

9   McGuinness and Johnstone, pp. 18–19.
10 Hawkins, p. 886.
11 Hawkins, p. 887. Hawkins appears to contradict himself over Immyns' voice. Having first described it as strong he later said that it was 'cracked'.
12 One of whom was Thomas Vincent; see p. 153.

among its members, with strengthening from a handful of professionals. Ten years later the 'Concert of Ancient Music' (defined as any music more than twenty years old) was formed, with King George III as patron, reflecting perhaps the dwindling energies of the old Academy, which gave place to the 'Concert' during the 1790s. The Concert, at the king's suggestion, took on the responsibility for an annual performance of *Messiah* after the original 1784 Commemorative Festival, the musicians to give their services free and all proceeds to go to the Royal Society of Musicians. Its late patron's instructions were observed by the Concert until its demise in 1848.[13]

Some time around 1730, to this formidable list of social, patronal, organisational and performing bodies, one very ancient institution was added, the Worshipful Company of Musicians, which appears to have then turned itself into something more akin to a musical society, as its former role and purpose were rapidly evaporating.

Although it was a dramatic change of direction for the Company, it was by no means unique in the history of livery companies at that time. Many of them had lost control of their trades or craft, and those which were well-endowed, like the Drapers and Grocers, were concentrating more on the administration of their charitable funds, while maintaining their customary forms of hospitality and engaging in City politics. The Musicians were however in a rather different position, as the change was quick and sudden, and was brought about by the failure to obtain the new Charter which would have given the Company's Dancing Masters an active supervisory role beyond the limits of the City.[14]

For the first time in this narrative the events described are traceable in the Company's own records, not yet by any means complete, but clear enough in their general picture. The surviving records begin, in the form of Renter Wardens' Accounts, in 1712.[15] These continued until 1754, by which time there is supporting evidence from Registers and Quarterage books, as well as the Clerk's Accounts, and no lack of primary sources thereafter, the Court Minute Books beginning in 1772. The irony is that as the records become more detailed, the company's activities become less interesting, at any rate until near the end of the 19th century.

We should therefore pause for a moment, before moving forward with the Company into Georgian times, and pick up what smatterings of information we can find about its activities during its last years as a craft guild. We have already noted the reinvigorating participation of the dancing masters, and can safely assume that this continued until the bad moment in 1718 when they were admonished by the Court of Aldermen for trying to obtain a new Royal Charter for the Company without first approaching the Aldermen. This was a turning-

---

[13] Betty Matthews, *The Royal Society of Musicians of Great Britain: A History, 1738–1988* (London: published by the Society 1988), p. 24.

[14] See pp. 127–8.

[15] Guildhall Library MS 3091.

point for the dancing masters who sink into insignificance thereafter, so far as the Company is concerned. But what of the 'professors', the practising musicians? During this period the Company dominated the City Waits, as it had done during the last part of the previous century. Between 1700 and 1720 eight of the ten City Waits appointed were members of the Company, some of whom appear in the contemporary Livery lists. The Company, it seems, was being run as an active partnership between and for the benefit of these two groups. The numbers were small, and one suspects that it was quite an exclusive society.

The City musicians and the dancing masters appear to have had at least one common interest, because the concert records for this period show that most of the City concerts were given in the Dancing Rooms.[16] It was the custom throughout the 18th century to give 'benefit' concerts for individual musicians, and one of the Dancing Room concerts, given on 28 February 1710 was held at Couch's Dancing Room in Walbrook for the benefit of James Graves and John Garee [or Geare]. Nicholas Couch and the two musicians were all Liverymen of the Company.

The Court and Livery had fought some hard and expensive battles during the 1690s. Beginning with the petition in 1694, which eventually produced an Act of Common Council in 1699, they then went on to sue John Groscourt with the object of closing down his unlicensed dancing school. Having lost the case, it was necessary to amend the Act, and this was achieved with the cooperation of the Court of Common Council at the end of 1700.[17] We do not know the cost of all this activity, but to persevere to the end would have needed a lot of mutual support within the small Company, and would have created a strong sense of camaraderie. One little custom of which we are given a glimpse before it was abandoned, in the first year of the Renter Warden's Account Book, and which may have reflected the bond which had united the members during this period, was the practice of selling a silver spoon to each new freeman of the Company, for the sum of thirteen shillings and fourpence. Another tantalising piece of information comes from a book entitled 'Pietas Londiniensis or The Present Ecclesiastical State of London', where it is said:

A Musick-Sermon on St Cecilia's Day, or November 23, given now by private Gentlemen of the Parish; but formerly it was kept up by the Company of Musicians and Parish Clerks in London.[18]

This was written in 1714, and referred to St Bride's, Fleet Street. Until 1703, as has already been mentioned, it was the Musical Society which ran this event, together with the concert and feast at Stationers' Hall. Either the writer, James Paterson, was confusing the parties involved (which seems unlikely as he men-

---

16 See Tilmouth for some of the references, e.g. pp. 43, 44, 48, 58, 64. From 1715 onwards the concerts were mostly held in City Livery Halls.
17 See p. 127.
18 James Paterson, *Pietas Londiniensis* (1714).

tions the Parish Clerks) or the Company and the Parish Clerks assumed responsibility for the service at St Bride's for a certain number of years from 1703.

Two lists survive of members of the Livery between the years 1696 and 1720. Neither of them are Company documents. The first is an 'Association Oath' in which the members of the Company declared their loyalty to King William III and to his heir Princess Anne.[19] The second is an extract from a master list in alphabetical order of all the Livery of the City in 1700. A collation of the two lists appears in Appendix 8. It will be noted that the names included eight (or possibly nine) Dancing Masters and five City Waits. There were more Waits who belonged to the Company but were not of the Livery.

From the lists it appears that there were thirty-two Liverymen in 1696 (although there is a note at the foot of the document which reads: 'The rest of the members are in the King's service or could not be found'!) and thirty-four Liverymen in 1700, plus or minus one or two.[20] By an Act of Common Council of 1697, regulations were in force prohibiting any freeman of an 'inferior' company from being elected to the Livery of his company unless he had an estate of at least £500 (for the Great Twelve the minimum was £1,000).[21] We do not know how many liverymen of the Musicians had been elected before this qualification was brought into effect, but one suspects that some of the thirty-four in 1700 might have had difficulty in showing the necessary wealth. We are looking at a currency in which £5 would buy dinner at a City tavern for the whole Court, and it cost £6 to entertain the Livery on election day!

Four members on the 1700 Livery list subsequently held the office of Renter Warden, Richard Stanton from 1712 to 1714, Joseph Mackeness for only a month or so in 1714, Thomas Nicholl from 1714 to 1715, and Richard Loyd from 1720 to 1721. Although the Renter Warden was in a sense the Company's treasurer, it was not yet the practice to appoint people to that office for their wisdom and financial acumen. It was a dogsbody job, to be undertaken by someone who was keen to be elected to the Court, and was willing to do penance to get there. The ability to keep a good set of accounts therefore varied considerably from one holder to the next, and it is not surprising that in the 1740s regular entries begin to appear: 'Paid the Clerk for making up this account'. Nevertheless although the Clerk may have produced the rough notes, the actual inscribing in the book was still done by the Renter Warden.

The Renter Warden had to collect and record all the quarterage received from freemen, as well as the fines, which were not just for the freedom or livery, but also included one shilling fines levied on Assistants (Court members) for lateness or non-attendance. Fees were collected on the binding of an apprentice or the 'turning-over' of an apprentice to a new master. Once the issue of silver

---

[19] PRO C213/171/50.
[20] Alastair Crewdson gave the number of Livery in 1700 as nineteen, but does not mention the source of his information.
[21] Johnson, vol. III, p. 432.

spoons had been abandoned in 1713, the freeman's fine was fixed at eighteen shillings and fourpence.

Summarising the Renter Wardens' Account Book as a whole, three things stand out and deserve to be examined in more detail. The first is the activity of a small number of women who were free of the Company, and who were busily binding apprentices throughout the period of the book. The second is the frequent reappearance throughout the book of Richard Sleep, who became Charles Burney's father-in-law in 1749, and about whom his granddaughter Fanny had not a good word to say. The third is the remarkable intervention of Thomas Eyre, who should be the first to receive our attention, because on the evidence of the Account Book (and there is none other) it was due to his energies and, probably, his vision that the Company was saved from extinction and found its new role.

The evidence for the chaotic state to which the Company had been reduced before Thomas Eyre took over can be briefly described. A Mr Joshua Shepherd was Renter Warden from 1716 to 1718. The last entry in his accounts, for 10 October 1718, reads 'for defraying the Charges of obtaining the New Charter: £22 3s 11d'. The account was duly audited on 13 October by six members of the Court. Then there is a gap. No new Renter Warden was appointed for 1718/19 and only eight entries were made for a four-month period in 1720 by the next Warden, 'Sone' Nicholl. These were left unaudited. The accounts for 1720/1 when Richard Loyd was Renter Warden are short, but complete and audited. Then there is a blank page, and the next heading, in a fine and disciplined hand, reads as follows:

THE ACCOUNT of Mr Thomas Eyre Renter Warden and present Master of the Worshipful Company of Musicians London

and runs from 1725 to 1734, a period of nine years. Allowing for one or two assumptions, it appears that first a substantial payment, equivalent to eleven livery fines, had to be made in 1718 in connection with the failed attempt to obtain a charter. As the Company at this time appears to have had inadequate reserves this left it in debt, and in great disfavour with the City Corporation, and as a result no one was prepared to take on the job of Renter Warden in 1719. Sone Nicholl made an attempt at it in 1720, but gave up after three months, although a Michaelmas dinner was held at the Swan Tavern during that time. The next year looks more normal, the only special feature being the 'continuance' of the Master (whose name we do not know); in other words he agreed to serve a second year in that office. Then apart from one eloquently blank page there is absolutely nothing on record in the book from October 1721 until November 1725, a gap of four years. It must have been a very bleak time. Richard Loyd in 1720 records in the book the only instance of a Liveryman, Mr Walker, being fined for refusing to come on the Court of Assistants. The good standing in which the Company had been held in the City before the events of 1718, as evidenced by the number of members appointed to the City Waits, was now lost. In the period from 1720 to 1730 there were five admissions to the Waits, only one of whom was a Musician. One of the new Waits in the 1720s was John Lucket, who was described as a 'Scrivener'. In 1715 he is shown as a Liveryman of the Musicians, who had taken advantage of the Company's practice of making small loans to its members. He must have lost all hope of being appointed a City Wait as a Musician by the time the vacancy arose in 1724, and joined the Scriveners instead.

Just to complicate matters the City Waits, of whom the Musicians were now a minority, were responsible in 1724 for a lawsuit in the name of the Company (or 'the Chamberlain of London') against the blind organist of St Giles Cripplegate, Henry Green, not because of his duties there, but because he had been employed by the stewards of the Festival of the Sons of the Clergy, and for that reason, it was claimed, should have taken up the City Freedom. Judgment was given for the Company, but not surprisingly Green became a freeman of another Company, the Leathersellers.[22] If the case had been heard one year later we would have had a note of the Company's costs, but it may be that the Waits underwrote the costs themselves.

How valuable a Court Minute Book would now be for these years. One can only guess what may have happened. Were there voices on the Court, perhaps some of the senior members, who were lamenting that nothing could ever be the same again, and that there was no point in carrying on? Had the Dancing Masters in the Company been blamed for what had occurred, lost interest and migrated westwards? Would any more City musicians join the Company now that the City Corporation had taken offence and was selecting its Waits from other companies? Was there any way in which to stem the flow of the Italians who were taking all the business away?[23] It must have been clear to a few at least of the Court members that the Company had three options; either to shut down, or to struggle on as a guild of professional musicians, effectively limited to those working in the City who lacked the ambition to join the Waits, or to open up the Company to music-lovers like any other new music society, at the same time providing a cheap entry for people of any description and occupation who wished to carry on business in the City and needed to acquire the Freedom (this remained a statutory requirement until the 19th century).[24] There was also the benefit available to Liverymen of the parliamentary and City franchise and the right to attend Common Hall at Midsummer and Michaelmas.

Enter the White Knight, Thomas Eyre. We know very little about him except that he was elected to the Livery in 1715 and to the Court in 1720, and by his own statement was Master in 1725. It is a fair assumption that he was the champion of the third option, and in taking on the task of Renter Warden/Treasurer

---

22 Donovan Dawe, *Organists of the City of London, 1666–1850* (London: published by the author, 1983), p. 8.

23 Exactly two hundred years later a Court Committee was appointed 'to stem the tide of foreign musicians'! (Court Minutes, 14 July 1925)

24 See p. 164.

for nine years he was prepared to accept the challenge of making it work. The Account Book shows a dramatic change in the level of admissions to the Freedom and election to the Livery from the date that he took office. During the years 1712–20 the number of new freemen each year had varied between nil and four, the total number being fifteen. From 1725–54, 568 new freemen were admitted, an average of nearly twenty a year. Eyre himself brought in thirty-nine freemen during his Wardenship, but his successor John Elmes recorded one hundred and twelve in two years, nearly three times the average rate.

The question naturally springs to mind: 'How did Thomas Eyre pull it off?' The bare accounts tell us nothing about his personality; but it is likely that he was a charismatic person who identified an opportunity and proceeded to exploit it. He seems to have decided to popularize the Company by providing a lot of entertainment. Whereas the normal pattern of Company feasting was to have a Stewards' Feast once a year, and a party of some kind on 'Election Day' at Michaelmas, Eyre appears to have doubled the amount of feasting in 1726 and 1728. The entries do not specify whether the costs incurred were for Court or Livery functions, but in either case it is likely that guests were invited who may have been potential candidates for the freedom and, in appropriate cases, the Livery as well.

The Company obviously had a 'fast lane' procedure which they would operate when a suitable candidate came into sight, whereby all or most of the relevant fines could be paid at the same time, and the candidate might find himself in the Livery, on the Court and saddled with Stewardship all on the same day. This happened to John Bosworth, later to become City Chamberlain, in 1716, although he appears already to have been a freeman of the Company. He paid £8 for his Livery, Steward's and Assistant's fines. Edward Bott, in 1729, went through the freedom as well, paying £7-18-4 for 'freedom and all offices.' Bott appears to have been given a £2 discount, as the Livery fine and Assistant's fine at that time were both set at £2, and the Steward's at £5, so he should have been charged £9-18-4. Robert Holmes in 1735 was less fortunate, as he had to pay for his freedom, his livery and his stewardship all on the same day, which cost him £12-18-4, and he would still have his Court fine to pay if elected. The Livery and Assistants' fines were increased in that year to £5 each, and the Steward's to £7.

In helping to put the Company back on its feet, Thomas Eyre had another card to play, although the accounts suggest that he only put it on the table just before his tenure of office came to an end. It was a financial 'carrot' of which any 20th century salesman would have approved. If one is interpreting the Renter Wardens' book correctly, it had been the practice to collect the freeman's fine or fee (disregarding the silver spoon) of 18s 4d, and against this entry small items of expense sometimes appear on the debit side, which relate to the cost of arranging for the freeman to take up the City freedom. Eyre continued this practice until 1734; for example in that year he made an entry: 'Paid expenses making four free by redemption 11s 8d'. Then suddenly on 20 August 1734 there appears the statement: 'Paid for twenty-five members made free by redemption £26-5-0d'. This corresponds to the sum of one guinea per head which was thereafter paid to the Clerk by the Company, leaving the Clerk to arrange for the freeman's enrolment in the Chamberlain's Court. The new arrangement meant that the new freemen, including the 112 admitted during the period of office of John Elmes, paid the Company 18s 4d for the freedom, and the Clerk was then paid an inclusive sum of £1 1s on their behalf out of the Company's funds. Effectively therefore they were receiving a contribution of 2s 8d from the Company towards the Clerk's fees and expenses. Thomas Eyre and his colleagues must have recognised that by increasing the other fines from £2 to £5 and from £5 to £7 respectively, and by the big increase in quarterage collected, at two shillings a quarter, from all members of the Company including the freemen, the concessions made to new members would be easily affordable, and would yield a greater return, the more so as the number of freemen continued to increase. The increase in numbers would also ensure that more apprentices would be bound within the Company, thereby providing an element of continuity. There were in fact 259 apprentice bindings during the period of the Account Book, of whom twenty-nine were pre-Eyre and therefore likely to be predominantly apprentice musicians. In the latter period there was a sprinkling of musical apprentices. These will be considered with the professional musicians who still belonged to the Company around the middle of the 18th century. Most of the Company's apprentices would have been in other trades.

To complete the picture, during the years 1725–55, 115 members of the Company were elected to the Livery, but there was only a handful of musicians among them.

One of John Elmes' first entries in 1734 relates to the purchase of 'a Book to enter the Members'. This book does not appear to have survived, but its sequel, dating from 1743–69, is in the Guildhall Library[25] and gives the address and occupation of the persons who joined the Company during that time. The trades represented within the Livery are very diverse. Of the traditional City occupations, there were seven Drapers, four Grocers, five Mercers, five Haberdashers and three Vintners. The Company was also distinguished by the support of Thomas Gates, the City Marshal, the Keeper of the Guildhall, and a gentleman from the Lord Mayor's Office. There were two 'Gentlemen' or 'Esquires' and fourteen with no description, who may or may not have been persons of substance who had no need to work. Among the more exotic trades there were three cheesemongers, five brokers, four tobacconists, one excise officer, one oyster-seller, one indigo-maker and two oilmen. There were nineteen musicians in the list of newly admitted freemen, who will be reserved for closer consideration, but first we must return to the year 1711 when Richard Sleep was appointed a City Wait, and follow his rather chequered career through to 1755 when he surren-

---

[25] GL MS 3097.

dered that office, and was no longer being paid for 'bringing the instruments to the Stewards' Feast'.

On 23 October 1711, Sleep, described as 'citizen and musician', was 'admitted' a Wait, in place of Thomas Sharples, a vintner, who surrendered the same date.[26] At that date Sleep was, it appears, a freeman of the Company.

Four years later it is evident that Sleep was in trouble. The Accounts of Renter Warden Stephenson show that on 18 November 1715 he paid out 2s 8d for the expenses of 'those members who attended the Lord Mayor with Mr Sleep', and on the next day another 11s 6d for those 'members that attended the Lord Mayor with Mr Sleep and the Officer in the morning and afternoon'. Whatever had occurred made it necessary for the Company to take Counsel's Opinion, and Stephenson paid 10s 9d to Mr Major the 'Councellor' on 7 December. Two months later, on 7 February, there was more money to be paid for those who attended the Court of Aldermen with Mr Sleep, and 3s 6d 'for summoning Mr Sleep before the Court of Aldermen'.[27]

It looks as though the Aldermen fined Sleep for his offence, whatever it was, because on 24 February he borrowed £5 from the Company on his bond, which was then repaid by him the following November. The fact that the Company had become so involved suggests that Sleep's offence in some way implicated the Company, and if the Renter Warden was willing to lend Sleep the money to pay the fine, it is possible that this meant that the Company's hands were not absolutely clean.

The accounts for 1718 show that the Company had to attend the Lord Mayor once again, for reasons unknown, 'with Mr Thompson and Mr Hall', but there is no reason to suppose that Sleep was involved also on this occasion, nor when the Court of Aldermen called up the Company early in 1719 in connection with the affair of the Charter.[28]

In October 1720 Richard Sleep paid his Livery fine of £2, a sign that past misdemeanours had been forgiven, although there is no clear evidence that he was ever asked to serve as Renter Warden or Steward. However there is a possibility that he came on to the Court and became Master during the blank years 1721–25, as this would explain why his name heads the list of auditors for Thomas Eyre's accounts in 1735. The case against Henry Green in 1724 brought by the City Waits in the name of the Company may suggest that Sleep was responsible for bringing these proceedings as one of the senior Waits and Master of the Company. His name next appears in a note of a petition recorded in the Repertories for 23 November 1725:[29]

---

26 CL Rep 115, p. 290. Sharples appears to have been reappointed in 1714.
27 A recent search in the City Records Office at Guildhall failed to locate any surviving record of this incident.
28 CL Rep 122, p. 97.
29 CL Rep 130, p. 26.

Petition of John Lewis, citizen and clothworker, that he had made an agreement with Richard Sleep and others of the City's Music to permit him to play at the Aldgate Watch at the usual hours of the night and at the customary seasons. Although he can fully comply with the terms of the agreement the Waits deny him the benefit of it and forbid him to pursue the same.

Order that both parties appear at the next Court.

There is no record that anything further was heard of this matter. One suspects that Sleep had exceeded his authority in delegating part of the Waits' duties and functions to Lewis, and it would have done neither party any good to have the case heard by the Court of Aldermen. Some settlement of the dispute must have taken place before the return date of the summons.

The next generation of the Sleep family now begins to appear in the records. On 21 November 1732, Francis Sleep 'citizen and musician' was admitted 'one of the eight City Waits'.[30] According to the account book he did not pay his Freedom fine to the Company until the following day, so there is a discrepancy in the records, either in his description as 'Musician' as of the 21st (the day before he was admitted), or in the date when he received his freedom (Father would no doubt have talked his way out of any difficulty which may have arisen). Esther, Charles Burney's future wife, and her sister Martha were admitted to the freedom by patrimony in 1747.

In 1736 there is an entry relating to the Stewards' Feast which reads 'Paid bringing the instruments to the George in Ironmonger Lane 5s'. Three years later a fuller entry for 21 March 1739 reads:

> Paid to Mr Richard Sleep as by order of the Court for defraying the charges of por-
> terage &c in carrying the instruments of music   £1 10s

Similar entries are repeated every time there was a Stewards' Feast until the end of the book, and indeed the last of such entries, in the year 1754, appears in the next account book. There appears to have been a mix-up in 1751 when Sleep put in a Bill which the Renter Warden queried, possibly on the grounds that there had been no feast to which it could relate. Sleep went away with 18s 6d instead of the usual thirty shillings.

Porterage charges for instruments of music are of little interest as items of expenditure in the normal way, but here it is noteworthy that during this period the accounts make no mention of any payment of musicians' fees. The first note of such payment was in 1756, when Sleep had given up and John Ward, a Livery-men and City Wait, was paid three guineas 'for Music at the Stewards' Feast'. Who then had been playing the instruments up to that time? Either it must have been visiting professionals who were prepared to give their services free (although in that case one would have expected to see some reference to their expenses), or it was the Livery themselves, and this was probably what did

---

30 CL Rep 137, pp. 31–2.

happen, and after each Dinner the party turned into an impromptu music session, in which all members who wished to take part could do so, whether professional or amateur.

In 1742 Sleep submitted his own petition to the Court of Aldermen. An entry in the Repertories for 24 February 1741 (old style dating) reads as follows:

> On the petition of Richard Sleep that he was admitted City Wait in 1711 and became senior in 1727 since which time the places are very much reduced in value by reason of the discontinuance of sundry entertainments, it is ordered that in consideration of his long service and the hardship in having lost the use of one of his eyes, he shall have the benefit of making one person free of the City by redemption.[31]

The award made by the Aldermen seems hardly worth making, but there must have been some special value in it for Sleep. The comment about the 'places being very much reduced' seems to be confirmed by the City's own records. Apart from their customary ceremonial duties when in attendance on the Lord Mayor and the Sheriffs, the only regular official events in which the Waits were now involved and for which they received special fees were the Courts of Conservancy, at which the Lord Mayor exercised his supervisory and judicial authority in relation to the lower reaches of the Thames as far as the Medway, going about on the official Barge in which he and his officers were provided with musical entertainment by the Waits. In 1734 this took six days and nights and the Waits were collectively paid £50. The usual amount was £20 per court once or twice a year, but in 1738 the Waits were only paid £23 3s 'with two French Horns at the four Courts of Conservancy'.[32] The amount was increased to £32 16s 6d in 1739 and reduced again to £26 6s in 1740, which indicates that the Waits were being paid according to the time actually spent in attendance.

In 1749 Richard Sleep and the other Waits submitted another petition, but 'no order was made',[33] so the substance of the petition remains undisclosed. The names of the Waits on that date are given as Richard Sleep, John Jenkins, Francis Sleep, Edward Jenkins, Corbett Neeves, James Smith, James Jenkins and William Jenkins. The Sleeps, father and son, and Edward Jenkins were Musicians, Neeves was a Butcher, Smith a Clothworker, and the other three Jenkins' were Haberdashers, although Richard Sleep had taken James as his apprentice in 1735 before turning him over to his father John. The Sleep and Jenkins families were therefore very close.

By that date Sleep would have been about seventy years old. He was a senior City Wait and a Liveryman, he had three children who were free of the Company, one of whom was also a Wait. He was blind in one eye, and not well off. He was one of the first subscribers to the Society of Musicians, appearing in the sub-

---

[31] CL Rep 145, p. 122.
[32] CL Rep 142, p. 468.
[33] CL Rep 153, p. 434.

scription lists for 1739, 1742, 1744 and 1755. For at least ten years Sleep had made himself responsible for the important but not very dignified task of getting the instruments to the Stewards' Feast. We cannot be sure that he had served on the Court or been Master (although he may have held this office at some time during the unrecorded years 1721–25), as there is no record of his having paid the Assistant's fine.[34] Nevertheless he was appointed quite regularly to the Audit Committee who had to approve the outgoing Renter Warden's accounts and sign them off. All other Committee members were Assistants. If therefore he had not served on the Court this would suggest some special status in the Company, although not a very enviable one. In 1749 his daughter Esther married Charles Burney, who in the same year became organist of St Dionis Backchurch in Fenchurch Street, and was the regular harpsichordist for the 'New Concerts' being given in the King's Arms, Cornhill. Because of these appointments and through his father-in-law's persuasion Burney took up the freedom of the Company on 3 July.

Sleep had had an eventful life. It was not particularly distinguished, but did it really deserve his granddaughter's acrimonious comment: 'the Male parent was not more wanting in goodness, probity, and conduct, than the Female was perfect in all'?[35]

What had he done – or, more precisely, what had Burney told his daughter Fanny that her grandfather had done? Burney was a terrible snob; he must have been only too pleased to have been 'obliged for health reasons' to escape from his father-in-law's influence in 1751 and move to Lynn in Norfolk. When he returned to London in 1760 it was not to the City.

In contrast to the Company membership at the beginning of the century when most or all were musicians or dancing masters, the lists fifty years later included just four or five professional musicians in the Livery, two of whom, Richard Sleep and Thomas Vincent, were very senior. More recent members were John Ward who provided the music in 1756, and had been admitted a City Wait the previous year, and John Young, who was violinist in the King's Band, Music Master at Christ's Hospital and organist of Christ Church Newgate. None of the other nineteen musicians shown in the second membership book (1743–69) came into the Livery, despite the fact that three of them, Timothy Smart, William Burnett and William Barton were City Waits, and two of them, Thomas Perkins and Timothy Smart, had been apprenticed in the Company. By 1794 there were only two professional musicians in the Livery, and fourteen in the list of freemen.

Any attempt to chart this drop in professional membership since the beginning of the century is made more difficult by the incomplete records in the early pages of the Renter Wardens' Account Book. From 1714 to 1720 the names of the

---

[34] Dawe (p. 12) states that Sleep was a Warden of the Company in 1747 and probably Master in 1749. I can find no evidence to support this in the Renter Wardens' accounts.

[35] *Memoirs of Dr Burney, arranged by his daughter Madame d'Arblay* (Edward Moxon 1832), vol. I, p. 63.

apprentices are not given, which if known would show which of the new freemen who had completed their apprenticeship during Thomas Eyre's 'reign' as Renter Warden were admitted as professional musicians. In Eyre's own accounts the names of the apprentices are given, but not their masters, which creates the same problem. What is apparent is that a very few of the professionals did take the training of apprentices seriously, and their names appear regularly through the book. First among these was the Holt family, who seem to have kept their Dancing School going long after the other Dancing Masters in the Company had faded away. It was obviously a family concern and there were six members of the family in the Company. There was Walter Holt senior, who had been Master in 1694, and whose widow may have been Ann Holt who took an apprentice in 1714. There was Walter Holt Junior who took one apprentice in 1715 and two more in 1717 (the old rule of only one apprentice seems to have been abandoned, although most masters limited themselves to not more than two at a time). There was Mary Holt, probably a sister of the younger Walter, who took apprentices in 1715, 1740 and 1744, William Holt (one in 1720), and Margaret Holt who was the most active, and was perhaps the daughter of the younger Walter. Between 1735 and 1752 she took seven apprentices, all girls who, one assumes, were aspiring professional dancers: Mary Cole, Estor Swynson, Honoria Lydgould, Susan Mulcaster, Elizabeth Ekins, Jane Burney and Eliza Ann Summers. There were other free-women in the Company who were taking apprentices, but there is nothing to indicate whether or not they were musicians. It seems however that for a woman living or working in the City at this time the principal advantage of being free of a Livery Company was the right to bind apprentices and teach them a trade or craft to their mutual benefit. The right to the freedom was limited to unmarried daughters and widows of freemen. By City custom an unmarried woman who was free of the Company lost her Freedom upon marriage. The custom was reflecting reality.

Of the 'serious' musicians, from the period beginning in 1734 when the names of both master and apprentice are known, the first to note is Abraham Adcock, who is shown in the RSM records as playing the bassoon, horn, trumpet, and violin, as well as being an organ-builder.[36] William Jenkins was apprenticed to him in 1737, although by the time of his appointment as a City Wait in 1747 he was a Haberdasher, like his brother James. Jenkins was a trumpeter.[37] Adcock's next apprentice in 1739 was Thomas Perkins, who took up the freedom of the Company in 1760. Adcock had another apprentice in 1752 named Eaton Pether, but his subsequent career is not recorded.

Thomas Vincent had been a City Wait since 1726, and became Renter Warden in 1738. He was a bassoonist and a military bandsman. He was one of the founders of the Society of Musicians (having been with Michael Festing and Charles

---

[36] *Members of the Royal Society of Musicians 1738–1984* (Royal Society of Musicians 1985) p. 14.
[37] *RSM*, p. 81.

Weideman in the Orange Coffee House on that famous day when the orphan children of their late colleague Kytch were seen driving donkeys through the Haymarket). In the same year, 1738, he took his son Thomas, an oboist, as an apprentice within the Company. The younger Thomas later became a pupil of Sammartini, the Prince of Wales' private composer, and rose to be one of the leading players of the day, as well as a composer of 'solos' which could be played either on the oboe or the violin.[38] By this time Thomas junior had left the City, and never entered the Company, even as a freeman. From 1765 to 1767 he tried his hand at theatre management as a partner at the King's Theatre, Haymarket.

In the Ward family John Ward senior apprenticed his son John in 1744, and after that it sometimes becomes difficult to distinguish between them, especially as the younger Ward became a City Wait in 1755, three months before his father, who took Richard Sleep's place when he surrendered. William Ward was apprenticed to one of them in 1754; the date suggests that he was a younger brother, and not the first of the next generation. John Ward junior was a violinist,[39] but what John senior and William played is not apparent.

Finally there are two organists, Goodwin Starling and William Selby. It was not strictly necessary for organists of City churches to be freemen, because their principal activity was religious and not commercial.[40] They may however had other occupations in the City, like Henry Green, or connections with one or other of the Companies. Goodwin was a former apprentice who actually became organist of two suburban churches, in Southwark and Bermondsey, and an organist at Ranelagh Gardens.[41]

William Selby was organist at All Hallows, Bread Street from 1756 to 1773, and also at St Sepulchre Holborn from 1760, but went to America for good in 1773.

Amongst these examples we have two apprentices who were unwilling to join the Company as freemen after the expiry of their apprenticeship, and it is clear that the professional musicians who were free of the Company were for the most part reluctant to join the Livery. These problems were not just short-term, because by the end of the century the situation was worse. There were good reasons for the serious decline in interest. The first has been mentioned several times before, namely that the centre of gravity for London music had now shifted permanently westwards, and for any musician regularly working in the West End the Company could provide no benefit or advantage whatever. It was only the City Waits and the few others whose appointment kept them in the City who were obliged to join a guild, whether they were in need of its support or not. Secondly the great inrush of amateurs and non-musicians must have had a deterrent effect on the professional. Professional musicians were obliged to

---

[38] Johnstone in *The Blackwell History of Music in Britain: The Eighteenth Century*, p. 183.
[39] *RSM*, p. 150.
[40] Dawe, p. 8.
[41] Dawe, p. 102.

coexist with amateurs in one way or another all their working life, often in somewhat menial circumstances. Social contact through the Company would be of no great advantage, especially if it made it difficult for them to fulfil their professional engagements.

These two reasons would have had their impact. But there can be little doubt that it was the existence of the Society of Musicians which had the greatest effect. Here was a new organisation, sponsored by the greatest musicians of their day, open only to professionals and offering benevolent assistance to any of its subscribers, if the Governors considered that a case for a hardship grant had been made. This was a genuine mutual benefit society, and a regular subscription was a good insurance. Why pay fines and fees and quarterage to a Livery Company which had nothing to offer but a small poor box? Apart from sentiment and family connections there was no case which the Company could make to match the attraction of the Society, and no evidence survives to suggest that much effort was made to increase the level of professional membership.

For the increasingly non-musical Livery, a good deal of feasting went on. The Court regularly dined together after their meetings, and there was a Stewards' Feast most years after 1736. The 'Election Day' feast in previous years may have been the Stewards' Feast in another guise, although it later became more common to have the Stewards' Feast earlier in the year and a separate function on or near Election Day (Michaelmas). But there was no obvious pattern, and Mr Sleep's instruments might be ordered up for either or both the annual festivities. The Dinners were never held in the Hall of another Livery Company, but always in a City Tavern, the most popular of which seem to have been the George in Ironmonger Lane, the Queen's Arms in Cateaton Street (now part of Gresham Street) and the King's Arms, Cornhill, which was a regular venue for musical activities around the middle of the century. Until 1742 the Renter Warden only paid half the cost of the Stewards' Feast, the Stewards presumably paying the rest, but from then on it looks as though the whole cost was borne by the Company, a sign of increasing prosperity.

After Sleep's retirement in 1754, John Ward was invited to provide music and was paid three guineas in 1756 and again in 1759 and 1761. After that not only is there no reference to music at the Feast for many years, but among the cumulative bye-laws of the Company printed in about 1769, there is one which must have been recently made, which positively bans music from the Stewards Feast:

> That the general meeting of the Livery of this Company at the Stewards' Feast be in future appointed by the Master – *that no Music be hired on that day* and that the Master quit the Chair on or before Twelve o'Clock at night and no more liquor be called for after that hour.

So far as the Livery was concerned therefore the transformation from craft guild to dining club was now complete. Strangely, this bye-law, perhaps because of the bad opinion of the Company which it could not fail to invoke, was omitted from the bye-laws which were periodically published with the membership lists during the next sixty years, but it was still felt necessary to rescind it formally by Court Resolution in 1830.[42]

It may seem surprising that a City Company which appeared to be running on a sound financial basis and was now almost exclusively committed to the epicurean pleasures of its members could run into problems, but this was to happen twice during the second half of the century. First, the Court discovered that they had appointed a dishonest and deceitful Clerk, and then when certain members of the Livery became curious about the Company's constitution the deceit spread to higher places.

John Crumpe was appointed Clerk in 1747 in succession to one who died the previous year, whose name is unknown, but who may have been responsible (soon after his appointment) for persuading Thomas Eyre to adopt the practice in 1734 of paying a guinea to the Clerk for each new freeman. If so, this anonymous Clerk must share the credit with Eyre and Elmes for the financial planning which put the Company on its feet again, and resulted in the huge increase in membership. Crumpe took over what the previous Clerk had begun, but also managed to persuade the Court that he could keep the books, and that the office of Renter Warden was no longer necessary. For this reason the Renter Warden Account Book faded out in 1754 and was replaced by a Clerk's cash book which, unlike the Renter Warden's annual accounts, was not audited – at least until the Court's suspicions were aroused that all was not well, and this did not happen until 1768. As the Minute Books prior to 1772 are no longer in existence, it is impossible to identify the full nature of his crime, but there is no doubt that Crumpe had embezzled Company money,[43] and his accounts did not balance. The Master and Wardens signed an audit report on 27 October 1768 which read as follows:

> MEMO that on 27th October 1768 this account was audited by us whose names are underwritten the balance due to the Company £53-1-7d besides a year's interest on £200 South Sea Annuities due 10th inst. NB Mr Crumpe has not recd.

Stephen Camm	Master
Ged. Gatfield }	
Heneage Robinson }	Wardens

The abbreviation 'recd' is perhaps an abbreviation for 'recompensed'. Crumpe appears not to have been discharged immediately. He may have been suspended while the enquiry continued. The first surviving Minute Book opens with Crumpe's discharge on 29 July 1772, and with an agreed settlement of fifty guineas

---

42 See p. 169. The original bye-law appears in the Charter, Ordinance and Memorandum book now in the Guildhall Library, MS 3101.

43 A Minute of 29 March 1773 records that 'The Committee continued their examination of the List of Freemen of this Company extracted from the City's Books and upon finishing the same are of opinion that many of the freemen inserted in the said list do not appear to be accounted for in the Cash Book of the said Company.'

payable by him to the Company. He eventually gave a Bill for this amount in April 1773 and the money was paid the following October, being used to settle nearly twenty years of arrears of the Orphans Tax accrued since the closing of the Renter Wardens' accounts in 1754. This was a tax charged on the binding of apprentices, and the Clerk was responsible for collecting it and paying it to the Chamberlain of London.

No sooner had the Company been restored to 'its regular and prosperous state'[44] under the guidance of William Cooper Keating, who had been Master in 1772 and was then appointed Treasurer, than the Court was faced with a new crisis, and although there is a slight inconsistency in the dating, one cannot help suspecting that Sir John Hawkins had a hand in it. His 'History of the Science and Practice of Music' was published in 1776, but the antiquarian curiosity of certain of the Livery as to the company's origins had been aroused two years before the publication date. One suspects that Hawkins had already completed his research for the book by then and had taken the opportunity, no doubt with mischievous intent, to give advance notice to someone in or close to the Company of what he thought that he had discovered and what he was going to write about it. Whether this happened or not the Court were asked in July 1774 to consider an innocent-sounding request from two Liverymen, Patrick Cawdron and Peter Bluck, present at the Stewards' Feast, that the Company's Charter be printed and distributed to the Livery 'so that they could see what respective powers the Court and Livery had'. The question was referred to the next Court when it was decided that the Charter should not be printed, as the Court, having read the Charter and Bye-laws, had found that 'they had exactly pursued the same'; members of the Livery should however be at liberty to read it. Within the closed circle of the Court there was obviously some unease about the situation, because a further Resolution was passed on 18 October 1774:

> that the Master Wardens or any other of the Court do not take up or mention at the next General Meeting, or at any other court the Motion of the said Mr Cawdron; but if called upon to give an answer, then the Master, or whoever presides do give in writing as shown.

In February 1775, the Court asked the Master and Clerk to go to the Record Office to look up the Charter, and Mr Cawdron was to be summoned to show why he refused to pay his quarterage.

When the Master and Clerk returned they reported to the Court in March on what they had found, and an account of their report and the ensuing debate four pages long was written into the Minutes. Barely credible though this may seem, these pages were then cut out of the Minute Book. There is enough left in the book to show that the Court had decided to advertise, with a reward, for any information relating to the old books and records of the Company. But the subsequent Minutes are silent about how the Court dealt with the inquisitive Livery-

---

[44] Minute of 20 January 1774, extending the Court's thanks to the Committee.

13. A great banquet at the City of London Tavern, Bishopsgate, in 1813, celebrating the liberation of the Netherlands from Napoleon. Although never used by the Company for its feasts, its great size puts a new dimension to the meaning of 'tavern' in the 18th and early 19th centuries. Note the fine setting of the musicians' gallery.

men, whose concern can only have been increased when Hawkins' book was published the following year. The mutilation of the Minute Book, an act of deliberate concealment, was no doubt kept secret by the Clerk and those members of the Court who were privy to the plot. But any members of the Company who had an interest in history and had read Hawkins' book would have wondered whether there was any legitimacy in the Company's existence at all. Others for whom the social activities of the Company were all that mattered would no doubt have shrugged the problem aside.

There does seem to have been a backlash of some sort, because the Minutes from 1777 until 1791 show a constant preoccupation with non-payment of quarterage and fines by members. By this time the office of Steward appears to have fallen into abeyance, and the Steward's Fine was now levied on all Liverymen as an extra charge; it was clearly unpopular and becoming difficult to collect. As there was a continuing economic problem of too many Liverymen attending Feasts which they had not properly subscribed to, the Court finally decided on reform at the January Court in 1780, when it was agreed to consolidate the Livery and Steward's Fines at fifteen guineas, although a Liveryman who had not yet paid his Steward's Fine was still liable to pay the fine at the old rate.

A Committee of Pastmasters was set up in the following year to consider how to implement the change, and ensure that outstanding fines were paid. The Court accepted the Committee's recommendation that only those who had paid their Steward's Fines should be invited to the Stewards' Feast. This had a dramatic effect on numbers dining the following year. During the previous four years attendance at the Feast had been 137 in 1778, 148 in 1779 and 1780, and 140 in 1781. In 1782 the number dropped to 71, and to 70 in 1783. Although there were odd years when the numbers reached treble figures they would not return to the old level until the 20th century.

As the 18th century passed into its last decades, the emphasis in relation to the membership of the Company began to shift from quantity to quality (in social terms), and this was achieved primarily through the special relationship which had long existed between the City Corporation and the Company through the City Waits. A majority of the Waits had been Musicians at the beginning of the 18th century, and were to become so again after 1750. By the time that the City decided in 1802 not to appoint any more Waits, all but two were freemen of the Company. Sir John Bosworth, City Chamberlain from 1734 to 1751, was an active member of the Company.[45] Henry Groome, Keeper of the Guildhall was admitted in 1761, and became a Liveryman the following year. In 1768 the City Marshal, Thomas Gates, joined the Company, and an officer of the Guildhall, James Green, was appointed Beadle. Thomas Whittell, appointed Clerk in 1772, was a Guildhall official, and the Guildhall was his official address as Clerk.

If the Company's reputation among its peers had been higher, it would by now have had its first Lord Mayor, because one of the most radical Lord Mayors of the 18th century, Brass Crosby, joined the Company as a humble freeman in 1748, on his arrival in London from Sunderland as a fortune-seeking young solicitor. He wasted no time in marrying three wives in succession, all wealthy, and this enabled him to pay his Livery Fine in 1752, and then to turn his back on the Company in 1756, when he was translated to the Goldsmiths. He then went on to buy his way into the office of City Remembrancer in 1760; he became a Sheriff in 1764, an Alderman the following year and MP for Honiton from 1768 to 1774. He was Lord Mayor in 1770/1, and achieved his greatest fame by supporting John Wilkes in his fight to publish the Parliamentary Reports. For his defiance of the Government, Crosby spent some time in the Tower of London, but he and Wilkes triumphed in the end.

Perhaps it was the frustration of losing Crosby to the Goldsmiths which induced the members of the Court to recruit another Alderman, and on 17 July

---

45 Bosworth's popular support arose from the fact that he was by trade a tobacco merchant and had led the City tobacco merchants in their opposition to Sir Robert Walpole's much resented Excise Bill (see Betty Masters, *The Chamberlains of the City of London 1237–1987* [London: City Corporation, 1988]).

1776 Alderman Thomas Wooldridge, 'lately elected Alderman of Bridge', was chosen Assistant in place of the late Mr Cotterell. Unfortunately this was an improvident move. Wooldridge turned out to be a most irregular and unreliable attender at meetings; he was almost the only Court member at this time, when it was customary to elect the officers by ballot (the senior and next senior in line being put in nomination on most occasions), to fail to achieve election to any office except Renter (or Junior) Warden. By 1782 he was in the New Prison, Clerkenwell, as an uncertificated bankrupt, accused of fraud, extortion and embezzlement, and on 25 February 1783 the Court of Aldermen stripped him of his office and appointed a new Alderman for the Ward of Bridge.[46]

Wooldridge must still have had friends on the Musicians' Court, because a real problem arose when the next Alderman on the Court of the Company, Alderman Turner, was elected Sheriff in 1783. The custom at this time was for the Livery Company or Companies to which the Sheriff-elect belonged to nominate sixteen of their number to support the Sheriff during the ceremonial proceedings at Michaelmas, at the beginning of the shrieval year. This included a dinner after the swearing-in. Alderman Turner was a Haberdasher as well as a Musician, so the dinner was to be held at their hall. Despite his appalling record Wooldridge was included in the sixteen nominated members of the Musicians. Just a week before the dinner Turner asked for a Special Court to be called, at which he informed the Court that he could not be seen to be inviting Wooldridge to his dinner 'under the situation he at present stood in with respect to the Court of Aldermen'. He asked the Court to exclude Wooldridge's name, and agreed to write personally to him. At this point Wooldridge disappears from the Company's records, except that on 25 July 1787 it was noted that he had been absent 'upwards of two years, and was therefore disqualified' from membership of the Court.

Alderman Turner did not rise to the mayoralty, but the Company achieved its first Lord Mayor in Alderman Sir Brook Watson, who was elected to the Court in January 1785, and became Sheriff in the same year. He was Master in 1790/1, and Lord Mayor in 1796.[47] The not unusual consequence of the Company's participation in the Lord Mayor's Show was that its finances went into reverse, and there was no feasting or dining during the following year.

In all the Company's Minutes up to this date there is no mention of music. The J.C. Bach–C.F. Abel concerts, the 1784 and subsequent Handel Commemorations, Salomon's Haydn Concerts, and all the rest of the vigorous musical activity so well patronised in the West End, were taking place in a different

---

[46] The account of Alderman Wooldridge's examination and disgrace is covered extensively in CL Rep 186.

[47] In Sir Brook Watson's later years he suffered as a result of a terrible accident that occurred to him while on a visit to Cuba. He had fallen out of a small boat and while struggling in the water his right leg was bitten off by a shark. A caricature drawing shows him in old age, looking dishevelled and with a peg-leg.

world. When in 1801 two members of the Company, Robert Shaw and James Oliver, who happened to be City Waits, attempted to galvanise the Company into exercising its jurisdiction in the City to prevent 'foreigners' performing there, the Court simply responded by placing an advertisement. The Minute of the decision does not even note that the petitioners were City Waits; it just refers to them as 'professional musicians'. In 1701 the Company, as a craft guild, was about to go into decline; in 1801 the Company's ongoing connection with music must have been in serious doubt.

10

Near to Oblivion

UP to this point it has been possible, logically and without artifice, to chart the Company's history century by century, the most significant seminal events taking place at or near the turn of each. The Company was established in 1500, its first Royal Charter was obtained in 1604, and the final City of London Act was dated 11 December 1700. However the year 1800 and the decades that precede and follow it have nothing more significant to offer than the Company's participation in Alderman Watson's Lord Mayor's Show in 1796, and it was not until the 1870s that the first signs of a new sense of purpose for the Company began to appear. In the meantime we are left with a barren period during which there was little contact with the musical world, and a sharp decline in the Company's *alter ego* as an attractive club for self-respecting City personages to join. The Company was in a state of potentially terminal decay.

This can be clearly seen in the fall in numbers in the Livery as shown on the annual Livery Lists. In 1805 the Livery numbered 247; in 1830 the total was 147; in 1859 it was down to seventy, ten of whom were shown as 'address unknown'. In fact the numbers were still more depressed after the turn of the tide, but it was only a matter of time before they once more began to increase. The figures for annual admissions to the Freedom are even more startling. In the years from 1800 to 1831 there were seventeen years in which admissions were in double figures (although the highest number, seventeen, was in 1800, the first year of this survey). Between 1831 and 1880 there was not a single year in which double figures were reached, and there were twelve years in which there were no admissions at all.

Two questions need to be answered. The first is whether this sorry state of affairs was due partly to extraneous factors or was solely the responsibility of those who were running the Company. The second is whether there was some sort of 'pilot light' which kept the Company ticking over when by rights it should have become extinct, and if so, who was holding and tending that light.

If, in order to find an answer to the first question, one is looking for scapegoats, the first place to look is within the City itself, where three important changes took place between the years 1802 and 1834. The first of these, in 1802, was the decision of the City Corporation to appoint no more City Waits. Those

14. Alderman Sir Brook Watson, the Company's first Lord Mayor (1796–97).
A portrait attributed to John Singleton Copley.

in office were allowed to continue, but on death or retirement they would not be replaced. It is no exaggeration to say that in the second half of the eighteenth century the professional, musical membership of the Company was centred on the Waits, and their number was maintained by new members hoping in due course, on the retirement of those Waits who were members of the Company, to step into their shoes. There were of course still some Waits who belonged to other Companies, but the Musicians were the dominant source. When in 1802 this incentive was removed, the effect was dramatic. From 1780 to 1802 seventeen musicians had become freemen of the Company. From 1803 to 1832 only seven musicians joined, although another rather tenuous link with the world of music was now developing through the membership of music instrument makers and music sellers.

The second blow was struck by Parliament in 1832 with the first Act of Reform relating to the Parliamentary franchise. The Livery vote in the City of London was severely restricted and the perceived privileges of a liveryman of a City Company were thereby diminished.

Finally in 1834 the City Corporation decided that it was no longer necessary for persons desiring to take up the City Freedom to first become a member of a company. The Freedom could be obtained by direct application to the City Chamberlain. It was thus immediately devalued, because it was the Livery Companies who had been most concerned to enforce upon persons wishing to carry on business in the City the statutory obligation to take up the Freedom. For the companies it had been an important source of revenue, and provided some control for those which were still trade guilds. Once the companies had lost the incentive to uphold the law it became unenforceable and ceased to be of importance.

In 1834, for almost exactly one hundred years the freedom of the Musicians Company had been on offer to all and sundry as a cheap way into City trade and business. By this means the Company, like many others that had lost their mistery and were no longer trade guilds, was able to thrive. Now it had nothing to offer to the ordinary City worker, whether he be 'porter', 'oilman' or 'sworn-broker'.

The loss of this incentive might have been compensated for at this time if there had been some musical function which the Company could latch on to – some role which it could fulfil – despite its neglect of the 'art or science' for so long. Unfortunately the changes in the City had come just at a time when musicians were also in a state of osmosis. They were passing through a long process whereby the 'professors' were evolving into a music profession. It was an extended and complex experience, because simmering away in the cauldron there were various unrefined ingredients which had to be absorbed, and others which needed to be filtered out. Those to be absorbed included, first, the status of the professional musician in society, second the establishment of a proper system of music education, third the rights and role of women musicians, and fourth the exploitation of the universally popular new instrument, the pianoforte. What had to be ladled out were the discrimination in favour of foreign musicians, for whom London in the late eighteenth century had been like a great jar of nectar, and secondly the long-standing 'open access' for amateur musicians to perform on the same concert platform alongside the professionals.

It took the best part of a century[1] before an organised, structured and articulate profession could be presented to the world in the 1870s and 1880s, together with educational facilities which would rank with the best of Europe's conservatoires. Even then Utopia was still a long way off – women's rights were still being ignored and by this time the supply of competent home-trained musicians had overtaken demand. New problems were therefore added to some of the old ones, for which satisfactory solutions are still being sought. What eventually altered the situation from the Company's point of view (but not in the 1830s) was that the profession now had an energy source and a power network which the Company could plug into and supplement, and it was this that provided the new-found sense of purpose which underlies the last two chapters of this book.

Reverting to the first question with which this chapter is concerned, we should look for some more clues. Was the Company a victim of circumstance or was its plight foreseeable or avoidable? We have seen how the City put the Company at a severe disadvantage in the 1830s. Perhaps too the City of London's general attitude to life during the so-called 'Age of Enlightenment' was partly responsible. It bore all the hallmarks of complacency. Disasters ringed the world, empires were being lost and won, but at the commercial heart of it all, nothing was allowed to disturb the established custom of the City. From about 1750 the Arts in the City began a century of repression; there were no theatres, and no concert rooms apart from Livery Halls which were occasionally 'borrowed' for a musical occasion. Even the Dancing Masters' Rooms (a popular venue for 'consorts' in the earlier part of the 18th century) were in decline.

On the other hand the City cannot take the blame for an introspective Company which showed no interest at this time either in promoting music in the City or in extending its connexion into other more cultural parts of London. Under these conditions it is somewhat difficult to defend its good name. When one reflects on the fact that in 1763 the Company proceeded against one Barton Hudson for employing persons not free of the City for the Lord Mayor's entertainment at the Mansion House, and then at some point in the next six years passed a bye-law banning all music from its own annual dinner,[2] it is hard to reject altogether Charles Burney's withering judgment on the Company:

> The only uses that have hitherto been made of this charter seem the affording to aliens of an easy and cheap expedient of acquiring the freedom of the city, and enabling them to pursue some more profitable and respectable trade than that of

---

[1] See Cyril Ehrlich, *The Music Profession in Britain since the Eighteenth Century* (Oxford: Clarendon Press 1985), chapter 5.

[2] See p. 155.

fiddling; as well as empowering the company to keep out of processions and city feasts every street and country-dance player of superior abilities to those who have the honour of being styled the waits of the corporation.[3]

Burney, and Hawkins, it may be argued, were prejudiced; the one had been forced into the Company on his marriage by a father-in-law whom he despised, the other's incomplete researches had persuaded him that the Company was a fraudulent organisation. But Joseph Haydn was quite innocent of any such prejudices. Cyril Ehrlich in *The Music Profession in Britain* quotes from Haydn's private diary his comments on a lunch given by the Lord Mayor in 1791, after which there was 'dancing to a wretched dance band, the entire orchestra consisting only of two violins and a violoncello'. In another room 'the music was a little better, because there was a drum in the band which drowned the misery of the violins'.[4] Little wonder that the end of the Waits was in sight! This pathetic musical offering should be compared with a not dissimilar occasion which Haydn attended in Vienna one year later, a charity ball in the City's Redouten-saal, where there were two orchestras, one of forty-three musicians, and the other of twenty-seven.[5]

The Waits were important to the Company, and a poor performance at the Mansion House could not have failed to reflect on the Company. But to treat the Waits and the Company as synonymous, as Burney did, is misleading. They made up less than a third of the professional musicians in the Company at that time. During the period 1780–1830 there were thirty-two freemen of the Company who were professional musicians, only ten of whom were Waits. A majority subscribed to the Royal Society of Musicians (which had gained its 'Royal' title in 1785) as well as belonging to the Company. The published archives of the Society have made it possible to assess some of them in their professional capacity,[6] and this assessment helps to counteract the bad taste left by Burney and Hawkins.

As one would expect there is nothing to suggest that their work was confined to the City although they may have been trained there. Some, like the City Wait, William Hill, and George Nicholson, who was one of the little handful of professionals to progress from the Freedom and take up the Livery, are recorded as having served their seven years' apprenticeship. Most had been trained to play two or more instruments. The City Wait, James Aldwell Oliver, who became a Liveryman and was elected to the Court in 1817, is noted as playing the 'Violin, Tenor [viola], Clarinet and Hautboy', with the comment 'is a single man'. Martin

---

3   Charles Burney, *A General History of Music* (1935), p. 286.
4   Ehrlich, p. 27 (quoting from H.C. Robbins Landon, *Haydn in England* (London: Thames & Hudson 1976), p. 106).
5   Robbins Landon, p. 206.
6   All the details that follow (except those relating to the Company) come from *The Royal Society of Musicians List of Members 1738–1984*, compiled by Betty Matthews. The assistance which this book has provided is duly and gratefully acknowledged.

Platts who joined the RSM and became a freeman of the Company at the age of twenty-one in 1784 is shown as having served seven years' apprenticeship and 'plays violin and horn, engaged at Brithelmstone [Brighton]'.

Lewis Lavenu joined the RSM in 1792 and the Company in 1794. 'He is a single man, his engagements are at the opera, Ranelagh and Oratorios, his instruments are the violin and tenor.'

Arthur Betts was the son of another freeman, John Betts of 2, Royal Exchange, musical instrument maker and dealer; Arthur joined the RSM in 1798 and became a freeman of the Company the following year. His instruments included the violin, tenor, violoncello and pianoforte and he 'is engaged in the Opera & Opera Concert, Covent Garden Oratorios,[7] has scholars and other private engagements'.

Neville Butler Challoner became a freeman in 1805 and joined the RSM the following year. He 'performs on the violin, harp, pianoforte &c – is engaged (as leader of the band) at the Theatre Sadlers Wells &c, at the Oratorios Covent Garden, the Russell Square and other concerts'.

William Hudson Wilson 'was educated by Mr Hudson as a chorister in St Paul's until 14, then apprenticed to Mr Ashley, performs on the Pianoforte, violoncello and double bass, is engaged at Sadlers Wells, the Oratorios and other concerts, and has some private teaching'.

James Taylor, who joined both organisations in 1808, 'performs on the harp and violin, engaged at Sadlers Wells, has considerable teaching and other private business'.

Willoughby Theobald Monzani, another former apprentice (whose father was also a freeman of the Company, a famous flautist and music-publisher) 'is engaged at the Philharmonic Concert, as first flute at the King's Theatre [Haymarket], and Concert of Ancient Music'.

The *curricula vitae* of these and other freemen, as set out in the Royal Society of Musicians records, are of great interest, and demonstrate that Burney's comment that 'the company has ever been held in derision by real professors' was very wide of the mark, unless it referred only to the Livery. Like other 'real professors' these freemen of the Company behaved like typical London professionals of that time, and used their versatility as executants and teachers in accumulating sufficient income for their subsistence year by year, at a time when ordinary musicians were very poorly paid.[8] They had a very real problem also in competing with the hordes of Italian, German, Austrian and French professionals who had chosen London as their working base. In his 'first London Notebook', which he wrote up in 1792, Haydn listed thirty-nine of the best

---

7 The Covent Garden Oratorios were presented on Wednesdays and Fridays during Lent, as the performance of opera was forbidden by law on those days (see Roger Fiske in *The Blackwell History of Music in Britain: The Eighteenth Century*, p. 211).

8 See Ehrlich, chapter 2.

instrumentalists in London for his future reference. Only four were English, and two of those were Dr Burney and his daughter.[9]

It is easy to see that these 'professors' felt that they were too busy to concern themselves with the Company and its governance, but it was nevertheless unfortunate, from the Company's point of view, that so few of them thought it worth while paying their fifteen guineas in order to join the Livery, and so become eligible for election to the Court, where they might, should they have been so inclined, have been able to bring the Company closer to the real musical world.

Only three of the professional musicians of this era came on to the Court, James Aldwell Oliver, who has already been mentioned, and who died in 1818, the year after his election, and John Ashley and his son, Charles Jane Ashley. Both of them were part of the musical 'establishment' of the time. John had been admitted freeman in 1771; he was a City Wait and may have been an hautboy and bassoon player in the Guards band.[10] He was Joah Bates' assistant director at the great Handel Commemoration Concert in Westminster Abbey in 1784. In 1795 he started his own series of oratorio concerts, which were subsequently continued by his son. In 1803, the same year in which he directed the first London performance of the Mozart *Requiem*, he became Master of the Company. He died in 1805.

Charles Jane Ashley was elected to the Court in 1819, but does not appear to have shown much interest in the Company, because his place on the Court was declared vacant in 1821 on the grounds of his non-attendance for two years. This is not altogether surprising, because he was nearly fifty when elected and had spent most of his life as an active 'professor'. He was a distinguished cellist, an original member of the Philharmonic Society (founded in 1813), and had been Secretary of the Royal Society of Musicians from 1811 to 1819. Because of the lack of support shown by C.J. Ashley, the Ashley family cannot with justification be included in the short list of families who helped to maintain and reinvigorate the languorous Company in the 19th century. John Ashley had two other sons who became Liverymen, General Christopher and Richard Godfrey, both described as 'musicians', but there is no other record of them in the Company annals.

The second question now has to be answered, the matter of the 'pilot light', and who held it and kept it alight during the dark years. Although others whose achievements have been lost sight of may have some claim to be included in the roll of honour, in dynastic terms there were only two families who were preeminent, the Skilbecks and the Collards, and one individual, William Chappell.

The Skilbeck family, unlike the Collards and Chappells, had no professional connection with music, but their active interest and original thought, running

---

9   Robbins Landon, p. 183.
10 RSM List of members, p. 16.

through several generations, and their concern that the Company be efficiently run, can be detected in the Court Minutes from the various resolutions with which a Skilbeck was associated as proposer or seconder. It was for example John Joseph Skilbeck, Master in 1830, who was responsible for bringing music back to the Company's functions by proposing the rescission of the infamous 1769 bye-law.

The Skilbeck family carried on business as Drysalters (dealers in chemical products) in the City of London. The first recorded member of the family to join the Company was John, who became a freeman in 1766 and a liveryman in 1773. His son John Joseph was admitted in 1795 and clothed with the Livery in 1801. He was called on the Court in 1826 and was elected Master in 1829. Although he declined to serve a second term as Master in 1846, he continued to serve on the Court until January 1863, when he died of a stroke which he suffered at the Court meeting.

John Joseph's son, another Joseph, was elected to the Livery in 1823, and to the Court in 1838. He was Master in 1842/3 and again in 1856/7, but predeceased his father. In 1855 Joseph Skilbeck gave notice to the Court that he would be proposing a motion at the next meeting of the Court that each member of the Livery be allowed to introduce two ladies to the Livery Dinner at the member's own expense. Unfortunately the ensuing Minute is so ambiguous that it is not clear whether the resolution was carried or not. In 1858 he proposed that the professional musicians who played at the Company's Dinners be allowed to charge fees not exceeding twelve guineas, and this was agreed.

John Henry Skilbeck, who described himself as 'Merchant' rather than 'Drysalter', came into the Company in 1867, representing the next generation. This was the time at which the Company numbers were sinking to their lowest level, and Skilbeck came straight into the Company, being clothed with the Livery on the same day that he was admitted to the freedom, which seems to have become a fairly regular arrangement for those who could afford it. He was elected to the Common Council in 1869, and with other colleagues on the Council he was involved in the cultural reawakening in the City, and played a prominent role in the establishment of the Guildhall Art Gallery. He was elected to the Musicians Company Court in 1870, and became Master in 1876/7. During his year of office he attended a meeting of the City Guilds Association which had been set up to consider the need to take steps to promote technical education, which from his perspective would have included the making of musical instruments, as well as the training of musicians. He served a second term of office as Master in 1888/9, and continued on the Court for the rest of his life. He attended his last Court on 21 January 1919, by which time he was 'Father of the Company', and died a few weeks later on the 5 March.

Frederick William Collard, who joined the Company in 1799, was one of several music instrument makers who helped to compensate through their membership for the decline in the numbers of professionals around the turn of the century, and began a tradition which has continued until the present day (it is indeed reflected in the 1950 Charter). John Betts, who has already been mentioned as the father of the violinist Arthur Betts, and who was the leading London dealer for Italian stringed instruments of his day, had been a freeman since 1782. Collard's contemporaries included James Riggs and George Astor of Cornhill, and Christopher Gerock, a naturalised German from Weissberg, and they were followed in the next generation by Henry and Joseph George Hill of Waterloo Place. However unlike Collard and his partner David Davis, who were both admitted to the freedom on the same date in January 1799, the other instrument makers did not proceed to the Livery.

Collard and Davis became liverymen in 1810. By this time their firm, then known as 'Clementi Banger Hyde Collard & Davis' (or more simply 'Clementi & Co') was profiting greatly, being at the centre of the rapidly expanding piano industry, thanks to the genius of the firm's founder Muzio Clementi. Clementi had come to London from Italy in 1773, and had established a unique reputation with his versatility, not only as a pianist of the highest order, and a composer of over one hundred piano sonatas, whom Beethoven respected as his equal, but also as a teacher whose pupils included J.B. Cramer and John Field, and as a music publisher and piano manufacturer who was responsible for some important technical improvements to the instrument at a vital stage in its evolution. In the 1790s, mainly through his work as a soloist and teacher, Clementi had made a substantial amount of money, part of which he invested in the leading London firm of music publishers and instrument makers, Longman & Broderip. The money was lost in the firm's bankruptcy in 1795, but Clementi's self-confidence was such that he decided to set up his own firm with Longman and other partners, of whom F.W. Collard was one. Collard was entrusted by Clementi with the responsibility of running the business after Longman had left in 1800, and during the time Clementi spent on the Continent from 1802 to 1810. Although Clementi resumed his position as head of the firm on his return, his many other musical activities meant that the 'resident' partners continued to manage the business as they had during his absence. As well as F.W. Collard there were David Davis, and Collard's brother who was four years younger, and who had had the misfortune to be baptized with the same names as his brother, in the reverse order. William Frederick did not become a member of the Musicians Company, although his son Charles Lukey did. After the death of Davis in 1822 and Clementi in 1832, the firm was known simply as 'Collard & Collard'. Throughout the 19th century the firms of Collard and Broadwood were in constant competition to become the leading English piano manufacturer (Broadwood was always first in size), and to patent and produce the greatest number of improvements and innovations, such as the upright piano, which became an important part of Collards' business later in the century.

Given the concentration which this high performance firm must have required it is remarkable that F.W. Collard was able to devote so much time to the affairs of the Musicians' Company. His partner David Davis was called on to the Court first, in October 1819, but he was of an older generation than Collard and died in April 1822, whereas Collard continued in office until his death in 1860. He was invited to fill the vacancy on the Court caused by Davis' death, and took his seat at the next Court in July 1822. Two years later he took as his apprentice William Chappell, son of Samuel Chappell, music seller of New Bond Street. Just four years after joining the Court, F.W. Collard became Master for the first time. He would be elected again 1845, and re-elected for the following year, when John Joseph Skilbeck declined to serve a second term. The Court Minutes show that, throughout his thirty-eight years on the Court, Collard was one of the most regular attenders, and his absences were very rare. He was elected as Treasurer in 1838, and held that office until his death. It was during his tenure of this office that the practice began of making donations to charitable causes. For a great many years the Court had exercised benevolence towards individuals, mostly widows of members of the Company, and there are numerous records of so and so being 'relieved with a guinea'. Now the Court was beginning to look further afield, and donations are recorded for such objects as 'the Committee for promoting subscriptions for building churches in Bethnal Green parish' (ten guineas in 1840), and the Patriotic Fund (ten guineas in 1855 – at the time of the Crimean War). In 1854 the Court voted to provide the Master with a sum of ten guineas annually for him to appropriate at his discretion 'towards relieving the distress of the poor'. A regular donation of five guineas to the Royal Society of Musicians began in 1870.

F.W. Collard died in April 1860, and a quite exceptional tribute, moved by J.J. Skilbeck (whose son Joseph had also just died), was recorded in the Court Minutes:

> That the members of this Court have heard with great regret of the death of their much esteemed Treasurer, Frederick William Collard Esquire, and they take the earliest opportunity of recording their respect for his memory and their high appreciation of the benefit derived by the Musicians' Company from his long connexion with it – particularly for the valuable services for years rendered by him as its Treasurer and for his uniform friendly feeling and courtesy to his colleagues of the court and to the Livery at large.

Frederick William appears to have had one son John Arnold, who did not join the Company, but his nephew Charles Lukey served as his apprentice, and was admitted to the freedom in November 1831, on the same date as William Chappell. He joined the Livery in 1855, to be elected to the Court in 1858. On his uncle's death, he was elected Treasurer, and became Master in 1864, serving for two consecutive years. C.L. Collard had two sons, William Stuartson and John Clementi, both of whom served their apprenticeship and were admitted and clothed on the same day, 13 April 1871. W.S. Collard was elected to the Court in October of the same year! John Clementi was not so well-favoured, and in 1876 he failed for the second time to be elected to the Court. One detects a whiff of resentment against the Company from his father at this point; he absented himself from the Court, and said that he wished to resign, both as Treasurer and from the Court.[11] Attempts to dissuade him were made, but he persisted, and William Chappell, who had been elected to the Court in 1870, and was now half-way through his first term as Master, was elected Treasurer in his place. John Clementi Collard duly came on to the Court in 1886. He was elected Master in 1893, and again in 1899, and in the following year was asked to serve for the remainder of the year following the sudden death in March 1901 of Sir John Stainer, who had begun his second term. The initial delay in his being called on the Court worked in his favour, as it meant that he was elevated to the highest office just at the time when the Company's revival was approaching its most energetic phase, as will be apparent from the next chapter.

Frederick William Collard did much for the Company, but perhaps the most valuable service which he performed (although it may not have been apparent at the time) was to introduce the young William Chappell to the Company. He was the son of Samuel Chappell, who in 1810, in partnership with J.B. Cramer and others, had established his music publishing business in New Bond Street. William succeeded to the business in 1834 (with his widowed mother Emily) when he was only twenty-five, his father having died in that year. He was a man with very wide interests, but especially in folk-song and early music and other matters of an antiquarian nature. With his fellow antiquarian Edward Francis Rimbault and George Alexander Macfarren, at that time one of the Royal Academy of Music's most distinguished graduates, he founded the Musical Anti-quarian Society in 1840. When his younger brother Thomas reached the age of twenty-five in 1844, William left the firm in his hands and joined the rival firm of Cramer and Beale, which became known as Cramer Beale & Chappell, from which he retired in 1861.

For reasons which are not apparent (unless it was simply his reluctance because of all his other activities) Chappell had a long wait before he was called on to the Court. He became a freeman and liveryman in 1831, when he was twenty-two years old. He retired from business when he was fifty-two; he was elected to the Court in 1870, when he was sixty-one. As we have seen he was Master in 1875/6 and served another term in 1887/8, the last year of his life.

When Chappell joined the Court, there was a change of pace. It was almost as if during the long wait for election, he had become aware of the vacuum that existed at the heart of the Company and, through a consciousness of its past and of English music history in general, he was mentally alive to what it should stand for in the future. Being a mere dining club with some musical entertainment was

---

[11] There is an interesting entry in Arthur Hill's Diary, relating to J.C. Collard's death in August 1918. Hill clearly believed that the Collard family controlled the Company in the 19th century. He wrote that 'by restricting the membership of the Court to as few as possible they were able to control the voting and thereby to elect their friends and relatives.' The difficulties experienced by J.C. Collard in 1876 seem to demolish this theory, and certainly the Minutes do not suggest that the Collards abused their influence. Most resistance to enlarging the Court came from other members (see p. 177).

for him not enough. When the opportunity arose he had the vision and personality to ensure that the vacuum was filled, and the mixture of talent which he assembled within the Company was much richer than what it replaced, and bubbling with ideas relating to the Company's new role. We may however note in passing, with a wry smile, that he started off on the wrong track, reporting to the Court on a 17th century manuscript relating to the Company which he had discovered in the British Museum, for which he was duly thanked. What he had found was in fact the Minute Book of the *Westminster* Company referred to in chapter 7.

But this was a trivial error. Of real value were the 'eminent Victorians' who became associated with the Company through his efforts. In 1876, during his Mastership, Chappell persuaded the Court to bestow the Honorary Freedom and Livery on Sir Henry Cole, the organising genius behind the Great Exhibition of 1851 and the establishment of the Victoria and Albert Museum. Cole also had a great interest in music and music education, and about this time was concerned, as Secretary of the Government Office known as 'the Science and Art Department', with the establishment in South Kensington of the National Training School, which after an unsuccessful start as a free music school was transformed in 1882 into the Royal College of Music.

It was the first Honorary Freedom ever conferred by the Company (apart from John Chambre in 1510), and it indicated the new horizons which Chappell was encouraging his colleagues to aim for. One learns from the Minutes that the Editor of the *City Press* was to be invited to the ceremony. It was duly noted in Sir Henry's diary entry for 1 August 1876:

> Dined with the Musicians at the Albion. Freedom and Livery presented to me. Suggested that they should aim to get 400 liverymen instead of 40. The idea well received. Mr Theobald an old Master very warm, wanted to shake my hand and said he always had £5 up to £10 ready for any good object. We were not humbugs and understood each other. Home by rail from Blackfriars.[12]

In its traditional role as a provider of annual feasts for the Livery, the Company had never faltered since recovering from the expense of taking part in Alderman Brook Watson's Lord Mayor's Show in 1796, notwithstanding the fact that the Livery dined free of charge, and the Court felt obliged to appoint Committees from time to time to 'report on the state of the Company's finances' (no actual reports are recorded in the Minutes). In an effort to improve revenue, the Court, concerned at the drop in membership, tried on several occasions to induce all the freemen, or Yeomanry, as they were now more commonly called, to pay their Livery fines and become full members, but many failed to respond. Despite this failure the Dinners continued.

In the early years of the century the tendency was to choose a venue in the

---

[12] Extract from a letter to A.F. Hill from Philip James (Victoria & Albert Museum), 17 December 1934.

hilly suburbs to the north of the City – Canonbury House, Islington, was a favourite place, and numbers dining there were about one-hundred at first, falling away to less than seventy by the end of the 1820s. In 1830 a dramatic change of location was made, again outside the City, this time to the east. The new hostelry was the West India Dock Tavern, Blackwall, which would have been newly built, as the Dock itself had only just been constructed. The route to the tavern was via the new Commercial Road and Poplar High Street, a long journey for some of the older members. Sixty-six Liverymen dined on the first occasion, sixty-five in 1832, and sixty-four in 1833. By 1841 the numbers were down to forty-nine, but they increased the following year to sixty, when the Dinner was held at the Brunswick Hall, also in Blackwall.

In 1861 it was proposed in the Court that music should be provided at the Livery Dinner by 'Musical Friends' at a cost not exceeding thirty guineas. This was agreed, but then rescinded at a subsequent meeting. Nevertheless 'Mr Hatton' with whom previous negotiations on this subject had taken place was invited to provide the music for the Livery Dinner in 1863 at a cost not exceeding twelve guineas, and this arrangement continued for the next nine years, most dinners taking place at what was now called the Brunswick Hotel, Blackwall, at the far end of Poplar High Street, with a convenient railway station close by to take the diners back to town.

In 1872, the Company was summoned back to the City for its Dinner, the venue being the Albion in Aldersgate Street, where the Court had dined quite regularly for many years. This now became the regular meeting place for the Livery, an indication perhaps that whereas earlier in the century the City, with its slums and smoke and miserable communications, was a place to be avoided for social functions, the ambience was now sufficiently improved to be able to provide a suitable environment. One thinks of the major improvement works whose names disclose their date: King William Street, Adelaide House, Queen Victoria Street, the Albert Embankment, Holborn Viaduct (railway terminology, a more dignified antecedent to 'flyover'). Each of these, together with the Underground railways, had an immediate impact on transport to and from the City. Equally important, but concealed beneath the streets, were the great sewerage improvements, which removed the threat of typhoid and cholera that had previously hung over the densely crowded City.

An acceptable environment, and commercial wealth and prosperity, unequalled anywhere in the world, part of which filtered through to the coffers of the City Corporation, were 'feel-good factors' which helped to develop a new relationship between the Lord Mayor and the Corporation and the Livery Companies. Except in a strictly local government sense, the Companies were no longer governed by the Corporation,[13] as they had been for the previous six cen-

---

[13] The Court of Aldermen still retains some controls over the Livery Companies, notably in respect of the establishment of new Companies, and changes to bye-laws, which require the Court's approval.

turies. The Companies, especially the Great Twelve, had always enjoyed a reputation for their hospitality. The Lord Mayor was now indisputably the greatest host of all, and his hospitality involved Masters (and sometimes Wardens and Clerks) of all the lesser Companies, either as his guests, as recorded for the first time in the Musicians Company Minutes in 1872 ('the Lord Mayor's Dinner to the Livery Companies at the Mansion House'), or as part of the 'establishment', as happened the following year, when the Master was invited to attend a Banquet given by the Lord Mayor for the Shah of Persia.

By this time Dickens' London of *Oliver Twist* and *Our Mutual Friend* had given place to Trollope's, as described in *The Way We Live Now* and *The Last Chronicle of Barset*. With all its faults the City was now a grander, more dignified and healthier 'Square Mile', and there was a renewal of self-respect amongst the lesser Livery Companies, especially as those without halls of their own could now once again pleasantly entertain their guests within the City itself.

There were however other special reasons why the Musicians Company was on the point of rejuvenation. In 1876, the same year in which the Company honoured Sir Henry Cole with the Honorary Freedom and Livery, the Corporation of London took one of its first steps towards becoming a patron of the arts, by providing ten scholarships, with an annual value of £40 each, to the National Training School in South Kensington (with which Cole was closely associated). This was in response to an appeal from the Prince of Wales, who had decided to implement the scheme which his late father had devised as early as 1854, as one of the ways of using the land in South Kensington which had been acquired for the common good with the proceeds from the 1851 Great Exhibition. The Corporation agreed to continue the scholarships for a period of five years, and a 'Music Deputation' was formed in 1875 from the Councillors who had attended on the Prince of Wales, to supervise the selection of the ten scholars.[14]

One of the Councillors was John Bath, who had already been suggesting to the Court of Common Council that they should consider ways of improving the performance of music in the Guildhall and of patronising the 'science of music' in the City. This was in 1873, and nothing came of the proposal, although it was not long before the Corporation became involved with the National Training School. Further initiatives followed – a proposal to establish a music school within Gresham College; a concert in 1878 in the Mansion House given by National Training School students, followed the next year by another by students from the Royal Academy of Music; the establishment in 1879 of the Guildhall Amateur Orchestral Society. By the end of that year, John Bath had his plans ready for a music college in the City, and these were presented to and accepted by the Court of Common Council in April 1880. Following this decision the Guildhall School of Music, under the direction of the first Principal, Thomas Henry

14 See Hugh Barty-King, *GSMD: A Hundred Years' Performance* (London 1980), p. 15.

Weist Hill, was established later the same year in an old wool warehouse in Aldermanbury.[15] It cannot have been just a coincidence that Bath became a liveryman of the Company in April 1879.

The other remarkable change which took place in the City during the 1870s, which the Company cannot have been unaware of, was the transformation of musical standards at St Paul's Cathedral, following the appointment of John Stainer as Organist and Master of the Choristers in 1872. He succeeded John Goss, who was a great organist and an esteemed composer of church music, but a very inadequate choirmaster. After forty-four years under Goss's direction the St Paul's choir was a by-word for indiscipline.

Stainer was the opposite, an indifferent composer, but a brilliant director, of whom it was said that 'he could do anything he liked with the choir'.[16] It is hard to believe that prior to his appointment the Vicars-Choral were not obliged to attend choir rehearsals, but this was evidently common practice in cathedral choirs, until new standards were set by Stainer at St Paul's; fines were now imposed for non-attendance and unpunctuality, although these were balanced by increased salaries, and challenging levels of commitment.

What was happening to music in the City in the 1870s had started some thirty years earlier elsewhere in London, when the Company's pulse-rate was at its lowest. There was a great surge in musical awareness amongst the middle classes in London and other English cities in the 1840s and 1850s. Unfortunately it had left the Company quite unmoved. If it had been otherwise, some of the forgotten and unsung heroes of early Victorian music, like the great conductor Michael Costa, and the Reverend Thomas Helmore, Principal of St Mark's College Chelsea, where the Anglican Church choral revival began,[17] might have been welcomed into the Company. When the Company finally began to take an interest in music once more, under the influence of the City Corporation and its 'Music Deputation', and urged on no doubt by Chappell and Skilbeck, it invited John Stainer and his opposite number at Westminster Abbey, Frederick Bridge, to join the Company in 1878, together with the elderly John Hullah, who had indeed been one of those early heroes, teaching the world to sing during the 1840s, at Exeter Hall in the Strand.[18]

This was the beginning of a process whereby, during the next twenty-five years, the Company assembled the most active and distinguished group of musicians and music-lovers that had ever sat together round its Court table.

---

[15] Barty-King, pp. 16–20.
[16] 'Early Recollections of St Paul's' by W.A. Frost, quoted by Bernarr Rainbow in *The Choral Revival in the Anglican Church 1839–1872* (London: Barrie & Jenkins 1970), p. 310.
[17] Rainbow, pp. 48–74.
[18] Rainbow, p. 43.

11

'Westminster' Bridge and the Loan Exhibition

IT was a nice mixture of the two 'Establishments', Music and the City, which had the old Company's nerve-ends tingling as the new blood began to circulate. The therapy had come none too soon. The Company membership in 1882 was no more than forty-nine, and the Court, whose numbers were held at thirteen, were engaged in a merry-go-round, up to the top and back again. The Court fine, payable on election as an Assistant, was like a life-membership, entitling the members to a Court attendance fee and free Dinners for as long as they could keep going.

We have noted in the last chapter some meritorious families and individuals to whom is due the credit for keeping the Company in existence, but well into the 1890s there were others on the Court whose only claim to fame seems to have been that they took part in the 'follow-my-leader' path to the Mastership, twice if not three times. William Costall May, for example, became Master in 1873, and his turn came round again in 1886. Next in line was Henry Richard Frisby, whose first term as Master began in 1874, his second in 1885, and there was still time for one more in 1895. During all that time Frisby's only claim to distinction was to propose from the Chair that there should be music at Court Dinners. Perhaps it is invidious to single out any individual when the only evidence available is the Court Minute Book, and much good work may have passed unrecorded there; but what does clearly emerge from the Minutes is that while some Court members were anxious to introduce more people of talent on to the Court by enlarging its number, they were being frustrated by the circulating caucus who were alarmed that the Company's funds could not cope with the extra expense and free meals that this would entail. One member, Joseph Sidney Lescher, was so upset by the negative attitude of his colleagues that after two attempts at reform he resigned from the Court in 1886.

Writing his autobiography in 1918 Sir Frederick Bridge recalled:

In 1878 I became a member of the ancient City Guild, the Worshipful Company of Musicians, at the same time as Sir John Stainer and John Hullah. There was not much life in the old Company in those days, and it really did not do anything for music. But I was able to proffer a few suggestions which perhaps helped to start it on its present great and beneficent career of service to Music and musicians.[1]

The 'few suggestions' to which he referred will feature prominently later in this Chapter, but we should pay some regard first to his two colleagues, who both added lustre to the Company's complement, but actually proved to be lesser lights than the vigorous and vivacious Bridge. John Hullah was of course a much older man. He was sixty-six in 1878, compared to Bridge who was thirty-four and Stainer who was thirty-eight. Hullah was an educationalist and a teacher who by the time he joined the Company had become semi-retired, although he was still 'government inspector of music'. He died in 1884 before a vacancy had occurred on the Court.

Dr John Stainer, as he then was, had already established his reputation at St Paul's by the time he joined the Company, and he had also assisted Sir Frederick Ouseley with the formation of the Musical Association (now the Royal Musical Association), which would have brought him into contact with William Chappell. He was the first professor of harmony at the National Training School for Music, and had the dubious distinction of presiding over its demise in 1882, having been appointed Principal the previous year in succession to Arthur Sullivan. The failure was more apparent than real because it was in fact a reconstruction (or, in musical terms, a 'resolution'[2]) leading immediately to the opening of the Royal College of Music in the same premises, the first Director being George Grove. If Stainer was offered the Directorship of the Royal College, he declined it, preferring to devote his time to the Cathedral where he himself had been a chorister. In 1888 however he was obliged to give up his appointment at St Paul's due to problems with his eyesight, having been blind in one eye since an accident in childhood. He received a knighthood on his retirement.

In January 1889 Stainer was elected to the Court of the Company and, following the death of Sir Frederick Ouseley later in the year, succeeded him as Professor of Music at Oxford. He was Master of the Company in 1894/5 and then again in 1900/1, but died in office while on holiday in Italy in March 1901. He and Bridge had been lifelong friends, and in due course of time a Mr Stainer married a Miss Bridge.

Despite his youth, Dr Bridge had been elected to the Court four years before his good friend, and attended for the first time in April 1885. He was a man of remarkable energy. He had the disposition of a diplomat, well-endowed with social graces and with a huge circle of friends, commanding support, personal and financial, wherever it was needed for whatever cause was uppermost in his mind. He was a keen sportsman (although by his own account his enjoyment ran well ahead of his expertise) and his autobiography contains photographs of

---

1   Sir Frederick Bridge, *A Westminster Pilgrim* (London: Novello & Co. 1918), p. 118.

2   'The conversion of a dissonant configuration (e.g. a suspension) into a consonance': *The New Grove Dictionary of Music and Musicians*, vol. 15, p. 756.

15. Sir Frederick Bridge.

16. Sir Homewood Crawford.

17. Arthur Hill.

himself dressed for shooting and fishing as well as in his robes a Doctor of Music. One feels an infectious sense of fun radiating from the pages of his book. In the closing chapter he expressed his life's philosophy as follows:

> Some there may be who will see in my chronicle a too frequent propensity to extract humour from all manner of situations. The experience of a long life has however taught me that sweet reasonableness ever waits on humour, whose warm radiance searches and dispels many shadows.[3]

Sir Frederick was one who well understood how to 'preserve harmony'.

He had come to Westminster Abbey just three years before his election to the Company, having previously been organist at Manchester Cathedral since 1869. His predecessor at the Abbey, James Turle, had held the appointment of organist since 1831, and was to retain the nominal title until his death in 1882. In reality he was actively employed in that office for forty-four years. Bridge served as organist for forty-three years, retiring in 1918. During that time he directed the music at two Coronations, and at the Golden Jubilee Service in the Abbey in 1887. It was not surprising that he became affectionately known in royal circles as 'Westminster' Bridge.

In some years choral services exceeded seven hundred in number, and for the first twenty years of his appointment Bridge had no official assistant, although he relied greatly on his articled pupils. Even so, the amount that he crammed into his already full life was astonishing. In the field of education he taught at the National Training School and at the Royal College, where he was the first Professor of Counterpoint. He became Gresham Professor of Music, Chairman of the Board at Trinity College and the first Professor of Music at the University of London. In 1878 he was invited to become assistant conductor of the Madrigal Society, of which he was already a member, and soon became the conductor. He was President of the Society in 1904, and by 1918 was the most senior member. The appointment which brought him the widest acclaim was with the Royal Choral Society, whose conductor he became in 1896 after the death of Sir Joseph Barnby, who had merged his own choir with one founded in 1871 by Charles Gounod to form the Royal Albert Hall Choral Society, renamed the Royal Choral Society (by royal command) in 1888.[4] He resigned after twenty-two years in 1922. He received a knighthood in the Diamond Jubilee year ('a Jubilee knight').

Despite all his other preoccupations Bridge was a most regular attender at the Company's Court meetings, and after William Chappell's death in 1888 he became the source and inspiration for most of the Court's new projects, which became more numerous from one year to the next. In fact it was at the very Court at which Chappell's death was recorded, in October 1888, that Bridge proposed that the Company should institute the presentation of a gold medal each year, in rotation, to the most distinguished student at the Royal Academy, Royal

[3] Bridge, p. 345.
[4] Bridge, p. 273.

College, and Guildhall School, a proposal which was referred to a Committee. Out of this first suggestion by Bridge, the customary presentation by the Company of annual medals at every British music conservatory of note has gradually evolved.

It was hardly surprising that after thirty years on the Court, and having twice served as Master of the Company, some of his younger colleagues were a little in awe of Sir Frederick. One of them in 1915, in a confidential note to a newly elected Court member, complained that there were two members 'who have tried to rule the roost', one of them being Bridge, 'who at times quite overwhelms one with his torrent of words'.[5] Nevertheless even if he had by then overstayed his welcome, it would be hard to find any other single person in the Company's history who had done so much to revive it and set it upon a proper course for the future.

During the 1880s there were others joining the Company who would in due course provide moral and, more importantly, financial support for the new initiatives. Joseph Edward Street, Under-Sheriff Homewood Crawford and Charles Thomas Daniell Crews were all admitted and clothed with the Livery in 1880. Street was the first of his family to join the Company, although his family had been associated with the Madrigal Society for several generations, and he was its Honorary Secretary. Crawford was a man who was at the very centre of City life. In 1874 he had married Louisa Truscott, daughter of Sir Francis Truscott, who was to be Lord Mayor in 1879/80, the first of three generations of Truscott Lord Mayors, all members of the Company. Homewood Crawford was Solicitor to the Vintners Company from 1877 to 1885, when he became City Solicitor, an office which he held until 1924. He was Master of the Fanmakers Company three times and of the Glovers Company five times, and the first Master of the City of London Solicitors Company. He received a knighthood in 1900. He was to become a prominent member of the Court and, having previous experience of exhibitions organised by the Fanmakers, he was chosen to be Chairman of the Loan Exhibition Committee. Charles Crews was a wealthy stockbroker, and was an exceptionally generous benefactor to the Company. All three were active amateur musicians.

The only new member in 1882 was Edward Ernest Cooper, who was closely associated with the Royal Academy of Music and was Honorary Treasurer of its Management Committee. He was a City man also, becoming an Alderman in 1906, Sheriff in 1912/13 and Lord Mayor in 1919/20.

During 1884–86 four notable but diverse recruits were added to the Livery. Thomas Lea Southgate was a writer and journalist, who became the editor of *Musical News* and then became greatly involved in fighting the scandal of the purchase of fake music degrees. This led to the formation of The Union of

---

5   Arthur Hill's Diaries (unpublished), entry for 20 February 1915.

Graduates in Music in 1893, of which Southgate was the Honorary Secretary and principal spokesman. Sir John Stainer was its first president.[6]

The Reverend Robert Henry Hadden was Vicar of two City parishes, and then moved to St Mark's, North Audley Street, subsequently being appointed Honorary Chaplain to King Edward VII. It was his death, when he was Junior Warden of the Company, which led to the writing of the 'Dirge'.[7]

Two distinguished professional musicians made up the quartet, Charles Santley, who had by then abandoned the operatic stage and restricted his performing career to recital and oratorio, and Otto Goldschmidt, who is principally remembered (unfairly) for being the husband of Jenny Lind, but was also the founder of the London Bach Choir, and the reviver of Handel's great 'Ode for St Cecilia's Day'. Neither Santley nor Goldschmidt were elected to the Court, although Goldschmidt and Bridge were very close friends and fellow-members of the Athenaeum.

Last chronologically, but by no means least, must be added the names of Alfred Henry Littleton, and Arthur Frederick Hill. Littleton joined the Company in 1889, having succeeded his father Henry as Chairman of Novello & Co two years before. He was therefore preeminent within the music publishing fraternity. He was also a great expert in and collector of early printed music. Arthur Hill was the second son of William Ebsworth Hill, who had perfected the art or craft of violin restoration in England. He and his brothers were the fifth generation to carry on the business, then at number 38 New Bond Street. He became a liveryman in 1891. Littleton and Hill were to play an important part in promoting the Company, particularly in relation to the Loan Exhibition. They were both elected to the Court on the same day in January 1905, Hill having already done the Company a great service by effectively managing the Exhibition, in his capacity as Joint Secretary to the Committee.[8] Littleton had been a member of the Loan Exhibition Committee; he was Master in 1910/11. Hill followed as Master in 1911/12, and became Treasurer in 1923. He was also a great antiquarian, and was responsible for the discovery of most of the old records relating to the Company in the City archives and elsewhere. If it had not been for his interest and labours the writing of this present book would have taken ten times as long.

This was the team which included the principal players during the revival of the Company. One must not however overlook the ongoing representatives of the Skilbeck and Collard families, who were active as always. There was John Henry Skilbeck, a Court member from 1871 to 1919, Master in 1876/7 and again in 1888/9. He was still signing off the Treasurer's accounts as one of the trustees in 1908. His son, Clement Oswald, was the designer of the swan on the

---

6 See Ehrlich, pp. 136–7.
7 See p. 224.
8 The other Joint Secretary was Sir John Stainer's son, J.F.R. Stainer, who Hill complained to his diary 'was leaving all the work to him'.

Company's Livery Badge.[9] The two Collard brothers, William Stuartson and John Clementi, served as Treasurer in succession, W.S. Collard taking over from William Chappell when he resigned the treasurership in July 1887, and J.C. Collard taking his brother's place in January 1904. He held the office until his death in August 1918.

There should have been another Chappell, Edward, who was elected to the Court in 1887, only a year after his admission into the Company. Unfortunately he seems to have been plagued with ill-health, declining to serve as junior Warden in 1892, then elected the next year, but having to give up the office, and finally resigning from the Court in 1897.

Others who should have played a more prominent part as members of the Court were denied the opportunity because of the refusal of the 'old guard' to increase the numbers. John Bath, who was the driving force behind the establishment of the Guildhall School of Music, was one of the excluded ones, and we have noted that neither Charles Santley nor Otto Goldschmidt were called on to the Court. Joseph Edward Street was another who was not elected although he had been considered for election, and this was the cause of a quite acrimonious dispute between members of the Livery and the Court in 1894, it being alleged that undertakings had been given and then broken. It reached the point at which Sir John Stainer, who was then Senior Warden, offered to resign from the Court in order to make room for Street. Stainer was told that his resignation would not be accepted, and the principal agitator finally acknowledged that there had been a misunderstanding and that the member of the Court who had indicated that Street would be elected had no authority and was in no way 'an ambassador' for the Court. Unfortunately Street's name continued thereafter to be omitted from the list of potential Court members, but this may have been at his own request. He was certainly highly regarded, and closely associated with Bridge at the Madrigal Society.

There were also one or two 'big fish' which the Company failed to catch, most notably Sir Arthur Sullivan, who was elected in October 1888. There is a marginal note in pencil in the Clerk's handwriting alongside this entry: 'Refused to join'. Another reluctant member was the distinguished lawyer Edwin Freshfield, the founder of the firm of that name. He was elected in 1880, but deferred taking up the freedom and livery for twenty-five years, first appearing on the Livery list in July 1905! The success of the Loan Exhibition may have persuaded him that this was an organisation worth joining.

It was inevitable that with eminent professional musicians joining the Company just at the time the London music colleges were being set up, or reestablished with sufficient patronage to survive, the Company would be drawn into the business of providing financial support. In 1880 this was still a completely novel concept for the Company, the only help that it had previously given to the profession being the intermittent subscription to the Royal Society of

---

[9] See pp. 196–7.

Musicians and the payments to certain individuals for relief from poverty and distress. The Company's finances were very limited, and barely sufficient to meet the regular attendance and dining expenses of the Court and Livery. There were as yet no funds specifically designated for charitable use. Nevertheless the appeals for help from the new colleges were beginning to reach the Clerk's office. The Corporation Music Deputation (which became the Music Committee in 1882) was appealing to the Livery Companies to help to establish scholarships at the Guildhall School, and (although it was much more soundly based than the National Training School, which had been intended to provide free music education maintained by voluntary contributions) the Royal College of Music still needed funds for exhibitions and scholarships for outstanding pupils who could not pay the fees.

The first appeal to the Livery Companies for the Guildhall School achieved only one response, from the Salters Company.[10] A second appeal in 1882 was more successful, but the Musicians Company, for reasons which are not apparent, decided that such money as they could spare should go to the Royal College and not to the Guildhall School, and a landmark decision was taken by the Court that a donation of one hundred guineas should be made, to be paid at the rate of twenty guineas per annum over five years.

Just at the expiry of those five years, John Bath makes one more appearance in the Company's annals, presenting an Address to the Court in April 1887 from eight of the Livery, asking for permission to convene a meeting of the Livery 'to consider if it was proper and expedient for the Company to undertake any movement in relation to the cause of Musical Science and Art in this Country'. The Court responded that the memorialists should formulate more definitely their views and objects in convening such a meeting, and nothing further is recorded on this subject, but it was only a little more than a year before Dr Bridge put forward his proposal for the gold medal referred to earlier in the chapter. It seems more than likely that this idea grew out of discussions that Bridge would have had with the members of the Livery who wanted to see the Company more active. The Committee which the Court set up to consider the medal proposal took a year to report back, but in the meantime, at the request of the Court, they had obtained designs and tenders for the medal, and finally recommended that the design by C.B. Birch A.R.A. should be accepted, and that the sum of £80 should be approved for the design and the making of the die. This was agreed and the design has been used for the Company's medal since 1889, the original die being still in use.

Dr Bridge, who had been a member of the Medal Committee, was allowed to present its report in the form of a revised Resolution, which the Court accepted. The Committee had come to the conclusion that to present a gold medal every year would be too expensive, and the new proposal was in two parts; first that a *silver medal* be awarded annually in rotation at the three institutions – the candi-

---

[10] Barty-King, p. 28.

date to be nominated without competition or examination by the Principal, assisted in each case by two of his principal professors; second, that a *gold medal* be awarded from time to time to some distinguished British-born subject 'who shall add a valuable contribution to musical composition or musical literature and in the case of very distinguished merit the Freedom of the Company may be conferred with the gold medal'.

The award of one annual silver medal was within the financial capability of the Company, but until additional funds were available it would have to be taken in turn by the Royal Academy, the Royal College and the Guildhall School, in that order. The heads of each institution gratefully accepted the proposal, and the first presentation was made to H. Stanley Hawley at the Royal Academy in 1889.

A possible clue to the unwillingness of the Company to help the fledgling Guildhall School may be found in the fact that when Sir Joseph Barnby was appointed in April 1892, after the death of the first Principal, Thomas Henry Weist Hill, Dr Bridge lost no time in proposing that the new Principal should be invited to dine with the Company, Barnby being Bridge's old friend, whereas Hill does not even rate a mention in his autobiography. At the following Court, in October 1892, Bridge asked the Court to agree to provide enough money each year for a scholarship at the Guildhall School of Music to provide free education in one subject. Sir Joseph was to be consulted on the details of the proposal. This was agreed by the Court without demur, and a year later, in October 1893, when he was Master, Bridge announced that the scholarship would be for Composition, and that the award should be competed for. The amount of the scholarship was to be nine guineas per annum. This was the first of the Company's permanent scholarships. No further attempt was made to fund any other recurrent awards out of the Company's ordinary resources. All medals and scholarships subsequently established were dependent on the generosity of donors who were prepared to provide an endowment fund for them. These are discussed in the next chapter.

It was now more than two hundred years since Charles II had stripped the City of London of its Charter, the ultimate low-point in relations between the Monarch and the City of London. Since that time the Livery Companies had been taking whatever opportunities presented themselves to honour successive members of the Royal Family, as one means of raising their self-esteem and justifying their continued existence. It was possible and acceptable for the 'Great Twelve' to enlist members of the Royal Family into their guilds; to take just one example, the Grocers Company had by this time successively elected, as Freemen, King William III, (who was also elected 'Sovereign Master' in 1689), the Duke of York, brother to George III, and his younger brother the Duke of Gloucester, Queen Victoria's first cousin the Duke of Cambridge,[11] the Prince of Wales and

---

[11] Commander-in-Chief of the Army from 1856 to 1895, and personally responsible for the successful establishment of the Royal Military School of Music at Kneller Hall.

Prince Alfred, Duke of Edinburgh. The Livery Halls of the Great Twelve and lesser Companies were conspicuous for their portraits of kings, queens and princes. For the small Companies, especially those without halls, the circumstances in which royal patronage could be sought were much more limited and up to this point the Musicians Company had made no gesture of loyalty to their Sovereign, despite the fact that Prince Albert had been a keen amateur musician.

It will come as no surprise that Dr Bridge should be the man to remedy the deficiency. Whether he already had in mind, when he made his proposal regarding the Gold Medal in 1889, that he was likely to be elected Master for the year 1892/3, and that there could be nothing more prestigious for the Company (under his direction) than to award its first Gold Medal to the Prince of Wales, we shall never know, but it is self-evident that in his position as Organist of the Abbey, and having been made a Member of the Victorian Order in appreciation of his Golden Jubilee Service in 1887, he was uniquely placed to request and be granted the occasion for the presentation of the medal on behalf of the Company.

The project was set in motion early in 1893, and at the April Court the following Resolution was proposed by the Master and carried unanimously:

> That the Worshipful Company of Musicians in order to express its deep appreciation of the untiring interest shewn by H.R.H. the Prince of Wales in the progress of the art of Music in this Country which has resulted in the successful foundation of the Royal College of Music with its liberal endowments in aid of promising talent, respectfully begs His Royal Highness to accept the Gold Medal struck by the Company for the purpose of encouraging Music and Musicians. The Company cannot but feel that should His Royal Highness graciously become the first recipient of their offering he will not only confer an honour on them, but will give a prestige and value to their Medal which will greatly enhance its value to future holders.

This effusive but loyal message was duly conveyed to Marlborough House, and at the next Court on 4 July it was announced that His Royal Highness had named the 19 July as the date when it would be convenient for a deputation to attend at Marlborough House to present the Medal.

The representatives of the Company who accompanied the Master on 19 July were led by the Junior Warden, Sir John Stainer, and the Immediate Pastmaster, Robert Warrick, and included W.S. Collard and Alfred Littleton, also Otto Goldschmidt and J.E. Street, neither of whom were Court members, but attended no doubt at the Master's special invitation. The Resolution was read, the presentation made, and the Prince of Wales expressed his thanks and best wishes for the spread and development of musical education, and his gratification that his efforts had been recognised by 'the ancient and interesting' Company of Musicians.[12]

---

[12] Bridge, p. 119.

Bridge had 'scored another first', which would be used as a precedent in various ways throughout the 20th century.

A quiet passage followed the completion of Dr Bridge's year of office as Master, although he would find himself back in the Chair six years later. He was succeeded by John Clementi Collard who in due course would surpass all previous benefactors of the Company with his magnificent bequest, but that was still many years away. Apart from the little difficulty relating to Mr Street already referred to, the most significant event in his year of office was the second award of the Company's silver medal at the Royal College – the recipient was a young singer whose name was Clara Butt.

In the following year, when Sir John Stainer was Master, although the matter does not seem to have been put to a vote in the Court, Pastmaster (twice) Wilkinson was on record as opposing any increase in the numbers on the Court because he was anxious about the state of the Company's finances. The much-needed increase was thus once again deferred. The Livery was however growing, with new members joining the Company at the rate of two or three each year, most of them with a much livelier interest in music than the previous generation. One important recruit in 1894 was Colonel Thomas Shaw Hellier, who had just retired the previous year as Commandant of the Royal Military School of Music, Kneller Hall. It was through his membership of the Company that its links with Kneller Hall were first established.[13]

The turn of the century passed quietly, no one in the Company being yet aware of the significance of the date 1500, although Arthur Hill in his first 'Handbook' of the Company, published in 1905, refers to the minstrels' petition without recognising it for what it was. 1904 was still earmarked as the year of celebration, even though the guilty secret of what happened to James I's Charter had once again been brought into the open and quickly buried. One of the many musical journals which were circulating at the time had published an article in 1887, based no doubt on a chance find in Hawkins' History, casting doubts on the origins of the Company. The Court appointed a Committee to search the archives, and they found a marginal note on the Patent Roll for 2 James I (1604) alongside the inscribed Charter, stating that 'These Letters Patent together with the enrolment of the same are void'. The note which was in Latin and had clearly been written in that same year went on to describe in detail the physical surrender of the Charter and its cancellation on 22 April 1635.

The Committee's Report to the Court consisted of four short paragraphs, the last of which read:

Under these circumstances your Committee consider that they should not proceed further without reporting these facts to your honourable Court.[14]

13 See p. 208.
14 The Report is held with the Company's documents at the Guildhall Library, MS 3102.

The Report was not minuted, and the Committee was not asked to pursue the matter further. There was a shrug of the corporate shoulders and what happened in 1635 was treated as a non-event. It was sufficient that the Company had been given a charter in 1604, and by some means or other was still going strong.

Before the Court could put its mind to the Tercentenary, Queen Victoria died at the age of eighty-two, and it was not long before its members were thinking about the forthcoming coronation of their king, who had accepted the Company's Gold Medal, and what extra honour or compliment the Company could pay him. It was decided to hold a competition for a Coronation March suitable for performance in the course of the Coronation Festivities. The winner of the competition would receive a prize of Fifty Guineas. The competition was announced on 1 August 1901, and that the Adjudicators would be Sir Frederick Bridge, Sir Walter Parratt (Master of the King's Music) and Sir Hubert Parry (Director of the Royal College of Music). There were 189 competitors. The winner of the competition was Percy Godfrey, Master of Music at the King's School Canterbury, and his composition was played at the Coronation Service (which was dramatically delayed at the last moment as a result of the king's attack of appendicitis) on 9 August 1902. Godfrey was made a member of the Company at no expense to himself, the fines and fees having been donated by Mr Crews, one of his many acts of benevolence to the Company.

The sheet music of the Coronation March had a tremendous sale, raising the sum of £866 for the Company, which was donated to the King Edward VII Hospital Fund. A cheque for this sum was presented to the Prince of Wales at York House, St James' on 12 February 1903.

Crews' next act of generosity was to provide the prize money for a competition held in 1904 for the best setting of a given text, to be used as the Company's Grace. The prize was won by the celebrated Cambridge composer and lecturer, Charles Wood, with a most beautiful short piece which is still used regularly at its banquets by the Company.[15] A second competition for a variety of musical compositions took place the same year to mark the Tercentenary, with four prizes awarded by the Rev Henry Cart, a member of the Livery.

These relatively small but generous 'private initiatives' demonstrate the enthusiasm with which the members of the Company welcomed the Tercentenary. The Company's own celebration was conceived on a much greater scale, and for an institution which had so recently come out of its 'cocoon' it was very ambitious indeed. The proposal was made at the Court in January 1903 by Sir Homewood Crawford, and unanimously agreed, that the Tercentenary should be marked by an Exhibition, to be held under the auspices of the Company, of ancient musical instruments, manuscripts, autographs, portraits, books and other musical mementos of music and musicians. Crawford was elected Chairman of the special Committee set up to arrange and present the Exhibition. It

[15] See pp. 223–4.

was a large Committee of twenty-one, of whom ten were Court members, and it included the newly appointed Clerk, Thomas Collingwood Fenwick. The Joint Secretaries were Arthur Hill and J.F.R. Stainer. The Chairman, with his experience and connexion as City Solicitor behind him, and Arthur Hill, at the heart of antiquarian music, both professionally and privately, were the driving forces behind the massive undertaking, which was achieved without any technical or specialist assistance, apart from the generous help received from the staff of Fishmongers Hall, where the exhibition was held. Other Livery Companies as well as the Fishmongers (who bore most of the cost of the opening ceremony) provided financial help; those listed in the official report were the Goldsmiths, Clothworkers, Mercers, Grocers, Skinners, Merchant Taylors, Haberdashers, Vintners and Leathersellers, and financial help came also from members of the Company. But it was the unhesitating supply of exhibits from very many sources, including the Royal Collection, which ensured the great success of the exhibition, 'many of which' as the report put it, 'had never before been exhibited nor are they likely to be gathered together again'. An illustrated catalogue was published after the exhibition as a memento of the occasion.[16] Another personal memento was preserved by Arthur Hill in his diary, written by the 'general dogsbody' who Hill relied on to a very great extent in the setting up and dismantling of the exhibition and its smooth running from day to day. His name was F.E. White and he was a dealer in old music. Mr White's short account is reproduced in Appendix 9. It shows the casual but remarkably effective way in which the exhibition was administered.

Not without some initial difficulty it was arranged that the Exhibition would be opened by the Prince and Princess of Wales. According to Arthur Hill's diary[17] the Prince 'dislikes speaking very much and anything ceremonious'. However, the actual opening ceremonial on 27 June was quite simple, and the royal party were able to make their tour of the exhibits privately with an entourage of about twenty people, including the Lord Mayor and the Lady Mayoress, the Master of the Company, William Herring, and the Prime Warden of the Fishmongers, Henry Chinnery. On entering the Great Hall their Royal Highnesses were entertained with a short recital of 'Shakespearian Music' played on authentic instruments and on their way around the stands and cases they would have seen a remarkable collection of early musical instruments, missals and other illuminated manuscripts and early printed music books. Light relief was provided by Sir Frederick Bridge, who undertook to play the National Anthem on a reproduction of a Graeco-Roman water-organ. Bridge said that the effect was 'rather ludicrous' but caused considerable amusement.[18]

While it was open to the public the exhibition was brought to life by a series of seventeen lectures on instruments and early music, nine of which were given by

[16] 'Catalogue of the Loan Exhibition held in Fishmongers' Hall 1904'.
[17] Arthur Hill's Diaries, 10 February 1904.
[18] Bridge, p. 151.

18. The Great Hall at Fishmongers' Hall set up for the Musicians Company Loan Exhibition which continued through June and July 1904.

members of the Company. Thanks to Mr Lett's skills in shorthand[19] and Mr White's initiative, the lectures have been published and preserved for posterity,[20] an invaluable quick reference guide to the state of technical and antiquarian knowledge at the beginning of the 20th century. The lectures were illustrated with demonstrations and musical examples.

It would be impossible to do justice to the erudition and scope of the lecturers or their subject-matter, in a précis in this chapter. So far from being archaic, the lecturers' ability to review and explain complex topics with clarity and simplicity (not to mention humour) remains impressive and exemplary. Just a few references must suffice to demonstrate this.

[19] See p. 276.
[20] *English Music, Being the Lectures given at the Loan Exhibition of the Worshipful Company of Musicians held at Fishmongers Hall, London Bridge June–July 1904* (published in London by Walter Scott Publishing Co. Ltd and in New York by Charles Scribner's Sons, 1906).

Dr W.H. Cummings, Principal of the Guildhall School of Music and Drama, delivered the second lecture, and chose for his subject 'Our English Songs'. He claimed the credit, no doubt with perfect justification, for first attributing the tune of the National Anthem to John Bull. He told the audience that there was no basis for the claim, reported a few weeks before in the *Evening Standard*, that Wagner wrote 'Rule Britannia'. The American National Anthem was based on the Anacreontic Society Ode with music by John Stafford Smith. These were facts that were not widely known at the time. It was a good way of introducing a talk which then traversed the whole range of English song from 'Sumer is i-comen in' to 'Annabelle Lee'.

Dr Henry Watson of Manchester shed a great deal of light on a subject which was not generally understood by music enthusiasts of the time – the relationship and differentiation between viols and the violin family and their music. It is a subject which is still not entirely free from controversy. A series of three lectures then covered 'Our Dances of Bygone Days', 'Masques and Early Operas', and 'English Opera after Purcell'. It is only in the last of these, when the lecturer, Dr Frank Sawyer of the Royal College of Music, attempted to divide the operatic works of the last two hundred years into three groups, that one feels tempted to question whether this was done for convenience, or desperation, or whether there were substantial reasons for it. Perhaps a hundred years on there is some food for fresh thought here. Fifty years ago the classification would have been dismissed as having no weight or merit. What Sawyer did was to group together Gay and Pepusch with Arne, Storace, Dibdin and Bishop in Group 1. Group 2 consisted of Balfe, Wallace, Macfarren and Benedict, and Group 3 was to include Alexander Mackenzie, Goring Thomas, Corder, Stanford and Sullivan. A certain lack of confidence is detectable towards the end of the talk. Sawyer was obviously waiting for something better to happen in English opera, and it is a pity that he did not live to see it.

Interestingly Sir Frederick Bridge, whose subject was 'Music in England in 1604', began his lecture with some Burney-bashing, whose 'large book' was 'in many ways admirable . . . but many of his remarks are extremely bitter and often ignorant'.[21] Bridge's first illustration was a piece arranged from *Morley's Consort Lessons* about which Dr Burney had written, with his knife as usual into the City,

> Master Morley – supposing, perhaps, that the harmony which was to be heard through the clattering of knives, forks, spoons, and plates, with the jingling of glasses and conversation of a city feast, need not be very accurate or refined – was not very nice in setting part of these tunes, which are so far from correct that almost any of the city 'waits' would, in musical cant, have vamped as good an accompaniment.

In fact Burney, according to Bridge, could never have heard Morley's arrangement of the tunes, because, at any rate since the Great Fire, no complete set of

---

[21] *English Music*, p. 171.

parts existed. Starting from the one known surviving copy of the viol part, he and Sir John Stainer had made a search and discovered two others, the recorder part in the British Museum and the cittern part in the Bodleian. There was no bass part – but that which Bridge had written before the discovery of the cittern part all but fitted the original. In connection with the Exhibition the bandora part had now turned up, so that only the lute part was still missing. Having cast considerable doubts on Burney's veracity Sir Frederick had the reconstructed piece played and sung; it was the now well-known Air, 'O Mistress Mine'.

The last lecture was delivered by Sir Ernest Clarke, a member of the Loan Exhibition Committee, on the subject of 'Music of the Countryside'. In his pre-amble, which had little to do with the title of his lecture, Clarke referred to Sir George Buck, Master of the Revels from 1603, just at the time the Company received its Charter, who wrote a book entitled 'The Third University of England; or a Treatise of all the Colleges, Ancient Schools of privilege, and of Houses of Learning and Liberal Arts, within and about the most famous city of London'. The following quotation, which does not appear to have been repro-duced elsewhere, comes from Chapter 38 of that book:

> Here be also the best Musicians of this kingdom, and equal to any in Europe for their skill either in composing, and setting, or in singing, or for playing upon any kind of musical instruments. The musicians have obtained of the King our sover-eign Lord, Letters patent for a Society and corporation.

Sir Ernest mentioned that Buck had then described the Company's arms exactly as they still were in 1904, and went on:

> It is our Company's object to restore to England that equality with other nations for the skill of its musicians 'either in composing, and setting, or in singing, or for playing upon any kind of musical instruments'; and the success of this series of Lectures will, I hope, convince Sir Homewood Crawford, our modern Sir George Buck, that in putting his hand to this great work, he has assisted very importantly to make the words of his prototype of three hundred years ago applicable to the present day.[22]

The exhibition closed on Saturday the 16 July, but everything was left in place until Monday morning, because the King had expressed a wish to view the exhi-bition privately on Sunday the 17th. Unfortunately no account survives of his visit. While the exhibition was open, the Company, their ladies and friends were well entertained with a *conversazione* with music given by the Wardens on 30 June, a special Banquet (paid for by the Master) to mark the Tercentenary on 8 July, and a closing reception on 17 July, provided by Sir Homewood Crawford, the Chairman of the Committee and Lady Crawford. There can be no doubt that in every respect the exhibition, which comprised over two thousand exhibits

---

[22] *English Music*, pp. 502–3.

from 193 lenders, and the series of lectures which illuminated it, were an out-standing success. On 23 July Arthur Hill wrote to the Clerk:

> So far, apart from the trifling mistake of three small items being sent to the wrong person, everything has gone all right, but I was naturally very anxious about the safe return of the Exhibits. Now that it is all over, I think I may say that never again will I undertake such a task![23]

The Company had however now gained its own momentum, and Hill was soon active again as one of its driving forces, together with Sir Homewood Craw-ford and Charles Crews, who succeeded William Herring as Master in November 1904. In the following year, Crews became President of the Livery Club, and these two years were celebrated with a period of imaginative giving, spending and innovation on his part, which were unique in the Company's history.

Charles Crews had been making donations and spending lesser sums before this time, and would continue to do so afterwards. In early 1904 for instance, he undertook to provide the Company with Gowns for the Master, Wardens and Clerk, which were worn for the first time in May, just in time for the Tercentenary festivities. Later in the year, to mark his election as Master he gave the Company a silver-gilt Loving Cup. During his year as Master, he underwrote the entire cost of a revival of a Jacobean Masque, 'The Masque of the Golden Tree' which was performed on 29 May 1905 in the theatre of the Guildhall School of Music, in the presence of Princess Christian of Schleswig-Holstein and her two daughters, together with the Landgraf of Hesse, the Lord Chief Justice and many other distinguished guests. The same month he presented a 'portrait of Handel by Rigaud'[24] to the Company.

In the meantime under his instructions the Clerk had been negotiating with the Stationers' Company for an arrangement whereby the Company could treat Stationers' Hall as its 'Headquarters', with the right to use it regularly for the Company's Court Meetings and its Dinners and Banquets; also for storage and a cellar for the Company's wines, and at a Special Meeting of the Court held on 11 May 1905 the Master was able to announce that an Agreement had been entered into embodying these terms on the basis of a 'Licence at Will'. So began the long-standing relationship with the Stationers' Company.

In the following year, during his presidency of the Livery Club, Crews informed the Court of his desire to pay for the installation, in the Company's name, of a stained-glass window dedicated to St Cecilia in the Lady Chapel of Southwark Cathedral. He also asked the Court's permission to arrange, in his capacity as President of the Livery Club, for a service to take place in St Paul's Cathedral on St Cecilia's Day, at which he hoped that the Bishop of London

---

23 Arthur Hill's Diaries, 23 July 1904.
24 Unfortunately, sixty years later the subject of this painting was declared on the best author-ity to be unidentifiable and certainly not G.F. Handel, and the Court decided to sell the portrait.

would preach a short sermon. The Court gave their full support to this proposal, and the event was recorded in the Minute Book. It shows that what was devised on that occasion remained virtually unchanged for ninety years:

Thursday 22nd November 1906: The members of the Company by arrangement with the authorities of St Paul's Cathedral attended Evensong at 4 p.m. at the Cathedral, when special music was given, this being the revival of an ancient custom of attending Church on St Cecilia's Day.

The Members met in the Lord Mayor's Vestry and proceeded in procession to the Chancel where Stalls were allotted to them, subsequently returning to the Lord Mayor's Vestry in the same order.

The procession was formed as follows:-

Cathedral Verger
Company's Beadle with Mace
28 Liverymen, two abreast
The President of the Livery Club
3 Honorary Freemen
The Clerk
Members of the Court who had not passed the Chair
Pastmasters
The Company's Banner borne by a cathedral official supported by the two
most junior members of the Company
The Chaplain
The Wardens
The Acting Master[25]

Livery gowns were provided[26] for those who did not bring their own gowns and hoods. The Livery Club gave a Banquet in the evening, following the service, to which the Cathedral dignitaries were invited.

Thus fully armed, adorned and harmonised there sprang into instant existence an annual celebration which has been firmly fixed ever since in the Company's calendar, even though conflict with the Musicians' Benevolent Fund St Cecilia Festival has necessitated a change of date in recent years, and the Masters, Prime Wardens and Clerks of the other Livery Companies are now invited to participate.

At the same Court, in October 1906, at which the St Cecilia service was proposed, a Committee which had been appointed for the purpose recommended the introduction of a Livery Badge, recalling the badge and collar worn in ancient times by the City Waits, and following the example of at least twelve other Livery Companies. The Treasurer, J.C. Collard, stated that he could not

---

[25] The beginning of Sir Homewood Crawford's year of office as Master was marred by a prolonged bout of illness which lasted until the following Spring. His place at the St Cecilia service was taken by the Immediate Pastmaster, Mr E.E. Cooper (subsequently Lord Mayor in 1919/20).

[26] These would have been the standard livery gowns without distinctive colour customarily hired out by Ede & Ravenscroft.

fund the cost of the dies from the Company's resources, and Charles Crews immediately undertook to cover the whole cost.

To complete his benefactions at this time Crews announced in January 1907 that he proposed to present a bust of Orlando Gibbons to Westminster Abbey in the name of the Company, his only stipulation being that he be allowed to make all the arrangements himself! He also announced that he was not satisfied with the plans for the St Cecilia window put up by Southwark, and he was now considering St Paul's Cathedral instead, a project which was confirmed at the following Court. The window was duly installed in the North Transept, but was completely destroyed in the Blitz, on 9 October 1940.

Many years after these great gifts were made to and on behalf of the Company, Arthur Hill indulged in some reminiscences in a letter to the Clerk. He claimed that the window and the St Cecilia revival had both been initiated at his suggestion. One other suggestion which Hill made to Crews had not been taken up:

> He was also sympathetic about another idea of mine which was to endow some almshouses for decayed musicians, but although he was at one time a millionaire, I failed to get him to carry this through. He left us, as you know, £500.[27]

---

27 Letter from A.F. Hill to H.A.F. Crewdson dated 18 October 1934.

12

A Twentieth-Century Panorama

A PHANTOM member of the Musicians' Company Court of 1907 who managed to put in a supernatural appearance at a Court Meeting of 1997 would have felt instantly at home in familiar surroundings. Apart from the Gowns (many more, to a different design), and the facial hair (much less) and the financial statements (a proliferation of noughts after every number), everything would have been much the same, the layout of the Court table, the procedure and the items on the Agenda – apologies, minutes of the last meeting, committee reports, accounts for payment, admissions and elections, any other business.[1] The Company, ninety years on, was bigger and richer, but otherwise it was very much as it had been at the beginning of the Century, whereas it would be difficult to prove that such similarities existed for any other matching period in the Company's history.

The homogeneity of the Company at the beginning and end of the 20th century lends itself to a panoramic survey. The Company can be examined within those parameters as if displayed like a map or tapestry, while at the same time one can usefully gather in one or two loose threads from earlier times which have so far been left dangling. This will be a less frenetic process than charting the Company's progress through ten decades, jumping from one topic to another as one goes. There will however be sub-headings to identify the subject-matter of each section, in what might otherwise be an unmarked trail.

The New Charter

During the course of the book it has become clear that the Court and Livery continued to attach a great deal of weight to the 1604 Charter which, until well into the 20th century, was the only document of origin of which they were aware. The fact that the Charter had been forfeited in 1635 had been hushed up on at least

---

[1]   Had the visit been delayed for two more years, the time-warped Court member from 1907 would have felt slightly less at home, finding himself in the presence of the Company's first Lady Assistant, Mrs Janet Lowy, and the Company's first Lady Assistant Clerk, Mrs Margaret Alford.

two occasions, even though anyone who had access to Sir John Hawkins' 'History' could hardly fail to have had grave doubts about the Company's supposed origins. By the time that Percy Scholes started lobbing his grenades into the Clerk's Office[2] something had to be done.

It was not just a cosmetic exercise. Since 1881, it had been the policy of the Court to invest much of the Company's surplus funds not in government stocks, but in freehold ground rents, which yielded an annual return two or three percentage points better than gilt-edged securities such as '2½ % Consols'. Over £10,000 had been invested in this way. Alastair Crewdson, being a Solicitor as well as Clerk, felt some concern about the status of these ground rents, and whether the Company had a right to hold them, and whether there was a latent problem in 'making title' when they were sold. The problem did not arise with the stocks and shares, because these were held by Trustees for the Company, and no one would be investigating their capacity to sell. But for freehold property the power to hold land *in mortmain* had been conferred expressly by the 1604 Charter, and *ipso facto* had been taken away again by its forfeiture. Was there any subsequent Act of Parliament which unequivocally applied to the Company, or any substitute Charter which could be proved to exist? If the incorporation of the Company was in doubt, its right to hold freeholds must also be in doubt. Even if the City's Act of 1500 had given the Company power to hold land within the City's own jurisdiction, this would have been of little assistance, as all the ground rents were in modern suburban London.

In 1949 it was decided that the obtaining of a new Charter was essential, and the old procedure, differing little from that followed in 1603, was once more put in train. First the permission of the Court of Aldermen had to be obtained. This was given and communicated by the Town Clerk on 23 February 1950. Then the Petition, in approved form, was submitted to the Privy Council Office, and on 8 December 1950 the Clerk of the Privy Council reported that:

> The King was pleased, at the Council held by His Majesty today, to approve the grant of a Charter to the Worshipful Company of Musicians of London.

The Charter and Bye-Laws are set out in Appendix 10. The Petition, to which these documents had been annexed in draft form, contained a brief account of the Company's constitution since 1500, and described the grant and forfeiture of the 1604 Charter, and the Charters obtained by the King's Musicians in the 17th century for the Westminster Company and its demise in 1679. It then stated that about the middle of the 18th century the City Company 'readopted the Charter of James I and has continued to use the same down to the present day'. The date of 1747 was the supposed date of the 'regrant', but 'new and diligent search has failed to bring to light the supposed re-grant of the said Charter'. The Company was therefore being 'hindered in the management of its common concerns and

---

2 See p. 101.

in its devotion to the Art or Science of Music'. Being persuaded of the necessity of disposing of any further doubts as to the regrant of the Charter *in perpetuum*, the Court had resolved on 19 July 1949

> to petition Your Majesty in Council for a new Charter of Incorporation to be granted them so that the efficiency of the Company may be promoted and they be enabled to pursue without hindrance the welfare of the said Art or Science of Music.

With the grant of the George VI Charter the long and untidy saga of the good-standing of the Company at last came to an end, and in due course the event was celebrated by the obliteration of the dates '1469' and '1606' from the Company's Badge and the substitution of '1500' and '1950'. The '1604' date was retained.

The new Charter and the Bye-laws are the current governing constitutional documents of the Company, and they have served the Company well during the fifty years since they became effective. The principal difference between these and the earlier Acts, Charter and Bye-laws (as might be expected) is the absence of any power to regulate City musicians or conscript them into the Company. It was replaced in the 1950 Charter by a principal object defined in terms of support rather than control:

> To foster and encourage the Art or Science of Music and the Craft of Musical-Instrument-making in the City of London the suburbs thereof and in the United Kingdom by the establishment and grant of prizes, medals, scholarships, fellowships and endowments; and the institution of examinations, competitions and certificates; the organisation of exhibitions and such other means as shall be judged from time to time by the Court of Assistants conducive to such objects.[3]

In other respects there was some simplification, but little change. The 1604 Charter permitted the Company to hold land up to an annual value of £20. This was increased in 1950 to £5,000. Fortunately, in the light of the inflation which has radically affected land values since 1950, the Company has abandoned its ground rents investment policy and has not acquired any other real estate. Any future decision to invest in freehold or leasehold property may require another application to the Privy Council.

The Company's Year

It is customary to record the Company's year according to the twelve months' period of office of successive Masters, so that the Company's year begins in November, on the date of installation of the new Master. The commencement in November rather than October is a fairly recent development, dating from the

---

[3] Worshipful Company of Musicians, Royal Charter of 1950, Clause 4 (ii).

separation in 1920 of the Installation Court from the statutory October Court, which under the old and new Bye-laws is required to be held within twenty days of the Feast of Michaelmas, for the purpose of electing the new Master and Wardens. Prior to 1920 the Installation and the Livery Dinner followed immediately upon the October Court meeting.

The 'Installation' or Livery Dinner is a very ancient institution, probably going back to the early 16th century, when there are records of the Company dining in Pewterers' Hall, and noted regularly in the 18th century account books (although the annual dinner for the Livery was sometimes held at a different time of year from the Installation, in which case only the members of the Court would 'dine-in' the new Master). During the 20th century it has customarily been an occasion for entertaining distinguished guests and the Master's own circle of friends, and also the winners of the Company's medals. The medals used to be presented individually after Dinner, but as they increased in number the ceremony became a little monotonous, and the presentation now takes place in the presence of the Court a short while before. This leaves more time for the music after (*never* through) Dinner.

The change of date to November has brought the beginning of the year much closer to the Company's Patronal Festival – St Cecilia's Day, 22 November. As mentioned in the previous chapter this was celebrated from 1906 to 1996 with a special Evensong in St Paul's Cathedral, but the popularity of the Saint and her Festival has reached the point at which it is necessary to share the choral resources available with a much wider circle of music-lovers, and the Company now participates in the Festival organised by the Musicians' Benevolent Fund on or close to the Saint's day, and has its own Evensong at St Paul's a month or so earlier. Despite grave doubts about her actual existence, and about her predilection for playing the organ, St Cecilia's Festival has become one of the most popular in the calendar, and the celebrations have grown and are likely to continue to grow, particularly in the City of London, where the precedent began in 1683, and became associated with Stationers Hall as soon as the rebuilding of the Hall after the Great Fire had been completed in the following year.

The Company now regularly participates in the 'three choir' Festival Service, held in rotation at St Paul's, Westminster Abbey and Westminster Cathedral, and is represented at the Luncheon after the Service, and at the Royal Concert given the same evening in aid of musical charities, at either the Barbican Hall, Festival Hall or the Royal Albert Hall. The Master of the Company is an *ex officio* member of the select party accompanying the royal guest.

Under the Bye-laws of the Company the Court is obliged to meet at least four times a year in January, April, July and October, and this regular pattern determines the administrative pattern for the Company's year, as meetings of the various Committees which report to the Court have to be arranged to fit in with the Court schedule. The Court maintains a long tradition of dining together after the April Court; a more recent innovation is the Dinner following the October Court which is known as 'the Masters' and Clerks' Dinner', and provides an opportunity for the Master to return the hospitality received by him from other Companies during his year of office.

For the Livery and their guests there is the Midsummer Banquet in mid-June, which in the days when all members of the Livery were male, and the event was colloquially known as 'Ladies' Night', was an opportunity to entertain wives and 'couples'. Now that the Livery is composed of ladies as well as gentlemen, the distinction between the Livery Dinner and the Midsummer Banquet has become somewhat blurred. There is perhaps still a feeling that the Summer function is an *Operetta*, whereas the Livery Dinner is *Grand Opera*; the latter is therefore a little more *serioso*, an opportunity perhaps for the Principal Guest to deliver a Message, and for the new Master to unfold his plans for the forthcoming year. But Masters and Principal Guests can have their own concept of what is right for an occasion, and the difference between the two functions is often imperceptible.

The tradition that the City closes down in August dies hard, and August is usually the quietest month in the year. The Company wakes up again in September in time for a Livery lunch, customarily preceded by the performance of a Bach Cantata in a nearby City Church to which the Company is specially invited.[4] A few weeks later, in early October, the Company attends its own special Evensong at St Paul's. This is now a service to which Masters and Wardens of the other Livery Companies are invited, and is followed by a Reception in the crypt of the Cathedral for the Company's guests.

Through the year, other less formal events occur in the calendar. Some of these will have been devised by the President for the Year of the Livery Club,[5] or the Master may wish to arrange something special to mark his year of office. More regularly there will be two or three Maisie Lewis Concerts, formerly given in the Purcell Room on South Bank, but currently at the Wigmore Hall, and an evening to celebrate the award of the annual Jazz Medal held at the 'Pizza on the Park'. The Committees of the Court meet regularly at the Clerk's office through the year, and there may be adjudications to attend and interviews to be held when fellowships fall vacant. The informal 'Phyllis Barrett lunches' for new and aspiring members take place through the year, and the Master's calendar will be full of invitations from musical institutions and from other livery companies.

Officers of the Company

With minor variations the establishment of livery companies conforms to a pattern that dates back to late mediaeval times. Since the early part of the 17th century the Musicians' Company's complement of officers has consisted of a head man, the Master, with his two chief advisers, the Wardens, an administrator,

---

4 At the time of writing the Cantata concert is one of a regular series given at the church of St Mary-at-Hill under the direction of Jonathan Rennert, Assistant.
5 See p. 238.

the Clerk, and an organiser and general factotum, the Beadle.[6] There has also been a Council to authorise and approve the work of the Master and Wardens and make strategic decisions concerning the well-being of the Company; this is the Court of Assistants, who have also provided a reservoir from which future wardens and masters are elected. The Master, Wardens and Court of Assistants together constitute the sovereign authority of the Company, subject only to the Court of Aldermen. The Master and Wardens have from earliest times been elected annually, although for a limited period after 1519 a two-year period of office was instituted, but it is not clear how long this continued.[7]

All this was in accordance with the custom of the City, but it was not until the second half of the 18th century that the Company elected its first Treasurer. The Court of Assistants is first mentioned in the 1604 Charter, and the first reference to the Clerk comes in a Will of 1629. It is impossible therefore to say whether the Court of Assistants was in existence before the James I Charter, or when the first Clerk was appointed. There is also some doubt as to the election of the first Master, as the 1500 Act referred only to the two Wardens. The 1519 Ordinances do imply however that this occurred in the first year of the Company's existence, as they refer to the power given to the Company in the year of Sir Nicholas Alwyn's mayoralty (1499/1500) to choose the Master and Wardens.[8] There is a discrepancy therefore between this statement and the wording of the 1500 Act as preserved in the City records.

Whether there was a Master *ab initio* or not, it is important, when considering the different functions of the various officers, to bear in mind the responsibility given to the Wardens in 1500 to keep the 'common box' of the Company in which its money was placed (although it would appear that the two keys to the box were kept by two other freemen[9]). The Wardens therefore jointly undertook the Treasurer's function at this time, as indicated by the title of their office. Two hundred years later, at the time of the Company's first surviving records, it had become the sole responsibility of the Renter Warden to keep the accounts and the funds to which they related.[10] We do not know when this practice began, but it continued, as we have seen, until John Crumpe had settled into the Clerkship, and managed to persuade the Court in 1752 to allow him to take over the Renter Warden's special function. Twenty years later the Company's finances were in chaos, Crumpe had been dismissed for embezzlement, and the first Treasurer, William Cooper Keating, was appointed.

The role of the financial officer, whether he was Renter Warden, as in the first

---

6 In the 17th and 18th centuries the Beadle's most onerous task was to collect the quarterage (the annual subscription, paid quarterly) from all members of the Company including the yeomanry.

7 See p. 42.

8 See p. 41.

9 See p. 7.

10 See p. 144.

half of the 18th century, or Treasurer, after 1772, has always been one of great importance in the Company, and it is therefore appropriate that for the first time the list of Treasurers should be included in Appendix 11 with the names of the Masters, Clerks and Beadles.

Although most Renter Wardens held office for only one year, there were several who continued in office for a longer period. Treasurers on the other hand have always been re-elected from year to year for as long as they were willing to accept the responsibility. It was natural therefore that they and the Clerks, also reelected annually, should develop an ongoing working relationship, which has been greatly to the benefit of the Company. The Company's Treasurers since the 'revival' have served it with distinction over many years, and for their dedicated service in that office John Clementi Collard, Arthur Hill, Sir Victor Schuster, Graham Wallace, Derek Lockett and Walter Ficker deserve particularly to be remembered. Credit is due especially to Derek Lockett for recognising, in the early 1960s, the risk of leaving the Company's funds invested entirely in gilt-edged securities and other fixed-interest stocks, and the need to diversify into equities, as the national economy began to move into an inflationary phase. His foresight at a critical time put the Company into a more favourable financial position than many of its peers.

As the principal salaried officer of the Company, one would have expected successive Clerks to have made a greater impact on the records than in fact they have. Even from the date of the earliest surviving Minute-Books (1770), the Clerk is rarely mentioned, except in regard to the carrying out of some instruction from the Court, and it was not until T.C. Fenwick's Clerkship (1902–27) that the Minutes regularly recorded that the Clerk had addressed the Court on some matter which he had been asked to investigate, or had given advice as to a City custom, or reported on some event that had occurred, or some correspondence which he had had. Perhaps it was more a question of change of style of minute-taking, but the impression given is that the earlier Clerks played very little part in the deliberations of the Court. And yet it had been the Clerk's duty to submit annual returns to the City Corporation in relation to the Livery from the 1690s onwards, and it was probably John Leadbetter or the unknown Clerk who succeeded him who worked out the new system of enrolling freemen into the Company.[11] In the days of the Renter Wardens it was frequently acknowledged in the accounts that the books had been written up by the Clerk.

Despite the general 'low profile' of the Clerks it is clear from the Minutes that one of them had a very high opinion of himself. Frederick Augustus France was Clerk from 1858 to 1866, and his first Minute recalls the fact that there were two Candidates for the Clerkship, 'Frederick Augustus H. France and Mr Rawll'. Notwithstanding the fact that Rawll had been a Liveryman of the Company for nearly twenty years, and France was new to the Company, there is no further ref-

---

[11] See pp. 147–8, 286.

erence to Rawll in the Minutes, which record loftily that France accordingly 'took the accustomed seat'. When he died in 1866, it was found that he had failed to pay accounts at the London Coffee House and elsewhere for which the Treasurer had supplied him with money, the amount owing being £93. 4s. Legal proceedings had to be initiated against his estate to recover the money. There is no suggestion that France's conduct as Clerk was anywhere near as heinous as that of John Crumpe, but it compared unfavourably with the long and loyal service of a number of Clerks, all of whom served the Company for twenty-five years or more – Thomas Whittell Sr (1770–97), Daniel Wood (1802–33) James Huxley (1833–1857) John T. Theobald (1871–1902) T.C. Fenwick (1902–27) and Alastair Crewdson (1930–67).

The list of officers in Appendix 11 is more comprehensive than in either the 1905 Handbook or the 'Short History'. It is however a little speculative in regard to Masters in the 18th century before 1770, being based mainly on the entries in the Renter Wardens' accounts relating to the payment of assistants' and wardens' fines. This provides an order of seniority which can be put into chronological sequence by reference to those years when the Master's name is known. The numbers almost match; there is one too many, and we cannot be sure which Warden failed to take the Master's Chair. For the 16th and 17th centuries there are very few years when the names of Masters are known, but where possible these have been included.

The Hall Fund

One of the consequences of the rapid revival of the Company in the early years of the century was the renewed desire to build a Hall. At the time the City of London was not just a financial centre; it was a centre for trade as well, with a huge amount of business in actual commodities taking place each day. This meant that the City was not yet dominated by a mass of self-important office blocks, and property prices were not much higher than in other parts of London. To raise funds to acquire a site and build a Hall was not therefore a totally unrealistic objective, and it was in fact Arthur Hill, when Treasurer of the Company and at a time when he exercised great influence over the Court's decisions, who proposed the establishment of a 'Hall Fund' for the purpose. The first reference to this project is in the Court's Minutes for 11 October 1929. By the following July nearly £2,500 had been raised. What would have happened if the Great Depression had not wiped out so much surplus wealth is impossible to assess, but Sir Ian Malcolm,[12] who was Master in 1930/1, persevered in throwing his weight behind the Treasurer's efforts, and circulated a letter to the Livery proposing an annual subscription to the Hall Fund from every member of the Livery of one guinea. Sir Ian was Master again in 1935/6 and returned at once to the same

---

[12] Sir Ian Malcolm K.C.M.G. (1886–1944) was a diplomat who became Private Secretary to Arthur Balfour.

objective, proposing an extra guinea to be added to the Freedom Fine on admittance.

The response from the Court and Livery was inadequate. Although the Court Minutes are silent on the subject there may have been a 'party' amongst the Court membership who felt that the last thing that the Company should be encumbered with was its own Hall. Nevertheless enough capital was amassed in the Hall Fund to provide sufficient income, until the steep rises in hire charges of recent years, to pay the charges of hiring Stationers' Hall for Livery and Court functions. The Hall Fund has now been amalgamated with the General Fund, the Court having decided that the original objective was utterly unattainable.

Endowments and Awards

In the 1870s the Company had just enough income to meet its annual expenditure, which consisted mainly of providing one free dinner to the Livery and several to the members of the Court. We have observed in Chapter 11 how the Company in the early 1880s came to recognise its new role – instead of being a regulator and controller of all who practised music in London, its objective in the 16th and 17th centuries, it was now to become a benefactor of young musicians, limited initially to those training in London. In the years from 1882 to 1892 a very substantial sum was voted by the Court for scholarships at the Royal College of Music, an annual Composition Scholarship was established at the Guildhall School of Music, and a Silver Medal was awarded annually in rotation at the three London Conservatoires. All these payments were charged to the ordinary revenue of the Company, but it was then recognised that if any more permanent awards were to be established, they would need to be separately endowed. For this purpose donors would be needed, but it was not until 1904, the date of the tercentenary of the Charter, that the first endowment was received. This was the beginning of a slow process continuing throughout the 20th century whereby, as a result of the generosity of a great number of benefactors, the Company, which started with nothing but its current account and a few ground-rents by way of investment, has become sufficiently well-endowed to meet the expense of the charitable purposes to which it is already committed.

The Company regularly has available a leaflet which sets out all the Company's awards, with a brief note on each, including the date of the gift, the donor and the purpose of the award. All the awards serve a most valuable purpose, and the Company's gratitude to all its donors knows no bounds, but it would, I think, be tedious to repeat all the information that can be found in the leaflet (which can be obtained from the Clerk's office). Instead there follows a brief account of how some of these awards came into existence. Lists of the major award winners appear in Appendix 12.[13]

---

[13] The list also includes the Special Award of the Silver Medal for Services to Music or to the

The first donor, in 1904, was none other than the famous 'Robber Baron', Andrew Carnegie, President of the United Steel Corporation, who had success-fully manoeuvred his Company into prime position in the US Steel Industry at the expense of his competitors. He was, it seems, a personal friend of the Master for 1902/3, Frank Lescher. Carnegie gave the appearance to his friends of being at heart a religious and rather romantic, homesick Scot. In order to satisfy his spiri-tual yearning he had spent substantial sums of money on providing more than five hundred churches in America, England and Scotland with organs, and had given great assistance to public libraries in the UK to enable them to develop their music services. He had preserved his links with his homeland by buying Skibo Castle and its vast estate in Sutherland, which he aimed to visit every year.

In 1903 it was agreed that the Master should approach his friend, offering him the Honorary Freedom of the Company in recognition of his services to music. The following letter dated 14 May 1903 was received in reply from Carnegie:[14]

> You propose a great honor indeed, but based upon my love of Music, I do feel that few men owe more to it than I – To me Confucius did not exalt it unduly when he said 'Music, sacred tongue of God, I hear thee calling and I come!' It is the highest form of expression yet attained by Man.
> Next season when we are in London if your Guild still desire to extend the 'Free-dom' I could not decline it.
> We reach London in May and remain as this year a week or more in London en route for the mountains and Moors, and the Music of the running waters.

A special banquet was arranged by the Company for Mr and Mrs Carnegie at Clothworkers Hall on 12 May 1904 during which he was made an Honorary Freeman. At Dinner it appears that Carnegie asked Lescher 'what he would do with £1,000' if it was offered to the Company, and Lescher wisely replied that a Committee of the Court would consider how it could be put to best use to help young musicians. Carnegie asked to be kept informed about the Committee's decision, which was a recommendation that two students should receive three years' free tuition at the Guildhall School of Music. On receiving this informa-tion Carnegie transferred $5,000 worth of United Steel Corporation Gold Bonds to the Company, and so it received its first endowment.

Another distinguished industrialist whose principal recreational interest was music was Ernest Palmer, whose Union Jack biscuit tins could be found wherever in the world the flag was flown. He had established a Scholarship (the 'Berk-shire Scholarship') at the Royal College of Music and had added to the College's Patron's Fund the immense sum of £20,000 to help British composers. On 8 July 1904, at the Company's Tercentenary Banquet, he too was made an Honorary Freeman, and the following year offered the Company £1,000 to establish two

Company, which evolved from the original Medal Committee's second proposal (see pp. 186–7).
[14] The letter is copied into the Minutes for the Court of 7 July 1903.

more scholarships at the Guildhall School of Music, one of which was to be awarded to an ex-chorister of either St Paul's or Westminster Abbey and the other to a girl student not more than seventeen years of age with a particular aptitude for sight-reading. In the following year Mr Palmer supplemented the capital of his fund by £250, and continued throughout his life to give his generous patronage to causes associated with music. It is clear that he enjoyed his link with the Company, and regularly accepted its invitations to attend special events.

The Carnegie and Palmer funds are still applied for the benefit of GSMD students, the award of £1,500 now being made in alternate years, Carnegie in one year and Palmer the next. Various changes in the detailed regulations have been made over the years to ensure the best use of the grants. The beneficiaries of both funds are now post-graduate students.

As will become apparent later in the chapter, the Edwardian era was a period of lavish gift-making to and on behalf of the Company, and also of commissioning new compositions from British composers. The wealth that lay behind these acts of generosity was conspicuous, and it is a little surprising therefore that only one other endowment for a prize was provided at this time, and that no one on the Court or Livery felt the need to supplement the Silver Medal awarded at each conservatoire triennially. One would have thought that the obvious unfairness of leaving each of the institutions without an award for two years out of every three would have inspired those with the resources to provide the small extra endowment required. As it happened, half a century was to pass before the medals were endowed so that they could be awarded annually at each institution. In the meantime the Royal College of Organists and Trinity College of Music had joined the triennial group,[15] but the Royal Military School of Music had had an annual medal award since 1908 and the Royal Marines School of Music (formerly the Royal Naval School of Music) since 1910.

The medal for army musicians seems to have been the result of second thoughts on the part of Colonel Shaw-Hellier, formerly Commandant at Kneller Hall and by this time a member of the Court. At the April Court in 1908, Dr Southgate, who was then Senior Warden, informed the Court in Shaw-Hellier's absence that the Colonel had been regularly donating a prize of five guineas annually, which was competed for by the Kneller Hall students, and he now wished to endow the Company with sufficient funds to enable the Company to continue to award the same prize. However at the following Court, Colonel Shaw-Hellier proposed the annual award of the Silver Medal to 'the most distinguished student of the Royal Military College of Music as the Commandant might recommend', and this was agreed. Through some oversight no record in the accounts appears of any cash payment to the Company by Colonel Shaw-Hellier to cover the endowment, whereas in 1909 the sum of £100 is shown as

---

[15] It was not until 1970 that the establishment of the Allcard Fund made it possible for the awards at the RCO and TCL to become annual.

having been received from Hugh Wyatt, Liveryman, to endow a similar medal at the Royal Naval School.

The one prize which was endowed was the Leo Stern Memorial Prize, instituted on the initiative of Arthur Hill for the benefit of a 'poor student of the Violoncello at the Royal College of Music'. The annual value of the prize was five guineas. Leo Stern was a distinguished solo cellist, who died at the early age of forty-two in 1904. Perhaps the greatest event in his life was to 'première' Dvořák's cello concerto under the composer's baton at a London Philharmonic Society Concert on 19 March 1896. He owned an early (large) Stradivarius cello, and played on a later (small) one, and would therefore have had a close relationship with the Hill brothers.

The Alice Prendergast Gift, made in 1913 in memory of her brother Arthur, arose indirectly from the production of the 'Masque of the Golden Tree' in 1905 under his direction. He was a noted authority on the 17th century masque and an honorary Fellow of St Michael's College, Tenbury. 'The Golden Tree' was originally written by Thomas Campion on the occasion of the marriage of the Earl of Somerset and Lady Frances Howard, but the 1905 Handbook noted that:

> it was the custom for several composers to unite in providing suitable music. It so happened in this case, the names of Lawes, Byrd, Coperario, Lanier and Holborne appearing in the score. Mr Prendergast not only rearranged their music for the little orchestra led by Miss Kate Chaplin, but also wrote some charming additional pieces quite in the olden style. With the exception of the Principals, the cast was composed mainly of students of the Guildhall School of Music.

The principal and original object of the Gift was to help choirboys from City churches to obtain apprenticeships in some useful trade (not as professional musicians), and some elaborate regulations were drawn up relating to the administration of the trust, which was carried on in this way until the beginning of World War II. After the war, there were no eligible candidates left for the award, and in any event the practice of apprenticeship was in steep decline. The secondary object of an award at the Royal Academy of Music was therefore substituted. The object has recently been changed again, and the fund now helps with fees for courses at the Royal School of Church Music.

The Benevolent Fund was set up in 1914, but some members of the Court had made an abortive attempt to get the Fund going six years previously, in 1908. First reactions had been favourable, but the Committee set up to consider the proposal reported that, having had the work of the Royal Society of Musicians explained to them in detail, they recommended that the proposal be deferred *sine die*. It was finally C.J. Ash, one of the most generous Liverymen of that time, who informed the Court in 1914 that he wished to give the Company the sum of £500 for the purpose of setting up the Benevolent Fund, and hoped that other members of the Livery would contribute also. By the end of World War I the value of the Fund had increased to over £2,000, making it possible for the Company, from the annual income of the Fund, to resuscitate a function that dated back to the 14th century fraternity, the assistance of musicians and their dependents in need. An honorary Almoner has been appointed in recent years[16] to ensure that due attention is paid by the Court to cases of hardship among members of the Company. Any surplus income of the Fund is customarily divided between the Musicians Benevolent Fund, the Music Trades Benevolent Society, the Incorporated Society of Musicians Benevolent Fund, the Organists Benevolent Fund, the Royal Society of Musicians Henry Wood Fund, the Corporation of the Sons of the Clergy and the Sheriffs' and Recorder's Fund.

The name of Walter Willson Cobbett will crop up again in connection with the Company's commissions from composers. Cobbett was an extremely competent amateur violinist, and his enthusiasm for chamber music, which at the beginning of the century he believed to be a forgotten art-form, amounted almost to an obsession – one that not only proved to be of great benefit to the Company, but was also said to have been 'important to the development of the English musical renaissance'.[17] His final act of benevolence was to present the Company in 1924 with £50 as an endowment, the income from which was to be used each year for a silver-gilt Company medal known as the 'Cobbett Medal' to be presented to a musician whose distinction lay in his or her services to chamber music. A list of the winners of this award can be found in Appendix 12.

Until 1930 there was no major award available to the Company which could be offered to an impoverished musician who had left studentship behind, but still needed help at a crucial stage in his or her career. Too many musicians with a great potential, particularly composers, were forced to spend too much time teaching, just in order to make ends meet. An opportunity for the Company to do something to help with this problem arose when it finally received the legacy bequeathed to it by John Clementi Collard who had died in 1918. The sum of £8,500, which was the Company's biggest legacy up to that date, was received in 1930. There were no precise instructions as to how the bequest was to be used, and a Committee was set up to make a recommendation, which was that the 'John Clementi Collard Fellowship' should be available, subject to nomination and interview, to one British-born musician at any one time, who would be aged between twenty-seven and fifty on application. The candidate must have shown undoubted excellence either in Composition, Research or Performance. The Fellowship was to be held for a period not exceeding three years. When first awarded it was worth £400 per annum, and now provides an annual grant of £10,000. At the conclusion of the Fellowship, the retiring Fellow is offered full membership of the Company as a free gift.

A list of the Collard Fellows, headed by the name of the first holder, Herbert Howells, can be found in Appendix 12. The Fellowship has been of considerable

---

[16] The Reverend Donald Baker was the first Almoner to be appointed, and being a lively and active nonagenarian (92 at the time of writing) continues to hold the honorary office.

[17] See the article on W.W. Cobbett by Frank Howes in *The New Grove Dictionary of Music and Musicians*, vol. 4, p. 507.

mutual benefit, as all its holders have been able to give up for a time, and sometimes permanently, what has been most unproductive in their lives, in order to concentrate on creativity in composition or excellence in performance, while some have subsequently made an important contribution to the work of the Company in relation to the 'Art or Science'. Outstanding in this respect was Dr Herbert Howells, whose love for the Company was very deep and fruitful. Sir Jack Westrup and Sir Lennox Berkeley, both of whom, like Howells, had been Collard Fellows and ultimately became Master of the Company, will be remembered also for their active involvement in Committee work and the Court's deliberations.

At the end of World War II the Master, the Rt. Hon. Sir Felix Cassel K.C., gave the Company a sum of money to mark the six years of his Mastership during the War, to be used 'for the encouragement of music in the Royal Navy, the Army and the Royal Air Force'. The money was used to endow the 'Cassel Prizes' (in the form of silver and bronze medals) at the music schools of the three services, together with a silver cup awarded annually to the best RAF band.

The first substantial post-war endowment came to the Company in the form of a gift from Cyril Davis, a Liveryman who was later called on to the Court, with the object of establishing an annual scholarship for opera singers, which was known at first as 'the Opera Singing Scholarship'. It was to be a competitive award, and the winner of the first competition was the celebrated Australian soprano, Marie Collier. However after the first year the administration of the award proved more difficult than anticipated, and the donor decided, with the approval of the Court, to reestablish the scholarship as a closed award at Glyndebourne, and in 1964 the 'John Christie Award' was set up. Ryland Davies was the first holder of the scholarship in its new form. The list of the award-winners can be found in Appendix 12.

A somewhat idiosyncratic legacy reached the Company in 1956, under the Will of John Mewburn Levien, who had been a Liveryman of the Company since 1912 and was briefly a member of the Court from 1932 to 1934, when he resigned on grounds of ill-health. Levien was a singing teacher, whose principal distinction had been to be appointed Treasurer of the Royal Philharmonic Society in 1915, and then to be its Secretary from 1918 to 1928, during a very tempestuous period in its history. Thomas Beecham had effectively 'taken over' the London Philharmonic Orchestra during the First World War, and it seems that Levien was one of the prime movers in securing Beecham's resignation and re-asserting the Society's control in 1918, a move which was much criticised by the media, with allegations of incompetence being frequently aimed at the new management.[18]

J.M. Levien bequeathed two separate gifts to the Company. The first was a legacy of £2,000 in memory of Sir Charles Santley. Under the terms of the Will the income from this money when invested was to be used to make annual gifts

---

[18] See Cyril Ehrlich, *First Philharmonic* (Oxford: Clarendon Press 1995), pp. 194–8.

to distinguished singers who upheld the Santley tradition. The gifts were to be in kind and not in cash, and this has given the Company the opportunity to invite those nominated for the award to make their own choice of gift for presentation at a suitable occasion. The recipients of the award are shown in Appendix 12, and it will be seen that when the income of the fund was sufficient two awards have been made each year, one to a male and the other to a female singer. The Santley Gift has been used by the Company not only to recognise great singers at the peak of their career, but also to recall, often from deep retirement, those who might otherwise have been quite forgotten until the publication of their obituaries. One memorable example was the celebrated soprano Carrie Tubb, who received her award in 1969, at the age of 93, having first sung for Beecham at Covent Garden in 1910.

The residue of Levien's estate was left to the Company to establish a scholarship for an advanced student of the organ, and was to commemorate W.T. Best (1826–97), the virtuoso organist at St George's Hall, Liverpool, and the first to play the great Willis organ at the Royal Albert Hall. He was pre-eminent in England in demonstrating the capacity of the new Victorian instruments, not just for the standard organ repertoire, but as a medium for rivalling the power of a symphony orchestra. He was a populist and a flamboyant performer. It is not clear what led Levien to wish to commemorate him (perhaps he had had early but frustrated ambitions of becoming a concert organist himself), but it provided the Company with a most valuable award, greatly sought after by young organists, and competed for by audition. Like the Collard Fellowship it is normally held for three years, and since the 1980s the outgoing scholar has enjoyed the same privilege of free admission to the Company. The holders of the scholarship are listed in Appendix 12.

Three years later some more little idiosyncrasies were to be found in relation to the gift of Ethel Mary Percival-Hart, who bequeathed a substantial legacy to the Company in memory of her father. A Fund was to be established bearing his name, to be used for the encouragement of singing, with special reference to Manchester and Sheffield, but 'not to be used in Wales'. Many grants have been made from the Fund, respecting the donor's wishes.

By the mid-1960s it was becoming apparent that while the Company had an increasing amount of money available to put toward specific objects each year in accordance either with the donor's wishes or with the terms originally determined by the Court, there were still no funds which could be used to respond to 'one-off' appeals of a musical nature, the number of which was constantly increasing. Two gifts had been received for this purpose in 1959 from members of the Court, but in 1966, during the Mastership of Derek Lockett, it was felt that a general appeal to the Livery should be made in order to build up a fund, to be known as the Foundation Fund, to a serviceable size. The response to the appeal produced a sum in the region of £11,000, and it was hoped that additions and accruals would over the years substantially increase this amount, which was felt to be a disappointing result and not enough to deal adequately with the inflow of deserving causes and their requests for help. However the problem was shortly afterwards overcome in an unexpected way.

Victor Allcard in his later years was the 'Father of the Company'. He had joined the Company in 1905, became an Assistant in 1924, and Master in 1929/30 and again in 1949 following the death of the incumbent Master, Sir Stanley Marchant. In 1970 Allcard assigned his interest in land (which was shortly to be sold for development) at Horsham in Sussex to the Company, to be held in trust 'for the general charitable purposes of the Company', and by his Will he also left the residue of his estate to the Company subject to a life interest which came to an end in 1998. The land was sold in 1972 for a considerable sum, and the Company received as its share of the proceeds a sum in excess of a quarter of a million pounds. Victor Allcard lived on until 1978 (he died in his 98th year) so that he was able to share in the delight of the members of the Court that this exceptional sum of money had been made available to the Company as an endowment for its 'general charitable purposes', making possible the meaningful response to musical appeals which had been desired for so long. A small part of the capital was also used to provide endowments for those medals which still had none or where the endowment was insufficient, so that every medal could now be awarded annually. Another part of the income was set aside for grants to be made to individual advanced music students, and to fund a music scholarship at the City of London School and the City of London School for Girls.

One of the most opportune uses of the Allcard Fund was the purchase in 1975 of the Library of the late Sir Jack Westrup, Heather Professor of Music at Oxford and Master of the Company in 1971/2. This was a very sizeable library, consisting of about 4500 books which he had acquired either by purchase or as a leading reviewer of music books over a period of thirty years or more. At the time of his death the new Guildhall School of Music building in the Barbican was under construction, complete with Library, but the school had an inadequate stock of books. It was therefore of mutual benefit for the Company to be able to buy the Westrup Library and to place it on indefinite loan at the GSMD. At first it formed the core of the collection, requiring the addition of an extra floor at roof level to accommodate it, but the Library's own stock has since been greatly increased, quite apart from the huge amount of tapes and disks which it now has for study purposes. These are stored and played within the enlarged roof-level floor which might never have existed if it had not been for the Company's action.

At about the same time as the Allcard Fund was established, another tailor-made Trust was established which throughout its existence has required a great deal of active management, all of which has been provided from within the resources of the Company itself. This is the Maisie Lewis Young Artists Fund, set up in 1969 with a generous gift of Sir Edward Lewis, the Chairman of Decca Records, in memory of his wife. Sir Edward was a close friend of Jack Iles, who was Master in that year. The specific object of the Fund is to provide 'platform experience' for young musicians who are reaching the end of their training, and

19. Herbert Howells.

20. Sir Jack Westrup.

21. Sir Lennox Berkeley.

from the outset it has been the invariable practice of the organising Committee to use the principal recital rooms in London for this purpose. For many years the Purcell Room on South Bank was the preferred venue, but at the time of writing the Wigmore Hall has taken its place. Two or three recitals are given each year, usually shared by two young artists, who are selected annually by audition. The recitals are well supported by members of the Livery and by invited guests from other Livery Companies, as well as the concert-going public.

In what so far has been for the Company a unique participation in a joint project, it took part in the preliminary discussions which led to the founding of the Loan Fund for Musical Instruments, and in 1979 became one of the founding Trustees together with the Arts Council of Great Britain, the Royal Society of Arts and the Musicians Union. This is a charitable fund which was established under the patronage of H.R.H. The Prince of Wales to help talented young professional musicians to purchase instruments of the quality they need, which they otherwise could not afford to buy. Assistance has been provided by making loans at a notional rate of interest, mostly repayable over five years. The Fund has operated throughout at a minimal cost in terms of administration, and loan repayments are therefore available for re-lending to new applicants. In the ten years 1988–97, 553 applications for assistance were received, of which just under 50% were successful. In 1997 (a typical year) all the loans made were in excess of £1,000, but none exceeded £20,000. The Executive Committee applies a stringent set of criteria in each case, which up to the present time has ensured that no loans have had to be written off.

On completion of his year as Master (1981/2), Sir Andrew Carnwath, who was himself an outstanding amateur pianist, endowed a scholarship for advanced students of the piano, to be held for a maximum of two years and to be competed for by audition. The income is also used to supplement the biennial Maggie Teyte Prize for singing, which is not one of the Company's awards, but is one with which the Carnwath family has been closely involved.[19] A list of the holders of the Carnwath Scholarship is included in Appendix 12.

In 1987, Richard Croucher, a friend of Anthony Rubinstein (Master 1979/80), decided that there was need for a new prize for composition, and asked the Company to administer the prize, which would be an amount of £10,000. There would be an open competition, with entrants submitting works already written by them. The winner of the prize would hold a fellowship for two years during which he or she would be required to write an orchestral piece as agreed with the Chairman of the adjudicating panel; the Company would then arrange for the first performance of the new work. The award was known as the Gemini Fellowship, and attracted much interest, hundreds of scores being submitted each year. These were read by an eminent group of composers and music administrators in

---

[19] The Administrator of the competition at the time of the gift, and currently, is Mrs Felicity Guinness, Sir Andrew's daughter.

order to select as short a final list as possible, from which the winner was finally chosen. The holders of the Fellowship are shown in Appendix 12. Unfortunately the list is now closed, as the award was discontinued in 1998. It was the only award made by the Company which has not been endowed, and its termination confirmed the wisdom of a policy, to which the Company normally adheres, of requiring an endowment for all its awards.

The composer Priaulx Rainier was the first woman to become a Liveryman of the Company. She was also the first woman to be awarded, in 1952, the Collard Fellowship. She was admitted to the Company as a Freeman in 1955 when her tenure of the Fellowship expired, but the Court of the day was not ready to honour its moral obligation to elect her to the Livery. Priaulx was however quite a determined lady, and never allowed the Clerk to forget what was due to her. The gradual change of climate leading to the abandonment of sexual discrimination will be historically recorded as a feature of the 1960s and 1970s. By the end of that time most members of the Court felt that the entry door for women into the Livery, which had been closed for centuries (but never legally barred), was now wide open, and that there could be no more suitable first lady Liveryman than the outspoken and persistent (in the nicest possible way) Priaulx Rainier, who was duly elected and clothed with the Livery on 13 October 1983. At about the same time she asked the Clerk, in his legal capacity, to draw up a will for her, leaving her estate to the Company in trust to establish a Fund which was, first of all, to provide a prize in alternate years for the South African College of Music at the University of Cape Town (where she had first trained), and the Royal Academy of Music (where she completed her musical education), and secondly to be used for the promotion of concerts by young artists of contemporary music including, where possible, her own. She always believed that her estate would be of no great value, but in fact the endowment fund when received was worth about £113,000.

The latest of the large bequests, the Constant and Kit Lambert Fund, also happens to be the biggest, and this too came into the administrative hands of the Company through the good offices of Anthony Rubinstein, who had a professional connection with the Lambert family. Mrs Camilla Hole, who was the first wife of Constant and the mother of Kit, wished to commemorate them by making a gift which would benefit students at the Royal College of Music, where both Constant and Kit had been students. Although Constant Lambert is remembered as a composer his actual output was small, because his principal service to British music was as a ballet conductor, having been appointed musical director of the Vic-Wells Ballet in 1931 and continuing in that office for the Sadlers Wells Ballet, as it became, until his retirement in 1947. From then until his early death in 1951 he carried on as a guest conductor for Sadlers Wells and the Royal Ballet. In terms of royalties therefore, Constant's contribution to the Fund, which was established in 1989, was comparatively small, and it was the royalties that flowed through Kit's estate which inflated the value of the Fund beyond all expectation. Kit was not himself a musician, but through his experience as an assistant film director he became involved with the emerging pop group The Who, and was appointed their manager in 1964. It was the rock opera 'Tommy', written and composed by the lead guitarist Peter Townshend, but containing a substantial creative contribution from Kit Lambert, that produced a massive inflow of fees and royalties for Kit which continued to accrue after his death in 1981. In 1998 the Constant and Kit Lambert Fund was valued at over one and a quarter million pounds.

This remarkable resource has made it possible for the Company not only to provide annual prizes of £1,000 each for twelve students at the R.C.M., and a Fellowship of £10,000, tenable for one or two years, but also to support a new and experimental project enabling post-graduate students to work with the next generation of first-degree students to their mutual advantage.

This account of the Company's awards is not exhaustive, and the reader is again referred to the Company's leaflet which contains a list of all the awards currently being made at the date of its publication (in addition to the Company's silver medal at each of the conservatoires, the twenty-two medals awarded annually include the Iles Medal for services to the Brass Band Music and the A.F. Bulgin medal which is given each year to a member of the National Youth Orchestra). However it is worth noting that even since the last publication date (1994) there have been three new awards, a prize for French song, a competition for classical guitar and a harp competition.[20] So long as the Company can continue to demonstrate its impartiality in the making of awards, there is in effect no limit (apart from the complement and capacity of the Clerk's office) to the number which it can administer.

The Company's Plate

The Master's and Wardens' badges, which would be more accurately described as 'jewels', were acquired in 1879/80. In 1900, the only piece of plate which the Company possessed was the Beadle's Mace, which bears the inscription 'The gift of Richard Loyde, Master of the Worshipful Company of Musicians, 1729'. It is a fine piece of Georgian silverwork with the Company's arms engraved on a square medallion that rises vertically from the centre of the head of the mace.

The lack of ornaments to adorn the Company's banquets in 1900 can be contrasted with the situation in 1922, when the retiring Master, Sir William Lancaster, wrote to the Clerk:

> We already possess so many beautiful and valuable pieces of plate, contributed by my predecessors, that no addition to these gifts seems really necessary.[21]

---

[20] The donors or promoters were respectively the late Myra Verney, Ivor Mairants (who died before the prize could be presented for the first time) and Clive Morley.

[21] Extract from a letter copied into the Minutes for the Court Meeting held on 17 October 1922.

The Master presented a cheque for one hundred guineas instead, to be used in connection with the music for the St Cecilia Festival. There had therefore been a plethora of gifts of plate during the early years of the century. By citing the occasion on which some of the gifts were made, the motivation of these and later donors, which was interestingly varied, can be appreciated:

The Charles Crews first silver-gilt Loving Cup: 25 October 1904 – on election as Master

The Charles Crews/Mario Tankard: 1905 – to celebrate his Presidency of the Livery Club

Sir Homewood Crawford's silver-gilt 'Elizabethan' Ewer and Rose Water Dish: 28 October 1907 – to mark the end of his year as Master

The Charles Crews second silver-gilt Loving Cup: 28 April 1908 – to celebrate his second term of office as Master

The Master's Chain of Office: 27 October 1908 – presented by Mr Crews to wear with the Master's Badge

The Treasurer's Cup: 26 January 1909 – presented by the Treasurer, Mr J.C. Collard, the names of all subsequent Treasurers to be engraved on the Cup together with the predecessors in that office of the Collard family, beginning with his great uncle, F.W. Collard, who was elected Treasurer in 1838

The Ash 'Steeple' Cup: 26 October 1909 – to commemorate Mr W.H. Ash's Presidency of the Livery Club

The Lord Mayor's Cup: 26 October 1909 – subscribed for by members of the Court and presented to Sir George Wyatt Truscott Bt, Lord Mayor and Master of the Company, 1908/9

The Alfred Littleton Loving Cup: 25 October 1910 – on election as Master

The Collard Snuff Box: 24 October 1911 – presented by Mr C.L. Collard; the actual silver snuff box presented by the Court to Frederick William Collard in 1834, and inscribed at that time

The Duckworth Bowl: 23 January 1912 – the silver bowl previously presented to the late Canon Duckworth (formerly Honorary Chaplain to the Company) by Mr Charles Hoblyn (Master 1901/2) and his family in 1906; now presented to the Company by Canon Duckworth's nephew, Mr John Troutbeck, on his taking up the Livery

The Meade-Falkner silver-gilt Loving Cup ('Coronation Cup'): 23 January 1912 – presented by Mr J. Meade-Falkner (a Liveryman) to commemorate the Coronation of King George V and Queen Mary (a reproduction of an Irish cup of 1728)

The Arthur Hill Dish and Porringer: 23 January 1912 – to celebrate his year of office as Master

The Charles Hoblyn silver-gilt Porringers: 23 April 1912 – to celebrate twenty-two years' connection with the Company (copies of late 17th century originals)

The William Fuller Candelabra: 15 July 1913 – to celebrate his year of office as Master

The Collard Cup: 24 October 1916 – presented by C.L. Collard on completion of his year of office as Master to commemorate the winning of the Victoria Cross by five Bandsmen since the commencement of the War

The Wyatt 'Peace Cup': 14 October 1919 – presented by the Master, Hugh Wyatt, at the conclusion of his term of office; the Cover of the cup was surmounted by the figure of Victory

The Boyton silver-gilt Loving Cup: 12 October 1926 – presented by Lady Boyton; the Cup, made in 1750, had been purchased at Christies by her late husband Sir James

Boyton when Senior Warden of the Company, with a view to presentation during his
    Mastership, to which he should have been elected on that day

The Bridge Cup: 15 October 1929 – presented in memory of Sir Frederick Bridge by Mrs
    R.F. Stainer (daughter) and Mr R.T. Bridge

The Leslie Porringer: 9 July 1929 – presented by Mrs W.H. Leslie in memory of her
    husband (Master, 1923/4). The hall-marking on the cup shows a date of 1680.

The Pearce Salver: 22 January 1935 – presented by Miss E.K. Pearce; this was a salver
    bearing the arms of the Company which had been presented by the Company to
    her late brother, the Rt. Revd Ernest H Pearce, Honorary Chaplain to the Company,
    on 29 April 1919, following his consecration as Bishop of Worcester. He died on 28
    October 1930.

The Viscount Astor silver-gilt Pilgrim Bottles: 7 July 1936 – to mark the conclusion of his
    term of office as Master

The Alfred Waley 'Monteith' Punch Bowl: 12 October 1937 – to mark the conclusion of his
    term of office as Master. The Bowl dates from the year 1709.

The Victor Allcard silver-gilt Rose-Bowl: 5 July 1955 – presented by Mr Allcard (Senior
    Pastmaster) to mark the 50th anniversary of his election to the Livery

Gifts

The gifts made by Charles Crews in the name of the Company, the St Cecilia
Window at St Paul's and the Orlando Gibbons bust at Westminster Abbey have
already been mentioned in the previous chapter, as have the Master's and Wardens' Gowns, which he gave to the Company in its Tercentenary year. In the same
year Colonel Shaw-Hellier gave the Company a richly embroidered Banner
depicting St Cecilia playing on a bass viol while a naked cherub holds above its
head a small book of music which the Saint, enraptured by her own playing,
appears to be ignoring.[22] The pillars supporting the canopy under which she
plays are each decorated with a lyre, and at the foot there are two coats of arms,
of the Company and of the donor's family. The banner is illustrated in the Company's 1905 Handbook. It was embroidered by Mary Digby, who had had much
experience in needlework, but it would seem that the Company's banner was her
pièce de resistance. On her death in 1924 the following epitaph was inscribed on
her tomb in the churchyard of France Lynch in Gloucestershire:

> This lowly stone doth mark the spot
> Where Mary Digby's soul is not
> She passed in 1924
> To Jesu's purgatorial shore
> . . .
> In London on Cecilia's day
> If in St Paul's your eye should stray

---

[22] It was said to be modelled on a painting in the Louvre by Domenico Zampieri
    (1581–1641).

> And on Cecilia's banner fall
> T'was Mary Digby made it all.

It is sad that the eye can no longer fall on the banner because it suffered so much damage from fire and water in Stationers Hall during the blitz as to be irreparable. At the time when the new banner bearing the Company's arms was presented by the Master, W. Graham Wallace, in 1952, it was decided not to replace the Shaw-Hellier banner.

Another casualty of the same fire was a carved oak Master's Chair, covered in velvet and bearing the arms of King James I, which Mr Crews had presented on 28 January 1908, the first Court of his second term as Master.

Charles Crews, the most munificent of donors of tangible things, died in 1914, and a long period elapsed before any other gifts in kind were received by the Company. However in the previous year the Company had itself made a gift, subscribed for by individual members of the Court and others, of a small stained glass window at the Guildhall in Londonderry. It was unveiled on 31 July 1913 by the Duchess of Abercorn and commemorates the Company's participation in the Plantation of Ulster, from which it had withdrawn just 300 years before.[23]

On 9 July 1929, the Treasurer, Arthur Hill, presented the Company with one of its most precious possessions, a portrait of King James I. Very little is known about the provenance of the painting, but it is thought to be contemporary.

After World War II the damage to its possessions suffered in the blitz, together with more humdrum wear and tear, needed remedying and repair and a new generation of generous donors saw to it that this was done. The presentation of the Banner depicting the Company's arms in 1952 by the new Master, W. Graham Wallace, has already been mentioned. In 1955, H.F.B. Iles, when Master, gave the Company ten gowns with thirteen hoods, the gowns with furred hoods to be worn by Pastmasters, and the remainder to be available for clothing ceremonies for new liverymen. More gowns were presented by other members of the Court in subsequent years, and in 1968 J.B. Iles followed his brother's example by presenting a new Master's gown and refurbished Wardens' gowns.

In 1966 Viscountess Astor presented the Company with a new Master's Chair, which had been ordered by her late husband during his year of office (1964/5). It has the Company's arms worked into the back of the Chair in fine needlework.

In 1974 Derek Lockett (Master 1965/6) gave the Company a painting by Leslie A. Wilcox recording the moment when, at a Special Court in Fishmongers' Hall on 12 July 1966, H.M. Queen Elizabeth the Mother had received the Honorary Freedom.[24]

To mark the conclusion of his year of office as Master (1988/9) Sir Vivian Dunn gave the Company an antique Royal Marines side-drum.

---

[23] See p. 73.
[24] See pp. 228–9.

Music and Manuscripts

The Company possesses a large collection of manuscripts, mostly of 20th century works, which could best be described as 'unfocused'. This is because they came into the hands of the Company in several ways. Some, which had an intrinsic value of their own, were gifts; others were received as entries for prize competitions; and the most select group were works commissioned by the Company.

In the first category the most valuable manuscript is undoubtedly 'The Lost Chord' by Sir Arthur Sullivan, which was presented to the Company in 1950 by the famous singer (and husband of Clara Butt) Kennerley Rumford, who had been Master of the Company in 1933/4. There are also a number of manuscripts of compositions by Percy Godfrey, who, it will be remembered was the winner of the Coronation March Competition of 1902. His subsequent career as a composer brought him little success,[25] and his wish that the Company should hold the manuscripts of his other works was thought by him to be a way of ensuring their survival, with a remote prospect of their possible posthumous success.

The prize entries mostly relate to the two Cobbett 'Phantasie' Competitions promoted by W.W. Cobbett in 1905 and 1907. The manuscripts include a quartet by Frank Bridge, and another by Haydn Wood. There was a spate of commissions and competitions under the Company's auspices during the Edwardian era, and the manuscripts that have remained in the Company's possession are few compared with the number which actually passed through the Clerk's office at the time. The names of John Ireland, Ralph Vaughan Williams, Adam Carse and Percy Fletcher (outstanding composer of military marches, and winner of the Company's competition in 1909) stand out among the prize winners but their manuscripts were passed to and retained by their publishers. The Clerk did report to the Court on 25 October 1910 that he had taken steps to obtain the original manuscripts of Compositions written for the Company, and 'had received several', but no details are given.

It is curious to note that despite the huge success of the Coronation March Competition in 1902, and the Company's continuing interest in military music, a similar Competition which the Company organised in 1911 to celebrate the forthcoming Coronation of King George V produced no entries which the adjudicators felt able to recommend for the prize.

In the last category there are six pieces which the Company can claim as its own. Two are well known to every active member of the Company, the Charles Wood 'Grace' and the Elgar 'Dirge'. It has long been assumed that the original manuscript of the prize-winning Grace was in the Company's possession, the gift of Dr Wood's widow, but on a recent inspection it has been found that the piece which it holds is a different setting by the composer of the same words. There

---

[25] In a letter to the Clerk dated 2 March 1938 Godfrey wrote 'It may interest you to know that for the past fifteen years, if I make an average of £10 a year, I consider myself fortunate.'

can however be no doubt about the autograph manuscript (marked by a large red ink splodge on the first page) of Elgar's 'Dirge' or 'Elegy', which has been regularly played for many years at the Company's annual service in St Paul's Cathedral, in commemoration of the members of the Company who have died during the previous year. Accompanied by correspondence relating to the gift (including an apology for the 'red ink disaster'), this is a precious item in the archives.

It is not generally known that another setting of the Grace was awarded an extra prize for its excellence in the 1904 competition, and was printed for use by the Company. It was written by Arthur Henry Brown and is a setting of the same words for Alto, Tenor and Bass.

Of more recent origin is the manuscript of the beautiful Hymn to St Cecilia written by Herbert Howells with words by Ursula Vaughan Williams. This was first performed in the St Cecilia Service at St Paul's in 1961. It was commissioned by the Livery Club of the Company, whose activities are referred to later in the chapter.

The last two items are less well-known. The first was a commission accepted by Elgar in 1907 for a 'Marching Song', which the more jingoistic members of the Court of the time hoped would rank with 'Rule Britannia' and 'Tipperary' and be sung on the march by squads of every battalion and company in the Army. With words by W. de Courcy Stretton, a former Royal Artillery Captain, the piece was completed early in 1908, and was first performed by a Kneller Hall Band for the Court on 28 April. The thanks of the Court to Kneller Hall are recorded in the Minutes for the next Court, and Sir Edward Elgar presented the manuscript to the Company in 1910, but little more is heard of the work. It was sung at an Albert Hall concert in October 1914, and 'enthusiastically received'[26] but as a popular work, it failed where 'Pomp and Circumstance No 1' had succeeded.

The other composition was a commission from Gordon Jacob, a former Collard Fellow, to celebrate the Coronation of Queen Elizabeth II in 1953. The work which Jacob wrote was entitled 'Laudate Dominum', and was first performed the following year at the Albert Hall by the Royal Choral Society under Sir Malcolm Sargent, in a programme which also included the 'Dream of Gerontius'. It is dedicated to the Company and the autograph score is in its possession.

The sponsorship of new music has been continued in recent years. A proposal from Sir Vivian Dunn in 1984 that the 1909 Composition Competition for a suite for Wind Band be repeated was warmly welcomed by the Court, and Sir Vivian proceeded to make all the arrangements with his customary energy and efficiency. A prize of £1,000 was offered for the winning entry. Twenty-one entries were received, and a final short-list of three pieces were selected for performance by the Royal Marines School of Music Band at the City University on 4

---

[26] Court Minutes, 27 October 1914, recording an informal report by Sir Frederick Bridge.

December 1984. The adjudicators, Vilem Tausky, Harry Mortimer and Victor Fleming (all members of the Company), awarded the prize to Bram Wiggins, with his entry entitled 'Big Sky Country', which was performed again by the massed bands of the Royal Marines at the Mountbatten Concert in the Albert Hall the following February.

In 1998, on the initiative of Sir Alan Traill, the Company participated in the sponsorship of the international 'Masterprize' competition sponsored by Coutts Bank. The Company's prize was a commission worth £10,000 for a work to be specially written for performance during the Quincentenary year. The winner of the prize had to be under thirty years of age at the date of the Masterprize Competition. In the event the first prize and the Company's prize were awarded to the same finalist, the English composer Andrew March, who is engaged on the new commission as this book goes to press.

The Two World Wars

The impact on the Company of the two great wars which left their scars across the world in the 20th century is notable for the contrast between what happened in 1914 and 1939. The Court, in 1914, saw itself as a corporate body with a responsibility to render assistance and encouragement to the nation, in the name of the Company, in whatever way it could. It therefore continued to meet regularly, and to help to sustain morale both within the Company and more widely. The fact that London was from time to time the object of Zeppelin air-raids was no deterrent to the daily life of the City, which continued almost as normal. Every member of the Company in London was strongly urged to make a special effort to attend the annual St Cecilia Service. Livery Dinners were however suspended and on the two occasions when the Livery were invited to attend a special function, its response was very poor. The first of these was a Concert in the Mansion House to entertain wounded soldiers, which took place on 28 February 1916. The second was a *conversazione* especially for the Livery on 10 April 1918 when only fourteen attended.

The Court decided early in the war to present a gold watch to every military musician who was awarded the Victoria Cross, and five presentations were made (all but one by the Lord Mayor), one to a bandsman, three to drummers, and one to a piper.

In 1914 the Company also gave a set of drums, fifes and bugles to the 10 Battalion The Royal Fusiliers (City of London Regiment). Unfortunately the Bandmaster of the Battalion decided to form a full-blooded military band, and there were insufficient resources in the unit to run two bands; after some difficult correspondence when it was discovered by the Company that the bandmaster had tried to trade in the fifes and drums at Messrs Hawkes in exchange for brass instruments, the fifes and drums were returned and given instead to the National Guard Band in the City of London.

At the end of the war members of the Court prepared a record of the Livery's involvement in it, of which a single copy has survived among the Company's papers.

Considering how close the nation was to the outbreak of World War II, it is strange to read in the Court Minutes for 10 July 1939 an account of the conferment of the Honorary Freedom on the Prime Minister, the Rt. Hon. Neville Chamberlain, who had a great love of music. Only three weeks later Nazi Germany invaded Poland, thereby precipitating the Declaration of War on 3 September. Chamberlain died of cancer about eighteen months later. In reply to a letter of condolence from the Master, Mrs Chamberlain wrote to say that shortly before her husband's death they were listening together to a performance on the wireless of Beethoven's Septet in E flat, and he had commented that it was that work with which he had been entertained by the Company when he had received the Honorary Freedom.

We have already noted the damage done to the Company's physical heritage in London during World War II – the destruction of the St Cecilia window in St Paul's Cathedral, and the loss of the St Cecilia banner and the Master's Chair in Stationers Hall (the Beadle's Gown was also burnt). It was not however just its possessions which were lost because the Clerk, Alastair Crewdson, was immediately called up for military service, first commanding a Territorial Brigade (which was hurriedly deployed in North-East France just at the time of the German breakthrough) and then an anti-invasion 'sub-area' in North-West England.

The Company was therefore effectively 'mothballed' from the start. The St Cecilia Service was abandoned because of the lighting restrictions (St Paul's could not be blacked out), and all social activity was suspended during the first three and a half years of the war. The surplus income which this created was applied to 'musicians seriously afflicted by the War' and the Musicians Benevolent Fund and the Incorporated Society of Musicians' Samaritan Fund were delegated to distribute about £400 per annum for this purpose. In other ways, thanks to the determination of the Master, Sir Felix Cassel (who held that office throughout the war), and his two Wardens, Sir Victor Schuster and A.W. Fitzsimmons, together with the Deputy Clerk, William Winterbotham, who was the Clerk's elderly Senior Partner, and the Beadle, George Godwin, an organist and choirmaster as well as a 'confidential clerk' in the Clerk's office, the Company's essential business continued without interruption. Courts were held regularly, but with the quorum reduced temporarily to five. On 15 October 1940 the Court meeting was held at the Clerk's office as Stationers' Hall had been badly damaged in an air raid the previous night, but the 'Stock Room' at the Hall appears to have been usable again by the following January, as Court meetings were again held there throughout the War from January 1941.

Awards were made in the usual way and silver medallists during the War included Owen Brannigan at the Guildhall School of Music, and the pianist Ronald Smith at the Royal Academy. Jack Westrup in 1940 and Gordon Jacob in 1943 received the Collard Fellowship, and the Cobbett Medallists included Isolde Menges, Sidney Griller and Dame Myra Hess.

On 12 October 1943 H.R.H. the Duchess of Kent, whose husband (an Honorary Freeman) had been killed in an air crash the previous year, was herself made an Honorary Freeman of the Company.

The Clerk was released from military service in 1944, and was able to pick up the Company's papers once more, although the continuing danger to London from flying bombs and rockets and the difficulty of laying on any formal functions in central London effectively inhibited the renewal of its customary social activities until the War was over. A luncheon was however arranged at the Connaught Rooms in April 1944 (this was before the V1 ('Doodlebug') bombardment began). The first post-war 'Ladies Night' Dinner (in those days regarded technically as a Court function, although the Livery were always invited) was held at Goldsmiths' Hall in July 1946, and the first Livery Dinner took place at Vintners' Hall in October 1947. The war damage to Stationers' Hall delayed the Company's return there until 1956.

Eminent People And Special Events

The record of the Company during the 20th century is peppered with accounts of special occasions for celebration or conferment of awards, which sometimes involved a departure from the Company's regular calendar of events. In most cases they were initiated or arranged by the Master of the day to mark his year of office, as it has always been the Master's privilege to provide something out of the ordinary if he wishes to do so.

Many of the Company's special events have been associated with the Honorary Freedom, which is the Company's highest award. It will be remembered that the first recipient of this honour was Sir Henry Cole in 1876.[27] This was the only award of the Honorary Freedom during the 19th century, and it was not until 1904 that the procedure was revived for Andrew Carnegie and S. Ernest Palmer. There followed a period when it might appear that no opportunity was lost in making the award, although the recipients were mostly of great distinction, as will be seen from the list set out below. During the second half of the 20th century, the award was less liberally bestowed, and a unanimous decision of the Court became a prerequisite for the proposal to proceed, with plenty of time being allowed for dissenters to convey their views privately to the Master or Clerk. This accounts for the fact that the majority of the admissions to the Honorary Freedom took place in the first half of the Century.

The Company has been particularly fortunate in being able to secure the gracious acceptance of the Honorary Freedom by no fewer than eight members of the Royal Family:

1905	H.R.H. Prince Christian of Schleswig-Holstein
1921	H.R.H. The Prince of Wales

---

[27] See p. 173.

	H.R.H. The Duke of Connaught and Strathearn
1935	H.R.H. The Duke of Kent
1943	H.R.H. Princess Marina, Duchess of Kent
1966	H.M. Queen Elizabeth the Queen Mother
1989	H.R.H. Prince Philip, Duke of Edinburgh
1993	H.R.H. The Duchess of Kent

A precedent had been set, with the presentation of the Company's Gold Medal to the Prince of Wales (later King Edward VII) in 1893 and observed again in 1920 when King George V accepted a similar Gold Medal, for the ceremony to take place in private at the Palace, and despite best efforts by the Master, H.T. Cart de Lafontaine, this was how the admissions of the Prince of Wales and the Duke of Connaught were made in 1921. A deputation made up of members of the Court attended at York House and Clarence House respectively for the presentations and a brief informal discussion afterwards. It was perhaps through the powers of persuasion of William Waldorf, 2nd Viscount Astor, who was Master in 1935, that the protocol was then changed and the Duke of Kent agreed to attend a Court at Stationers Hall on 9 July, to be first admitted to the Honorary Freedom and then to dine with the Court and Livery. After Dinner the Duke replied to the Toast of 'the Guests' with a speech which must have been somewhat unexpected because it developed into a eulogy of the work of Delius, who had died the previous year. The Duke urged those present to familiarise themselves with Delius's early works.

Following this last precedent, the conferment of the Honorary Freedom on Queen Elizabeth the Queen Mother at Fishmongers Hall on 12 July 1966 was a very splendid occasion, devised with great care and forethought by the Master, Derek Lockett. It was his inspiration to have invited Sir John Barbirolli to accept the Honorary Freedom earlier on the same evening, taking part in the subsequent proceedings and providing, with Lady Barbirolli and Lady Fermoy, the Queen Mother's Lady in Waiting, the programme of music after Dinner. The Master was also able to persuade Princess Marina, Duchess of Kent to accept an invitation to the ceremony and the Dinner.

Fishmongers Hall was filled to capacity with the Livery, their ladies and the Company's guests (a ballot had been necessary as the Livery's demand for places exceeded the number of seats available). It was literally 'a glittering occasion', as the chandeliers were alight and the order had gone out (to those who were able to comply with it) 'tiaras will be worn'. The Queen Mother's arrival was marked by a flourish of trumpets. After the ceremony a specially bound copy of the 'Short History', containing an inscription recording the presentation and the names of the Company's Officers, was given to her instead of the usual Honorary Freeman's scroll. Kneller Hall trumpeters sounded another fanfare as the Queen Mother took her place for Dinner, and when the meal was over she graciously proposed the toast to 'The Company'. The music consisted of an oboe sonata by J.B. Loeillet played by Lady Barbirolli (Evelyn Rothwell) and Lady Fermoy, and the first Piano Quartet in C Minor by Fauré, performed by Lady Fermoy, Martin Milner, Ludmilla Navradil and Sir John Barbirolli (cello).

In 1989, when Sir Vivian Dunn was Master, he grasped the opportunity to offer the Honorary Freedom to Prince Philip, Duke of Edinburgh, who had come to know Sir Vivian well through many years of naval association. Colonel Dunn, as he then was, had directed the Royal Marines Band during the Royal Commonwealth Tour in 1953, and on many occasions conducted the massed bands of the Royal Marines in the presence of royalty.

The fact that music was not thought to be one of Prince Philip's foremost interests was no deterrent to his willingness to accept Sir Vivian's invitation, and it was arranged that the Honorary Freedom should be conferred upon him on 30 March 1989 at Stationers Hall, and that the Duke should dine with the Court and their guests after the Ceremony. It was something of a challenge for the Master to devise a programme for the evening which the new Honorary Freeman would find most enjoyable. Sir Vivian's solution was to follow the formal ceremony with a brief examination of some of the Company's more unusual possessions (including a pair of scissors believed to have belonged to Beethoven), and then make time for completely informal conversation before Dinner. Prince Philip took full advantage of this and there were very few members of the Court or guests with whom he did not speak. When the assembled company had proceeded to their places for Dinner, musicians from the Royal Marines School of Music, Deal, dressed in uniforms of the 1790s, played the March from 'Scipio' as the Master escorted Prince Philip to his place at the top table. Following Dinner the same musicians performed on baroque instruments a selection of English songs, arranged specially by the Master for the occasion, and John Heddle Nash (Master 1984/5) sang three songs by Mozart, Stanford and Sullivan.

Forty-nine other Honorary Freemen have been admitted up to the present time. These are listed below, with the year in which the honour was conferred on them and a brief note of their profession, office or service to the Company:

1876   Sir Henry Cole; civil servant, much involved with music education in schools

1904   Andrew Carnegie; US industrialist, philanthropist
        S. Ernest Palmer; Industrialist, benefactor of music

1905   William H. Cummings; Principal, Guildhall School of Music
        The Rev. F.W. Galpin; antiquarian and collector of early music instruments
        Arthur H.D. Prendergast; expert on the masque

1908   Sir Alexander Mackenzie; Principal, Royal Academy of Music
        Sir Hubert Parry Bt; Director, Royal College of Music
        Sir Walter Parratt; Master of the King's Music

1909   Brig. Gen. Sir Alfred G. Balfour; Commandant, Royal Military School of Music

1911   The Rt. Hon Lord Alverstone; Lord Chief Justice ('in recognition of his interest in Music')

Sir Thomas Vesey Strong; Lord Mayor ('for services rendered at the recent International Music Congress')

Sir Edward Elgar; composer

1912 Sir Charles V Stanford; composer, Professor of Music, University of Cambridge

1913 Sir Landon Ronald; Principal, Guildhall School of Music

1918 Lt.-Col. J.M. Rogan; Director of Music, Coldstream Guards

1919 Col. T.C.F. Somerville; Commandant, Royal Military School of Music

1920 Lady L.C. Cooper; for services to the Red Cross (amateur musician and wife of Sir Ernest Cooper, Master and Lord Mayor 1919/20)

1921 The Very Revd W.R. Inge; Dean of St Paul's

1925 Col. J.A.C. Somerville; Commandant, Royal Military School of Music

Sir Frederic H. Cowen; composer and conductor

1931 Sir George Henschel; singer and conductor

1933 Harry C. Colles; music historian and critic (The Times); editor of Grove's Dictionary of Music (3rd and 4th editions)

1934 Sir Donald Tovey; music analyst and essayist

1935 Sir Edward German; composer

H. Plunket Greene; oratorio singer

1936 Sir Milsom Rees; royal laryngologist; consultant to Royal Opera House, Guildhall School of Music and Musicians Benevolent Fund

1937 The Revd E.H. Fellowes; scholar, librarian and editor of madrigals and lute-songs

1938 William Charles Smith; Assistant Keeper, British Museum Music Room, Handel specialist

Sir Henry Wood; conductor

1939 The Rt. Hon. Neville Chamberlain; Prime Minister, amateur musician

1944 Sir George Dyson; Director, Royal College of Music

1945 Ralph Vaughan Williams; composer

Sir Arnold Bax; composer; Master of the King's Music

1949 Sir George Franckenstein; former Austrian diplomat

Sir Reginald Thatcher; Principal, Royal Academy of Music

1952 John Christie; founder, Glyndebourne Opera

Sir Arthur Bliss; composer; Master of the Queen's Music

1957 Dr Harold Darke; organist

1962 Frank S. Howes; music critic (The Times) and historian

1965 Benjamin Britten; composer

1966 Sir John Barbirolli; conductor

1971 Sir William Walton; composer

1972 The Rt. Hon. Sir Edward Heath; Prime Minister, amateur musician

1982 Sir Michael Tippett; composer

1986 Sir Reginald Goodall; conductor

1987 Sir Yehudi Menuhin; violinist, conductor

1997 Sir Harrison Birtwhistle; composer

The procedure for the conferment of the Honorary Freedom is no different from the ordinary admission ceremony, except that the recipient is greeted by the two Wardens and escorted by them to the Master, and will usually be given an illuminated scroll as a memento of the occasion. It is the normal custom for the ceremony to take place at the end of a Court Meeting, and the new Honorary Freeman is invited to dine with the Court or the Livery. Two exceptions deserve to be mentioned, because on each occasion a composer of the greatest distinction was being honoured.

In 1911 the Court determined to give the Honorary Freedom to Sir Edward Elgar, but he found it very difficult, due to his other commitments, to attend a Company function in order to receive the honour. A private Dinner was therefore arranged at number 50 Lancaster Gate, the house of Alfred Littleton, Immediate Pastmaster and Elgar's publisher, on 14 December 1911. The ceremony took place at a Special Court before Dinner, and against all established protocol at the time Lady Elgar and the four other ladies present were permitted to watch the ceremony.

Benjamin Britten, whom the 3rd Viscount Astor particularly wished to distinguish with the Honorary Freedom during his year of office, also found it difficult to conform to the Company's calendar, and a Saturday in July, 17 July 1965, was therefore selected for a Special Court to be held at Cliveden, Lord Astor's home in Berkshire. As part of the ceremony the Court and their ladies, together with the Master's invited guests, were entertained with music sung by the choir of St George's Chapel, Windsor. The programme included Britten's own 'Hymn to St Cecilia' conducted by the composer, and 'Rule Britannia' from Thomas Arne's 'The Masque of Alfred' which was first performed for Frederick, Prince of Wales at Cliveden. A buffet lunch concluded the proceedings.

A few days later the Master received a letter from Britten (which he presented to the Company) which reflects the humility and warm sincerity which endeared him to so many friends:

My dear Bill,   The Red House, Aldeburgh
                                                   July 19th 1965
Thank you so much for that ceremony. I was really deeply touched that you arranged it for me, and most particularly for your words. It was a most memorable occasion, for me, and I was completely serious when I said that I was encouraged to go on and try to do better in my work as a result of it. . . . I thought that you had got a most easy and sympathetic lot of people to meet me too. In fact thank you most sincerely for all the thought you had put into the occasion – I hope you are not feeling any the worse for it; you must go on and get better and better.
                                                   Yours ever
                                                   Ben

There have been many other special events not related to the Honorary Freedom. In fact in 1965, just three months after the Cliveden occasion the Company was able, through the generosity of the Master, to entertain delegates attending the Commonwealth Arts Festival to Dinner at Stationers Hall, after which a dazzling display of African music was performed by the Legon Orchestra of Ghana.

Going back to the early years of the century, Charles Crews decided in 1907 that he wished, in the name of the Company, to present to Westminster Abbey a bust of Orlando Gibbons, who was organist at Westminster, but died in Canterbury after taking part in the formal ceremony of welcome for Charles I's future queen, Henrietta Maria. The bust, in black marble, was to be a copy of the one in Canterbury Cathedral, and would be unveiled by Princess Christian of Schleswig-Holstein. The ceremony took place in Westminster Abbey on 5 June 1907, and was the first time that the Company had processed, robed, outside the City. The music for the service, which marked the 282nd anniversary of Gibbons' death, consisted entirely of his music, and was sung by a large choir of about 300 singers accompanied by a 'large string band', under the direction of Sir Frederick Bridge. Taking part in the service with the Company were Sir Hubert Parry, Sir Alexander Mackenzie, Dr W.H. Cummings, Sir Walter Parratt, Sir George Martin (organist of St Paul's Cathedral), Sir Charles Stanford, Dr E.H. Turpin (President, Royal College of Organists) and Dr Charles Harriss (Director of the McGill University Conservatoire of Music and a Liveryman of the Company).

Another event takes us from the sublime to the delightfully ridiculous. It was the Ladies' Night Banquet in 1958, when Sir Denis Truscott, who had completed his first term of office as Master the previous November, was now Lord Mayor, and invited the Company to hold the banquet in the Mansion House. The musical entertainment after Dinner was a performance of Malcolm Arnold's 'Toy Symphony', conducted by the composer. Serious work was required to be done by the string section of the orchestra, represented by the Entente String Quartet and by Dr Clarence Raybould at the piano. The 'line-up' of virtuosi was as follows:

Quails: Dr Reginald Jacques, Stanley Rubinstein
Cuckoo & Guard's Whistle: Sir Adrian Boult, Leslie Woodgate
Nightingale & Whistle in C Sharp Minor: J.S. Morley (Master), Lt.-Col. D. McBain
Toy Trumpets: The Lord Mayor, Dr Greenhouse Allt, Dr Thomas Armstrong, Dr J. Dykes Bower
Dulcimers: Trevor Burnett-Brown (Senior Warden), Dr Herbert Howells (Junior Warden), Alastair Crewdson (Clerk)
Triangle: Priaulx Rainier
Cymbals: Harry Vowles
Drum: George Godwin (Beadle)

A second performance of the 'Toy Symphony' at a Company banquet was given by the Ad Hoc Orchestra[28] on 7 June 1982, when the Master, Sir Andrew Carnwath, entertained the Lord Mayor, Sir Christopher Leaver, and the Lady

---

[28] The names of the performers seem to have been lost, but they certainly included John Heddle Nash and the author. Sir Denis and Lady Truscott, Sir Gilbert Inglefield, Mr and Mrs John Street, Mr and Mrs Lockett and Victor Fleming may have completed the ensemble.

Mayoress to Dinner at Stationers Hall. The symphony was again conducted by the composer, a Liveryman of the Company.

A rather more serious and substantial evening of food and music was arranged on 13 May 1969 at Middle Temple Hall, in commemoration of the grant of the Charter to the King's Minstrels five hundred years before. This was during the Mastership of Jack Iles, and his principal guests were H.R.H. Princess Alice, Duchess of Gloucester, and Jennie Lee, Minister of Education. The intention of the evening was to give a flavour and impression of a late 15th century banquet, and on consulting Philip Pickett and Ian Bent of the Guildhall School of Music and Drama, it was apparent that courses of music would typically have been sandwiched between courses of food. The evening was programmed accordingly and the assembled company was entertained to some hurdy-gurdy music before the main dish of roast poussin (the swan, being a protected bird, was 'off') which in turn was followed by some more 15th century instrumental music. The sweet course which came next, in which the swan was presented in the form of a meringue, was the prelude to some Elizabethan Consort Songs. This still left time after the Feast for a selection of 16th century music, including music for brass consort, viol consort and partsongs, performed by the Jaye Consort and other musicians under the direction of Adrian Thorne.

On 25 October 1985 the Company presented a Concert at Merchant Taylors' Hall in aid of the Lord Mayor's Appeal for St Paul's Cathedral Choir School. Under the direction of Jonathan Rennert the programme, which extended from Christopher Tye to Sir Michael Tippett, was given by the Elizabethan Singers, members of the St Michael's Singers and the Phoenix Chamber Orchestra. Full advantage was also taken of the fine organ in the Hall which was played by Christopher Dearnley. The concert was the first point of contact between the Lord Mayor, Sir Alan Traill, and the Company, and was to lead a few years later to Sir Alan joining the Company and becoming increasingly involved in the Company's affairs. He is Master of the Company during for the Quincentenary year.

The Livery Club of the Worshipful Company of Musicians

The Livery Club was founded on 10 March 1902, and in the same year it was responsible for the private publication of the first 'Handbook' of the Company, which was extended and reissued in 1905, and again in 1915. The 1905 edition explained that the Club had been founded by some members

> who felt that the Annual Livery Dinner did not afford sufficient means of personal intercommunication between the Members, and that the interests of the Company and its usefulness to the Art of Music would be enhanced by the formation of a Club or Union of Members whereby more frequent opportunities for social intercourse would be afforded.[29]

---

[29] *The Worshipful Company of Musicians*, 1905, p. 174.

22. H.M. Queen Elizabeth the Queen Mother receiving and accepting the Honorary Freedom of the Company from the Master, Derek Lockett, at Fishmongers Hall on 12th July 1966.

23. 13th May 1969: H.R.H. Princess Alice, Duchess of Gloucester, receiving a specially bound copy of the 'Short History' from the Master, Jack Iles, with its author, Alastair Crewdson, and the Beadle, Roy Day, on the occasion of the Feast at Middle Temple Hall, commemorating the King's Minstrels' first Charter granted in 1469.

24. H.R.H. Prince Philip, having received the Honorary Freedom from the Master,
Sir Vivian Dunn, in conversation with the Treasurer, Walter Ficker (31st March 1989).

25. H.R.H. the Duchess of Kent, the latest royal recipient of the Honorary Freedom, examining some of the Company's treasures with the Master, John Iles, and the Author. The music is the autograph score of Sullivan's 'The Lost Chord'.

With this objective in mind the Club sprang into action, with about 60 per cent of the members of the Livery joining in the first year. Not only was the Livery Club responsible for the first Handbook, but it also took the initiative in persuading the Company to attend Evensong at St Paul's Cathedral on St Cecilia's Day 1906. A regular programme of musical events for the Livery Club members, some of which must have outshone the Company's own more formal functions, continued from 1905, when there was a display of 'Ancient Dances' at Queen's Gate Hall, until the outbreak of war in 1914. At the Presidential Dinner of the Club in 1906 ladies were invited for the first time and the winning entries in W.W. Cobbett's 'Phantasy' Competition were given their first performance. Two years later the Club was entertained to a demonstration of English Folksong and Morris Dancing under the direction of Cecil Sharp, who was then at the peak of his activity.

During the early years of the Club the principal musical interest seems to have been the rediscovery of Cecilian Odes from the late 17th and early 18th centuries. In 1910 there was a performance of Italian music (Pergolesi, Scarlatti and Palestrina – in that order) and in 1913 a programme of French music including Lalande, Lully and Rameau, together with traditional airs.

The annual pattern was abruptly broken by the war, and when it was over the enthusiasm for supplementary activities seems to have been lacking. The Club continued, but its membership fell and many subscriptions remained in arrears. In the 1930s it was little more than a memory. Its second incarnation in 1952 was due almost entirely to the energy of the Company's Treasurer, W. Graham Wallace, who was worried at the time about the shortage of new members wishing to join the Company, and who realised that the social activities of the Livery Club, if revived, would be more likely to attract potential recruits to the Company than the Company's own formal events. His concern was a financial one, it being then still the custom of the Company to permit members of the Livery to dine free of charge once a year at the Livery Dinner. A note circulated by the Treasurer at the time compared the balmy days of twenty years before (i.e. in the early 1930s), when the annual income produced by the investment of Livery Fines covered the cost of the Livery Dinner as well as some special events and 'casual donations of a charitable nature', with the current conditions when high prices and taxation meant that this income did not even cover the cost of the Dinner. This denied the Company the opportunity of 'taking part in any outside activities requiring cash'.

Wallace pointed out that in the early days of the Club 'guests and observers' at its functions became attracted to join the Company, so that the membership was materially increased, and he believed that by re-forming the Club the 'same spirit of goodwill and adventure' could be revived. New members would mean more income for the Company, and the crisis would be resolved.

As in 1902, there was a good response to the Treasurer's appeal, and by 1954 there were more than fifty members of the Club. The Livery, who numbered 155 in 1952, increased steadily to over two hundred by 1960. Unfortunately the beginnings of inflation during that time meant that the increased income from the investment of Livery Fines was overtaken by the chronic increase in dining costs, and the free Livery Dinner passed into history. The purpose of the Club's revival was therefore thwarted, but this had no effect on the enthusiasm with which it began, and continued, to engage in an annual programme of miscellaneous events, for which the annually-elected Club President, supported by the Honorary Secretary and a Committee, was primarily responsible.

The new Club was fortunate to have as its first Secretary Stanley Creber, whose position at the Royal Academy of Music enabled the Club to organise several of its early events around the senior students' music-making, for example a performance of 'Suor Angelica' and 'Gianni Schicchi' in 1955 and a Mansion House Soirée in 1958. There were also visits to the BBC in 1956 and 1961, and to the London docks in 1957 and 1962. It was at the request of the Club that Dr Herbert Howells wrote the 'Hymn to St Cecilia' in 1961.

By this time the Club, like the Company, had certain regular fixtures written into its calendar; these were the annual dinner, usually in February, an invitation to a Kneller Hall Garden Party and Concert in midsummer, and a party after the St Cecilia Service, which was held at first in Stationers Hall, but later in the St Paul's Cathedral Chapter House.

In 1967 the chivalrous, incorrigibly eccentric Reggie Beloe was elected Honorary Secretary, and held that office for the next seventeen years. The Club's programme continued as varied and adventurous as ever. One of its grandest moments was in Beloe's first year as Secretary, when Walter Ficker, who succeeded Derek Lockett as Treasurer and became Master in 1982, was the Club President. Sir Gilbert Inglefield, who had joined the Company the previous year, was Lord Mayor. He was a passionate devotee of Handel, and was delighted to accept the invitation of the Livery Club to attend its annual dinner, at the Mansion House on 23 February 1968, when all the music was by Handel, whose birthday anniversary it was.

Reggie Beloe was succeeded as Honorary Secretary by Stephen Barrett in 1985, and for the next four years the Club was as active as ever, and its programme now included a social evening arranged around one of the Company's annual Maisie Lewis Recitals. Some concerns were however being expressed at about this time that the Company and the Club were drawing too far apart, and that it might be better if the Club were simply the *alter ego* of the Company under the auspices of a Social Committee drawn from the Court and the Livery. In this way every member of the Livery would be a member of the Club, and the events of both Company and Club could be better coordinated. After a great deal of discussion it was decided to make this change, which coincided with the transfer of responsibility from the Club to the Clerk's office for such functions as the annual visit to the Guildhall School of Music and Drama's Opera production, and the party after the St Cecilia Service. At the time of writing the Club has effectively ceased to exist as a separate body, and it will have to wait for a new group of Liverymen (and a sympathetic Court) to prise it away from the

Company once more. It is of course important that a Livery Club should function in close cooperation with its parent body at all times, but as well as being the best way of bringing members of the Livery together informally, there are many things that the Club can do which would be outside the scope of the Company.

Fin de Siècle

The reader with the stamina to have fought his or her way through this long chapter will have been left in no doubt about the huge amount of archival material which charts the Company's progress through the 20th century. This is not just due to improved record-keeping; it is an indication also that this Century has been the most fertile and productive period in the Company's history, even though its objects have changed greatly from those of the original craft guild. Increased activity and effectiveness have produced their own integral growth and at the time of writing the Company is stronger than it has ever been, both economically and in the size of its Livery, which now numbers 360.

In the last years of the Century, some additional benefits, initiatives and changes have given the Company extra life and new opportunities, which have helped its standing within the fellowship of the minor Livery Companies, and made it possible to play a more active part in the field of musical patronage.

A generous bequest under the Will of Reggie Beloe has enabled the Court to repay the hospitality enjoyed each year by the Master from other Companies, by holding an additional Dinner for this purpose after the October Court. A gift by Stephen Barrett in memory of his late wife, Phyllis, provides for a series of informal lunches to be held each year in the Clerk's office for new and intending members. The residue of the late Victor Allcard's estate which was bequeathed to the Company subject to a life interest, has now vested in the Company, and will add over two hundred thousand pounds to its charitable funds. It may form the basis of the 'New Foundation Fund' planned as a Quincentenary commemoration, with the object of helping young musicians as they progress from student status into the profession, the difficult so-called 'wilderness years'.

The problem of public relations, which is always troublesome for livery companies, as they are so little understood outside the City of London, has been solved to a large extent through the initiative of John Iles (Master 1993/4) and Adrian Davis (Master 1994/5) in founding a 'House Journal', taking as its title the Company's motto 'Preserve Harmony'. This semi-annual broadsheet has been sent free of charge to all members of the Company since 1990, and copies are now sent also to the Clerks of all the other Livery Companies. Each year it includes a profile of the new Master, the latest Company news including some of the recent events and awards, and contributions by members of the Livery covering a wide range of musical topics. In an age when everyone wants to know what everyone else is doing, it has proved an ideal medium for ensuring that no one can justly complain that they 'have been left in the dark'.

Perhaps the most important change has been the upgrading of the amount of

26. On 17th July 1965, the Court assembled at Cliveden, the home of the Master, Viscount Astor, to confer the Honorary Freedom on Benjamin Britten. Included in this commemorative photograph are the following (from left to right): H.F.B. Iles, the Author (Assistant Clerk), J.S.P. Morley, Henry Willis, W. Graham Wallace, Benjamin Britten, Trevor Burnett-Brown, Alastair Crewdson (Clerk), Lord Astor (Master), Roy Day (Beadle), Victor Allcard, Frank Wright, Herbert Howells, Sir John Dykes-Bower, David Loeb, E.H.T. Broadwood, Stanley Rubinstein and Sir Jack Westrup.

time which the Company now requires the Clerk to spend on the Company's affairs. The long tradition of Solicitors serving as Clerks to the Company in their spare time, which goes back to J.T. Theobald, who became Clerk in 1871, was beginning to buckle under the strain of the much more intensive time pressures to which all professionals in London have been subjected during the last quarter-century, and also the demands of an increasingly active Company. Michael Fletcher, who had served the Company loyally since 1988 was caught in this vortex and by mutual agreement made way for Simon Waley, who was employed in 1993 on the basis that he would give half his time to the Company and the other half to the Honourable the Irish Society, which looks after the interests of the City Corporation in Northern Ireland, as it has done since the

Londonderry Plantation.[30] Although some optimistic estimates that the change would not result in an increase in administrative costs have not been realised, the work of the Clerk's office has increased beyond all expectations, and it would be hard to justify an argument in favour of a return to the old regime. The Company has reached a point where it needs the additional administrative support which the change has provided, and with the turn of the century this requirement is likely to increase still more, especially if the celebration of the Quincentenary puts the Company under the spotlight, with a consequential extra involvement in musical activities.

A historian is not supposed to speculate on what these might be, but the sowing of one or two seeds is as good a way as any of ending the book. The 'New Foundation Fund' has already been mentioned, and the widespread support which this proposal has received suggests that aid and encouragement to young musicians through prizes and grants will continue to increase as it has done for the last one hundred years, even if the demand can never be wholly satisfied. The desire to provide help in this way is almost instinctive. The great number of benefactors who are keen to participate in this work means that it will never be the Company's sole prerogative. The Company will always be one of many such benefactors, even if it is able to spread its help more widely than most.

The beginning of a new Millennium could therefore be the moment at which the Company recognises that, as the oldest surviving musical institution (outside the royal household) in the country, it may have other responsibilities. Should it be looking backward as well as forward? Should it be using the musical past to enrich the future? Should the increased size of the Livery be exploited by the setting up of working groups to examine those issues and problems which are of most concern to those of the Livery who have volunteered for this work?

It would be wrong for the Company to acquire an antiquarian image, and it cannot hope to compete with the expertise of the academicians who have made musicology such a precise science. What it would perhaps be able to do is to give regular support to performers who have an interest in reintroducing modern audiences to 'ancient' English music (with its old meaning of 'not-contemporary'), so much of which has lain undeservedly in limbo since its first performance.

Then there is the legacy of the Dancing Masters, who wore the same livery and bore the same arms as today's and tomorrow's Liverymen of the Company. Their dances, both courtly and 'country', are long overdue for a popular revival. Those who have practised it would say that there is just as much addictive power in the rhythm of baroque dance as in any African-American import. Is the Company neglecting its heritage in paying so little regard to the art or science of dance, especially as the Dancing Masters went on to become the pioneers of classical ballet?

---

[30] See p. 88.

Like all other Livery Companies the origins of the Company lay in a Christian fraternity, and the links between the Anglican Church and the Company have been maintained through the 20th century. However the Anglican Choral Tradition, as revived in the 19th century by Thomas Helmore and others, is now once again at risk, with the sharp decline in the number of parish choirs, the lack of organists and the impact of charismatic music. It would be a terrible thing if in the 21st century the only place where one could hear an anthem by Purcell or Wesley was a Cathedral or a concert platform. It could be a declared objective of the Company or a dedicated group of its members to look for ways of reversing this decline and of helping to set standards for church music, both as to the music itself (modern and ancient) and its performance. Efforts could also be made to link this with the ongoing problem of maintaining a proper level of group training in music in primary (particularly Church of England) schools.

The 21st century will be an age of instant world-wide communication, and it will become difficult for a City Livery Company not to attract international interest, or to ignore the possibilities of 'outreach'. For the Musicians Company this could be a pleasant and rewarding activity. In Europe there are more than sixty cities which are known to have had Guilds of Minstrels or Musicians at some time in their history. In India, China and elsewhere in the world there are probably hundreds, if not thousands, more. Contact with these cities, face to face or through the Internet offers amazing possibilities.

Finally, in the last fifty years, the remedial power of music in a controlled medical environment has been the subject of intense research, and Music Therapy is now a recognised form of treatment for persons of all ages who suffer from brain disorders and many other conditions. It is particularly effective in the case of children with severe problems of communication. The United Kingdom is among the leaders in terms of research, but is slow in creating the opportunities for Music Therapists (all of whom have a first degree in music) to practise. It is a profession to which the Company could give its special consideration and support.

In its five hundredth year, it is good to be able to record more of the Company's History than has been done before, and to give credit to those who have led it through its many years, and who have brought honour to the name of the Company. At the same time one stands blindfold and helpless on the threshold of the next five centuries, but not without hope that the Company will have a continuing role to play in 'preserving harmony'.

APPENDIX ONE

Statutes of the Paris Guild of Minstrels, 1321[1]

1. No minstrel shall hire out any other performers than himself and companion, this is to overcome the exploitation of inferior and outside players at extra low rates.

2. *Trompeurs* or *autres menestreurs* who have been engaged for a function must wait until it has ended before they move on elsewhere.

3. They may not send a deputy, except in the case of illness, imprisonment, or other emergency.

4. No *menestreurs* or *menestrelles* or *aprentiz* may tout for custom at feasts or weddings in Paris, or else be fined.

5. In taverns no apprentice minstrel should recommend any player, or discuss his profession, and should direct any enquiries to headquarters with the words 'Sir, the laws of my profession forbid me to engage anyone but myself, but if you seek minstrels or apprentices, go to the *rue aus jougleurs*, and there you will find good ones.'

6. When a prospective customer appears in Minstrel Street, he is to be allowed to approach whatsoever performer he chooses without interference from rivals.

7. Apprentices must observe the same rules.

8. All minstrels, whether from Paris or without, must swear to obey the Statutes.

9. Any outside minstrel arriving in Paris must be required to swear to the Provost of St Julian or to a royal appointee in charge of the Guild that he will obey the Statutes, or else be banished for a year and a day.

10. Two or three worthy representatives of the profession shall be chosen to impose fines on offenders, half of such income to go to the Guild, and half to the Crown.

---

[1] As set out in Wilkins, *Music in the Age of Chaucer*, p. 138.

The Charter of Edward IV

(Translated from the Latin)

The Brotherhood of the King's Minstrels

THE KING TO WHOM ALL THOSE TO WHOM ETC., GREETING

Be it known that we have learned from the complaint of our beloved Walter Haliday (Marshall), John Cliff, Robert Marshall, Thomas Grene, Thomas Calthorn, William Cliff, William Christean, William Eynsham, our Minstrels, that certain ignorant rustics and craftsmen of various callings in our Kingdom of England have falsely represented themselves to be Minstrels. Of whom some assuming our licence which has in no way been granted to them, represent themselves as our Minstrels; under the colour of which licence and of the said art or occupation of Minstrels they in various parts of our Kingdom collect and receive large sums of money from our subjects.

And although they are in that art or occupation by no means learned or skilled, and practise divers arts and callings on holidays and ordinary days and derive a sufficient living therefrom, they nevertheless move from place to place on festival days and collect all those profits by means of which our aforesaid Minstrels and our other Minstrels for the time being, sufficiently learned and instructed in the aforesaid art or occupation, and practising no other craft, trade or calling, should obtain their living.

Furthermore we learn that much disgrace is thus brought upon that art or occupation, and manifold and manifest deterioration of our Minstrels practising the said art or occupation, and moreover no slight loss and grievance to our people engaged in agriculture or otherwise.

Therefore our Minstrels have humbly besought us that we would of our grace and special favour deign to provide for them a suitable remedy in this matter.

We considering the foregoing and being favourably inclined to their reasonable supplication in this matter, have of our own favour, certain knowledge and of our own motion, granted and given our licence and by these presents do grant and give licence for ourselves and our heirs as far as in us lies to the said Walter Haliday (Marshall), John Cliff, Robert Marshall, Thomas Grene, Thomas Calthorn, William Cliff, William Christean and William Eynsham, our Minstrels, that they to the praise and honour of God, and that they may be the more specially bound to pray for the well-being of us and our most dear Consort

Elizabeth Queen of England so long as we live and for our souls when we shall have departed from this world; as also for the soul of our most dear lord and father Richard late Duke of York, and for the souls of our renowned progenitors and for all the faithful departed, both in the Chapel of the Blessed Virgin Mary within the Cathedral Church of St Paul in London and in our own Royal Free Chapel of St Anthony in our same City of London, to found, to continue and to increase a certain perpetual Brotherhood or Guild (such as we learn that brothers and sisters of the Fraternity of Minstrels of our Kingdom in times past formed, established and ordained) and that they may be enabled to receive, to admit and to accept as brothers and sisters of the said Brotherhood or Guild, whatsoever persons, both men and women, adhering to them with loyal intention;

And that our aforesaid Marshall and Minstrels who now are as well as our other Minstrels and those of our heirs in perpetuity, shall be able at their pleasure to name, elect, ordain and successively constitute from among themselves, a Marshall capable and fit to remain in that office for the term of his life, and also each year two Wardens to rule and govern the said brotherhood or guild;

And furthermore we will and by these presents grant for the support and increase of the said brotherhood or guild that no Minstrel of our Kingdom, even though he be sufficiently instructed in the art or occupation, shall henceforth in any way practise or publicly exercise the art or occupation within our Kingdom aforesaid, unless he belong to the said Brotherhood or Guild and shall have been admitted to the same and shall have contributed to it with the other brethren (provided that none of the aforesaid brethren or those to be admitted shall pay for entrance or admission more than three shillings and four pence); and if he should do otherwise or should in any way contravene he shall by the aforesaid Marshall and Minstrels of ourselves or our heirs for the time being be fined according to their discretion;

And that our aforesaid Marshall and Minstrels and their Wardens and their successors shall be able lawfully and with impunity to summon, make and ordain lawful and orderly meetings and communications among themselves and lawful statutes and rules for the proper government and the advantage of the Brotherhood or Guild when and as often as it may be necessary;

And if any of our Minstrels or those of our heirs should depart or die or should on account of shortcomings or offences or other cause whatsoever be released, removed or deposed from our service, then the Marshall and other Minstrels at the time existing shall on our behalf elect and nominate another Minstrel, fit and sufficiently learned and skilled in the art or occupation wherever in our Kingdom, whether within or without the Liberties, they may chance to find him (the County of Chester excepted) in the stead and place of the one departed, released, removed or deposed, and to instal him as one of our or our heirs' Minstrels to be retained in our service, to receive our pay, our royal assent thereto having been obtained.

And moreover we will and by these presents grant to the aforesaid Marshall and Minstrels that they and their successors shall have the power and faculty to inquire by all reasonable and lawful ways, methods and means throughout the whole of our aforesaid Kingdom, as well within as without the Liberties (the aforesaid County of Chester excepted) concerning each and every person pretending to be a Minstrel and falsely claiming our Licence and improperly and illegally professing or exercising the aforesaid art or occupation, or not belonging to the aforesaid Brotherhood or Guild; and concerning all other matters and circumstances regarding the foregoing;

And from time to time, as often as may be necessary, as well within as without the Liberties (the County of Chester excepted) to supervise, to examine, to rule and to govern all and each of those persons practising the art and occupation of Minstrels and to justly and properly correct and punish any one of them for offences or shortcomings in respect of the foregoing.

And all penalties, fines, forfeitures or damages whatsoever (if in accordance with the foregoing any such should be properly or probably adjudged, assessed or imposed by reason of such inquisition, examination or scrutiny, upon anyone pretending to be Minstrels or otherwise offending) shall be collected, applied and expended for the use and advantage of the Brotherhood, for the continual and perpetual maintenance of certain wax candles (commonly called tapers), for the expenses in the aforesaid Chapels of the Brotherhood at present existing or which may come to exist in the future,

Shall be held, occupied, exercised, enjoyed all and singly the aforesaid inquisition, scrutiny, supervision, rule, government, correction, punishment and other things aforesaid in the ways and forms above cited by the aforementioned Walter, John, Robert, Thomas Grene, Thomas Calthorn, William Cliff, William Christean and William Eynsham our Minstrels and their successors for ever without let, hindrance, impediment, molestation, disturbance, or injury of us, our heirs, justiciaries, escheats, ministers or others whatsoever.

The Charter is printed in Rymer's Foedera *(vol. XI, 642).*

APPENDIX THREE

The Lord Mayor's Precept

7th March 1555

On the behalf of our Sovereign Lord and Lady the King and Queen's Majesties we straitly charge and command you immediately upon the sight hereof, calling before you all Vinteurs keepers of Taverns alehouses and other victuallinghouse-holders within your said ward and also all keepers of dancing houses and keepers and maintainers of unlawful games and plays called 'white and black' and such other like, do furthermore give in most earnest wise like charge and commandment to every of them that they the said Vinteurs keepers of taverns Alehouses and Victualling houses that they or any of them do not permit or suffer at any time hereafter any minstrel or minstrels or any other whatsoever person or persons to sing any manner of song or songs or to play upon any manner of instrument or to make or play any manner of interlude or plays within his or their house or houses or other whatsoever place or places within the said City and Liberties thereof, Singing and playings at any marriage or marriages to be kept in any such house or place only excepted, upon pain to be clearly sequestered and discharged for ever from the keeping of any such tavern alehouse or other victualling house or place whatsoever within the said City and Liberties, and also upon such further pain as by the Court of Aldermen of the same City shall be thought meet and convenient and to every of the said keepers of dancing houses and unlawful games that they or any of them do not from henceforth keep or maintain any longer within the said City and Liberties any such dancing or unlawful game or games not only upon pain or imprison-ment of their bodies but also upon such further pains as are provided by the law for such offenders

Fail ye not hereof as ye tender the Commonwealth and honour of the said City and the Advancement of justice and as ye will answer for the contrary at your peril

Given at the Guildhall of the City of London the viith day of March 1554[5]

L. Blackwell

(CL Jor 16, fol. 328)

APPENDIX FOUR

The Charter of James I (1604)

(translated from the Latin)

JAMES, by the Grace of God King of England, Scotland, France, and Ireland, Defender of the Faith, &c. To all to whom these present letters shall come, greeting: Know ye that of our special grace, certain science, and mere motion, and at the humble petition of our faithful subjects the freemen of the Society of Minstrels of our City of London, we have willed, ordained, constituted, declared, and granted, and by these presents for us, our heirs and successors, do will, ordain, constitute, declare, and grant, that they, the foresaid freemen of the Society aforesaid, or by what other name or names the same Society is called or named, and their successors, from henceforth for ever may be and shall be by force of these presents one body corporate and politic in substance, deed, and name, by the name of master, wardens, and commonalty of the Art or Science of the Musicians of London, and them, by the name of the master, wardens, and commonalty of the Art or Science of the Musicians of London, one body corporate and politic in substance, deed, and name, really and fully for us, our heirs and successors, we do erect, make, ordain, appoint, confirm, and declare by these presents; and that by that name they shall have perpetual succession, and so from henceforth shall be named, called, and accepted in our City of London and elsewhere, and not otherwise: And that they and their successors, by the name of the master, wardens, and commonalty of the Art or Science of the Musicians of London, be and shall be at all times for ever to come persons able and capable in law to have, purchase, receive, and possess messuage, lands, tenements, liberties, privileges, jurisdictions, franchises, and hereditaments, of what nature, kind, or property soever the same shall be, to them and their successors in fee and perpetuity, or for term of year or years, or otherwise howsoever, and also goods and chattels and other things whatsoever, of what kind, name, nature, quality, or property they shall be: And to give, grant, demise, alien, assign, and dispose of lands, tenements, and hereditaments, and to do and execute all and every other deeds and things, by the name aforesaid; and that by the same name of the master, wardens, and commonalty of the Art or Science of Musicians of London they shall be able and may plead and be impleaded, make answer and be answered, defend and be defended in whatsoever courts and places, and before whatsoever judges and justices, and whatsoever other persons and officers of ours, our heirs and successors, in all and singular actions, pleas, suits, plaints, causes, matters, and

248

demands whatsoever, of what kind, nature, quality, or form they be or shall be, in the like manner and form as any other our liege people of this our realm of England, persons able and capable in law, or any other body corporate and politic within our realm of England, can or may have, purchase, receive, possess, enjoy, retain, give, grant, demise, alienate, assign, and dispose, plead and be impleaded, answer and be answered, defend and be defended, do permit or execute: And that the master, wardens, and commonalty of the Art or Science of Musicians of London aforesaid shall have for ever a common seal to serve for the dispatching of the affairs and business whatsoever of them and their successors; and that it shall and may be lawful to the same master, wardens, and commonalty of the Art or Science of Musicians of London aforesaid from time to time, at their pleasure, to break and change that seal, and to make a new one, as to them shall be thought meet: And, moreover, we will and by these presents for us, our heirs and successors, do grant to the foresaid master, wardens, and commonalty, and their successors, that there may be and shall be for ever one of the commonalty aforesaid, to be chosen in form hereafter in these presents mentioned, who shall be and shall be named the master of the said Art or Science of Musicians of London: And that likewise there may be and shall be two of the commonalty of the same art or science, to be named and chosen in form hereafter in these presents mentioned, who shall be and shall be named wardens of the Art or Science of Musicians of London aforesaid: And that likewise there may be and shall be thirteen or more, not exceeding the number of twenty in the whole, to be chosen of the commonalty aforesaid in form hereafter in these presents mentioned, who shall be and shall be named assistants of the Art or Science of Musicians of London, and shall be from time to time aided and assisted to the same master and wardens for the time being in all causes, business, and matters touching or concerning the said commonalty: And, moreover, we will and by these presents for us, our heirs and successors, do grant to the foresaid master, wardens, and commonalty of the Art or Science of Musicians of London aforesaid, and to their successors, that the master, wardens, and assistants of the Art or Science of Musicians of London for the time being, or the greater part of them, upon summons of the master and wardens for the time being, or the greater part of them (being gathered together for this purpose), on that behalf to be made, may have and shall have full power and authority to frame, appoint, ordain, and make from time to time reasonable laws, statutes, constitutions, decrees, and ordinances whatsoever, in writing, which to them, or the greater part of them, according to their good discretions, shall seem to be good, wholesome, profitable, honest, and necessary for the good rule and government of the master, wardens, and commonalty of the art or science aforesaid, and of all other minstrels and musicians of the City of London, and within three miles of the same city, for the time being, and for the declamation in what manner and form the same master, wardens, and assistants, and all and singular persons of the commonalty aforesaid, shall bear and behave themselves in their office, art, and science, for the further public weal and common profit of the same master, wardens, and commonalty of the art or science aforesaid, and in all other affairs and causes whatsoever touching or in anywise concerning the art and science aforesaid: And that the same master, wardens, and assistants of the art and science aforesaid for the time being, or the greater part of them, as often as they shall make, frame, ordain, or establish such laws, statutes, institutions, ordinances, and constitutions in form aforesaid, shall and may make, limit, and provide such pains, punishments, and penalties, by imprisonment of body, or by fines, amerciaments, or by both of them, towards and upon all offenders against the same laws, statutes, institutions, ordinances, and constitutions, or any of them, as to the same master, wardens, and assistants for the time being, or the greater part of them, shall be thought necessary or requisite for the observation of the same laws, ordinances, and constitutions; and the same fines and amerciaments to have to the use of the said master, wardens, and commonalty, and their successors, without impediment of us, our heirs or successors, or of any officers or ministers of us, our heirs or successors, and without any account therefore to be yielded to us, our heirs or successors: All and every which said laws, ordinances, statutes, and constitutions so as aforesaid to be made we will shall be observed under the pains therein contained, so that the same laws, ordinances, constitutions, imprisonments, fines, and amerciaments be reasonable, and not repugnant, nor contrary to the laws, statutes, customs, or rights of our realm of England: And for the better execution of our will and grant in this behalf we have assigned, named, created, constituted, and made, and by these presents for us, our heirs and successors, do assign, name, create, constitute, and make, our beloved Phillip London to be the first and present master of the foresaid Art or Science of the Musicians of London: Willing that the same Phillip London shall be and continue master of the art or science aforesaid from the date of these presents unto the Feast of St. Michael the Archangel next following after the date of these presents, and from the same feast until one other to the office of master of the art or science aforesaid shall be in due form chosen and elected according to the orders and provisions hereafter in these presents expressed and declared, if the same Phillip London shall so long live: We have also assigned, named, and appointed, and by these presents for us, our heirs and successors, do assign, name, and appoint, our well-beloved Isaac Thorpe and Thomas Carter to be the two first and present wardens of the said Art or Science of the Musicians of London, to continue in the said office of wardens of the said art or science from the date of these presents unto the foresaid Feast of St. Michael the Archangel next coming after the date of these presents, and from the same feast until two others to the same office of wardens of the same art or science shall be elected and chosen according to the ordinances and provisions in these presents expressed and declared, if the said Isaac Thorpe and Thomas Carter shall so long live, unless in the meantime they, or either of them, shall be removed from that office for their evil government or evil behaviour in that behalf, or for some reasonable cause: And we have assigned, named, created, and constituted, and by these presents for us, our heirs and successors, do assign, name, constitute, and make, our well-beloved Anthony Tindall, James Sherman,

Walter Lowman, William Warren, Arthur Norton, Tristram Waters, William Benton, Rowland Rowbedge, Robert Baker, John Mitchell, John Popson, Vincent Johnveryn, John Bickley, and Simon Hopper to be the first and present assistants of the same master, wardens, and commonalty of the art or science aforesaid, to continue in the same office during their natural lives, unless they or any of them shall be in the meantime amoved from thence for their evil government or evil behaviour in that behalf, or for any other reasonable cause: And that it shall and may be lawful to the same master, wardens, and assistants for the time being, or to the greater part of them, for the time being, at their pleasure, to elect, name, and admit from time to time such and so many of the ancientest and most worthy freemen of the same commonalty as to them shall be thought meet to be the assistants of the same master and wardens, and their successors; and that he or they, after he or they shall be so elected and named, shall take a corporal oath before the master and wardens for the time being to execute that office rightly, well, and honestly in all things touching that office (so that the number of the said assistants do not at any time exceed the number of 20 persons); and to remove any of the said assistants for the time being or which hereafter shall be for any reasonable cause, and to choose, appoint, and admit others of new:

And, moreover, we will and grant by these presents for us, our heirs and successors, to the said master, wardens, and commonalty, and their successors, that the said master, wardens, and assistants of the art or science aforesaid for the time being, or the greater part of them, from time to time, at all times to come, shall and may have power and authority every year for ever at the Feast of St. Michael the Archangel, or within 20 days after that feast, to name and choose, and that they shall and may name and choose, one of the freemen of the commonalty aforesaid, and which shall be master of the Art and Science of the Musicians of London for one whole year then next following: And that he which shall be elected and named to be master of the art or science aforesaid shall, before his admittance into that office, take his corporal oath before the last master, his predecessor, and the wardens of the art or science aforesaid for the time being truly, well, and faithfully to execute that office in all things touching the same office; and also two others of the aforesaid commonalty of the art or science aforesaid which shall be wardens of the same art or science aforesaid for one whole year then next ensuing: And that he which shall be elected and chosen as aforesaid into the office of the master of the art or science aforesaid shall and may execute the office of the master of the art or science aforesaid for one whole year then next following; and that they shall be elected and chosen as aforesaid into the office of the wardens of the art or science aforesaid shall execute the office of the wardens of the same art or science for one whole year then next following, and take a corporal oath before the master of the art or science aforesaid, the last wardens, their predecessors, and so many of the assistants as shall be then present to execute the office of wardens of the art or science aforesaid well, uprightly, and honestly in all things touching that office: And, further, we will and by these presents grant for us, our heirs and successors, to the aforesaid master, wardens, and commonalty, and their successors, that if the master and wardens of the commonalty aforesaid, or any of them, shall happen to die or to be removed from their office at any time within one year after they shall be elected and chosen as aforesaid to the office of the master or to the office of wardens of the art or science aforesaid (which said master and wardens and every of them we will be caused to be removed for evil government or for any other reasonable cause, by the greater part of the same master, wardens, and assistants), that then and so often as it shall and may be lawful for such and so many of the same master, wardens, and assistants who shall then survive or remain, or the greater part of them, at their pleasure, to elect and choose one other to be master, and one or two others to be warden or wardens of the art or science aforesaid, according to the ordinances and provisions before by these presents declared, to execute and exercise the said office of master or the said office or offices of warden or wardens aforesaid until the Feast of St Michael the Archangel then next following, the like corporal oath being taken as aforesaid in form aforesaid, and so as often as any such occasion shall happen: And, more-over, of our more abundant special grace, certain science, and mere motion we have given and granted, and by these presents for us, our heirs and successors, do give and grant, to the said master, wardens, and commonalty, and their succes-sors, special free license, lawful power, faculty, and authority to have, purchase, receive, and possess to them and their successors for ever messuages, lands, tene-ments, meadows, feedings, pastures, woods, underwoods, rectories, tithes, rents, reversions, and other hereditaments whatsoever within our dominions, as well of us, our heirs and successors, as of any other person or persons which are not im-mediately held of us, our heirs or successors, in capite or by knight's service, so as the same lands, tenements, meadows, feedings, pastures, woods, underwoods, rectories, tithes, rents, reversions, services, and other hereditaments do not exceed in the whole the yearly value of twenty pounds over and above all charges and reprises. (The statute of lands and tenements not to be put into mortmain or any other statute, act, ordinance, or provision heretofore had, made, or provided, or any other cause, matter, or thing whatsoever to the contrary thereof in anywise notwithstanding): And also we give and grant for us, our heirs and suc-cessors, by these presents to every subject and subjects of us, our heirs and suc-cessors, free and special license, lawful power, faculty, and authority that they or any of them may give, grant, sell, bequeath, or alienate messuages, lands, tene-ments, meadows, feedings, pastures, woods, underwoods, rectories, tithes, rents, reversions, services, and other hereditaments whatsoever which are not held of us, our heirs and successors, in capite or otherwise by knight's service unto the said master, wardens, and commonalty of the Art of Science of the Musicians of London, and to their successors, so that all the same messuages, lands, tene-ments, meadows, feedings, pastures, woods, underwoods, rectories, tithes, rents, reversions, services and other hereditaments so to be given, granted, bequeathed, or alienated to the said master, wardens, and commonalty, and their successors, by virtue of these presents do not exceed in the whole the clear yearly value of twenty pounds by year above all charges and reprises; the statute of lands and tenements not to be put into mortmain, or any other thing, cause, or matter whatsoever before this time had, made, ordained, or provided to the contrary thereof in anywise notwithstanding: And, moreover, we will and by these presents for us, our heirs and successors, for the better rule and government of all those which in our City of London, and within three miles of the said city, do profess and exercise and hereafter shall profess and exercise the art or science of music, we give and grant to the said master, wardens, and commonalty of the Art or Science of Musicians of London, and to their successors, that the said masters and wardens, and their successors, for the time being at all times to come shall have the survey, search, correction, and government of all and singular musicians and minstrels within our said City of London, or within the suburbs, liberties, and precincts of the same city, or within three miles of the same city, and within all liberties, franchises, jurisdictions, and places, as well exempt as not exempt, situate and being within the said city, suburbs, and three miles of the same city: Also we will and by these presents grant to the said master, wardens, and commonalty of the Art or Science of Musicians of London that they may have and shall have these our letters patent under our great seal of England in due manner made and sealed without fine or fee, great or small, to be yielded or paid unto us in the Hanaper of our Chancery, or otherwise to our use howsoever, albeit express mention of the true yearly value or certainty of the premises, or any of them, or of other gifts or grants by us or any of our ancestors or progenitors before this time made to the foresaid master, wardens, and commonalty of the Art or Science of Musicians of London be not mentioned in these presents, or any statute, act, ordinance, provision, proclamation, or restraint to the contrary thereof before this time had, made, ordained, or provided, or any other thing, cause, or matter whatsoever in anywise notwithstanding. In witness whereof we have caused these our letters to be made patents. Witness ourself at Westminster, the eighth day of July, in the second year of our reign of England, France, and Ireland; and of Scotland the seven and thirtieth.

BYELAWS

CONFIRMED BY THE LORD CHANCELLOR ON 25 AUGUST 1606

TO all people to whom these presents shall come, Thomas Lord Ellesmere, Lord Chancellor of England; Thomas Earl Dorset, Lord Treasurer of England; and Sir John Popham, Knight, Lord Chief Justice of the Pleas before His Majesty to be holden, send greeting in our Lord God everlasting. Whereas in a certain Act or Statute in the Parliament holden at Westminster the five and twentieth day of January, in the nineteenth year of the reign of the late King of famous memory after the Conquest, Henry the Seventh, made and ordained for the weal and profit of the subjects, it was, amongst other things, ordained, established, and enacted that no master, wardens, or fellowships of crafts or mysteries, or any of them, nor any rulers of guilds or fraternities should take upon them to make any act or ordinance, to execute any acts or ordinances by them theretofore made in disheritage or diminution of the King's prerogative, or any other, or against the common profit of the people: But if the same acts and ordinances were examined and approved by the Chancellor Treasurer of England, the chief justices of either bench, or three of them, or else before both the justices of assize in their circuit or progress in that shire where such acts or ordinances be made, upon pain of forty pounds for every time that they do the contrary, as in the said Act of Parliament more plainly doth and may appear.

Know ye that Tristram Waters, master of the Art or Science of Musicians of London, and William Benton, Vincent Janvrin, now wardens of the said art or science, with the whole assent and consent of the assistants of the same, willing and desiring the said Act of Parliament in all and every thing to be duly observed and kept, the first day of August, in the year of the reign of Our Sovereign Lord James, by the Grace of God King of England, France and Ireland, Defender of the Faith, the Fourth, and of Scotland the Fortieth, have exhibited a certain petition containing divers articles for acts and ordinances for the better rule and government of the Art or Science of Musicians of London dwelling and inhabiting or which hereafter shall dwell or inhabit in the said city, the suburbs thereof, and within three miles of the said city, in the Art or Science of Musicians of London aforesaid, and for the common weale and conservation of the good estate of the said Art or Science of Musicians, and have instantly desired us that we all and every their acts and ordinances hereafter mentioned to us exhibited would examine and approve and those and every of them correct and amend in due and convenient manner and form as the said recited Act of Parliament requireth:

We well perceiving and considering their said supplication to be good and acceptable according to their desires, and by authority of the said Act of Parliament to us given all and every their acts and ordinances to us exhibited, have seen, read, and well understood, and all and every of them examined, corrected, and reformed, the tenor whereof hereafter followeth:

Imprimis, be it ordained that from henceforth, yearly, at the Feast of St. Michael the Archangel, or within twenty days next after the same feast, the master and wardens of the said Art or Science of the Musicians of London, with the assistants of the same fellowship, or the greater part of them, shall from time to time elect and choose out of the freemen of the said Company one master and two wardens of the same art and science to rule and govern the same fellowship for one whole year then next ensuing: And if any of the master or wardens so chosen or to be chosen shall happen to die or for reasonable cause be removed or deprived from his place and office within one year next after he shall be so elected, that then, within fourteen days next after such death, deprivation, or removing of any of the said master or wardens, one other or others of the freemen of the said Company shall be in like sort elected and chosen by the rest of the wardens and assistants of the same fellowship to serve in the place or stead of such of them as shall so happen to die, be deprived, or removed until the Feast of St. Michael the Archangel then next ensuing: And the master and wardens so newly elected and chosen shall take a corporal oath for the due execution of their offices and places in manner and form hereafter prescribed, and according to the limitation of the letters patents granted to the said master, wardens, and commonalty by our now Sovereign Lord the King: And whatsoever person or persons of the said fellowship being chosen by the said wardens and assistants, or the more part of them, to be master or any of the wardens of the said art or science, if he shall refuse to take upon him the said office of master or warden and the charges thereunto belonging, or to take the said oath, being thereunto required, he shall then presently pay to the commonalty and fellowship of the said Art or Science of Musicians for his or their refusal for every fine he or they shall so refuse the sum of five marks, to be levied of his or their goods and chattels, and to be employed as hereafter is specified.

Item: be it ordained and established that, according to the ancient custom of the City of London, the master and wardens and assistants of the foresaid Art or Science of Musicians of London for the time being, and their successors, may and shall elect and choose, at all such times as shall seem good unto them, so many of the said fellowship into the livery and clothing of the same fellowship as shall seem unto them meet and convenient for the worship of the said City and the credit of the said Art, Science, and Commonalty of the Musicians of London: And whatsoever person or persons of the said science or fellowship shall be at any time hereafter enabled and called by the said master and wardens and assistants for the time being, or by the said master and wardens and eight of the said assistants at the least, to be one of the livery of the said fellowship, and of his obstinacy and frowardness shall refuse and deny to take the same upon him at the time appointed unto him by the said master and wardens and assistants, that then he so refusing shall forfeit and pay as often as he so refuseth forty shillings; and that also all and every person and person being called and chosen into the assistants or livery as aforesaid, and taking upon him or them the said calling, shall pay to the said master and wardens of the said fellowship, to the use of the said fellowship, twenty shillings.

Item: be it ordained that if any person or persons of the said Art, Science, or Fellowship of Musicians, of his own motion or forwardness, or by the procurement of any other person or persons at any time hereafter, shall go out of the said fellowship to any other mystery, fellowship, or occupation without the express consent of the master, wardens, and assistants of the fellowship of the said Art or Science of the Musicians of London for the time being, or the more part of them, in writing under their common seal to be had and obtained, shall forfeit and pay ten pounds of good and lawful money, to be levied of his or their goods and chattels.

Item: be it ordained and established that every person and persons of the said art or science shall be obedient to all manner of lawful summons and warnings given to him or them in the master and wardens' names for the time being by the beadle or other common officer of the said art or science and commonalty, or otherwise in the behalf of the said master and wardens of the said art or science for the time being, and shall be always ready to come and shall come unto them in such lawful and decent manner as he shall be assigned to do, at the hour and place to him conveniently appointed, for such causes and matters, either concerning the affairs of the King's Majesty, his heirs and successors, Kings and Queens of this realm, or the estate of the City of London or anything concerning the said art or science, or any brother or sister of the same fellowship, whereof he shall have further knowledge at his coming, or for the burial of a brother or sister of the said fellowship; and if he will not come upon such warning, and in such manner, at his hour and place appointed him, that then he shall forfeit and pay for every default, for not keeping his hour and place, twelve pence; and if he shall not come at all upon such warning to the place of assembly while the master or wardens and assistants shall be there together, but shall willingly absent himself without a reasonable excuse, to be allowed of by the said master and wardens, he shall forfeit and pay for every such offence two shillings.

Item: be it ordained if any person or persons of the said fellowship, art, or science, or any other person whatsoever, shall use or exercise the said Art or Science of Musicians, or any faculty thereof, or make that any means toward the getting of his living within the said City of London and suburbs thereof, or three miles compass of the said city, without the license or consent of the said master, wardens, and assistants, or the more part of them, in writing under their common seal first had and obtained, or shall not observe and obey the orders to be set down by the said master, wardens, and assistants, or the more part of them, every one so offending shall forfeit and pay such sum or sums of money or fines as shall by the said master, wardens, and assistants, or the more part of them, be imposed upon them for every such offence, so as the same exceed not the sum of forty shillings.

Item: it is also ordained that the master and wardens of the said Art or Science of Musicians of London for the time being shall or may yearly keep four quarter days in the year; and also within every quarter of the year quarterly for ever two other courts or assemblies, or more if need so require, at their common hall or other convenient place of meeting, as well for reformation of the defaults or abuses used in the said art or science as to hear the complaints of all such as shall find the aforesaid grievances concerning the same, and determine thereof according to their knowledge, wisdoms, and discretions; all which quarter days, courts, and assemblies shall be kept at convenient times to be appointed at the discretion of the said master and wardens of the said art or science for the time being: And every brother or widow of the same art or science shall pay for quarterage at every of the said quarter days quarterly for ever sixpence: And if any of the said master and wardens absent themselves and come not unto the common hall of the said fellowship at every such quarter day, and to every of the said other courts or assemblies, and shall not keep every of the said courts or assemblies according to the times or in form abovesaid, that then for so doing or electing to do so aforesaid he or they shall forfeit at every time in the name of a pain five shillings, without a reasonable excuse proved and allowed by and before the residue of the said master, wardens, and assistants of the said art or science, or the more part of them: And also every one of the said assistants that shall be at any time hereafter lawfully warned to come to such day and place appointed for the said courts and shall make default shall forfeit and pay for every such default, without a reasonable excuse proved and allowed by and before the said master and wardens, two shillings and sixpence.

Item: be it ordained that no person of the said fellowship shall unseemly revile, rebuke, smite, or abuse any brother of the same fellowship, either by facing, bracing, evil reproaching, or affraying, in the presence of the said master and wardens or elsewhere, nor in anywise disorder or misbehave him or themselves toward the master or wardens of the said fellowship, nor to any other of the said fellowship, upon pain to forfeit for every such offence forty shillings.

Item: be it ordained if any person or persons that do or shall use the said art or science shall, at any time or times, in any place, by any means, directly or indirectly, supplant, defeat, or put out, or wittingly practice to supplant, defeat, or put out, any musician free of the said fellowship, being first hired or spoken to serve at any triumphs, marriages, revels, feasts, dinners, suppers, banquets, meetings, guilds, or brotherhoods, or for any such like occasions, to the hindrance of any brother of the said fellowship that was formerly bespoken, that then every person so offending shall forfeit and pay for such offence forty shillings, and suffer imprisonment of his or their bodies till he or they do pay the same.

Moreover, be it ordained that the master and wardens of the said art or science, or such other discreet and skilful persons of the said Company as for the time being shall be by the said master and wardens assigned or appointed, shall and may at all times hereafter, so often as they shall think needful and requisite, call before them to the common hall of the said Company, or to such other convenient place of meeting as the said master and wardens or the parties by them assigned shall appoint, all persons, as well free of the said fellowship as all others, which do or shall use or exercise the said Art or Science of Musicians, or the teaching of musick or dancing, or any faculty belonging to the said art or science of musicians or musick, and used for their maintenance, gain, or living within the City of London, and in the liberties or within three miles of the same city, and there to examine, approve, and allow the said parties and every of them for their sufficiency and skill in the said art or science, or to reject and disallow of any party for his insufficiency and want of skill; and that no person or persons, whether he be master, servant, or apprentice, so called before the said master and wardens, or before the parties by them assigned, and being by them disallowed as insufficient and unfit, shall presume to use or exercise the said art or science thereby to make any gain or have any reward for the same until he shall afterwards be allowed, upon pain to forfeit for every time he shall so offend the sum of twenty shillings: And it is ordained that if the said master or wardens, or their deputies, shall find any abuse or disorder used or practised in the said art or science, or any the faculties or qualities aforesaid, within the limits aforesaid, to the slander, hurt, or prejudice of the said art or science, or shall find any foreigners to use or practise the said art or science within the freedoms and liberties of the said city, or three miles compass of the same; or if any person summoned or warned to appear at the said common hall or other convenient place of meeting to be examined, opposed, approved, allowed, or disallowed as aforesaid shall refuse to appear or obey what shall be done and set down by the said master and wardens, or the persons that by them shall be assigned, that then all and every such person and persons so offending shall forfeit and pay to the said master and wardens and commonalty for every such offence twenty shillings, and shall suffer imprisonment of his or their bodies, at the discretion of the said master and wardens: And that the same penalty of twenty shillings for every offence committed by any apprentice or servant contrary to this ordinance or the ordinance next preceding, with the privity and allowance of his or their master, shall be levied and paid of and by the master of the said servant or apprentice.

Item: it is ordained that all persons not being free of the said Company that shall use or exercise the said art or science, or any faculty or quality touching and concerning the same, toward the getting of his or their living within the said city or liberties thereof, and all others allowed to use the same within three miles of the said city, and getting his or their living thereby, to their own use shall forfeit and pay to the said master, wardens, and commonalty at the four quarter days, at or in their common hall or other convenient place in that behalf assigned, sixpence quarterly: And if any of them shall fail to present themselves to pay the said quarterage at the said common hall or other place aforesaid at the said quarter days, having such sufficient warning thereof as the freemen of the said Company are to have, then he or they so failing shall forfeit and pay for every such default one shilling, except he show such reasonable cause in excuse of his default as shall be allowed by the said master and wardens.

Item: it is ordained that all and every persons free of the said commonalty that shall entertain or take any apprentice shall, at the assembly of the said master and wardens at the court or quarter day next and immediately after the sealing of the indentures to be made between them, present the same, his apprentice, to and before the master and wardens of the said Art or Science of Musicians of London for the time being to the intent the same master and wardens may have due examination of the said apprentice whether he be free born or not, and to see that he be clean and whole limbed; also to know what age he is of, and, further, to understand the number of years that the said apprentice shall serve, and when the same shall begin and end; and that every master shall pay to the master and wardens and commonalty of the said art or science two shillings sixpence for the presentment of every such apprentice, according to the ancient custom of the said city; and that every person that shall do contrary to this ordinance shall pay for every time offending twenty shillings.

Item: it is ordained and established that from henceforth no person or persons whatsoever that now or hereafter shall be master or wardens of the said Art or Science of Musicians of London shall take, have, or keep above two apprentices using the said art or science at any one time: And that none other person or persons of the same art or science not being or having been warden of the said Company shall either take, have, or keep above one apprentice at once using the said art or science until the said apprentice hath served with his master until the last half year of the term of his apprenticeship mentioned in his indenture; and then the same master may take one other apprentice: And that no person or persons which are not free of the said commonalty that do or shall use the said art or science within the city or the liberties thereof, or within three miles of the same city, shall at any time hereafter, directly or indirectly, have, take, or retain to be brought up in the said art or science any more apprentices than only one apprentice at one time, unless the master of such apprentice shall have continually used the same art or science to his own use for his maintenance and living by the space of fourteen years after the expiration of his term of apprenticehood: In which case it shall be lawful for any such person to have and keep two apprentices at one time, and not above; and that every person which shall offend against the true meaning of this act shall forfeit and pay the sum of twenty shillings for every month that he shall continue the keeping of any such apprentice.

Item: it is ordained that no person using the said Art or Science of Musicians of London, or any quality or faculty of dancing, shall teach, keep, or play, nor hand, exercise, or use, any dancing in any school of dancing upon any Sabbath Days within the said city or liberties thereof, or within three miles of the same city, upon pain to forfeit for every such offence.

Neither shall any person sing any ribaldry, wanton, or lascivious songs or ditties at any time or place within the City of London or liberties thereof; or within three miles of the same city, whereby God may be dishonoured, or any slander or infamy may arise or be given of or to the said science, upon pain that every person offending against the true meaning of this branch of this Act shall forfeit for his offence ten shillings, and suffer imprisonment of his or their bodies for such convenient time as shall be thought fit by the discretion of the master and wardens of the same society for the time being.

Item: it is ordained that no person or persons of the said science or fellowship from henceforth shall present any of his apprentices before the Chamberlain of London, or his deputy, to be made free of the said city after his years be expired until he have presented his said apprentice before the master, wardens, and assistants of the said Art or Science of Musicians of London, or the more part of them, for the time being at their common hall or meeting place to be examined of his service and continuance of the same: And if upon due proof, as in such case is used, it shall appear unto the said master and wardens that the said apprentice hath duly served and continued as an apprentice during the term of his years, as in such case is used, then the same apprentice to submit himself to the rules and ordinances of the same fellowship in manner and form hereafter specified, and then to lay down and pay for his admission to the said master and wardens three shillings and fourpence: And after that the same master and wardens shall present the same late apprentice before the said chamberlain, or his deputy, for the time being, and thereupon shall cause the said late apprentice to be admitted into the said society and into the freedom of the said city, upon pain to every master of such apprentice doing contrary to this ordinance to forfeit for every such offence.

And it is further ordained that if hereafter any person or persons of the said Art or Science of Musicians of London, being a freeman of the said commonalty or any other, using or that shall use the said art, science, faculties, and qualities aforesaid, or any of them, within the said city and liberties, or within three miles compass thereof; having an apprentice bound unto him in the science or mystery aforesaid, be minded and will sell the term of years of the same, his apprentice, to any other man of the same art or science, or to any other, that then he shall first bring the same, his apprentice, to and before the master and wardens of the said Art or Science of Musicians of London for the time being that they may note and write the selling and turning over of the same apprentice in their hall book: And the master that so shall make sale of his apprentice shall forfeit and pay two shillings; and that every person of the said art or science that shall offend contrary to this ordinance shall pay for every such offence twenty shillings.

Item: it is ordained and established that no person or persons free of the said art or science, or any their servants or apprentices, or any other person or persons professing the said art or science, or any their servants or apprentices, either in consort or otherwise, shall at any time or times hereafter play upon any kind of instrument or instruments, either evening or morning, at or under any nobleman, knight, or gentleman's window or lodging in the street, or the window or lodging of any other person or persons whatsoever, within the City of London, suburbs, liberties, and precincts aforesaid, without license and leave of the master, wardens, and eight of the assistants at the least of the said Art or Science of Musicians of London for the time being, upon pain that the master of every such servant or apprentice shall forfeit. and pay for every person so offending and for every time that he or they shall so offend the sum of three shillings and fourpence.

Item: it is likewise ordained and established that no person or persons free of the said Art or Science of Musicians, nor any their servants or apprentices, nor any other person or persons using or exercising the said art or science, or any their apprentices or servants whatsoever, shall play at any weddings, feasts, banquets, revels, or other assemblies or meetings within the City of London, suburbs, or precincts aforesaid, under the number of four, in consort or with violins, upon pain that the master of every such servant or apprentice shall forfeit and pay for every person, servant, and apprentice, and for every time he or they shall offend contrary to this ordinance, the sum of three shillings and fourpence.

Item: it is ordained and established that the master and wardens of the said Art or Science of Musicians of London for the time being shall not at any time hereafter demise, grant, let, or sell any lands or tenements which shall hereafter belong to the Company of the said Art or Science of Musicians of London to any person or persons by lease for terms of years or otherwise, nor shall receive any fine or fines or incomes, nor shall do any act whatsoever which shall bind, charge, or hinder the said Company, and the master, wardens, and commonalty thereof, without the special agreement, will, consent, and assent of all the assistants of the same Company for the time being, or of eight of the same assistants at the least, and of the same master and wardens, upon pain of forfeiture of twenty pounds for every time they or any of them shall do contrary to the meaning of this ordinance: And that all and every demise, grant, act and acts hereafter to be made, procured, or done by the master or wardens to the contrary shall be utterly void and of no force.

Item: it is ordained that if hereafter the master and wardens of the said Art or Science of Musicians for the time being, or any of them, during the time of their continuance in their office, shall be found partial, remiss, negligent, or not indifferent in executing any of the said Acts or ordinances comprised in this book shall favour any person or persons in his or their offences, or for meed, favour, affection, or dread shall not execute the said ordinances and every of them indifferently to and upon every person after their offences according to the meaning of this book and the ordinances herein comprised, that then, upon a due proof thereof had before the other master, wardens, and the assistants of the said art or science for the time being, or before the other wardens and eight of the same assistants at the least, every person so found partial, negligent, or not indifferent as is aforesaid, shall forfeit and pay for every time so offending forty shillings, more or less, at the discretion of the other wardens and of the said assistants.

Item: it is ordained that the master and wardens of the said Art or Science of Musicians of London for the time being, and their successors master and wardens of the said art or science for ever, shall, within one month next and immediately after the expiration of their office of wardenship and the admission and oath of the new master and wardens that shall supply their place, make and yield up yearly unto the same new master and wardens for the time being, and to the assistants of the same company or fellowship or eight of the same assistants at the least, a true, whole, plain, and perfect accompt, payment and delivery of all

261

and all manner sums of money and of all other things whatsoever which have been delivered unto them, or otherwise by any whatsoever means come or ought to come to the hands, possession, order, or custody of them, or any of them, to the use of the commonalty of the said Art or Science of the Musicians of London during the year of their office and charge, and of the office and charge of every or any of them, upon pain to forfeit and pay at every time for doing contrary to this ordinance ten pounds.

Item: it is also ordained that every year, yearly, against the foresaid day of account to be made to the new master and wardens of the said Art or Science of Musicians of London for the time being by them that last were in the same office, before there shall be chosen by the same new master and wardens, with the advice of the said assistants, four or more to audit, hear, try, and examine the same account with auditors, shall be chosen out of the aforesaid assistants of the said art or science; and such person or persons being chosen as aforesaid which shall refuse to take upon him or them the said office of auditor shall forfeit and pay every of them five shillings.

Item: it is ordained and established that all and every of the same penalties, fines, amerciaments, forfeitures, and sums of money by these ordinances limited and appointed to be taxed, forfeited, or paid shall be sued for, levied, and recovered by the said master, wardens, commonalty, and fellowship of the said Art or Science of the Musicians of London, to be employed by the said master and wardens of the said art or science for the time being in and about the relief of the poor of the commonalty and fellowship of the said Art or Science of the Musicians of London, and to the sustentation of the charge to be borne by the master, wardens, and commonalty of the said art or science in the common occasions of the said Company:

And if any person or persons, of his or their froward disposition or otherwise, shall hereafter refuse or deny to pay in good and lawful money of England any quarterage, penalties, fines, forfeitures, or other amerciaments whatsoever, set or assessed, or to be set or assessed, upon him or them, that then it shall be lawful to the said master and wardens, and their successors master and wardens of the said art or science, to command and commit all and every such person and persons to ward until he shall agree with the master and wardens for the time being for his contempt and misbehaviour in that behalf; and have paid the same: Provided always, that the said master, wardens, and assistants for the time being, by their discretion, may mitigate, diminish, or abate the said forfeitures, penalties, and amerciaments, or any of them, as the case shall require, according to equity and good conscience: Provided also, that these Acts or ordinances, or anything herein contained, shall not in anywise extend or be construed to extend unto the King's Majesty's musicians in ordinary being not free of the said commonalty of the musicians of London, anything herein contained or expressed to the contrary in anywise notwithstanding.

Item: it is ordained that all and every person and persons, being of the full age of 21 years, which now are or hereafter shall be of the said Art or Science of Musicians of London, now using or exercising or which hereafter shall use or exercise the said art or science, as well masters as journeymen and apprentices, and every of them, within the places and precincts aforesaid, shall, upon reasonable warning and monition to them given personally, appear at the common hall, at the time and times for the purpose appointed, before the said master, wardens, and assistants, or the greater part of them, and then and there shall in willing and obedient manner, under their hands, submit themselves and yield their consents to the true and due performance of all and singular the ordinances, laws, constitutions, and orders above in these presents, upon and under the pains in them and every of them mentioned, specified, contained, and set down.

Ye shall swear that ye shall be true to our Sovereign Lord the King, and to his heirs and successors Kings and Queens of the realm of England: And that you and every of you, effectually and diligently, during the time and season you shall be or remain in your said office, shall, as far forth as you lawfully and conveniently may, see to and keep the said Art and Science of the Musicians in good order, and rule and execute your office in every case thereunto appertaining truly, justly, and indifferently. So help you God, and by the contents of this Book.

Ye shall swear that ye shall always, in what lawfully and conveniently you may to your power, faithfully aid and assist the master and wardens of the Art or Science of Musicians of London for the time being, and every of them, as well in the execution of the rules and ordinances made and ratified for the good order and government of the said art as in all other affairs whatsoever concerning the same art, good and faithful counsel to the best of your knowledge from time to time shall ye give unto them. You shall not procure nor consent that the lands, revenues of, or goods of the foresaid Company shall be inordinately spent, consumed, or embezzled, but to the best of your skill and power ye shall the same let and withstand. So help you God, and by the contents of this Book.

All which acts, ordinances, constitutions, and oaths in manner and form aforesaid, as well at the request of the said Tristram Waters, now master of the said Art or Science of Musicians of London, and of the said William Benton and Vincent Janvrin, now wardens, and the commonalty of the same, by the authority and virtue of the same Act of Parliament made in the nineteenth year of King Henry the Seventh, we, the said Chancellor, Treasurer, and Chief Justice aforesaid, have seen, perused, read, examined, and approved, and for good, laudable, and lawful ordinances, constitutions, and oaths we do allow and approve. In witness whereof to these presents, we, the said Lord Chancellor, Lord Treasurer, and Chief Justice, have subscribed our names and set our seals, the five and twentieth day of August, in the fourth year of the reign of our Sovereign Lord James, by the grace of God King of England, France, and Ireland, Defender of the Faith, and of Scotland the fortieth.

This would appear to be the end of the original Bye-laws and the remainder to be Addenda: but the copy in the possession of the Company runs on without a break.

Ye shall swear that ye shall be faithful and true to our Sovereign Lord the King's Majesty, and to his heirs and successors Kings and Queens of Great Britain; ye shall not do nor consent to be done any treasons or felonies, but all such as you shall know ye shall duly to your power do to be revealed and known to the King or his Council: And ye shall be obedient unto the master and wardens of the Art or Science of Musicians of London for the time being in all things concerning the same art and science, being agreeable to the ordinances of the said art and customs of the City of London, and shall come duly and truly upon every lawful summons to any assembly to be made for any matter or cause to be treated and communed upon by the master, wardens, and assistants of the said art or science, except ye reasonably or lawfully be, or else to pay such penalties and fines as ye shall forfeit by reason of your default: And also ye shall be at all times contributory to all manner of charges done or to be done by them in and about the weal and continuance of the said art or science to your power: Also well and truly after your power ye shall in all things obey, keep, and observe all the acts and ordinances made for the governance and good order of the said art and science, and confirmed according to the laws and statutes of this realm in that case provided. So help ye God, and by the contents of this Book.

Item: be it ordained if any person or persons of the said fellowship, art, or science, or any other person, either free or not free, whatsoever, that shall use or exercise the said art or science of musick or musicians, or any faculty thereof, shall go himself, or suffer his servant or apprentice to go, in any open street within this city or liberties thereof, or within three miles of the same city, from house to house with any instrument or instruments uncased or uncovered in any part, to be seen by any passing by, upon pain or forfeiture of twelve pence for every such offence.

Item: be it ordained that if any person or persons of the Art, Science, or Fellowship of Musicians, or any other person whatsoever that shall use the said Art or Science of Musicians within this city or liberties thereof, shall by themselves, their servants, or apprentices play upon or with any instrument, or use the said art or science of music, or any other thing concerning the same in consort, or any other kind of instruments whatsoever of or with any foreigner or foreigners, servants, or apprentices, within the city or liberties thereof and not elsewhere, upon pain to forfeit and pay for every such offence three shillings and fourpence.

Item: be it ordained if any person or persons, free or not, of the Art, Science, or Fellowship of Musicians shall suffer their servants or apprentices to serve by themselves with any music within this city or liberties thereof; or three miles of the same, at any feasts, banquets, weddings, huntsup, or at any other assemblies, triumphs, or occasions, either to go abroad in the streets or to play at any taverns, victualling houses, or any other place whatsoever, except they do go in or with the company of two freemen at the least well and sufficiently exercised and experienced in the said art or science of music, whereof one to be the master of some one of the said apprentices or servants, as also foreigners without the city and liberties and within the three miles of the same city, shall in like manner observe the same orders as the freemen of the same city doth, whereby they may be the better guided and directed in that science for the laud, honour, and commendation thereof; and that the freeman or foreigner being master of the said apprentice or servants shall himself, or the other freeman or foreign master, offer and present the music, and not any other his apprentice or servant, upon pain to forfeit for every offence contrary to this act three shillings and fourpence.

Item: be it also ordained that if any person or persons professing the said Art, Science, or Fellowship of Musicians of the City of London or the liberties thereof; or three miles of the same city, shall at any time hereafter by any means, directly or indirectly, by himself or wittingly know or suffer his servant or apprentice to use or practice any manner of unlawful games at any time or in any place with any freeman's servants or apprentices, either of the said art or science or being free of any other company whatsoever, or any foreigners, within three miles of this city, shall in anywise or by any means countenance him or them therein, upon pain of forfeiture of every such offence being justly proved against them or him, shall for every time he or they shall so offend forfeit and pay to the master and wardens and commonalty ten shillings, or suffer imprisonment of his or their bodies till he or they have paid the same.

It is also ordained and established, consented, and agreed that if hereafter any person of the said art or science be grieved with any other person of the same art or science, that then he that is so grieved shall first complain to the master and wardens of the said Art or Science of Musicians of London for the time being, and show his cause of griefs unto them without any his further complaint, to the intent that the same master and wardens may understand the same and the circumstances thereof; and thereupon to take order for good agreement, peace, and concord to be had between the said parties, according to the right, equity, and good conscience, either by mutual agreement of the parties themselves or else by way of arbitrament: And also that no person of the said art or science maintain any matters or quarrels against or between any persons of the same art or science, nor that any of the same art or science shall arrest, sue, or molest any other of the said art or science for any matter of controversy, evil words, or debt not exceeding ten pounds, before such time as the master and wardens of the said art or science for the time being do give licence unto the same parties to enter into the law if reasonable order cannot be by them therein taken, upon pain that every person that shall do contrary to the intent and meaning hereof shall pay for every such offence twenty shillings.

It is also enacted, ordered, consented, and decreed that there shall be chosen every year two stewards, to provide for one whole year upon the four quarter days four dinners for the master, wardens, and assistants of the said Company, unto which charge it is also enacted, ordered, consented, and agreed that any assistant that shall come to every or any of the said dinners shall contribute and pay to the stewards towards the charge of the said quarter dinners twelve pence: And also it is further enacted, ordered, consented, and agreed that every person refusing to hold steward as aforesaid shall pay unto this Company the sum of forty shillings for his fine for every time that he shall so refuse the same steward-ship, being thereunto chosen by the master, wardens, and assistants, or the greater part of them: And it is further ordered, consented, and agreed that the said four quarter dinners, and every of them, shall be from time to time kept and held at such place as the master and wardens for the time being shall think fit, meet, and convenient, and shall nominate the same place unto them the said stewards.

APPENDIX FIVE

Special Status of the County of Chester

The following account is given in the 1915 *Handbook*

It will be noted that the Minstrels of the county of Chester were exempted from the jurisdiction of the Guild. The exemption was due to the curious fact that authority over the Minstrels and 'other Vagrants' of that county had previously been conferred, in the time of King John, upon Hugh de Dutton, of Dutton, in Cheshire, and his heirs, by Randle, third Earl of Chester, under the following circumstances:

Randle among the many conflicts he had was distressed by the Welsh and forced to retreat to the Castle of Rothlent in Flintshire about the reign of King John, where they besieged him. He presently sent to his Constable of Chester, Roger Lacy, surnamed 'Hell' for his fierce spirit, that he would come with all speed and bring what forces he could to his relief. Roger having gathered a tumultuous rout of fiddlers, players, cobblers, both men and women, out of the City of Chester (for it was then the fair time in that City) marched immediately towards the Earl. The Welsh, perceiving a great multitude coming, raised the siege and fled. The Earl coming back with his constable to Chester gave him power over all the fiddlers and shoemakers, but John, his son, conferred this authority on his steward, who was then Hugh de Dutton, and his heirs.

Out of this concession arose a custom of licensing the Minstrels of the county, for which purpose a Court was held annually at Chester on Midsummer Day, when each Minstrel who sought for a licence had to give four flagons of wine to the representative of the Dutton family, who presided, and pay 4½d. The right of the Duttons in this matter was tested by the Crown by writ of Quo Warranto and was admitted, and it was subsequently recognised in various Acts of Parliament relating to vagabonds. The last Court was held in the year 1756.

Fuller details will be found in Sir John Hawkins' *History*, vol. V, chapter 42 (edn of 1875, vol. I, p. 191).

APPENDIX SIX

Ordinances of 24 July 1638

To the right Honourable the Lord Mayor & Court of Aldermen

According to an order of this honourable Court of the fifth of April last we whose names are subscribed have taken into consideration the matters contained in the petition of the Master Wardens & Comminalty of Minstrels London and thereupon do humbly certify:

That it appeareth unto us that the petitioners are and have been an ancient Brotherhood of this City by the name of Minstrels and that they have been so governed by the acts and orders of this honourable Court.

And we are of the opinion that the same fraternity be called as well by the name of the Master and Wardens and fellowship of Minstrels of London as of the Master and Wardens and fellowship of Musicians of London.

We have also taken consideration of the orders indicated in their petition and thereby desired to be approved by your lordship wherein we made some alteration and present them to the further judgment of this honourable court viz:

That according to an order of this honourable Court the 15th year of King Henry 7th the choice of Master and Wardens may be made once every year. And that they may take their apprentice for such term of years as by the Master and Apprentice shall be agreed *non obstante* any other order so that the same be not for any lesser term than seven years from the date of the Indenture. Also that the fine of xxs of him that refuseth to accept the place of Master Wardenship may be from henceforth the sum of Vli. And the election of the Master & Wardens to be on the feast day of St Michael the Archangel in every year from henceforth, And if any Master or Warden do not give a just account to the Court of Assistants within one month next after the expiration of their Master and Wardenship then the party failing therein to forfeit and pay the sum of Vli a piece.

Also it is ordered That it shall be lawful for the said Master and Wardens at their next meeting to choose seventeen of the gravest and most discreet persons of the said Brotherhood to be Assistants to the said Master and Wardens. And that from henceforth after the death or removal of any the said Master Wardens and Assistants the greatest number of them from time to time to choose another Master Warden or Assistants in the place or stead of him or them dying or removed. And that every Assistant at the taking upon him the said place pay unto the said Brotherhood xls And if any Assistant shall refuse to accept and take upon him the execution of the said place unto which he shall be so elected and chosen that then he shall pay to the use of the said Brotherhood the sum of IIIli vis viiid any former order to the contrary notwithstanding. And that the greatest part of them the said Master Wardens and Assistants shall be a full Court. As also that every Warden and Assistant if he do not come and appear to do the affairs of the Brotherhood upon every Court day according to his summons by the Beadle That then he forfeit and pay the sum of iis or less at the discretion of the Master and Wardens and most parts of the Assistants unless he shall have a lawful excuse to be approved of by them or the greater number of them to the use of the said Company.

The Court days to be kept at such time and on such days as the Master and one of the Wardens shall appoint and think fit.

Also it is ordered that every Brother at his making free shall pay iiis iiiid and every freeman of the said Brotherhood shall pay iis per annum for quarterage and every Journeyman xiid to the use of the said Company, that is to say upon every quarter day the freeman vid and the journeyman iiiid which if they fail then to forfeit and pay for every time so offending for the use of the said Brotherhood iiis iiiid.

Also it is ordered every person free of the said Brotherhood shall upon the presenting of his Apprentice pay unto the use of the said Brotherhood iis vid And that if any person free of the said Brotherhood shall assign over his Apprentice without licence of the Master & Wardens that then he shall pay the sum of xxs to the use of the said Brotherhood.

Also it is ordered that the Master Wardens and Assistants or the greatest number of them shall and may once every year choose two of the said Brotherhood to be Stewards for one whole year for the four quarter days and to bear the charge thereof (every Master Warden and Assistant allowing xiid thereunto) the same to be kept at the place appointed by the Master Wardens and Assistants or the greatest number of them. And every one refusing to hold Steward shall forfeit & pay to the use of the said Brotherhood the sum of Vli.

And we further think fit that Robert Gill be and continue Master and Samuel Pickering & John Starling Wardens of the said Brotherhood until Michaelmas day next and so until others shall be duly admitted & sworn in their several places.

All which nevertheless we humbly submit unto your Lordship's and Worships' graver judgments
      Samuel Cranmer   Henry Platt   Gilbert Harrison   John Stone

The which Report being here openly read was allowed of & ordered to be entered into the Repertory & to be accordingly performed

Act of 11 December 1700

(CL Rep 52, fol. 358–9)

Whereas the Master Wardens Assistants and Commonalty of the Art or Science of Music in the City of London freemen of the said City have been an ancient Brotherhood and Company And Whereas by the ancient custom of the City of London (confirmed by divers Acts of Parliament) no person not being a freeman of the said City ought to use or exercise any Art occupation or mistery for lucre or gain within the said City and Liberties thereof Notwithstanding which many persons as well aliens as other foreigners to the said City do take upon them to teach practise and exercise the Arts of Music and dancing; and also keep Public Schools in Halls and other places within this City and the Liberties thereof, And do publicly use, exercise and teach the art, mistery or Occupation of Dancing, not being free of this City, nor member of any Company or fraternity and so not Subject to any of the rules or Government of the Same; Whereby debauchery and many disorders are much promoted and in danger of being committed, And the Youth of this City much abused in their Education, to the great dishonour of the good Government of this City: and whereas the dancing Masters have of Ancient times, and for many years last past, been under the rule, inspection and Government of the Company of Musicians; But being under no obligation to be free or members of the same, the Company has no power to correct or punish the Abuses by them committed. For remedy and redress whereof for the future, and to the intent the aforesaid inconvenience and mischiefs may be prevented for the time to come, and that the said Company may have the oversight and punishment of all offences committed by any of the members professing and keeping of Schools, for teaching of Music or dancing, within this City and liberties thereof for the future:

Be it Enacted Ordained and Established, by the Right Honourable the Lord Mayor, Aldermen and Commons of the City of London in Common Council Assembled: and by the authority of the same, That an Act of this Court made the Eleventh day of September, in the Mayoralty of Sir William Ashurst Knight and Lord Mayor of this City, relating to the said Musicians and Dancing Masters, and every clause, matter and thing therein contained, shall be, and is hereby absolutely Repealed and made void. And be it further Enacted and Ordained, that all and every person or persons using practising or exercising, or which shall hereafter use practise, exercise or teach the Arts, Misteries or occupations of Music or dancing, or either of them, for lucre or gain within the City of London or Liberties thereof, who hath already served an apprenticeship in the said arts and Misteries, or in either of them, and not yet made free of this City and having a right to his freedom in any other Company within this City; And also all and every other person or persons, using, exercising or teaching the said Arts or either of them for lucre or gain, That then all and every such person and persons so doing and offending, in all, or any, or either of the said cases, shall forfeit and pay for every such offence, the sum of forty shillings of lawful money of England. And be it further Enacted by the authority aforesaid that from and after the twenty-fifth day of December 1700 if any person or persons not being free of the said City and Company nor free of the said City nor any other Company within the said same city shall for lucre or gain Publicly use, exercise or teach the said arts, misteries or occupations or either of them within the said City or Liberties thereof That then all and every such person or persons so doing and offending shall forfeit and pay for every such offence the sum of four pounds of lawful money of England. And be it further enacted and ordained by the Authority aforesaid That all Dancing Masters and Musicians as shall take Apprentices or Servants to teach them the said arts, or either of them, and all others that are free of the said Company shall from henceforth bind their Servant and Servants apprentice and apprentices in the said Company to a freeman thereof Under the penalty of forty shillings for every Apprentice he shall bind in any other Company. And no freeman of the said Company shall teach and instruct any such Intended apprentice in the said arts or either of them above the space of three months before he be bound an Apprentice to a freeman of the said Company as aforesaid under the like penalty of forty shillings. All which pains, penalties, sum and sums of money to be forfeited by this Act shall be recovered by Action of debt Bill or plaint to be commenced and prosecuted in the name of the Chamberlain of the City of London for the time being in some one of His Majesty's Courts of Record within the said City and that the Chamberlain of the said City for the time being in all such suits to be prosecuted by virtue of this present act against any offender shall recover his ordinary Costs of Suit to be expended in and about the prosecution of the same. And be it further enacted by the Authority aforesaid That one moiety of all forfeitures to be recovered by virtue of this Act (the costs of suit for the recovery of the same being first deducted and allowed) after recovery and receipt thereof shall be from time to time paid into the Chamber of the City of London for the use of the Mayor Commonalty and Citizens of the said City of London and the other moiety to the Master Wardens and Assistants of the said Company for the time being for the use of the poor of the Company. And be it further enacted by the authority aforesaid That no person or person using, practising or exercising for lucre or gain the said arts, Misteries and occupations of Music and Dancing or either of them who shall have a right by patrimony or Service, shall from henceforth be admitted by the Chamberlain of this City into the freedom thereof in any other Company than the said Company of Musicians; and that the said Chamberlain shall not admit any using or exercising the said Arts of Music or Dancing Masters into the freedom of this City, Until such persons are first admitted into the freedom of the said Company of Musicians Any Usage or Custom to the contrary in any wise notwithstanding.

APPENDIX EIGHT

Liverymen of the Musicians Company 1696–1700

This list is a compilation from the Association Oath of Loyalty subscribed to by liverymen of the Musicians Company in 1696 and a complete alphabetical list of City Liverymen in 1700 preserved in a typescript document entitled 'An INDEX to the liverymen of London in 1700' and compiled by T.C. Dale in 1933 – Typescript in the Guildhall Library.

The names of those in both lists appear in the first group.

Dancing Masters are identified with an asterisk – City Waits with a 'W'.

At the end are the names of the City Waits who at this time were members of the Company, but not of the Livery.

*	George Barker	*	Walter Holt snr
	Charles Blackmore	*	Walter Holt jnr
*	Nicholas Couch		William Hughes
	Brian Courthope (Clerk)		Richard Lowe
	Thomas Cox		John Mason
W	Caesar Duffield		Edward Morris
*	John Geary		Charles Pratten
	James Graves		Richard Price
*	George Hill		John Wade
	Francis Howard		

1696 List only:

W	Walter Cole		Michael Lee
	Thomas Cox		Thomas Maryan
	Thomas Eaglesfield		John Munson
	Thomas Hornby	*	Francis Pendleton
	Alex Johnson		Nabul Smith
	Charles Kendick		Thomas Spencer
	Isaac Layfell		John Tisdell

273

1700 List only:

	John Counley		Thomas Nicholl
W	Friend Hale		William Nicholson
*?	Henry Hart	*	Joseph Priest
	Dan Holden		Anthony Rous
W	George James		Richard Stanton
	Richard Loyd		Edward Stone
	Joe Mackeness		John Tappin
W	William Meares		

City Waits – Musicians, but not of the Livery:

John Lenthall (1688)   Richard Robinson (1687)
Henry King (1689)   William Smith jnr (1704) William Stevenson (1687)

APPENDIX NINE

Extract from Arthur Hill's Diary for 17 July 1904

(Mr White's account of the Exhibition)

17/7/04 The following was written by Mr. F.E. White, who, like his father, was a dealer in old music. Their traditional knowledge was considerable, and I see no one today who can fill their place. I engaged the son to help me place many exhibits in their correct order, particularly the books. Stainer did much in this direction, and Alfred Littleton also assisted, but Mr. White was so trustworthy that I relied upon him to superintend matters when I was not there, for I could not possibly be at Fishmonger's Hall all and every day. Another real worker was Mr. Shedlock, but for the help of whom the Guide Book, which was ready for the opening day of the Exhibition, could not have been completed.

Sir Frederick Bridge interested himself particularly in the cupboard which he had made out of wood from Purcell's house, but as usual, he used to gather the carpenters & other workers round him, & with his stories and jokes, delay the work!

[Mr White's account]:
In the early part of 1904, Mr A F Hill asked me if I could spare a week, he was on the Committee for a Loan Exhibition in connection with the Worshipful Company of Musicians & he would be expected, to a certain extent, to be present for the week. They were preparing, but if I could represent him, he would be able to get away. I agreed, and according to arrangement, I went to Bond Street to go with him to Fishmonger's Hall. When I reached there, he told me he had an appointment for one hour later, and he asked me to take the plans and get the men to put the place in order. There were three lots, the men with the upright cases, the men with the flat table cases, and the carpenters who were to put up the screens for hanging portraits; he said he would follow in about one hour. I found the men waiting and asked who was the Foreman, it appeared there were three, one to each lot of cases, and one to the carpenters, they soon got the place into order.

One humorous scene occurred during the Exhibition, Sir Frederick Bridge had his Westminster Boys one day, and after he had shown them round The Exhibition, they finished up at the Committee Room; there was an old instrument, a recorder, on the mantelpiece. Sir Frederick caught sight of it, took it down, and was explaining the instrument to the boys and began to play it, I was at the door and the Rev. Mr. Galpin came along; he took in the situation at a glance and turned to me to unlock the case that was close to us and took out one of his instruments and played an accompaniment to Sir Frederick.

The Exhibition was opened by our present King and Queen (they were then the Prince & Princess of Wales) and after the ceremony, I saw Mr. J. Lea Southgate, a member of the Committee, and I told him I was leaving that evening, as I had only been engaged for a week. He asked me not to go until he came back, he brought a message from Sir Homewood Crawford - I had seen everything, come in, couldn't I stay for the three weeks of the Exhibition and another week to see them out again. I was first in with the plans for the workroom and the last out with a Viol da Gamba, which I took to Mr. E.J. Payne, I think to Amersham, on the Great Central Railway.

On my arrival at the Exhibition on Thursday morning, Mr. Jowse (now Sir Jowse) said 'You know who is coming this morning'. I told that it had been arranged that I left before closing time on Wednesday, and I had not heard of anyone coming. He told me then that Lord Alverstoke (Lord Chief Justice) was coming and to my surprise, it was only a few minutes later, His Lordship arrived with his sister, Miss Webster. I apologised for the absence of [?] and said they would require catalogues when to my great relief, Sir Homewood Crawford and Mr. Southgate came running up the opposite staircase.

On the Friday afternoon, before the last day of the Exhibition, Mr. Charles Letts [the diary maker], one of my customers, asked me if I thought the Committee would like to see his transcripts of the Lectures; he had had a shorthand writer there each day. I told him I could not interrupt the committee, who were then sitting as it happened. When I went into the room, Sir F Bridge and another member were conversing away from the Committee and I was able to tell him the Lett's message and he said it was the very thing they were talking about, and he told Sir Homewood Crawford my message, then turned to me and asked me to introduce him to Mr. Letts. Sir Homewood Crawford said 'I am Chairman' and I had the pleasure of introducing both to Mr. Letts. They had not had a shorthand writer, so Mr. Lett's series of Lectures was of great use.

APPENDIX TEN

Charter of King George VI

GEORGE the SIXTH by the Grace of God of Great Britain, Ireland and the British Dominions beyond the Seas King, Defender of the Faith:

To all to whom these Presents shall come, Greetings!

WHEREAS the Master Geoffrey Hawkes the Senior Warden Hilary Philip Chadwyck-Healey the Junior Warden Sydney John Loeb and Victor Allcard John Henry Iles Alfred Joseph Waley Sir Felix Cassel Baronet Sir Felix Victor Schuster Baronet William James Phillips Denis Henry Truscott and Geoffrey Trevor Burnett-Brown being members of the Court of Assistants of the Worshipful Company of the Musicians of London have by their Petition humbly represented unto Us that the said Company is an ancient Fellowship of the City of London and was constituted a Company of the same City by the Court of Aldermen in the year of our Lord 1500 and were granted a Charter by Our Royal predecessor King James I in the year of our Lord 1604 but such Charter was revoked by Our Royal predecessor King Charles I in the year of our Lord 1634 and although re-granted some hundred years later as was supposed no record of any such re-grant has in spite of diligent search in recent times been found wherefore they have petitioned Us on behalf of themselves and all other Members of the Court of Assistants Liverymen and Freemen of the said Company for a new Charter of Incorporation for the better management of their common concerns:

AND WHEREAS WE are minded to comply with the prayer of such Petition

NOW THEREFORE WE of Our special grace certain knowledge and mere motion do hereby for Us Our Heirs and Successors will grant appoint and declare as follows:

1.   That the present Master, Senior Warden, Junior Warden, Members of the Court of Assistants, Liverymen and Freemen of the said Worshipful Company of the Musicians of London and all such persons as may hereafter become Masters, Senior Wardens, Junior Wardens, Members of the Court of Assistants, Liverymen and Freemen of the body corporate hereby constituted pursuant to the provision of these Presents or the powers hereby granted shall forever hereafter be

one body corporate and politic by the name of The Worshipful Company of Musicians (hereinafter referred to as 'the Incorporated Company') and by the same name shall have perpetual succession and a Common Seal with power to break, alter and make anew the said Seal from time to time at their will and pleasure and by the same name shall and may sue and be sued in all Courts and in all manner of actions and proceedings and shall have power to do all other matters and things incidental or appertaining to a body corporate.

2. We do also for Us Our Heirs and Successors licence authorise and for ever hereafter enable the Incorporated Company or any person on its behalf to acquire any lands tenements or hereditaments whatsoever within Our United Kingdom of Great Britain and Northern Ireland (such lands tenements or hereditaments not exceeding at any one time in annual value calculated as at the times of the acquisition thereof respectively the sum of £5000) and to hold all or any lands which the Incorporated Company is hereby authorised to acquire in perpetuity or in lease or otherwise and from time to time to grant demise alienate or otherwise dispose of the same or any part thereof

3. And We do hereby also for Us Our Heirs and Successors give and grant Our licence to any person or persons and any body politic or corporate to assure in perpetuity or otherwise or to demise to or for the benefit of the Incorporated Company any lands tenements or hereditaments whatsoever within Our United Kingdom of Great Britain and Northern Ireland within the limits of value aforesaid hereby nevertheless declaring that it shall not be incumbent upon any such person or persons or body to inquire as to the annual value of the property which may have been previously acquired by the Incorporated Company.

4. The objects for which the Company is incorporated are as follows:
    (i) To carry on the duties and objects of a Livery Company of the City of London.
    (ii) To foster and encourage the Art or Science of Music and the Craft of Musical-Instrument-making in the City of London the suburbs thereof and in the United Kingdom by the establishment and grant of prizes, medals, scholarships, fellowships, and endowments; the institution of examinations, competitions and certificates; the organisation of exhibitions and such other means as shall be judged from time to time by the Court of Assistants conducive to such objects.
    (iii) To take over all the lands securities moneys and property of every description whether real or personal of or to which the Worshipful Company of the Musicians of London is at the present time possessed or entitled and the same to manage maintain and dispose of in good order and sort.
    (iv) To accept any gifts of property, whether subject to any special trusts or not, for any one or more of the objects of the Incorporated Company.

(v) To undertake and execute any trust which may lawfully be undertaken by the Incorporated Company and may be conducive to its objects.

(vi) To invest any moneys of the Incorporated Company not immediately required for any of its objects in such manner or on such security as may from time to time be determined. Provided that moneys subject or representing property subject to the jurisdiction of the Charity Commissioners or the Minister of Education shall only be invested in such securities and with such sanction (if any) as may for the time being be prescribed by law.

(vii) To provide in whole or in part for the salary maintenance superannuation or pensioning of any necessitous members of the Incorporated Company or their dependants, or of any servants of the Incorporated Company or their dependants.

(viii) To petition for Supplemental Charters, obtain provisional orders or legislative or other measures not inconsistent or at variance with the lawful customs of the City of London to enable the Incorporated Company to carry any of its objects into effect or for effecting any modification of its constitution or for any other purposes which may seem expedient; and to take part in any proceedings, measures or applications, which may seem calculated directly or indirectly to affect the interests or objects of the Incorporated Company.

5.   The first Master, Senior Warden and Junior Warden respectively of the Incorporated Company shall be the present Master, Senior Warden and Junior Warden of the Company, that is to say Hilary Philip Chadwyck-Healey Master Sydney John Loeb Senior Warden and William Graham Wallace Junior Warden and the Members of the first Court of Assistants shall likewise be the present Members of the Court of Assistants and the first Treasurer, Clerk and Beadle respectively shall be the present Treasurer, Clerk and Beadle to hold office till Michaelmas next and the subsequent Masters Wardens Court of Assistants and other officers shall be such persons as shall from time to time be elected in accordance with the Bye-laws.

6.   The Bye-laws set forth in the Schedule hereto shall be the Bye-laws of the Incorporated Company until the same shall be repealed altered or added to as provided in the same Bye-laws. And We hereby grant to the Incorporated Company that they may repeal, alter and make additions to the Bye-laws according to their discretion, yet so that no such revocation, alteration or addition, be in diminution of Our Royal Prerogative, or contrary to the law of the land or the lawful customs of the City of London or against reason and good faith, and so that no such revocation, alteration or addition shall come into operation until the same shall have been approved by Our Privy Council and a Certificate under the hand of the Clerk of Our Privy Council shall be conclusive evidence of such approval.

And lastly, We do by these Presents for Us Our Heirs and Successors grant and declare that this Our Charter shall be in all things valid and effectual in law according to the true intent and meaning thereof and shall be taken construed and adjudged in the most favourable and beneficial sense for the best advantage of the Incorporated Company as well in Our Courts of Records as elsewhere by all Judges, Justices, Officers, Ministers and other Subjects whatsoever of Us Our Heirs and Successors any non-recital mis-recital or other omission defect or thing to the contrary notwithstanding

IN WITNESS whereof We have caused these Our letters to be made Patent

WITNESS Ourself at Westminster the 29th day of December in the fifteenth year of Our Reign.

BY WARRANT under The King's Sign Manual.

SCHEDULE

BYE-LAWS

1.   The Master and Wardens shall be chosen yearly on the Feast of St. Michael the Archangel or within 20 days thereafter and upon any refusal to hold either of the said offices and take the Oath prescribed the refusing Party shall forfeit £3 6s. 8d. In case of Death or Removal others are to be elected in their Stead.

2.   The Court of Assistants shall consist of the Master, Senior and Junior Wardens and not less than thirteen nor more than twenty Assistants and upon resignation or demise others are to be elected.

3.   (a) Assistants shall be selected by the Court from amongst the Members of the Livery either by Seniority or by worthiness and shall on election make the customary declaration, sign the Roll and pay the prescribed Fine.

(b) If after election to the Court any Assistant shall refuse to serve the offending party is to pay a fine of forty shillings as often as he refuses. Any Assistant upon neglecting to attend the duties of the Office for two years successively is to be considered as having resigned from the Court and a new member shall be chosen in his room.

4.   (a) No Liveryman of the Company shall be elected to the Court of Assistants unless he has previously given to the Master an assurance in writing that he is prepared to proceed to the offices of Junior and Senior Warden and Master of the Company on being elected thereto unless excused from doing so by the Court for good reason acceptable to the Master.

(b) If an Assistant having given such assurance declare himself on being chosen for one of the offices aforesaid unable for good reason acceptable to the Master to take office he may be excused by the Court from serving that office for the period of one year and he shall forfeit the sum of £3 6s. 8d

(c) If at the end of the said period the Assistant shall not be prepared to accept the same office on being chosen therefor he shall be deemed to have resigned from the Court and a vacancy therein shall be declared.

5.   The Court shall meet quarterly in the months of January, April, July and October and as often additionally as shall seem meet to the Master and Wardens.

6.   The Master or failing him the Immediate Past Master shall be the Chairman of all Meetings of the Court but if neither of them be present a Chairman shall be elected first from the Past Masters who are present and if there is none present then the Chairman shall be elected from the Assistants present.

7.   (a) Seven Members present shall form a quorum, but no dealing with the real or personal property of the Company shall be passed unless by a majority in the proportion of two to one of the Members present and voting upon the resolution.

(b) The Chairman shall have a casting vote.

8.   (a) Admission to the freedom shall be according to the customs of London by Patrimony, Apprenticeship, or Redemption. On admission to the freedom candidates must pay the prescribed Fines and Fees make the customary declaration and sign the Roll of Freemen.

(b) Candidates for Admission to the Freedom by redemption shall be nominated in writing by a Freeman of the Company and proposed and seconded by Members of the Court of Assistants and elected in open Court by a majority of the Members present.

(c) Every Freeman of the Company being a Freeman of the City may take apprentices and shall present every person to be apprenticed to him to the Master, Wardens and Court of Assistants or to such person or persons as they shall direct to be duly bound by indentures according to the custom of London, the apprentice paying therefor such fees as may from time to time be prescribed. The indentures of every such apprentice shall within the first year of the term be enrolled in the Chamber of London according to the Custom of London and if the apprentice shall be turned over or assigned such turn over or assignment shall take place first as the Master, Wardens and Court of Assistants shall direct and afterwards in the Chamber of London according to the Custom of London. Every apprentice having reached his term's end and being of full age shall upon proof of faithful service and of the due performance of all the covenants of his indentures be admitted to the Freedom by virtue of his service, paying therefor such fees as may from time to time be prescribed.

9.   The Court may call upon the Livery as many of the Freemen of the Company as are Freemen of the City of London and as they shall think fit and

every Freeman before taking upon him the Clothing shall pay the prescribed Fines and Fees.

10.　The Company's Treasurer Clerk and Beadle shall be elected annually by the Court at its October meeting.

11.　The Accounts of the Company shall be audited annually by one or more duly qualified auditors elected from time to time for the purpose by the Court.

12.　The Common Seal of the Company shall be affixed in the presence of the Master or a Pastmaster; the Treasurer or Deputy Treasurer and the Clerk or Deputy-Clerk.

13.　All securities of the Company shall be placed in the care of the Bankers of the Company. A schedule of all such securities shall be obtained from such Bankers annually and produced to the Auditors.

14.　Notice of Motion to repeal alter or add to the Bye-laws may be given at any meeting of the Court of Assistants and shall be placed on the Agenda for consideration at the next Court. Such Motion shall be declared carried only by the votes of two-thirds of the Members then present, and such Motion shall not be put unless there be fifteen Members of the Court then present. No amendment of the Bye-laws shall be effective until approved by the Court of Aldermen.

APPENDIX ELEVEN

A List of the Officers of the Musicians Company

MASTERS

(with the year of their installation at a date between Michaelmas and mid-November – those marked with an asterisk are unconfirmed)

1519	John Clyn	1745	Richard Bosworth *
1594	William Warren	1746	John Nottingham *
		1747	Edward Burton *
1596	Robert Strachey	1748	George Hindmarsh *
1603	Phillip London	1749	William O'Brien *
		1750	Benjamin Cleeve *
1605	Tristram Waters	1751	Jonathan Barnard *
1633	Thomas Chamberlain	1752	Man Griffith *
		1753	Samuel Bosworth *
1637	Robert Gill	1754	Henry Pointer *
1648	Robert Gill *	1755	Nathaniel Hill *
		1756	Thomas Pattle *
1687?	John Dyer	1757	John Trotman *
1693	Walter Holt	1758	Robert Thirsk *
		1759	John Henley *
1695	Charles Pratten	1760	John Hutchinson *
1725	Thomas Eyre	1761	Richard Lewis *
		1762	Heyland Bigger *
1728	Richard Loyd	1763	Hinchley Phipps *
1736	Thomas Vincent *	1764	Maurice Griffith *
1737	John Beckwith *	1765	Henry Spencer
1738	Jonathan Key *	1766	William Jackson
1739	Miles Nightingale *	1767	John Walker *
1740	Henry Spencer *	1768	Stephen Camm
1741	John Rayner *	1769	Gedaliah Gatfield
1742	Samuel Story *	1770	Heneage Robinson *
1743	George Courtness *	1771	William Cooper Keating
1744	Heneage Robinson *	1772	Thomas Ashton
		1773	William Stagg

1774	Robert Sidall	1818	Joseph Delafons
1775	John Hardy	1819	Alexander Glennie
1776	Robert Clark	1820	John Chaplin
1777	William Gibson	1821	Richard Jones
1778	John Salte	1822	Thomas Bingham
1779	Edward Williams	1823	Alexander Glennie
1780	Robert Holder	1824	Joseph Todd
1781	William Garsed	1825	William Suttaby
1782	Thomas Weston	1826	Frederick William Collard
1783	Henry Evan	1827	Thomas Fellows
1784	William Chivers	1828	Edward Batten
1785	Isaac Holmes	1829	John Joseph Skilbeck
1786	William Rix	1830	William Ward, M.P.
1787	John Rutter	1831	Thomas Fellows jnr.
1788	Richard Ackerman	1832	John Strachan Glennie
1789	John Crozier	1833	Henry Wadd
1790	Ald. Sir Brook Watson	1833	Thrower Buckle Herring
1791	Richard Humphreys	1834	Giddes Mackenzie Simpson
1792	Joseph Harrop	1835	William Chaplin
1793	Solomon Wadd	1836	Robert Albron Fellows
1794	William Moore	1837	Thomas Herring
1795	Thomas Weston	1838	Henry Patteson
1796	Jonathan Key	1839	William Ward
1797	Joseph Stede	1840	John Evans
1798	Thomas Ellis	1841	Edward Wiggins
1799	Joseph Cough	1842	James Southby Bridge
1800	William Huson	1843	John Skilbeck
1801	Thomas Cross	1844	James Wedderburn Simpson
1802	James Smith	1845	Frederick William Collard
1803	John Ashley	1846	Frederick William Collard
1804	Job Williams		(re-elected)
1805	Thomas Fellows	1847	William Ward
1806	Thomas Ashby	1848	Thomas Fellowes
1807	John Rutler	1849	Thrower Buckle Herring
1808	William Moore	1850	William Chaplin
1810	Joseph Gough	1851	Thomas Herring
1811	Thomas Wood	1852	Thomas Herring (re-elected)
1811	John Axford	1853	John Evans
1812	Joseph Staines	1854	Edward Wiggins
1813	Joseph Green	1855	James Southby Bridge
1814	Job Williams	1856	Joseph Skilbeck
1815	John Axford	1857	Robert Philip Jones
1816	Joseph Staines	1858	John Wood
1817	Joseph Green	1859	Thomas Fellowes

1860	William Chaplin		1901	Charles Dennis Hoblyn
1861	Thomas Herring		1902	Frank Harwood Lescher
1862	James Southby Bridge		1903	William Cordy Herring
1863	John Evans		1904	Charles Thomas Daniell Crews
1864	Charles Lukey Collard		1905	Edward Ernest Cooper
1865	Charles Lukey Collard (re-elected)		1906	Sir Homewood Crawford
			1907	Charles Thomas Daniell Crews
1866	John Hilditch Evans		1908	Sir George Wyatt Truscott (*Lord Mayor*)
1867	Robert Philip Jones			
1868	John Peter Theobald		1909	Thomas Lea Southgate
1869	John Barnwell Herring		1910	Alfred Henry Littleton
1870	Thomas Prowett Jones		1911	Arthur Frederick Hill
1871	Joseph Sidney Lescher		1912	William Palmer Fuller
1872	George Wood		1913	Clifford Blackburn Edgar
1873	William Costall May		1914	Adrian Charles Chamier
1874	Henry Richard Frisby		1915	Charles Lukey Collard
1875	William Chappell		1916	Sir George Wyatt Truscott, Bt.
1876	John Henry Skilbeck		1917	Alexander Burnett Brown
1877	William Stuartson Collard		1918	Hugh Wyatt
1878	Walter Meacock Wilkinson		1919	Sir Edward Ernest Cooper (*Lord Mayor*)
1879	Robert Betson Warrick			
1880	John Hilditch Evans		1920	Henry Thomas Cart de Lafontaine
1881	John Peter Theobald			
1882	John Barnwell Herring		1921	Sir William John Lancaster
1883	Thomas Prowett Jones		1922	Henry Thomas Cart de Lafontaine
1884	George Wood			
1885	Henry Richard Frisby		1923	William Henry Perry Leslie
1886	William Costall May		1924	Edward Barclay Hoare
1887	William Chappell		1925	Henry Dexter Truscott
1888	John Henry Skilbeck		1926	Herbert Sullivan
1889	William Stuartson Collard		1927	George John Bennett
1890	Walter Meacock Wilkinson		1928	Walter Willson Cobbett
1891	Robert Betson Warrick		1929	Victor Allcard
1892	Professor John Frederick Bridge		1930	Sir Ian Zachary Malcolm
			1931	Henry Saxe Wyndham
1893	John Clementi Collard		1932	John Henry Iles
1894	Sir John Stainer		1933	Robert Kennerley Rumford
1895	Henry Richard Frisby		1934	The Rt Hon Viscount Astor
1896	William Stuartson Collard		1935	Sir Ian Zachary Malcolm
1897	Walter Meacock Wilkinson		1936	Alfred Joseph Waley
1898	Sir John Frederick Bridge		1937	Sir Hugh Percy Allen
1899	John Clementi Collard		1938	Alec Raven Briggs
1900	Sir John Stainer		1939	Sir Hugh Percy Allen
1901	John Clementi Collard			

1939–44   The Rt Hon Sir Felix
 Cassel, Bt
1945   Sir Felix Victor Schuster, Bt.
1946   Arthur William Fitzsimmons
1947   William James Phillips
1948   Sir Stanley Marchant
1949   Victor Allcard
1949   Geoffrey Hawkes
1950   Hilary Chadwyck-Healey
1951   Sidney John Loeb
1952   William Graham Wallace
1953   Evelyn Henry Tschudi
 Broadwood
1954   Henry Frederick Bird Iles
1955   Cecil Winton Maudslay
1956   Sir Denis Truscott
1957   John Sebastian Morley
1958   Geoffrey Trevor
 Burnett-Brown
1959   Professor Herbert Howells
1960   Charles Evelyn Boosey
1961   Henry Willis
1962   Henry Alastair Fergusson
 Crewdson
1963   Alfred Robert Stock
1964   The Rt. Hon Viscount Astor
1965   Gerald Derek Lockett
1966   Stanley Rubinstein
1967   Sir John Dykes-Bower
1968   John Bird Iles
1969   David Jack Loeb
1970   Frank Joseph Wright
1970   Sir Denis Truscott

1971   Sir Jack Westrup
1972   Benjamin Angwin
1973   W.S. Lloyd Webber
1974   Sir Gilbert Inglefield
1975   Sir Lennox Berkeley
1976   Nathan Abrahams
1977   Ronald William Mein Atkin
1978   Leonard John Digby Halcrow
1979   Antony Benno John Stanley
 Rubinstein
1980   John Edward Street
1981   Sir Andrew Carnwath
1982   Ronald Francis Walter Ficker
1983   Hubert Frank Winckler
1984   John Dennis Heddle Nash
1985   John Stewart Pownall Morley
1986   Sir Bernard Lovell
1987   William Richard Inge
 Crewdson
1988   Sir Vivian Dunn
1989   Malcolm James Hubble
1990   Jeffery Bannerman Lockett
1991   Henry Willis 4
1992   John Clive Iles
1993   Anthony Presgrave Pool
1994   Adrian Maurice Wolf Davis
1995   Francis Anthony Armstrong
 Carnwath
1996   Anthony Maxwell
 Burnett-Brown
1997   Frank Norman Fowler
1998   Professor Malcolm Troup
1999   Sir Alan Traill

CLERKS

1629   James Brook

Before 1697 – after 1712   Brian
 Courthope

 –1728   Charles Allen
1728–35   John Leadbeater

1735–46   name not known
1747–70   John Crumpe
1770–97   Thos. Whittell, Snr
1797–1800   Thos. Whittell, Jnr
1800–02   Henry Woodthorpe
1802–33   Daniel Wood

1833–57   James Huxley
1858–66   Frederick Augustus France
1867–71   John Wood
1871–1902   John Theophilus Theobald
1902–27   Thomas Collingwood Fenwick
1927–29   Charles Keith Phillips

1929–30   Athro Charles Knight
1930–67   Henry Alastair Fergusson Crewdson
1967–87   William Richard Inge Crewdson
1987–93   Michael James Gwynne Fletcher
1993–   Simon Francis Norman Waley

TREASURERS

1772–93   William Cooper Keating
1793–1801   John Hardy
1801–18   Solomon Wadd
1818–19   Joseph Steele
1819–31   Joseph Gough
1831–60   Frederick William Collard
1860–76   Charles Lukey Collard
1876–87   William Chappell
1887–1904   William Stuartson Collard
1904–18   John Clementi Collard

1918–23   William Palmer Fuller
1923–39   Arthur Frederick Hill
1945–51   Sir Victor Schuster, Bt
1951–62   William Graham Wallace
1962–78   Gerald Derek Lockett
1978–93   Ronald Francis Walter Ficker
1993–97   Francis Anthony Armstrong Carnwath
1997–   Maurice George Hart

BEADLES

(an asterisk indicates some uncertainty about dates)

1618   James Smyth
1629   Philip Richman
1696   Robert Nicholls
1712–14   Cox *
1717–25   Hale *
1736–40   George James *
1741–48   William Glanister *
1749   William Pamplyn
1768   James Green
1776–80   Richard Bygrave

1781–99   John Wilkinson
1799–1830   James Stamper Messenger
1831–60   Henry Delafons
1860–98   Nathan William Walker
1899–1936   Ernest Hills
1936–62   George Henry Godwin
1962–76   Leslie Roy Day
1976–88   Jack Vernon Hayhow
1988–95   Philip Chancellor
1995–   David Barnes

APPENDIX TWELVE

The Company's Major Awards and Award-Winners

THE WALTER WILLSON COBBETT MEDAL
for Services to Chamber Music

(* indicates awarded posthumously)

1924	Thomas Frederick Dunhill	1953	Sir Arthur Bliss
1925	Mrs Frederick S. Coolidge (USA)	1954	Leon Goossens
1926	Alfred Joseph Clements	1955	Edmund Rubbra
1927	Harry Waldo Warner	1956	Arthur Benjamin
1928	Sir Edward Elgar	1957	Thurston Dart
1929	Frank Bridge	1958	Kathleen Long
1930	Ralph Vaughan Williams	1959	Yehudi Menuhin
1931	Arnold Bax	1960	George Malcolm
1932	John Ireland	1961	Lennox Berkeley
1933	Professor Charles Wood*	1962	Anne Macnaghten
1934	C. Armstrong Gibbs	1963	Norbert Brainin
1935	Richard H. Watkins	1964	Emmanuel Hurwitz
1936	Sir Donald Tovey	1965	Joan Dickson
1937	Senor Don Pau Casals	1966	Howard Ferguson
1938	Ivor James	1967	Dr Kenneth Leighton
1939	Herbert Withers	1968	Elizabeth Maconchy
1940	Isole Menges	1969	Hugh Bean
1942	Dr Ernest Walker	1970	Cecil Aronowitz
1943	Sidney Griller	1971	Watson Forbes
1944	Dame Myra Hess	1972	Denis Matthews
1945	Herbert Walenn	1975	Janet Craxton
1946	Lionel Tertis	1976	Gordon Crosse
1947	William Walton	1977	Ivor Newton
1948	Michael Tippett	1978	Wilfrid Parry
1949	Gordon Jacob	1979	Edwin Roxburgh
1950	Denis Brain	1981	Hugh Maguire
1951	Gerald Moore	1985	Christopher Hogwood
1952	Frederick Thurston	1986	Philip Jones
		1987	Sir Peter Maxwell Davies

1988	Lady Evelyn Barbirolli	1994	Irvine Arditti
1989	Jack Brymer	1995	Levon Chilingirian
1990	Sidonie Goossens	1996	Amelia Freedman
1991	Eileen Croxford	1997	Yfrah Neaman
1992	Elgar Howarth	1998	David Takeno
1993	Nona Liddell		

THE JOHN CLEMENTI COLLARD FELLOWSHIP

1931	Herbert Howells	1965	Adrian Cruft
1934	Constant Lambert	1968	Alan Ridout
1937	William Alwyn	1971	Bernard Roberts
	Edmund Rubbra	1974	Christopher Brown
1940	Jack Allan Westrup	1977	Hamish Milne
1943	Gordon Jacob	1980	Edwin Roxburgh
1946	Lennox Berkeley	1983	Justin Connolly
1949	Alan Rawsthorne	1986	Alec Roth
1952	Priaulx Rainier	1989	Benedict Mason
1955	Bernard Stevens	1992	Ann Mackay
1958	Peter Racine Fricker	1996	Robin Grant
1962	John Gardner		

THE SIR CHARLES SANTLEY MEMORIAL GIFT

1957	Norman Allin	1969	Owen Brannigan and Carrie Tubb
1958	Isobel Baillie and Roy Henderson	1970	Peter Pears and Joan Hammond
1959	Agnes Nicholls (Lady Harty) and Clive Carey	1971	Gwynneth Jones and Alfred Deller
1960	Keith Falkner and Elsie Suddaby	1972	Charles Craig and Elizabeth Harwood
1961	Richard Lewis and Astra Desmond	1973	Harry Secombe and Jennifer Vyvyan
1962	Geraint Evans and Eva Turner	1974	Dame Lilian Stiles-Allan
1963	Parry Jones and Maggie Teyte	1975	Thomas Hemsley
1964	Alexander Young and Heather Harper	1976	Josephine Veasey
1965	Hervey Allen and Joan Cross	1977	Norman Bailey
1966	David Ward and Gwen Catley	1978	Helen Watts
1967	George Baker and Olive Groves	1979	Robert Tear
1968	John Shirley Quirk and Janet Baker	1980	Norma Proctor
		1981	Benjamin Luxon

1982   Betty Bannerman
1983   Ian Wallace
1984   Constance Shacklock
1985   Alfreda Hodgson
1986   Michael Langdon
1987   Marion Studholme
1988   Derek Hammond-Stroud
1989   Valerie Masterson and Eric Shilling
1990   Felicity Lott and Norman Lumsden
1991   Elizabeth Bainbridge and Thomas Allen

1992   Ian Partridge and Sarah Walker
1993   Elizabeth Vaughan and Philip Langridge
1994   Anthony Rolfe-Johnson and Wendy Eathorne
1995   Richard Van Allan and Dame Josephine Barstow
1996   Rosalind Plowright and Willard White
1997   Ann Murray and Robert Lloyd
1998   Johanne Peters and John Tomlinson

W.T. BEST MEMORIAL SCHOLARSHIP

1957   Christine Waple
1960   Susan Landale
1963   Steuart Bedford
1965   Timothy Robert Warwick Farrell
1968   David Bruce-Payne
1971   Stephen John Cleobury
1974   Carys Mon Hughes
1977   Jonathan Stephen Holmes

1980   John Scott
1981   Jane Watts
1983   Andrew Lucas
1986   David Liddle
1990   Stephen Farr
1993   David Goode
1996   Neil Cockburn (2 years); Mathew Owens (1 year)

JOHN CHRISTIE AWARD

1965   Ryland Davies
1966   Neil van Allan
1967 }
1968 }   Jill Gomez
1969   no award made
1970   Teresa Cahill and Yvonne Fuller
1971   Anthony Roden
1972   Ian Caley
1973   Linda Esther Gray and John Tomlinson
1974   Elizabeth Gale and Anthony Johnson

1975   Anthony Rolfe Johnson and Alan Watt
1976   John Rawnsley
1977   Kate Flowers
1978   Fiona Kimm
1979   Keith Lewis
1980   Christopher Blades
1981   Helen Walker
1982   Glen Winslade
1983   John Hall
1984   Louise Winter
1985   Anna Steiger
1986   Peter Rose
1987   Alastair Miles

1988   Robert Poulton
1989   Alison Hagley and Gerald
        Finley
1990   Sarah Pring and Christopher
        Ventris
1991   Andrew Slater

1992   Edith Pritchard
1993   Julie Unwin
1994   Howard Quilla Croft
1995   no award made
1996   Lisa Milne
1997   Linda Tuvas
1998   Daniel Borowski

CARNWATH SCHOLARSHIP

1984   Nigel Hill and Jeremy Carter
1985   Andrew Bottrill
1988   John Adams
1990   Lucy Parnham

1992   Alexis Alexander French
1994   Jonathan Ayerst
1996   Alexander Taylor

GEMINI COMPOSITION FELLOWSHIP

1988   Simon Bainbridge
1989   Javier Alvarez
1990   Simon Holt
1991   David Sutton-Anderson (with
        additional prize to Jeremy Byers)

1992   Keith Gifford
1993   Helen Roe
1994   James Wood
1995   Julian Butcher
1996   Michael Zev Gordon

SPECIAL PRESENTATIONS OF THE SILVER MEDAL

1903   Sir Walter Parratt and Sir Hubert Parry, Bt: for acting as Adjudicators
        for the Coronation Prize March

        Charles Ernest Rube: in recognition of his gift of a Loving Cup

        James Munro Coward, Thomas Lea Southgate and Cyril Arthur Pearson:
        for services in connection with the Coronation Prize March

1905   Arthur Frederick Hill, John Frederick Randall Stainer and Col. Thomas
        Bradney Shaw-Hellier: for services in connection with the Tercentenary
        Exhibition

        William Hayman Cummings and Carl Hentschel: for services in
        connection with the 'Masque of the GoldenTree'

1907   Sir Charles Santley in honour of his Jubilee Year in Music

1911   Charles Albert Edwin Harriss for services to British Music

1914   William Henry Ash and Claudius James Ash: for services in connection with the foundation of the Benevolent Fund

1916   Lt Albert Edward Williams, Bandmaster, Grenadier Guards: for services to Music

Miss Phyllis Lett: for services to Music

1920   Walter Damrosch: for services to Music

1945   Lt David Crawley, Royal Papuan Constabulary: for raising and training a Band of Papuans and subsequent distinguished conduct in face of the Japanese Invasion of New Guinea

1966   Professor Nketia, Director of the Legon Orchestra of Ghana: for services to Music

1967   Henry Alastair Fergusson Crewdson, Clerk to the Company: for services to the Company and to Music

1978   Gerald Derek Lockett, Treasurer: for services to the Company

1988   William Richard Inge Crewdson, Clerk to the Company: for services to the Company

1993   Ronald Francis Walter Ficker, Treasurer: for services to the Company

1999   Antony Benno John Stanley Rubinstein: for services to the Company in encouraging and accomplishing some notable benefactions

Sir David Willcocks: for services to Music

BIBLIOGRAPHY

Books

Ackroyd, Peter, *The Life of Thomas More*, London, Chatto & Windus, 1998.

Ashbee, Andrew, *Records of English Court Music*, vols I–VII, Aldershot, Scolar Press, 1986–1993.

Aylmer, G.E., *Rebellion or Revolution*, Oxford, Clarendon Press, 1986.

Barty-King, Hugh, *GSMD: A Hundred Years' Performance*, London, 1980.

Bridge, Sir Frederick, *A Westminster Pilgrim*, London, Novello & Co., 1918.

Bromley, J., and Child, H., *The Armorial Bearings of the Guilds of London*, London, Frederick Warne, 1961.

Bullock-Davies, Constance, *Menestrellorum Multitudo: Minstrels at a Royal Feast*, Cardiff, University of Wales Press, 1978.

Burney, Charles, *A General History of Music from the Earliest Times to the Present Period* (4 vols, London, 1789)

Burney, Dr, *Memoirs of Dr Burney, arranged by his daughter Madame d'Arblay* (Edward Moxon, London, 1832)

Caldwell, John, *The Oxford History of English Music*, 2 vols, Oxford, Clarendon Press, 1991 and 1999

Catalogue of the Loan Exhibition held in Fishmongers' Hall 1904, London, Musicians Company publication.

Chambers, Edmund K., *The Elizabethan Stage*, Oxford, Oxford University Press, 1923.

Christ's Hospital Admissions, Vol. 1: 1554–1599, London, Council of Almoners of Christ's Hospital, 1937.

Crewdson, Henry Alastair Fergusson, *The Worshipful Company of Musicians: A Short History* (2nd edn), London, Charles Knight, 1971.

Curl, James Steven, *The Londonderry Plantation, 1609–1914*, Chichester, Phillimore & Co., 1986.

Dawe, Donovan, *Organists of the City of London, 1666–1850*, London, published by the author, 1983.

Duffy, Eamon, *The Stripping of the Altars: Traditional Religion in England c.1400–c.1580*, New Haven, Conn., Yale University Press, 1992.

Duffy, Maureen, *Henry Purcell*, London, Fourth Estate, 1994.

Dugdale, Sir Simon, *The History of St Paul's Cathedral*, London, 1818.

Ehrlich, Cyril, *The Music Profession in Britain since the Eighteenth Century*, Oxford, Clarendon Press, 1985.

———, *First Philharmonic: A History of the Royal Philharmonic Society*, Oxford, Clarendon Press, 1995.

English Music, Being the Lectures given at the Loan Exhibition of the Worshipful Company of Musicians held at Fishmongers Hall, London Bridge June–July 1904, published by Walter Scott Publishing Co. Ltd (London) and by Charles Scribner's Sons (New York) 1906.

Evelyn, John, *The Diary of John Evelyn*, ed. Guy de la Bédoyère, Woodbridge, The Boydell Press, 1995.

Fraser, Antonia, *King Charles II*, London, Weidenfeld and Nicolson, 1979.

Harvey, Brian, *The Violin Family and its Makers in the British Isles*, Oxford, Clarendon Press, 1995.

Hawkins, Sir John, *A History of the Science and Practice of Music*, London, Novello & Co., 1875 edn.

Hayward, Arthur L., ed., *Amusements Serious and Comical and Other Works by Tom Brown*, London, George Routledge, 1927.

Heath, Baron, *Some account of the Worshipful Company of Grocers*, London, private publication, 1869.

Hibbert, W.N., *History of the Worshipful Company of Founders, of the City of London*, London, privately printed, 1925.

Holman, Peter, *Four and Twenty Fiddlers, The Violin at the English Court 1540–1690*, Oxford, Clarendon Press, 1993.

Hotson, Leslie, *The First Night of* Twelfth Night, London, Rupert Hart-Davis, 1954.

Husk, William Henry, *Musical Celebrations on St Cecilia's Day in the 16th, 17th and 18th Centuries*, London, Bell & Daldy, 1857.

Hutton, Ronald, *The Rise and Fall of Merry England: The Ritual Year 1400–1700*, Oxford, Clarendon Press, 1994.

Johnson, A.H., *The History of the Worshipful Company of the Drapers of London*, Oxford, Clarendon Press, 1914.

Johnstone, H. Diack and Fiske, R. (eds), *The Blackwell History of Music: The Eighteenth Century*, Oxford, Basil Blackwell, 1990.

Lafontaine, H.C. de, ed., *'The King's Musick': A Transcript of Records Relating to Music and Musicians, 1460–1700*, London, Novello & Co., 1909.

Lasocki, David, *The Bassanos*, Aldershot, Scolar Press, 1995.

Latham, Robert, *The Shorter Pepys*, London, Bell & Hyman, 1985.

Leppert, Richard, *Music and Image: Domesticity, Ideology and Socio-cultural Formation in Eighteenth Century England*, Cambridge, Cambridge University Press, 1988.

Lindley, David, ed., *Court Masques, Jacobean and Caroline Entertainments*, Oxford, Clarendon Press, 1995.

Masters, Betty, *The Chamberlains of the City of London 1237–1987*, London, 1988.

Matthews, Betty, *The Royal Society of Musicians of Great Britain: A History 1738–1988*, London, published by the Society, 1988.

———, ed., *Members of the Royal Society of Musicians 1738–1984*, London, published by the Society, 1985.

Munrow, David, *Instruments of the Middle Ages and Renaissance*, Oxford, Oxford University Press, 1976.

Myers, A.R., ed., *The Household of Edward IV: the Black Book and the Ordinances of 1478*, Manchester, 1959.

Overall, W.H. and H.C. (eds), *Analytical index to the series of records known as the remembrancia. Preserved among the archives of the City of London AD 1579–1664*, London 1878.

Paterson, James, *Pietas Londiniensis*, London, 1714.

Ramsay, J.H., *Lancaster and York*, Oxford, 1892.

Rainbow, Bernarr, *The Choral Revival in the Anglican Church 1839–1872*, London, Barrie & Jenkins, 1970.

Reddaway, T.F., *The Rebuilding of London after the Great Fire*, London, Jonathan Cape, 1940.

Ridley, Jasper, *Henry VIII*, London, Constable, 1984.

Robbins Landon, H.C., *Haydn in England*, London, Thames & Hudson, 1976.

Schofield, John, *The Building of London from the Conquest to the Great Fire*, London, British Museum Press, 1993.

Scholes, Percy, *The Puritans and Music in England and New England*, London, 1934.

Shapiro, M. *Children of the Revels: The Boy Companies of Shakespeare's Time and their Plays*, New York, Columbia University Press, 1977.

Southworth, John, *The English Medieval Minstrel*, Boydell Press, Woodbridge, 1989.

Stow, John, *A Survey of London in 1598*, Stroud, Glos., Alan Sutton edn, 1994.

Strong, Roy, *Henry Prince of Wales and England's Lost Renaissance*, London, Thames & Hudson, 1986.

Unwin, George, *The Gilds and Companies of London*, 4th edn, London, Frank Cass & Co., 1963.

Wagner, Leopold, *London Inns and Taverns*, London, George Allen & Unwin, 1924.

Walker, Ernest, *A History of Music in England*, 3rd edn, ed. J.A. Westrup, Oxford, Clarendon Press, 1951.

Walls, Peter, *Music in the English Courtly Masque 1604–1640*, Oxford, Clarendon Press, 1996.

Ward, Edward, *The Dancing Master, A Satyr*, London, A. Moore, 1722.

———, *The Dancing School with the Adventures of the Easter Holy Days*, London, J. How, 1700.

Warwick, Alan, *A Noise of Music*, London, Queen Anne Press, 1968.

Wilkins, Nigel, *Music in the Age of Chaucer*, Cambridge, D.S. Brewer, 1979.

Wilson, Blake, *Music and Merchants: the Laudesi Companies of Republican Florence*, Oxford, Clarendon Press, 1992.

Wilson, John, ed., *Roger North on Music*, London, Novello & Co., 1959.

Wilson, J. Dover, *The Essential Shakespeare*, Cambridge, Cambridge University Press, 1945.

Wilson, Michael, *Nicholas Lanier, Master of the King's Music*, Aldershot, Scolar Press, 1994.

Woodfill, Walter, *Musicians in English Society from Elizabeth to Charles I*, Princeton, Princeton University Press, 1953.

Articles

Baillie, H., 'A London Guild of Musicians 1460–1530', in *Proceedings of the Royal Musical Association* 83 (1956–57).

———, 'Some Biographical Notes on English Church Musicians', *RMA Research Chronicle*, vol. 2 (1962).

Ingram, W., 'Minstrels in Elizabethan London: Who Were They and What Did They Do?', in *English Literary Renaissance* 14 (1984).

Lindenbaum, Sheila, 'The London Midsummer Watch', in Barbara A. Hanawalt and Kathryn L. Reyerson, eds, *City and Spectacle in Mediaeval Europe*, Minneapolis, University of Minnesota Press, 1994.

Lindley, Keith, 'London's Citizenry in the English Revolution', in R.C. Richardson, ed.,

Town and Countryside in the English Revolution, Manchester, Manchester University Press, 1972.

Mateer, David, 'William Byrd's Middlesex Recusancy', *Music and Letters* 78, no. 1 (February 1997).

Prior, R., 'Jewish Musicians at the Tudor Court', *Musical Quarterly* 69, No. 2 (1983).

Sutton, Anne, 'Merchants, Music and Social Harmony', *London Journal* 17, no. 1 (1992).

Tilmouth, Michael, 'A Calendar of References to Music in Newspapers published in London and the Provinces (1660–1719)', *RMA Research Chronicle*, No. 1 (1961).

Wood, Julia K., ' "A Flowing Harmony", Music on the Thames in Restoration London', *Early Music* (November 1995).

Unpublished Works

Dale, T.C., 'An Index to the Liverymen of London in 1700', transcribed and compiled in 1933 (copy in the Guildhall Library).

Kisby, Fiona, 'The Royal Household Chapel in Early Tudor London 1485–1547' (unpublished dissertation).

Martin, Jennifer, 'The English Dancing Master 1660–1728:, His Role at Court, in Society and on the Public Stage', unpublished dissertation, University of Michigan 1977.

INDEX